THE FOUNDING

OF THE

GERMAN EMPIRE

BY WILLIAM I.

BY

HEINRICH VON SYBEL

TRANSLATED BY HELENE SCHIMMELFENNIG WHITE

VOL. VII.

Auf rauhen Pfaden immer aufwärts

GREENWOOD PRESS, PUBLISHERS
NEW YORK

Originally published in 1897 by Thomas Y. Crowell & Co.

First Greenwood Reprinting, 1968

Library of Congress Catalogue Card Number: 68-31005

PRINTED IN THE UNITED STATES OF AMERICA

PREFACE.

THIS volume was already in print. when, on November 26th, I received a copy of *Figaro* of the 23d, containing the lengthy preface to Émile Ollivier's prospective history (in seven volumes) of the Liberal Empire; i.e., of the Ollivier Ministry, from January 2d to August 9th, 1870. As I have since heard, the first volume of this exhaustive work appeared on the 26th. Although I have as yet not seen it, the preface suffices fully to reveal both the character of the author and the nature and extent of his information. His main purpose seems to be to establish that the war of 1870 was the result of a diabolical intrigue devised by Bismarck; although the evidence he offers in proof of this is confined to a repetition of the inventions of the Duke of Gramont, an authority about as reliable as the author himself.

These assertions have long since been refuted, and may be found in full in the contents of this volume following page 285.

HEINRICH VON SYBEL.

BERLIN, November 29th, 1894.

CONTENTS OF VOLUME VII.

BOOK XXIII.

GERMANY AND FRANCE.

BOOK XXIV.

ORIGIN OF THE FRENCH WAR.

BOOK XXIII.

GERMANY AND FRANCE.

GERMANY AND FRANCE.

CHAPTER I

THE FIRST CUSTOMS PARLIAMENT.

IT is now our purpose to observe how the national idea asserted itself in our German Fatherland amid the varying movements of European politics during that turbulent year, 1868.

I. FIRST HALF OF THE REICHSTAG SESSION.

Whilst the elections in South Germany were still in progress, it was determined in Berlin to convoke the Reichstag for the 23d of March. With a short intermission for the Easter holidays, this would allow it to continue its deliberations for four weeks before its ranks would be increased by the addition of the South German members of the Customs Parliament for the session to be opened on April 27th.

In the speech from the throne with which, on the appointed day, King William opened the Reichstag, he confined himself to the formal announcement of the bills which had been prepared for its consideration. For the further development of freedom of migration

3

there was a bill regulating the carrying on of a trade or
business; by another, certain police restrictions upon
the right or contracting marriage were to be removed.
Besides these, there was a bill regarding the quarter-
ing of soldiers in time of peace, and one for the introduction of a uniform system of measures and weights,
based upon the metric and decimal systems.

These proposed measures all gave promise of further
advance in the direction of the reforms introduced
through the action of the previous session, and were
well adapted in their realization to promote prosperity,
facilitate intercourse, and insure personal freedom.

They were followed by a number of postal treaties,
the object of which was to extend the advantages of
the new postal laws to international intercourse.
Another treaty regulated the much-disputed lawful obligations of returning emigrants who had acquired the
right of citizenship in America, upon whom, however,
their native State had a claim for military service
avoided by emigration.

The budget for 1869 could not as yet be submitted,
since the estimates for some of the important items
could not possibly be made at this early date, or else
were dependent upon the action of the Customs Parliament.

Finally, the King commended to the consideration
of the Reichstag the proposed law regarding the administration of the Federal debt, which had been discussed
during the previous session. In connection with it
he expressed the hope that the difficulties which had

then presented themselves would be surmounted by a spirit of mutual concession.

At present, however, the political aspect of the House gave little prospect for the realization of this hope. The Liberal elements, it is true, were animated by the best of intentions, in so far as possible to go hand in hand with the Governments in common labor to complete and strengthen the interior equipment of the Confederation. No one could fail to perceive the degree of prosperity and security before the law which had even now followed, and would continue to follow, in the wake of uniform Federal legislation. To all proposals involving emancipation of economic labor and production, of internal and international intercourse, the Reichstag invariably devoted careful investigation, which frequently led to instructive discussion, not rarely to needless amendments, but hardly ever to party opposition on principle.

The convention with America, by which Prussia relinquished its right to claim military service of naturalized American citizens upon their return to their German fatherland, was approved, with little hesitation; even less opposition was encountered by the postal treaties, everywhere hailed with joy.

The report made by the Committee in charge of the bill providing greater freedom in contracting marriage presented a sad picture of the consequences attending the complicated restrictions heretofore in force, and the arbitrary interference on the part of magistrates and police authorities; of the legal insecurity in these matters to which especially the poorer classes were subject; of the many cases of illegal cohabitation which were the result, together with the increasing number of illegitimate children. Not a voice was raised in defence of these evils. There was a difference of opinion merely with regard to the means best adapted to their remedy, and this soon ended in an agreement which received general approval.

In addition to these measures, the benefits of which would be immediately reaped, a wide prospect of future advance was opened. In response to a request originating with Wagner and Planck for the introduction of an improved criminal code as well as a new criminal procedure, together with the change in the organization of the courts which this necessitated, the President of the Federal Chancery, Delbrück, at once announced the willingness of the Governments to comply with it, and the Federal Council forthwith appointed a number of committees to draw up the desired bills.

Another committee was charged with the drafting of a new law of domicile; another one, with the preparation of a revised civil procedure; a third, with a plan for improved regulations governing mortgages. In fact, the two organs of the Confederation seemed to be engaged in a rivalry for legislative production. "We are making too many laws; we are working too fast! Soon we shall have to devote all our time to learning the law, and have none left to live by it," exclaimed the highly conservative Councillor Bassewitz, who later became Minister.

This, however, was only one side of the situation. As willing as the liberal elements in the Reichstag were to further every tendency of Federal legislation toward promoting the welfare of the people, as little inclined were they to relinquish their efforts to extend parliamentary influence beyond the sphere to which the Federal Constitution limited it. This was but what was to be expected of the Extreme Left; but the attitude of the National Liberals too, who heretofore had been so well disposed toward the Government, was such as to make the second half of the party name appear more and more appropriate.

And so, in the Reichstag, fair weather and foul alternated continuously. Hardly had the assembly organized on April 2d, before the veteran Waldeck challenged to combat, by presenting a motion granting compensation to the members of the Reichstag. " We are the representatives of the entire population," he declared; " therefore the people, free from restriction of any kind, should have entire liberty in the choice of deputies ; thus only can the right man always be selected." He believed in the infallibility of the people as did the Ultramontanes in that of the Pope. " Our interests will be best served by a spirit of utmost liberality," he remarked further; " for thus alone can we win the South."

Bismarck opposed the motion with the remonstrance that it was highly unwise at this early day to tinker at the Constitution, as yet hardly a year old, and especially so to begin with this Article, which, as the result of a compromise between the Governments and the Reichstag, had made the adoption of the Constitution possible. And so far as the South was concerned, he declared that Waldeck, living only in his ideals, had no conception of the actual conditions.

" The South," he explained, "is averse to union with us, not because we are not liberal enough, but because we are much too liberal for its taste. Baden, the only liberal State of the South, is most eager to be admitted into the Confederation. It is the liberal South Germans, therefore, who desire union with us; those who do not are the reactionary parties. These I will not designate more particularly: the latest elections in South Germany have cast a strong light upon them, and it bespeaks an almost inconceivable ignorance of facts to dispute this condition of affairs. Should we guarantee to the parties now predominant in South Germany certain institutions of which their El Dorado, Austria, is about to rid itself, — and which would surely be no advance toward liberalism, — then, perhaps, we might hope to secure a South German majority favorable to union with us."

As powerful as was the impression made by this convincing exposition of the true state of affairs, and as strong as was the influence which the immovable attitude of the Government exerted, still it was only by the very slight majority of 97 voices against 92 that the motion was finally rejected in a very poorly attended sitting of the House. Almost all the National Liberals, and even a few Old Liberals, sided with Waldeck.

A much greater interest was evinced in a motion presented on the following day by Lasker, with the support of forty-five associates, proposing the enactment of a Federal law securing the members of the Representative Assemblies and Chambers of the several German States against prosecution for utterances made in the performance of their functions.

We have seen how in the preceding year Lasker's efforts for the enactment of a similar law for Prussia were crowned by success in the Prussian House of Deputies, whereas, when presented to the Upper House, the bill was rejected there by an almost unanimous vote. Thus deprived of all hope to achieve his desire through Prussian legislation, he resolved to bring this important question before the Reichstag.

The principal arguments for and against were developed anew in a long and interesting debate; the deciding question, however, was whether the Reichstag had authority by so momentous a decision to affect the constitutional rights of the individual States.

"The law which we desire," Lasker declared, "will be no infraction on the State Constitutions, but will simply bring about a modification of the criminal law, a province which as expressly as possible is placed within our jurisdiction. The Federal authority has the privilege to revise the entire existing criminal code; surely, then, it has the right to decree that certain acts, heretofore considered as violations of law, shall cease to be unlawful, and therefore no longer subject the perpetrator to legal prosecution. If for certain acts a deputy may be called to account by the law of the land, this presupposes that these acts are declared punishable by the criminal code there in force; therefore, by making the necessary change in the code, legal prosecution may no longer follow, even without a modification of the Constitution."

To this his opponents replied, that in spite of his seemingly correct deduction, the fact remained that by the proposed measure a privilege heretofore not generally conceded would be granted to the members of the several Chambers, whereby the position of the people's representatives would be materially strengthened, resulting in an increase of power for the Chambers, and consequently in a modification of the rights granted by the Constitution. Therefore, it was further argued, this measure also implied an extension of the competency of the central power, and a restriction of the individual independence of the States; to proclaim such a tendency would, under present conditions, be most disastrous, and would arouse a violent spirit of reaction.

An earnest remonstrance to this effect was added by the Weimar Minister, Herr von Watzdorff, to whom no one had ever ascribed reactionary or particularistic propensities. Windthorst declared himself ready to further the proposed measure in the Prussian Assembly, but believed that its adoption by the Reichstag would endanger the permanence of the Confederation. "Do not mistake the spirit of the times,"

he cried, "the flood tide of the German unity movement is past; the ebb has set in, and it therefore behooves us to be doubly careful!"

Bismarck's attitude was conciliatory. The time had
been, as we have seen, when he forcibly opposed the
deputy's privilege to calumniate; now, however, much
in need of the friendship as well as the moderation
of the middle parties, he volunteered to use his influence in Prussia to secure to the originators of the
motion the realization of their wish, upon one condition.   Although advocating that freedom of speech
should in no way be restricted with respect to those
present in the House, both Ministers and deputies, —
"for they can defend themselves," he said, "and moreover, no one is compelled to be a Minister," — he yet
felt constrained to stipulate for the continuance of
legal protection for the individual honor of all other
persons whose character had been defamed upon the
floor of the House.   Such a measure, he said, would
command his support in the Prussian Assembly; he
would, however, not promise to use his influence with
the Federal Council for the adoption of a Federal
law such as was proposed by the motion now before
the House, since it exceeded the competency of the
Confederation.

The House, however, was not to be moved; and
Lasker's motion was carried by a majority such as has
rarely been given in this assembly upon a political
issue, namely 119 voices against 65.   Bismarck had
been victorious over Waldeck with only a few votes

to spare, but upon this question he failed utterly to
carry the majority with him. In the Federal Council,
however, his influence sufficed to defeat Lasker's bill
by a unanimous rejection. Nevertheless, the opposition which the question aroused upon this occasion
was no longer of a vindictive nature; for although the
legal redress of the grievance was thus indefinitely
postponed, still, from that day forth, no deputy was
ever again prosecuted upon German soil for his parliamentary utterances.

These deliberations were not concluded until just
before the recess for the Easter holidays; after these
came six peaceful days, during which the common care
for the common good kept the two organs of Federal
legislation bent upon the same purpose, their tempers
unruffled by any question of power. But on the
seventh day the scene was suddenly changed; and
from an insignificant beginning a vehement Constitution strife was quickly developed, which in its bitterness was suggestive of the evil days of the great
conflict.

The order of the day for April 22d included the report of the Committee in charge of the bill regarding
the administration of the Federal debt, which had been
announced in the speech from the throne. It will be
remembered that in 1867 the Reichstag had made a
number of changes in the proposed measure, and upon
motion of Miquel had resolved upon an additional
paragraph empowering the Reichstag to make legal
complaint against all functionaries charged with the

administration of the public debt who had been dere-
lict in the performance of their official duty.

Although in framing the new bill the Federal Council had with great decision rejected this additional
clause, it had accepted all the other amendments, some
of them with a heavy heart, and now expected a like
spirit of friendly concession from the House. This
hope was, however, doomed to early disappointment.
In the Committee to which the bill was referred a motion was at once made to restore Miquel's clause; and
after Bismarck had emphatically opposed such a step,
the motion was lost by only seven votes against seven,
after which the clause was nevertheless again proposed
in the plenum by Miquel together with forty-four
associates.

Miquel at first treated it as an unimportant matter-
of-course, stating that according to the draft of the bill
the administration of the debt would be placed under
the control of a Committee on the Public Debt, which
would render periodic reports to the Reichstag, and
advise that body either to grant or to refuse discharge
to the officials intrusted with the administration of the
debt. Now, the purpose of the additional clause, he
explained, was evidently no other than to render this
control effective in every case, that it might be exerted
even should the highest authority of the administration,
the Federal Chancellor himself, fail to take the steps
required by the Committee's report. The application
was therefore only to a most exceptional case, from
which no further doubtful consequences could arise.

But against this construction a vigorous protest was made by his most ardent supporters, Reichensperger and Hänel. "Not at all," said they; "the merit of the clause lies chiefly in its greater and fundamental significance, since this will lead to an effective responsibility not only of the subordinate officials, but of the Federal Chancellor himself in case of faulty directions given to his subordinates, or of failure to take proper measures against those guilty of unlawful acts." That the Chancellor really was a responsible officer, they argued further, was distinctly stated in the Constitution; the principle being thus fully recognized, its practical application by means of the proposed clause was no deviation from the intention of the Constitution, but, on the contrary, was putting it into effect.

The theory that the responsibility provided by the Constitution was intended to be only a so-called moral one and not a legal one, they sneered at as mere child's play. The Constitution, said they, was neither a prayer-book nor a code of morals; it was a law, and as such could only provide legal duties and responsibilities. There was quite as little foundation, they held, for the criticism that the right to enter legal complaint which this clause bestowed upon the Reichstag was an innovation and an attempted extension of parliamentary power. Should a practical responsibility of the Ministry ever be brought about, the legal complaint in case of a violation of a constitutional right, namely a right of the people, must, as had heretofore been conceded by everyone, proceed from the body representative of the people. The proposed clause was therefore the means by which the most important right of the people could find an actual existence instead of one on paper only, even though, as yet, but in a limited sphere.

Those who opposed the measure declared this argument to be faulty from beginning to end. Not only, said they, had the Reichstag, to whose action the Constitution had been submitted, refrained from making the Chancellor's responsibility a legal one, subjecting him to prosecution by the law, but it had distinctly rejected a motion to that effect, namely, the assurance that a law regarding the procedure and tribunal for such a suit would be enacted in the future. To represent the consequences of the moral responsibility to be merely the judgment rendered by history, they declared to be a mistake, since, notwithstanding the absence of legal prosecution, the political and parliamentary consequences might be of a most serious nature, especially so at a time like the present, when there was still so much uncertainty regarding the jurisdiction of the highest Federal and State authorities.

The further conclusion they held to be indisputable, namely, that no matter how desirable the Reichstag's right to bring suit might appear with reference to the future, for the present the Constitution simply provided that a report regarding the Federal receipts and expenditures should be submitted to the Reichstag for the purpose of discharge, and in no way con-

ferred upon the body the right to instigate legal proceedings in case irregularities were discovered. Evidently, therefore, by Miquel's motion not only would
a specific conclusion be deducted from general principles recognized by the Constitution, but in reality
the motion implied a fundamental modification of the
Constitution, an extension of the Reichstag's power
to a degree almost incalculable in its effect.

Here Bismarck entered the conflict with the drastic
energy characteristic of his remarks. " It is your
intention," said he, " in the event of a dispute regarding the interpretation of the law, to place the
Federal Chancellor under the jurisdiction of the district judge ; in that case the Chancellor can feel
secure in his actions only by continued conferences
with the district judge, consulting him daily as a
sort of ' constitutional ' family physician. It might
instead be advisable to appoint the district judge as
Chancellor at once, although in that case you would
probably cease to intrust him with the further interpretation of the law."

He then pointed out the absurdity of making two
factors of legislation, both of the highest sovereign
power, subject, in case of a dispute between them,
to the decisions of a civil judge, who, although
doubtlessly well versed in the law of the Pandects,
was yet deficient in the technical knowledge of those
matters upon the proper appreciation of which the
final decision must depend.

In reply to the remarks of a previous speaker, who,

to convince his hearers that an effective control sustained by the right to bring suit was a necessity, had reminded them of the fact that at the outbreak of the last war the Government, without asking leave or license, had issued treasury notes to the amount of twenty-two millions, Bismarck now said, "Very true; had we not had the courage to undertake this step of which the district judge would most likely have disapproved, you would to-day still be subject to the ordinances of that most august body, the old Confederate Diet, and Prussia would be smaller by a number of provinces. Instead of censuring us, you should praise us ! "

But still more unfavorably did he regard the foremost demand of Miquel's proposed amendment, the Reichstag's right directly to prosecute subordinate officials. The principle which would thereby be introduced into our judicial system, he declared, would quickly spread, and soon result in the destruction of discipline and in a total lack of respect for those in authority. Every official made responsible in the proposed manner would feel himself authorized to criticize every order given him by his superior in office, as to whether it conformed to the parliamentary or judicial view. The administration would thus no longer be directed by the Minister, but by the courts of justice or the parliamentary majorities. It mattered little, therefore, from which side Miquel's motion was viewed, its object remained identical, — an extension of the Reichstag's power.

Bismarck concluded with a criticism of the tactics which the champions of the motion had adopted in choosing the time to secure their end. Twesten [1] had revealed them when he said that the House could with impunity insist unyieldingly upon its decision of 1867, since the loan of ten millions, approved at that time for the speedy establishment of a navy and for coast defences, could not be obtained by the Government except by the passage of the bill regarding the Federal debt. "Since the formation of a navy is an urgent necessity," he had said, "we are in the fortunate position of being needed by the Government, which will find itself compelled to concede to our demand if we remain firm." To this Bismarck now replied, "What would you say, gentlemen, should the Federal Government reverse your weapon, and use it against you? You take it for granted that the Federal Government is more vitally interested in the navy than are you. What would you say if we, assuming you to possess a degree of patriotism such as you ascribe to the Government, and which I have no doubt you do possess, although unevinced at the present moment, if we upon this supposition should announce, 'You shall have no navy, no telegraphs, unless you are willing to sacrifice one or the other of your parliamentary privileges; for instance, unrestricted liberty of speech.' You would, to express it mildly, consider that not very handsome of us. You are very sure, however, that we will not do this, and therefore feel quite free to resort

[1] Page 154 of the stenographic reports.

to this means of bringing pressure to bear upon the
Governments."

The opposition made a vigorous defence against this
accusation. "We are quite as ready to promote the
interests of the navy as are the Governments," it was
said. "Should the Governments make the loan impossible by persistently rejecting our perfectly just and
beneficial amendment, we will be found ready to provide the required amount in some other way. The
sum to be raised for this year is three and one-half
millions; should this be included in the budget in the
form of *pro rata* contributions, the result would be an
assessment of only three and one-half groschens upon
every person."

The question of how great a tax burden already
rested upon each individual was not taken into consideration. Bismarck closed with the suggestive remark, that as recently as the preceding day the Federal
Council had unanimously declared against accepting
Miquel's motion. The House, however, also remained
firm to its purpose, and cast 133 votes in favor of
Miquel's motion against 114 in opposition. Bismarck
immediately withdrew the bill; and the loan being
thus made impossible, the Government directed that
all work for the navy which was not absolutely necessary should be suspended.

II.   THE CUSTOMS PARLIAMENT.

Thus openly at variance with the Liberals, and feeling that the friendship of the Conservatives was his

merely at the dictate of necessity, Bismarck faced the crucial test of the first Customs Parliament. Notwithstanding the unfavorable results of the elections in South Germany, he remained firmly resolved to lessen the antipathy of the opposing elements by preserving as friendly an attitude as possible, and to guide them into the way leading to closer union by engaging them in labor for the common good.

His intention to evince a spirit of courtesy and hearty good will was shared by the Conservatives, although for wholly different reasons. German unity had never been an inspiration to them; the fundamental idea of their feudal system had ever rested upon a certain independence of the landed proprietors and town magnates; how, then, could they consistently oppose a corresponding desire for independence in the South German States?

With the National Liberals it was otherwise. They, too, desired to avoid contention; they were, however, deeply incensed by the ill-usage their party associates in the South had received, and were therefore little disposed to allow an opportunity to condemn such proceedings to pass unimproved. The members of the South German majority were prepared for such attacks, which, to say the least, was not conducive to a diminution of the distrust and sensitiveness which they felt upon their arrival in Berlin. In fact, every one believed that as it had been in the South German elections, so it would be in the Customs Parliament; the question of German unity would come to the front in every transaction. And so the atmosphere of the hall of assembly was surcharged with electricity, ready at any moment for the lightning's flash.

In the speech from the throne with which on April 27th King William, as bearer of the presidential dignity of the Customs Union, opened the session of the Customs Parliament, he directed attention to the expansion of the Union brought about by the force of the national idea, and to the unity of interests arising as a consequence to all its members. Until now, he said, it had not been possible to fulfil the well-justified demand of the German people for an effective share in the legislation of the Union, although the advisability of such a step had become more and more apparent with the increasing changes in the politico-economic life of the country. That to-day it was possible for the representatives of the whole nation to be assembled together for deliberation upon the common economic interests of Germany he believed to be the fruits of a natural development.

After enumerating the important bills to be submitted to the Parliament, the king concluded with the counsel: "In these deliberations, gentlemen, keep the common German interest ever before you; from this standpoint seek to harmonize the individual interests, and a result will crown your labors such as will earn for you the gratitude of the whole German nation." To this he added the hopeful expression, that the friendly relations maintained between the German Government and all foreign Powers seemed to assure the blessings of peace, for the protection of which the German States had allied themselves, and could at all times depend upon the united strength of the German people.

To these utterances no one could object, yet to the majority of the South Germans it was not pleasing to hear these repeated allusions to the aspiration for nationality, to the representation and gratitude of the people, and especially not to the undesired treaties of alliance. What, indeed, had all this to do with the Customs Union of the Prussian, Bavarian, and Swabian nations ?

Neither was it agreeable, although quite unavoidable, that whereas the members of the North German Reichstag, whose claims had long been verified, took their places in the Customs Parliament without preliminary formalities, the South Germans had to await the decision of a North German majority with regard to the validity of their election. Therefore it was with tempers already ruffled that on April 28th they proceeded to the choice of officers, which was destined not to pass without a violent clash of opposing spirits.

The election of the excellent President of the Reichstag, Simson, to the corresponding place of honor in the Customs Parliament was accomplished without a party struggle ; when, however, it came to the choice of the two vice-presidents the battle waxed hot indeed. To evince a spirit of friendliness toward their associates from the South, the North German majority had selected South German candidates for both these

offices ; for the first, the Premier of Bavaria, Prince
Hohenlohe; for the second, Baron von Roggenbach,
formerly Minister of Baden. To the Bavarian Clericals Hohenlohe was, however, most odious ; and they
opposed to him one of their own leaders, Baron von
Thüngen, who, to be sure, received but 59 votes (South
German Particularists and a few North German Democrats). But the National Liberal, Roggenbach, for the
very reason that he was a South German and yet was
nationally inclined, they regarded as a traitor, doubly
dyed, to the sacred cause of southern independence.
With shrewd calculation they turned to the Conservatives of the Reichstag, and proposed to them that their
First Vice President, the Duke of Ujest, be put in
Roggenbach's place, whereby they really succeeded in
excluding Roggenbach.

Encouraged by so happy a result, the South German
Particularists, re-enforced by a few Democrats from
Saxony, at once constituted themselves under Thüngen's leadership as the " South German " fraction, whose
openly avowed watchword was protest against every
expansion of the functions of the Customs Parliament,
but who in secret were resolved to allow as little fruit
as possible to ripen upon this field so entirely hateful
to them.

On May 1st a Committee of the House reported upon
the examination into the Bavarian elections. It appeared that the law promulgated in Bavaria to govern
the Customs Parliament elections had not in every
particular conformed to the directions of the Union

treaty of July 8th; however, in consideration of the very general participation in the elections, and the overwhelming majorities rendered in most cases, this was not regarded as sufficient cause to dispute the validity of the elections, or to make any further steps necessary. It afforded an occasion, however, for a display of the irritated mood of the National Liberals to which allusion has been made. Miquel moved that the House request the presiding officer of the Customs Federal Council to come to an understanding with the Bavarian Government, to the end that in the future such irregularities might be avoided. It was in vain that the Bavarian deputies, irrespective of party, endeavored to show how really insignificant and free from practical consequences the cause of complaint really was; all the Liberal fractions supported Miquel's motion, securing for it a majority. Otherwise calmness and moderation characterized the discussion, the objective point of which was simply the interpretation of a law.

But when on the following day, May 2d, the Würtemberg elections were reached, a vent was found for the discharge of the mutual displeasure. In this report the election law published in Würtemberg was criticised much as had been that of Bavaria, and especially were the orders for its enforcement, issued by the Ministry, disapproved. Although the report did not recommend that as a consequence the results be declared invalid, yet the House was advised to request Bismarck to endeavor to effect an agreement with Stuttgart as with

Munich, that a recurrence of the evil might be prevented.

Hereupon Minister von Mittnacht attempted to prove that the Würtemberg election measures had entirely conformed to the directions given in the treaty of July 8th, his reasoning being, however, more sophistical than convincing. Now Braun (Wiesbaden) took the floor, and giving the rein to his scathing and sarcastic wit, with a few short but effective sentences cut into shreds the Minister's carefully constructed web of legal argument. Then, in vivid colors, he set forth the Würtemberg campaign, in which, he said, three parties, each overflowing with venom toward the others, but now, prompted by their common disinclination to national unity, as well as by an artificially nurtured hatred of Prussia, had combined to prevent the election of every candidate who was known to be at all favorable to the Confederation. To this proceeding, he said, the Government had openly influenced its officials, and the officials in turn the voters; of this he then gave a number of examples.

Mittnacht's defence against these accusations was both energetic and skilful. A few of the examples cited he could prove to be without foundation; although, without doubt, much that was underhanded remained irrefutable. With reference to the irrational abuse of Prussia, he said, that whenever the populace is stirred by intense excitement, a great deal that is noxious rises to the surface; but to hold the Ministers responsible for this he declared to be the height of injustice. The real originators of the excitement were the men of the National Party, who upon every occasion had demanded that Würtemberg should seek admission into the Northern Confederation, and to that end had represented their own State as corrupt and hastening to its decline, whereby they had deeply offended the patriotic self-esteem of the people. " The greater number of our deputies," he said in conclusion, "surely do not belong to the Government Party; but that as a body they are truly representative of the opinions prevailing in Würtemberg, of this I can assure you."

In this spirit the debate was carried on for some time. The Conservatives expressed regret at the tone which Braun had introduced into the discussion, to which Lasker replied that a thunder-storm often clears the atmosphere. " We have told one another some plain truths," he said, "and we will gradually learn to know one another better. At all events, one thing has become evident; as in the elections so in the Customs Parliament, the German question can no longer be kept down; to-day, in spite of the greatest discretion, it forces itself to the front everywhere, whether we approve of this or disapprove it."

The motion presented by the Committee, expressing disapprobation of the course pursued by the Würtemberg Government, was then voted upon by roll-call, the parties being greatly divided; and the result showed that it had been carried by 162 voices against 105.

Encouraged by these victories, the National Liberals

determined to follow them up. Eleven of their South German associates, from Darmstadt and Baden, supported by their entire party in the Reichstag, moved that in reply to the speech from the throne the draft of an address prepared and submitted by them should be accepted. In response to the first sentence of the speech, namely, that as a result of the national idea the Customs Union, from a small beginning, had grown into a firm union of all the German States, the draft expressed the hope that the thought of nationality would uninterruptedly continue to exert its beneficent influence, so that soon, beyond the sphere of the Customs Union, the inalienable right of the whole German nation to a full representation of all the common interests might be realized.

They were soon to discover, however, that they had entirely misjudged the disposition of the House. Although it had not been possible to reject the criticism of illegality passed upon the Würtemberg election-law, nevertheless all the other parties were wholly disinclined to reopen the political strife; and at the close of the final deliberation upon the motion, two counter motions to set aside the one regarding the address, and to pass to the order of the day, with a statement of the reasons for this action, were presented, one by the Free Conservatives, the other by the Party of Progress; and even as many as three motions, simply to pass to the order of the day, without stating any reasons, were before the House, moved by the Conservatives, the North German Clericals, and the South

German fraction, all indicative of the same opinion, that the best way to promote all the common German interests was, for the present, to labor together in harmony to solve those problems by which, within the limits fixed to its activity by treaty, the Parliament found itself confronted.

It was in vain that on May 7th Bennigsen declared most positively that no one in the ranks of the National Liberals desired to violate existing treaties; that they, too, believed, as a matter of course, that any change in these treaties must depend upon the free consent of all the South German Governments and Chambers. But why, he asked, forbid the expression of patriotic desires and hopes, the future fulfilment of which no one doubted, and to deny which no one had the courage?

Baron von Thüngen fought his battle from behind the bulwark of the existing treaties, the stipulations of which the South would fulfil with perfect good faith, he declared (he himself, it will be remembered, had done all in his power to prevent their conclusion), and would therefore expect the North to fulfil its obligations quite as scrupulously. In the South, he said, ever since the war of 1866, a deep distrust of the powerful victor had taken possession of the people, and filled them with apprehension of further deeds of violence. Although this was not encouraging, it was but natural; and it would therefore be most unwise, by over-hasty expectations beyond the stipulations made by the treaties, to alarm and so check the growth of the friendship which as yet was in its earliest and tenderest stage.

The motion simply to proceed to the order of the day was then adopted by a vote of 186 voices, Conservatives, Clericals, and Democrats, in its favor, against 150 Free Conservatives and North and South German National Liberals, opposed.

Whilst these political battles were being fought, the actual business of the Customs Parliament had begun. At first came a number of proposed measures of minor importance, having no bearing upon the chief work of the session, and involving no disputed questions of principle; these were therefore disposed of both quickly and harmoniously.

The first one was a commercial and navigation treaty between the Customs Union and Spain, by which each of the two contracting parties granted to the other the privileges of the most favored nations, a measure securing to German commerce the advantage of as low entrance duties in Spain as that country had heretofore accorded to the French. When H. H. Meier of Bremen expressed regret that the advantageous conditions to arise to the Customs Union from the treaty had not been extended to include the Spanish colonies as well, President Delbrück was in a position to reply that this desire had been presented in the Congress of the Spanish Cortes, and that the Spanish Minister had thereupon transmitted to Berlin the announcement that such a step would be sanctioned.

It was with greater readiness, therefore, that the Parliament ratified the treaties, which it did by a unanimous vote.

It will be well to mention in this connection that a commercial treaty of like purpose between the Customs Union and the States of the Church was submitted ten days later, and was also sanctioned without occasioning a difference of opinion between the parties.

The object of another measure proposed by the Federal Council was to mitigate certain prescriptions of the customs penal code, and to facilitate the entrance of imports into the territory of the Union by simplifying the handling of the goods by the customs officers. This bill was also received with great favor, and an agreement between the Federal Council and the Parliament was quickly reached upon every point. Regret was even expressed that the Federal Council had confined its action to these individual, though doubtlessly beneficial, changes; and a resolution was adopted by the House expressing the hope that the Governments would as quickly as practicable undertake a comprehensive and liberal reform in the customs laws and penal code. To this the Federal Council made no objection.

Meanwhile the more important measures to be considered during the session had been reached, — a new commercial treaty between Austria and the Customs Union, as also a revision, based upon the principles of the treaty, of that part of the former Union tariff left untouched by the treaty; and finally a proposed law regarding uniform taxation of tobacco throughout the territory of the Union.

All these measures were closely related in a two-fold manner. Ever since the English-French commercial treaty of 1860, a great free-trade movement had spread through one-half of Europe, finding expression in a reduction or total remission of numerous impost duties, as well as in the extension of the privileges of the most favored nations to many new contracting parties. Since 1866 Austria also had relinquished the position theretofore maintained, and according to the more recent fashion had concluded treaties with England, France, and Belgium. When, in 1867, negotiations between the Customs Union and Austria were begun relative to a renewal of the commercial treaty of 1865, which had been set aside by the war, it became evident that here, too, the former desire for a great customs combination between the Union and Austria had been relinquished, and that the aim of the present treaty was simply to extend and facilitate intercourse in so far as this was compatible with self-interest.

Perhaps this view was even more generally held in Germany than in Austria. Owing to the circumstances of the time, Bismarck had been thus inclined ever since 1853, and more especially so after the French commercial treaty. Delbrück had always, both in theory and in practice, been an earnest advocate of the principles of free trade; and in the North German Reichstag the great majority shared his views. The Conservatives of that day were quite as enthusiastically eager to abolish the duties on iron as were their

followers of the next generation to increase the import duties upon grains.   Among the National Liberals
and the Party of Progress, those who advocated the
opposite theory formed but an insignificant minority.
This was also true of the representatives of Darmstadt
and Baden, and only among the deputies from Bavaria
and Würtemberg was a large group of determined
protectionists to be found.   On the whole, therefore,
the new tariffs were not only favorably received by
the Parliament, but were hailed with joy.

It was but natural that under these circumstances
the Governments should flatter themselves with the
hope that in gratitude for these desirable tariff rates
the second and less popular half of their proposed
measure would receive favorable consideration.   The
abolition or reduction of so many impost duties would,
for the next few years at least, cause a considerable
decrease in the revenues arising from customs; this
the Governments estimated would reach in round figures two and one-half million thalers annually, for
which they were most anxious to find reimbursement,
nay, even hoped to secure a surplus, since many of
them, and foremost among these Prussia, knew their
home budgets to be seriously embarrassed.   It was
therefore proposed that both the excise upon native
and the impost duty upon imported tobacco should
be increased, and that a duty should be levied upon
imported petroleum, at present untaxed.

The commercial treaty with Austria was the first to
be considered, and from the outset it was to be seen

that the deliberation would terminate favorably. Most auspicious for the result, however, was the fact that there was no opportunity to display the customary zeal to amend, since a motion involving an agreement with a foreign Power leaves no intermediate course open ; it must be either accepted or rejected. It, however, occasioned a division in the ranks of the South German fraction, whose members were so firmly resolved to hold together upon all other questions. They were all ardently devoted to Austria, were filled with indignation that Prussia had ousted their Austrian brothers from the German Confederation, and were inspired by the hope again to win the favor of Austria. Three-fourths of these gentlemen could not find it in their hearts to reject a treaty which promised to bring them into closer sympathy with Austria. And so the deliberations were more in the nature of an amicable exchange of opinion than of a controversy. Of the great number of reduced tariff rates, only those on three articles were exhaustively discussed, — those on linen yarn, pig-iron, and wine.

In reply to a prophecy made by Moritz Mohl, that these flourishing industries would be destroyed by diminishing the protection thus far afforded them against foreign competition, Otto Camphausen stated, that although the linen spinneries had, without doubt, needed protection for a time, to allow them to accumulate the capital required for the transition from hand to machine spinning, yet their present financial condition was such that, with proper management, they need fear no foreign

competition, notwithstanding the reduction in the protective tariff. With regard to pig-iron, this zealous
protectionist was informed by Herr von Henning that
at one time when iron was unprotected, a thriving iron
industry was developed in East and West Prussia because raw material could be imported from England by
sea much more cheaply than it could be obtained from
Westphalia by way of the long overland route; but that
this industry perished when the importation of English
pig-iron was rendered impossible by a high protective
duty.

A peculiar condition of affairs was revealed by the
debate upon the duty on wine. Mecklenburg and
Lübeck were not at that time members of the Customs
Union because they were still bound by an earlier commercial treaty with France. Now the French Government had consented to release them from this agreement
on condition that the Customs Union would make a
corresponding reduction in the impost duties upon
wines, and would also agree to remove all internal
excise duties from imported wines. Since Austria also
was very desirous of this reduction, the Federal Council had embodied it in the treaty; and the members of
the House who were most familiar with these matters,
especially those from the South, declared that the German vineyards need fear no competition, and that there
was therefore no reason why the duty should not be
lowered, and Mecklenburg and Lübeck be thus gained
for the Customs Union.

The representatives from Darmstadt and Mainz,

Metz and Bamberger, declared that they fully approved
such a step, but mentioned the fact that within their
own State there was an excise on wine which was
nearly as high as the proposed duty on that which was
imported; so that for Hesse the peculiarly unfortunate
circumstance was brought about that protection was
given the foreigner at the expense of the native producer, in regard to which they gave notice that they
would present a special motion.

The treaty was then voted upon by the House, and
was accepted by a vote of all voices except seventeen in
its favor. The latter were all stanch protectionists of
the South German fraction, who, much to their sorrow,
were obliged to admit that according to the doctrines
they held, greater freedom of intercourse with Austria
would result to the disadvantage of their own land.

According to the usual course, the deliberation upon
the second tariff bill submitted by the Federal Council
was now in order, for in this way only could a correct estimate be formed of the deficiency which the
reduction of the customs duties would occasion in the
receipts of the States; this would naturally lead to
the question of how the deficiency might be made
good by the imposition of new taxes. The South
German fraction feared, however, that in this way the
majority might perhaps be induced to vote for the
tobacco tax proposed by the Governments; and Moritz
Mohl moved that this be placed upon the order of the
day. He regarded it as so important a subject, he
said, that it ought to be considered in its consequences,

apart from everything else which might tend to influence the decision in regard to it.

Georg Vincke, who in this session preserved a remarkable silence, objected to such a proceeding, declaring it to be the invariable custom first to estimate the expenditures or deficiencies which might arise, and then to adjust the revenues to these demands. "However," he added, "since Mohl, as I understand, expresses the unanimous desire of our South German associates, we ought to be obliging and grant it."

Agidi lent his support to this expression of a fraternal spirit; and although Bamberger remarked, "We South Germans are never unanimous, neither is this a convent of the Knights of Malta with a North and a South German tongue, but a German Parliament," still Mohl's motion carried the day, and on May 15th the preliminary deliberation upon the taxation of tobacco was begun.

Since that time this question has frequently been discussed in our parliaments, and its solution sought in the most divers ways. To treat of it here in full would hardly be a pleasure to my readers; it will suffice to call to mind the leading points in controversy.

Whenever the subject arises, immediately is marshalled an array of interested disputants, tobacco plantters, manufacturers, and dealers. It was argued that by increased taxation this flourishing industry would be seriously crippled, if not totally ruined. This was especially to be taken into consideration, since the

producers were largely men of smaller means, such as
tobacco growers, factory employees, etc., who by the
proposed measure would suddenly be deprived of their
means of subsistence. As in the production, so in the
consumption, it would be the poorer classes who would
be chiefly affected by the heavier tax upon tobacco;
since, as was generally conceded, it was they who
shouldered the greater part of the burden imposed by
indirect taxes. It was declared to be both unjust and
cruel to add to the cost of the poor man's one luxury,
his pipe. This appeal in the name of philanthropy
was the more effective, since the men of the middle
class also preferred to pay a lower rather than a higher
price for their Bremen cigars, as did the rich man for
his Havana.

The advocates of the tax met these objections by
eclaring that tobacco was not one of the necessaries
f life, but a luxury, and as such, and because of its
peculiar nature, was especially well adapted to be an
article of taxation. The great quantities consumed in
Germany showed its use to be general in all classes;
therefore this tax, more than any other, would yield
a large revenue to the State without being seriously
felt by the individual consumer. Moreover, every one
ould, if he chose, avoid the slight increase of expense by smoking a little less. In so far as philanthropy toward the poor man was concerned, surely the
word was never more misapplied; for should the poor
man smoke a few cigars less each day and spend the
money thus saved for bread to feed his children, this

would be a benefit both to his family and himself.
With regard to tobacco, it happened to be the case
that the cheaper, and therefore poorer, kinds, and
above all others those raised in Germany, contained
much more nicotine than did the finer American
brands,[1] and therefore were much more injurious to
health. What, asked they, could be said against a
tax which, if consumption remained the same in spite
of its imposition, would fill the State treasuries, and
if it acted as a restraint upon consumption would
improve the health of the poor man?

To the further objection, that the manufacturers
would suffer, the reply was given that any material
change in the customs-system always resulted momen-
tarily to the detriment of some branches of industry
and to the advantage of others. Unless conditions
were doomed to remain at a complete stand-still,
changes must be undertaken in the hope that, judging by past experience, after a short period of transition the equilibrium would again be restored. At all
events, so small a revenue for national purposes as was
derived from the consumption of tobacco in Germany
was unexampled elsewhere in the civilized world.[2]

---

[1] According to Liebig's careful investigations.

[2] With regard to the conditions prevailing at the time, Michaelis
made the following statement: Duty on coffee per hundred-weight in the
Customs Union 5 thlrs., in England 9¼ thlrs.; on tea per cwt. 8 thlrs. in
the C. U., 18⅜ in Eng.; on 100 quarts of brandy 13 thlrs. in the C. U.,
an average of 86 thlrs. in Eng.; on a like quantity of wine 6 thlrs. in
the C. U., 8⅜ in Eng.; on beer, a like quantity, 1¼ thlrs. in the C. U.,
4⅜ in Eng.; on tobacco per cwt. 4 thlrs. in the C. U., 116 to 129 thlrs.
in Eng.

In France the State revenues arising from tobacco amounted in

In 1868 these arguments and counter-arguments were presented by the disputants with equal ardor. From the outset it was evident, as indicated by the number of speakers who desired to be heard, that the current of sympathy was wholly toward cheap cigars and against the imposition of the new rates of taxation. That which decided the question, however, was the circumstance that, besides the Party of Progress and the South German fraction, by ·far the greater number of the National Liberals also opposed the measure with as much acrimony as they had shown toward the bill presented by the Government on April 22d. It was by one of their leaders that the deliberations were given the turn leading to the final decision ; admitting that the essential features of the bill were well taken, he, however, denied the need of an increase in the State revenue.

It was the duty of every popular representative body, said Twesten, before consenting to increased taxation of the people, to require convincing proof of its necessity, or else to demand a binding agreement that corresponding relief would be afforded through the reduction of other taxes. Both of these conditions were wholly absent in this case. A previous speaker, he continued, had pointed out that by in-

---

1865 to 233 million francs, in the Customs Union to 2,700,000 thlrs., or 10 million francs. As based upon the average prices of that day, cane sugar was taxed in the C. U. at 55% of its value, coffee at 22%, rice at 25%, cocoa at 33%. As opposed to this, tobacco was taxed at 18.2%, which made it appear that the legislators desired to influence the people to purchase tobacco in preference to food materials.

creasing the tax on tobacco the more grievous tax on salt could be discontinued; this was very good, yet, as every one knew, it was much more difficult to effect the abatement of a tax than to establish one. Therefore the House ought not to relinquish its restraining power upon the tax on tobacco until the abatement of the duty on salt was an accomplished fact.

It was true, he said, that the reduction of duties proposed by the tariff reform was apparently very great; a closer examination would, however, reveal the fact that it was largely confined to duties which were as insignificant to commercial interests as they were to the Customs treasury. The hopes which in commercial circles had been placed upon the reform had by no means been realized. The question naturally arose why, for instance, the duty on pig-iron was lowered, and that on the various forms of manufactured iron remained unaltered. In fact, of all the long list of articles upon which the duty had been lowered, there were really only three, pig-iron, wine, and linen yarn, on which the reduction of duty threatened for the moment materially to affect the State treasuries. In connection with these, it was, however, more than probable that the decrease in duties would be quickly followed by a corresponding increase in importation, and thus an abundant return be made to the State treasuries for their momentary loss. Therefore the necessity of a new, and especially of so high a tax as that proposed to be levied upon tobacco, was by no means convincingly shown.

At the time of this discussion the situation was as follows : The duty upon imported tobacco amounted to 4 thalers per hundred-weight. In the North German Confederation native tobacco yielded a land tax, in four classes, of from 3 to 6 thalers to the Prussian acre. In South Germany no tax of any kind was levied upon tobacco-raising, but in exporting their production to North Germany the tobacco-planters were obliged to pay a transportation duty (*Uebergangs- steuer*) [1] of 20 silver groschens per hundred-weight.

What was now proposed by the Federal Council was to raise the duty on imported tobacco from 4 to 6 thalers, and to place a uniform tax of 12 thalers on tobacco produced within the territory of the Customs Union, which was double the maximum rate heretofore levied in the North ; in consideration of this the South would no longer be required to pay the transportation duty.

In opposition to this, Twesten proposed, for the reasons which have been stated, that the duty on foreign tobacco should remain unchanged, and that the tax on the home production should be fixed at 6 thalers per acre, or three silver groschens on every parcel of three square roods.

These rates would yield annually, instead of a rev-

---

[1] TRANSLATOR'S NOTE. — *Uebergangssteuer* is the tax which those States of the German Empire which levy a tax upon articles of consumption produced within their territory are permitted to levy upon like articles imported from other States of the Empire ; the rate of this tax is not allowed to exceed the legal rate of the excise levied upon the home production.

enue of 1,900,000 thalers as was desired by the Governments, about 450,000 thalers, of which, however, after deducting the South German transportation duty heretofore levied, and the cost of collecting, little would remain to be turned over to the Customs Union treasury.

Michaelis, as representative of the Governments, submitted a statement based upon exact figures, showing that unless the revenue of the North German Confederation were augmented by receipts from the Customs Union, the Confederation would be compelled to increase its *pro rata* assessments by two millions, in consequence of which the Prussian budget would close with a deficit of five millions. Nevertheless, Twesten won a complete victory.

After the proposed Government measure, as well as an amendment with a view to a compromise, had been rejected by an overwhelming majority, Twesten's motion was voted upon by roll-call, and adopted by 167 voices in its favor against 135 opposed. The minority consisted of those deputies who antagonized a new tax of any kind, of North German Progressists and Democrats, and South Germans of all parties.

Under these circumstances the National Liberals desisted from hostility to the Government as well as from all further opposition on principle. At least a part of the original bill would have been rescued by them despite the general disapproval. They declared that equalization of the taxes throughout the North and South was in itself a great advance ; more than this was,

for the present, impracticable. The newly created national institution, the Customs Parliament, would show
but little wisdom should it begin its activity by increasing the burdens of the people. Especially inju-
dicious would it be to alienate the South from the
national idea by diminishing the protection heretofore
extended the cultivation of the vine, and at the same
time placing a heavy tax upon the production of tobacco, so long as a continued deficit in the State treasuries was no more in evidence than it was at present.
Should such a condition come about, the National
Liberals, they declared, would not be found wanting.

In the Federal Council these fine promises created
but little confidence. Notwithstanding all the reasons
given, the No was plainly to be discerned in all that
was said. Nevertheless, the next day was destined to
bring with it a bright afterglow of the old sentiments,
and, strange to say, in connection with a budget question. To be sure, it was not one dealing with the
imposition of a new tax, but with the reduction of an
existing one.

On May 18th the final deliberation, or third reading,
of the commercial treaty with Austria was in order.
With regard to one of its positions, the reduction of
the import duty on wine, Bamberger and his associates
now brought forward the motion of which they had
given notice, asking that the Federal Council of the
Customs Union take steps toward a redress of the
grievance to which, in the Grand Duchy of Hesse,
the conflict between the reduction in the duty on wine,

and the existing system of indirect taxation gave rise. As has been stated, unless relief were afforded, the duty on French wines would be only a trifle higher than the tax on domestic wines in Hesse-Darmstadt; on the Hessian tierce the duty would be about twelve florins, the tax, a little over nine,[1] which, together with the greater expense connected with the cultivation of the vine in Hesse, rendered competition with the French wines simply impossible. Moreover, the complaint was made, by those presenting the motion, that the method pursued in collecting the duty was intolerable, and opposed to the principles of the Customs Union, impeding intercourse, occasioning the searching of houses by day and by night, provoking the people to smuggle and defraud.

Although these statements were not to be denied, Moritz Mohl, in the name of the South German fraction, rose to offer relentless opposition to Bamberger's request. "What existing treaties require of us in this matter is evident," said he. "The treaty of July 8th enumerates the articles upon which every State is free to levy an internal tax; wine is one of these, although the maximum tax which may be placed upon it is limited. Now, the present tax of nine florins levied upon wine in Hesse is less than this maximum allowed, ten

[1] According to a statement rendered by Fabricius, Tax Counsellor for Hesse (p. 253 of the stenographic reports); he, however, omits from the total amount of the taxes his own estimates regarding the wine-trade at wholesale and under grant of a charter, and therefore places the entire amount of the tax at seven florins and ten kreuzers.

Compare also the speech made by the Hessian Government Counsellor, Pfannebecker, to be found a few pages farther on.

florins, and therefore quite in conformity with the requirements of the Customs Union treaty. Consequently
if any actual grievance exists, it is wholly within
the province of the Hessian Assembly to relieve it.
The Customs Parliament has as little right to interfere in this matter as has the Customs Federal Council, and would by such a step unlawfully extend its
jurisdiction."

The Hessian representative in the Customs Federal
Council, Privy Councillor Hofmann, hastened to confirm the correctness of this view, denying the Parliament's jurisdiction in the matter, and reserving to
his Government all right to act.

The ardent zeal of these two gentlemen was not
destined to bring them much glory. Up to this point
Bismarck had taken no part in the discussion personally. Now, however, he made the plain yet effective
statement, that at the present moment he was not,
any more than was his colleague from Hesse, in a
position to say whether or not the Federal Council
would regard the subject of the motion just presented
as within its jurisdiction. "Since, however," he continued, "the competency of the Federal Council in
the matter under discussion has been questioned by
one of its members, I feel compelled to state that
this is the personal opinion of the gentleman, and
that neither of us is authorized to express an opinion
upon this question in the name of the Federal Council. Moreover, my impression *prima facie* is the reverse of that expressed by my Hessian colleague.

[Cries of "Bravo!"]   I can readily imagine that
should the Federal Council believe that the freedom
of intercourse in the interior which the institutions
of the Customs Union are designed to guarantee is
either restricted or endangered by the absence of uniformity in the tax system, it would no doubt consider
itself competent to undertake the remedy."   [Enthu-
siastic bravos.]

To this Bismarck added, after listening to a reply
made by Hofmann, "In my estimation the question is
not whether the Hessian laws conform to the requirements of the Customs Union treaty, but whether the
legislative organs of the Customs Union are authorized
to decide the question whether this is the case or not."

To-day it would be difficult to find any one in either
the North or the South to whom the objection of in-
competency would appear reasonable.   For example,
the Parliament resolves upon a certain tax on wine,
resulting in a serious disadvantage to one of the States
of the Union.   Shall this State not be privileged to
call the attention of the Federal Council to this grievance, leaving to this body the speedy redress?   The
Customs Union declares it to be its purpose to bring
about a general uniformity in all the inland duties on
articles of consumption.   Shall its Parliament be debarred from considering and deciding upon a case of
gross non-uniformity?

The treaty required co-operative action to prevent
smuggling and fraud in connection with the collection of excise duties; the Bamberger motion was

directed against a legislative measure which was constantly provocative of these abuses; and yet it was
questioned whether this step were one beyond the
jurisdiction of the legislative organs, and it was even
looked upon as evincing a systematic attempt to extend
their power.

Up to this point the discussion had at least been confined to the special question in hand, that is, whether
the Parliament were privileged to concern itself with
the Hessian wine-tax, so long as this did not exceed
the maximum of ten florins allowed by the treaty.
Now, however, after Bismarck had so plainly indicated
his approval of the motion, the suspicious irritability
of the South German fraction was doubly aroused; and
the Würtemberg Clerical, Probst, allowed his excitement to lead him to intensify to the utmost the ill-
feeling created by Mohl's political blunder, and so to
induce an important political discussion by the very
warning he uttered against it.

" There is in this House," said he, " a large party
which hopes by extending the competency of this assembly to open to the South the way into the Northern
Confederation. Our party is opposed to this. It is
our intention rigidly to uphold the limits set to the
competency of this body, and therefore to discounte-
nance every attempt to introduce the German question,
that our differences may not be noised abroad, nor
peace within this Parliament be disturbed. There is
yet another consideration. Over our heads hangs an
avalanche, which, by the concussion caused by our con-

flict, may be set to rolling. There is one who would
listen with lurking satisfaction should we be compelled
here to state whereby the antagonism between the
North and the South is maintained; why the elections
in the South gave evidence of so great disinclination
to Prussia; why we refuse to seek admission into the
Northern Confederation."

By this speech all the sluices were thrown open, and
a torrent of indignation rushed forth; for every member of the Majority was burning to refute every one of
these assertions.

Again Bismarck took the word. He directed attention to his well-known circular note of September 7th,
and the statement contained in it, that the North German Confederation would scrupulously refrain from
bringing pressure to bear upon the South to induce it
to seek entrance into the Confederation. Not until the
latter should of its own free will announce such a desire would the North give consideration to the question
whether its own interests would admit of such a step.
"For," said he, "we are not so anxious as you suppose us to be, gentlemen. Continue your deliberations
upon matters of taxation in peace of mind; we have
no thought to extend the power of this Parliament;
neither, however, will we allow it to be diminished."
Then, in conclusion, he uttered one sentence which fell
like a thunderbolt upon Probst's insinuation of danger
threatening from France, and shattered it: "Above all
else, I would advise you to remember that an appeal
to fear never finds a response in German hearts."

At once, and from all sides, the storm burst upon the
Southern fraction and their Ultramontane and Social-
democratic sympathizers. "Yes," it was declared,
"we do desire national unity; we intend to proclaim
that, both here and everywhere. We are not averse to
an honest encounter, for thus alone will we learn to
understand one another; we intend to carry the internal
struggle to its close, and at the same time to proclaim
abroad that even now we are united in the purpose to
forbid any foreign interference with the consummation of
German unity. But surely we do not seek it by way
of an extension of this assembly's competency. To
that end the Customs Union will not suffice; the con-
vocation of even a great parliament cannot call into
being a national political existence, such as will meet
our aspirations for Germany; this will require the institution of an established government such as we have
in the North German Confederation, and which the
Customs Union cannot supply."

Such were the leading thoughts that formed the
key-note of the many-tuned speeches of the parties
which, though usually so divided in their opinions,
were for the moment united through Probst's short-
sighted zeal — Old Liberals and National Liberals,
Progressists and Conservatives.

Probably the greatest discomfiture of the day was
caused the Southern fraction toward the close of the
debate by the appearance upon the orator's platform of
Völk, the representative of the Bavarian province of
Schwaben. In a speech overflowing with wit, enthu-

siasm, and good sense, he disputed the right of his associates from the South to make that entire section
responsible for their utterances by using the expression,
" we South Germans, we Swabians," since, as he clearly
demonstrated, it was solely due to the accidental distribution of the inhabitants in the election districts that
his opponents had been enabled to secure the larger
representation in the House, whereas the greater number of votes had really been cast for the national side.
As he closed with the exclamation, " Among us there
are some who still seem to enjoy throwing snowballs
at one another, but the time is at hand when the sun
with the increasing warmth of its rays will deprive
them of the material for their missiles. Yes, truly,
my friends, the springtime has come upon Germany!"
jubilant acclamation rang through the House ; and not
only the treaty with Austria, but Bamberger's motion
as well, was approved by an overwhelming majority.

This was the most vexatious day the Southern fraction had as yet experienced ; there was, however, ample
consolation in store for them. It soon appeared that
even in the nationally inclined majority, there still
remained much of the old spirit which · aised German
unity as its ideal high upon its standard, but decided
all practical action by local and material interests alone.
On May 18th enthusiasm had run high for a great
and united future; on the 19th the finances received
cool and careful scrutiny in the light of home interests.

The subject under consideration was the Government bill regarding the reform of the general customs

tariff, in so far as this had not already been modified in
favor of greater freedom of intercourse by the Austrian
commercial treaty.   There was a long list of commodities upon which the duty was either to be entirely
remitted or to be materially lowered, classed under 57
heads, including many subdivisions, and making a reduction in duties estimated at 200,000 thalers annually.   In this list, so pleasing to the eye of free-traders,
only one item stood forth conspicuously and annoy-
ingly; it was not the abolition of an existing duty, but
the restoration of one remitted in 1865, a duty of fifteen silver groschens on a hundred-weight of· coal-oil,
the annual revenue from which it was estimated would
amount to 500,000 thalers, and would probably grow
larger with every year.   All the liberal sympathizers
of the people who on the day before had voted with
Bismarck were on this point in perfect harmony with
the Southern fraction, whose intention it was to prevent
the Customs Parliament from passing a single new tax.

The House concerned itself but little with the other
positions of the tariff; all the interest was centred
upon petroleum.   It was even rumored that should its
general unpopularity result in the defeat of this Article
of the bill, the Federal Council would withdraw the
entire measure.   To gain certainty upon this point,
Braun (Wiesbaden), after a short general debate,
moved that the separate Articles should not be considered in the order in which they appeared in the bill, but
that the one regarding petroleum should be given the
precedence.   The House so decided, although President

Delbrück had declared that it was not the usage of
the Federal Council to make hypothetic decisions; it
would await the action of the House, and then declare
its intentions.

That the duty on petroleum would fare even harder
than had the tax on tobacco was not to be doubted.
For, to begin with, all the arguments which had been
arrayed against the latter applied with equal force to
petroleum: the insufficient evidence of an actual financial exigency, which could only be established by a
careful study of the completed budgets for both Union
and State for the coming year; the probability that
the reduction of the other duties would not result in
a deficiency of revenue, but by inducing greater consumption would eventually be to the advantage of the
Customs treasuries; further, the malicious imputation
that in this case, as in that of every indirect tax, the
burden would fall upon the shoulders of the poor man;
and, finally, the impossibility, politically, for the Customs Parliament to establish a continuous source of
revenue over the disbursement of which it had no
right of supervision.

" My vote," said the leader of the Bavarian National
Party, Marquard Barth, " will be cast against any
form of consent, so that the Federal Council will find
itself compelled to convoke this assembly again next
year, and grant us greater privileges, such as become
a true representation of the German nation. He who
keeps his purse-strings tied," he added in closing,
" holds power within his grasp, for he will find him-

self surrounded by suppliants; but he who has emptied out all that he has, is no better than a beggar himself."

There was still another argument against the duty on coal-oil, namely the indisputable fact, that, unlike tobacco, it was not an article of luxury, the consumption of which had no more desirable effect than to injure the health of the consumer; but that in consequence of its enormous importation and exceeding cheapness, it had become a means of labor, consequently a source of increased production and wealth; that it had become indispensable to all classes of the population, and, bringing light to the poorest hut, had made night-work possible to the occupants. "Will you," exclaimed Braun at the close of a flowery speech full of pathos, "will you, by raising the price of coal-oil, transform the people's light into darkness?"

This multiplicity of reasons was met by the former Prussian Minister of Finance of the new era, Herr von Patow, with the calm assurance of one who knows well that of which he speaks. He called Barth's attention to the possibility that a Customs Parliament habitually sterile of desired results would cease to be convoked at all by the Federal Council; he advised his adversaries not to use the Customs Parliament's official ignorance of the budget matters of the individual States as a pretext to deny the existence of public exigencies, since every one was fully aware that the members of the House were perfectly familiar with the budgets of their respective States. He set at naught

the complaints regarding the pernicious effects of the
tax on oil by showing how insignificant would be the
share falling to the individual. He had obtained from
both consumers and dealers exact data regarding the
quantity of oil used upon his estates, and had found
that for the poorest field laborers this averaged ten
pounds a year for each family. Since the tax proposed
was fifteen silver groschens per hundred-weight, the
average laborer would in consequence be burdened
with a tax of one and one half silver groschens, an
exaction which he could meet almost exactly by drink-
ing one pint of beer less each year.

Deputy von Wedemeier confirmed these statements ;
his statistics were based upon more extended research,
the books of both large and small oil-dealers having
been submitted to his examination, by which it was
clearly demonstrated that the consumption of petroleum increased materially with each ascending degree
of prosperity, until for the millionnaire it reached the
large amount of nine hundred pounds, entailing a tax
of four and one-half thalers, ninety times as large a
sum as that required of the poor man. It was therefore pre-eminently a tax of which it could not truth-
fully be asserted that it unjustly oppressed the small
consumers.

However, the majority was not to be influenced in
its decision, and the Article regarding petroleum was
rejected by a vote of 190 voices against 99. The
deliberations upon the other Articles of the bill passed
most smoothly ; all the proposed remissions of duties

were sanctioned despite Mohl's strenuous opposition.
The only action of sufficient interest to be recorded
here was a motion receiving the support of more than
one party, proposing that a clause be added asking the
Federal Council to submit a bill in the near future
dealing with a corresponding reform in the taxation
of sugar, since a decrease in the present rates would
most likely be followed by a much larger consumption,
and consequently by a proportionate increase in the
State revenues.

To this Delbrück replied that he fully appreciated
the grounds upon which the request was based. Since,
however, sugar was by far the most important item in
the whole system of taxation of articles of consumption, even a slight error in the arrangements concerning
it would have most serious financial consequences; the
desired action must therefore be preceded by a most
thorough investigation; and for this reason the promise to give the subject careful consideration was the
only one which he could at present make.

When, on May 23d, the House proceeded to the final
deliberation upon the tariff bill, Delbrück announced,
in the name of the Federal Council, that unless the
tax on petroleum were approved, the entire bill would
be unacceptable to the Governments. This had been
fully expected, and therefore made little impression.
The free-trade majority believed that by the time
another year had passed, the Federal Council would
find itself compelled to be less unyielding, and therefore definitively refused its consent to the tax on oil by

149 voices against 86, whereupon Bismarck at once announced that the Federal Council withdrew the entire bill.

This closed the business of the session; all that now remained was a series of courtesies to be extended by the North to the representatives from the South. In the speech from the throne, with which King William closed the session, he commended the results so far achieved, and presaged an auspicious future for the desired measures which had as yet failed of enactment. The labors shared during the past weeks, he hoped, had removed, or at least softened, dividing prejudices; in the future, as heretofore, his attitude would be prescribed not by the power vested in himself, but by a sacred regard for the rights of the several States of the Union and for existing treaties.

In honor of its South German guests, the City of Berlin gave a brilliant garden party; this was followed by an elegant banquet in the Exchange, the festivities being closed by a pleasure trip to Kiel, where the new Federal naval station and the beginnings of the German war marine were inspected.

Our South German friends gladly accepted all these evidences of friendship; their official thanks, however, appeared in the form of an address to their constituents, in which they rendered an account of their stewardship, taking much credit to themselves for having unyieldingly and effectively obstructed every attempted change in the nature of the Customs Parliament, as well as every proposed increase of significance in the taxes.   In conclusion, they declared that their observations in the North had but deepened their conviction that union with the Northern Confederation would require of the Southern States the complete surrender of their independence; that the Prussian tendency to excessive furtherance of military objects was prejudicial both to material interests and moral culture, and must rest as a crushing burden upon the people.

The only way of escape from all this, they believed, lay in the direction of a firm association uniting all the strength of South Germany on a basis of liberal institutions, namely, the formation at last of the Southern Confederation.

III.   CLOSING WEEKS OF THE REICHSTAG.

The idea of national unity had, as has been seen, made no converts in the first Customs Parliament. Bismarck who, as he had himself informed the South Germans on May 18th, could await their desire to be admitted into the Confederation without the least impatience, was little disturbed by this fact, and before many days had passed, on May 27th, authorized the re-assembling of the German Reichstag, that the work of promoting the public welfare, and consolidating the Confederation, so well begun, might be completed.

The first condition to such a result was that the uncertainty in matters of finance should be relieved, an end for which the action of the Customs Parliament had been as barren of results as it had been for the as-

piration after German unity, and for the achievement
of which Miquel's motion, accepted by the Reichstag on
April 22d, proved an effectual barrier by making an
agreement between that body and the Federal Council
impossible.

What was most necessary, therefore, was that an
understanding upon this point should be reached as
quickly as possible. Therefore, as the first step in the
desired direction, immediately after the close of Whit-
sun-tide week, the draft of the Federal budget for 1869
was on June 4th submitted to the House, which then
selected June 8th as the date for the preliminary deliberation by the plenum.

Although some complaints were heard that the time
thus allowed was much too short for a thorough study
of the budget, the great majority were desirous to escape from the heat of the dog-days in Berlin; and upon
closer inspection the budget was after all found to coincide so nearly with its predecessor in most points,
or else the reasons for deviation were so apparent, that
a more detailed examination was really not necessary.
Therefore, when the session was opened on July 8th,
every one felt convinced that the only hotly debated
point would be the additional clause proposed by Miquel to the bill regarding the Federal debt.

As has been seen, in the last discussion of the bill
Twesten urged insistence upon this clause; since the
Government could not afford an interruption in its
work of founding a navy, and through its dependence
upon the money to be realized by the loan would be

forced to accept the clause upon which this was conditional. To be sure, the other members of the National Liberal Party who were heard in the House
declared that now, as before, the party intended to
further the interests of the navy by a vigorous support,
and that, should the Government, through its persistent rejection of the clause, fail to obtain the loan, the
National Liberals would be quite willing to consent
to other means of raising the required amount; still,
since the party, in direct contradiction to these fine
phrases, by its attitude in the Customs Parliament had
denied to the Governments every increase of revenue,
but little credence was given these protestations of
good will.

The Conservative press daily developed the theme,
that it was the purpose of the Liberal Opposition to
deprive the Government of every source of supply for
the requirements of the navy, except that offered by the
loan, thus compelling it to accept the Miquel clause.
In every key the changes were rung upon the malevo-
lence of a course of action by which it was intended
to force an unconstitutional extension of power at the
expense of the country's safety, by refusing the necessary funds for the navy.

To this the Liberals, of course, made reply by revers-
ing the accusation, declaring the responsibility for re-
tarding the work upon the navy to lie wholly at the
door of the Government, which for the sake of retaining a reactionary and arbitrary power refused its sanction to this clause, emanating from a true conception

of constitutional government; in consequence, it found but 300,000 thalers at its disposal for expenditure upon the navy instead of the three and a half million of the loan.

In this warfare of charges and counter-charges, the position of the Government, which was simply that of insistence upon the retention of an existing provision of the Constitution, was far more tenable than was that of the Opposition, advocating, as they did, a fundamental change of existing conditions. Outside of the initiated few, the far-reaching consequences of Miquel's apparently inoffensive clause were little understood; and with the popularity at that time enjoyed by the aspiring young navy, the dispute by which its prospects were jeopardized caused much vexation among the people.

It was therefore with greater eagerness that the National Liberals reiterated their former assurance that they were far from intending to injure the navy; quite the contrary was true; should the Government insist upon making the loan impossible, they would see to it that the required funds were forthcoming from other sources.

What they expected to gain by their proposed course it is hard to discover. Should they provide the Government with the desired funds through increased taxation this would, to be sure, make a navy possible; but that the end had been achieved by means of a heavier tax burden instead of the loan would not be likely to add to the popularity of the party, besides

which, should the necessity of a loan be removed,
that of a law regarding the administration of the Federal debt, together with Miquel's clause, would also
disappear.

However, this course once adopted, must be pursued; and so, in reversal of the usual order, it was
the Liberal Left which now anxiously scanned the
items of the budget to discover a possible way of aug-
menting the revenue, whereas the Governments persisted in their refusal to lay additional burdens upon
the people.

To raise the three and a half millions which the
loan was originally intended to furnish, their first re-
course was to an increase of the *pro rata* contributions. Delbrück with decision pronounced this to be
infeasible; since it had already been found necessary
to fix the amount of the contributions at twenty-three
millions, three millions more than had been required
the preceding year. A still further increase would
completely demoralize the finances of the individual
States.

" Very well," was the reply, " then we will desist
from this proposed increase in the contributions. The
budget, however, affords other ways and means of
coming to the assistance of the navy. It is quite obvious that the principal receipts of the Confederation have
been estimated at too low a figure; the deficiency
apprehended as the result of the reduced postal rates,
as also that arising in consequence of certain reductions in duties, will not be as great as feared, but,

on the contrary, will be transformed into a surplus by the impetus given to intercourse."

Delbrück admitted that in a few years this might perhaps be the case, but directed attention to the fact that it was the budget for 1869 that was now being determined, and that for the coming year the continuance of a deficit was beyond question. The criticism had been made, that the half million to accrue from the tobacco tax in its new form had not been taken into account in the estimates. "Why should it appear in the budget for 1869," asked Delbrück, "for its amount is not decided upon until the summer of 1869, and it is not due until December of that year?"

No better success awaited a proposition made by Lasker. It had appeared that franking privileges had been extended to twenty-two per cent of all the letters passing through the mails during the past year; should this privilege be withdrawn a large sum would be realized by the Government, it was claimed. To this Delbrück remarked, that of these letters by far the greater number represented the official correspondence of the Government authorities; should postage be required upon them, the revenue realized from this source would be paid by the several States, and therefore would be equivalent to an increase in the *pro rata* contributions.

Thus the search in the ordinary budget for the means wherewith to meet the extraordinary demands of the navy had to be abandoned, leaving the realization of the loan as the only resource. The more apparent this fact became, the more animated grew the debate upon the Miquel clause, each party seeking to throw upon the other the responsibility for the disadvantage to be suffered by the country, should the condition made be insisted upon. Back and forth flew the charge of doctrinaire obstinacy, and lack of patriotism. A large part of the House, however, remained wholly unaffected by these polemic pyrotechnics. From various sides came the criticism that all this recrimination was useless; since all parties were united in the wish to see the German navy established in strength, and it was not possible that no way could be devised by which the nation's desire could be realized and yet neither party be forced to abandon its principles in the fulfilment.

In response to this appeal, rose Otto Camphausen, at that time one of the highest officials in the Prussian Ministry of Finance. He was as well known for his proficiency in matters of this department as he was for his skill as a parliamentarian; in his utterances there was generally little attempt at rhetoric elegance and oratorical effect, but, based upon extensive technical knowledge, and characterized by convincing logic and unerring judgment as to the attainable, they never failed to convince.

To a vehement utterance made by Schulze-Delitzsch, he now added the remark that it was most unreasonable of the Federal Council, which had but just derived its power, to authorize government loans from the Reichstag, in that the latter had embodied this provision in the Constitution, now to refuse the Reichstag the right to control the exercise of this power. Camphausen then directed attention to the circumstance, that in connection with this subject very different kinds, of official control were possible; that in Prussia, according to a law enacted in 1850, the administration of the public debt was placed under rigid supervision, and that this arrangement, after a test of eighteen years, had proved itself beyond objection. When in 1867 the Federal Council had announced, in connection with the loan for the navy, that the draft of a law regarding the Federal debt would be submitted, it had been the general understanding that this law, by conforming in its general features to the excellent one in force in Prussia, would secure the advantages of the latter to the administration of the Federal debt, and that it would be unopposed in the Reichstag.

" The Governments also were greatly surprised when the reverse of this appeared," he said, "and even more so when it was proposed to infuse into the bill a political principle of far-reaching significance. That they should refuse their consent was but natural."

He then exhorted the two parties not to exasperate each other by prolonged contention, not to tie their own hands for the future by rashly vehement asseverations, but instead, to direct their efforts towards an adjustment whereby an agreement would become possible.

His counsel was received with enthusiastic applause, but did not prevent a last wrathful battle of words between Wagener (Neustettin) and Count Schwerin.

This closed the general debate, and on June 9th the special deliberation upon the several items of the budget was begun. The estimates for the navy being set aside for the time, all the other sections were conferred upon on the 9th and 10th of June in a manner more suggestive of an academic discussion than of a parliamentary struggle. There was no lack of criticism or of hopes expressed with regard to the future, nor were a few harmless motions for amendment wanting; the result of each vote, always excepting the estimates for the navy, was, however, invariably favorable, until all the paragraphs of the budget were approved. Evidently the anticipated action of the Federal Council claimed the interest to the exclusion of the figures presented for consideration.

The Governments had, in fact, agreed upon a proposal of compromise after the manner suggested by Camphausen, for which they had obtained the sanction of the King as well as the approval of Bismarck, who was absent owing to illness. On the 10th, when the voting upon the budget by headings was drawing to a close, President Simson announced to the House that a bill of the following contents had been received from the Federal Chancellor: —

The administration of the loan for expenditures upon the navy as approved by the Reichstag in 1867 shall, until the enactment of a definitive law regulating the

administration of the Federal debt, be committed to
the charge of the Prussian central administration of
State debts, by which it shall be conducted according
to the law of 1850, and under the restriction that no
change shall be made in the rate of interest except
as may be provided by a special law. To the Federal
Chancellor shall be intrusted its supreme supervision ;
the oath required of the officials in accordance with
the Prussian law by which they engage not to execute
any unlawful order received from the Government
shall, however, henceforth apply to the administration of Federal matters as well. The administration
shall be conducted under the supervision of a Committee on the Federal Debt, consisting of three members of the Federal Council and three of the Reichstag,
elected by the members of the body to which they
respectively belong, together with the President of
the Prussian Court of Accounts. This Committee
shall have the unqualified right at any time to examine the records and accounts of the administration,
to make inquiry into the methods pursued by it, and
regarding the balance on hand ; with regard to all this
the Committee shall annually render an account to the
Reichstag for the purpose of discharge.

The proposed compromise consisted, therefore, in
that the general and permanent arrangements for the
administration of the Federal debt were not now to
be determined, since this would have required of one
of the two parties the renunciation of its principles
regarding the Miquel clause, but that for the present

only the administration of the loan of 1867 was to
be placed under a provisional management in a manner providing all necessary precautions for the protection of the State's interests.

The House at once decided upon a preliminary deliberation on the bill by the plenum, the date for which
was as yet left undetermined, since it was the general
wish that the public discussion of the decisive question
should be preceded by consultation within and between
the several fractions.   Of these discussions we have no
account; their results, however, soon appeared.

The Progressists had from the outset looked with
disfavor upon the assumption of a loan by the young
Confederation, and at the most had been willing to
consent to it only if responsibility of the Ministry could
be achieved in connection with it. They would, therefore, have nothing to do with the proposed compromise.
That its rejection entailed a complete stand-still in the
development of the navy mattered little to them.   The
navy was of no great interest to them under any circumstances ; and, moreover, that they should be expected to yield a great principle of political freedom for
fear of a war as yet invisible upon the political horizon,
they resented with indignation.   " A State that is willing to renounce liberty," was Waldeck's expression,
" does not deserve to exist ! "

In opposition to them the Conservatives, Free Conservatives, and Old Liberals had persistently voted against
Miquel's clause; but now, influenced by their interest
in the navy, and the hope of a reconciliation between

the two legislative organs, they were willing to accept the new proposition by which the enactment of the clause was at least indefinitely postponed.

Under these circumstances the deciding power lay in the hands of the large National Liberal Party. Up to this point, side by side with the Party of Progress, it had battled valiantly for responsibility of the Ministry; now, however, when through the inflexibility of the Government, and the pressure of the financial situation, it became a choice between giving up the navy or the Miquel clause, for an indefinite time, it became apparent at once how great a difference of disposition there really was between this and the radical parties, notwithstanding the great number of constitutional doctrines held by them in common. Germany's power at sea was dear to the National Liberals, and they decided in favor of the proposed compromise. " Since I must choose between inflicting an injury upon my fatherland, or relinquishing a right of freedom, I will vote to-day, as I shall always vote, for my fatherland!" exclaimed Lasker in striking contrast to Waldeck's utterance.

But, as wise as it was to abandon a position grown untenable, it was, nevertheless, especially after all that had preceded it, a surrender on the part of the National Liberals. And when, on June 15th, the deliberation by the plenum was begun, it soon developed into a vehement explanation between the former allies. With every possible shaft of ridicule and pathos did the Progressists point their representation of the weakness and want of principle evinced by the friends who had deserted them ; in bitter derision they showered upon them quotations from their former valiant speeches in which they had proclaimed that a retreat from the position which had been assumed with regard to this most important question was impossible for them.

As a matter of course, those upon whom this violent onslaught was made found abundant material with which to defend themselves and make counter-charges. At several points even Delbrück as well as a number of Conservatives entered the debate with effective arguments against the Party of Progress. Löwe (Kalbe) had deplored the wasteful expenditure upon the navy to which this bill would throw open the door. To this General von Moltke now replied,[1] " Where, indeed, is an intelligent person to be found who would not prefer that the enormous sums which all the countries of Europe expend for military purposes might be diverted into peaceful channels? An international agreement such as has often been proposed to this end will, however, never achieve the desired result. I can see but one way in which this can be accomplished, which is that in the heart of Europe a Power will arise which, without itself being one to seek conquest, will yet be so mighty that it can forbid its neighbors to enter into war. I believe, therefore, that should this beneficent condition ever be realized, it must be brought about by Germany. This, however, gentlemen, cannot come to pass until Germany is sufficiently strong,

[1] Stenographic reports, pp. 442 and 450.

which means when it is UNITED.   And to arrive at this
goal despite the disapprobation of Europe, we need an
army and a navy.   I trust, therefore, that you will
sanction the bill submitted by the Government."

Von Moltke's speech recalls the famous words of
Frederick the Great: " Were I King of France, not a
cannon-shot should be fired in all Europe without my
permission."   Moltke would have modified the saying to read: " When King William becomes Emperor
of Germany, he will not permit a cannon-shot to be
fired in Europe."

No more effective argument could have been made
against the short-sighted opposition to the so-called militarism.   It was a truly prophetic speech with which
the great soldier portrayed for the eyes of Europe the
coming era.   The Reichstag responded to his appeal by
hearty applause and a vote of 151 favorable against 42
dissenting voices.

Immediately afterward, feeling assured of a like result for the budget at its third reading, Delbrück
presented it in the altered form occasioned by the realization of the loan.   The final deliberation took place
on the 19th of June, and resulted in the approval, first
of the proposed compromise-bill, and then of the entire
budget as presented for its final reading without
amendment of any kind.   This was followed by the
election of the three members of the Reichstag who
were to represent that body in the Committee on the
Federal Debt.

Thus internal peace was restored, and after many

reverses the Government had at last won a great victory; an imposing sum had been appropriated for the
navy, and the aspirations of the Liberals to an extension of parliamentary power had suffered defeat. And
yet, that this presaged more peaceful days for the
future was by no means to be assumed; although the
advantages just won within the province of financial
politics were for the moment most agreeable, the general situation was nevertheless conducive of serious
* apprehension, even for the near future.

The Federal budget for 1869 showed a total expenditure of 77,700,000 thalers (of this sixty-six millions
were for the army, one and one-half for coast defences,
and eight and one-half for the navy). The receipts by
which this was to be met were from Federal sources
49,300,000 thalers; the deficit was covered by 5,100,000
thalers out of the loan and by *pro rata* contributions
amounting to 23,300,000 thalers. That the ordinary
receipts of the Confederation should be increased
seemed most necessary therefore; this, however, could
be brought about in a productive manner, only through
the action of the Customs Parliament; and, after past
experience, what could be expected of that body?

Thus the politico-financial activity of the Reichstag
was ended. We must, however, glance at the results
achieved in the sphere of legislation during these last
weeks.

First of all must be mentioned the ratification of new
postal treaties with Switzerland and Belgium, as also a
telegraph treaty with Luxemburg. Then there were

numerous and urgent demands that the arrangements
for the Federal administration should be perfected,
and upon every possible occasion attention was called
to the need of a collegiate and responsible Ministry.
Formal motions and resolutions with regard to this
were, however, not again attempted. The only motion
which was passed was one relating to the budget, and
proposed by Count Bethusy-Huc ; by it the Federal
Chancellor was requested to transfer such expenses for
the Foreign Office as were still charged to the Prussian
budget, to that of the Confederation.

In this connection two bills originating with the
Federal Council are still to be mentioned. The one
concerned the establishment of a well-regulated and independent system of accounts to insure lawful collection
and application of the Federal revenue. That there
was urgent need of such an authority it will not be
necessary to demonstrate. The present time was, however, much too limited to permit the careful thought
required to devise and perfect a wholly new plan.
The Federal Council therefore, proposed that a course
similar to that pursued with regard to the administration of the Federal debt should be adopted, and until
a definitive arrangement could be determined upon,
the conduct of the Federal system of accounts should
be placed under the management of the corresponding Prussian authority, the Chief Court of Accounts,
conducted under most careful restrictions.

Deputies Twesten and Kirchmann called attention to
the fact that the regulations governing this authority

had been devised in the year 1824, and consequently could not in all particulars meet the requirements of the principles of constitutional government. For this reason the House passed a motion offered by Twesten to the effect that the proposed arrangement should apply only to the years 1867, 1868, 1869, and, owing to the limited period for which it was to be in force, refused to discuss the objections of a technical nature suggested by Kirchmann.

The other of the two bills proposed by the Federal Council related to certain legal relations affecting all Federal officials. For the elaboration of a comprehensive system of regulations to govern the civil service, the time had also been found insufficient. It was therefore proposed that the House should confine its action to the solution of certain questions which would not permit of delay. The first matter to be considered was the frequent transfer of Federal officials from the territory of one State to that of another, and the questions of legal residence, rights of domicile, and tax obligations which this suggested.

The Reichstag expressed itself as agreed to all the provisions of the draft with one exception. That the Federal officials should with regard to the payment of taxes be subject to the same regulations as were the local officials of the State in which they happened to be employed met with opposition. It was pointed out that in Prussia as well as in a number of the smaller States, therefore in by far the larger part of the Confederation, the State officials, although subject to the same requirements with regard to State taxes as were all other residents, yet, in so far as municipal taxes were concerned, were assessed on a basis of only one-half of their salaries, and that this unjust distinction was now to be extended to Federal officials as well.

The debate soon became most animated. When Delbrück declared that it would hardly be seemly. to withhold from the Federal officials the privileges granted to those of the several States, he received the reply: " Nothing is easier than to place every one on an equal legal footing ; instead of conferring this privilege upon the officials of the Confederation, withdraw it from those of the States." This stand was persisted in ; and as a first step in the desired direction, the privilege was refused to the Federal officials.

There was a larger number of bills whose subjects were matters affecting the public welfare.

The repeal during the past year of all legal restriction upon rates of interest induced the Conservatives to introduce a motion providing that imprisonment for debt should be entirely abolished. Now that an unjust creditor was permitted to demand the most extortionate rate of interest, it was not to be tolerated that the law should be made instrumental to so atrocious a practice by decreeing the imprisonment of the debtor. The jurists of the assembly entertained serious misgivings with regard to the measure because of the further change in the law governing the order of procedure which it entailed ; and for this reason the Federal Council proposed to replace it by one of like tendency

but of more careful preparation, which was approved
by the Reichstag after a brief discussion.

A similar course was followed in the action upon
another bill originating, like the previous one, with the
Reichstag. It dealt with the co-operative associations
which during the past ten years had been called into
existence through the indefatigable efforts of Schulze-
Delitzsch, and by which, without assistance from the
State or marked revolution of any kind, a system of co-
operation had been inaugurated, the purpose of which
was to procure more advantageous economic conditions
for the members by seeking to place within their reach
cheaper raw materials, credit, and independent industrial plants. Most desirable results had been achieved,
and the associations had spread to every part of
Germany, their number having reached the imposing
figures of from thirteen to fourteen hundred; twelve
hundred of these were to be found within the limits of
the Confederation alone, and by them sums amounting
to more than sixty-seven thalers had been advanced
within the year to members.

This organization as it had been practically developed
was not provided for by any existing law. In some
respects it resembled an open, in others a secret, business partnership, in still others a stock company, or a
free public association. At all events, the proportions
which it had assumed peremptorily demanded the regulation by law of its legal, personal relations (relations
of the association to the authorities, to its members, its
officers, debtors, creditors, etc.); and therefore, in con-

sonance with Schulze-Delitzsch, the Prussian Government had in 1867 agreed with the Assembly upon a law which the associations generally regarded as to the purpose. Schulze (Delitzsch), therefore, now proposed to the Reichstag that this Prussian law, with as little modification as possible, should be adopted into Federal legislation.

To this the Reichstag consented; the Federal Council, however, before arriving at a decision in regard to the motion, referred it for careful examination to the Committee which it had appointed for the revision of the civil procedure, and which was already actively engaged in the performance of this duty. The result appeared in a few weeks in the form of numerous improvements in the text. "A contention about mere trifles," muttered Twesten. "Nevertheless," exclaimed Schulze, "I am willing to accept all that has been suggested without the slightest hesitation." And so did the Reichstag; on the very last day of the session this important measure was enacted.

The extreme but perfectly justifiable caution which induced the Federal Council to scrutinize every proposed measure with respect to its possible influence upon existing legal regulations, and by which its action was made most thorough, but also more deliberate than suited the taste of the impatient, led to a peculiar device to expedite matters with regard to a measure of greatest moment just before the curtain was dropped upon this session's labors.

Just after the publication of the law regarding free-

dom of migration, it became apparent that the permission
to change his domicile could little benefit a person if
he was prohibited from supporting himself by his trade
in the abode of his selection.   The endless multiplicity
of industrial and municipal regulations in force in the
several States, provinces, and communities of the Confederation made the enactment of a new and uniform
law for the regulation of industrial pursuits in the Confederation as difficult as it was necessary.   It had been
fruitlessly attempted in 1867 ; and in the next year the
Federal Council had submitted a comprehensive bill regarding it, consisting of 172 paragraphs, worked out
wholly upon the principle of liberty in industrial pursuits.   It was for just this reason that the Conservative
element in the Committee to which the bill had been
referred opposed it with renewed energy in every one
of its 172 paragraphs, so that, although the session was
fast approaching its close, there seemed no prospect of
ending these deliberations.

At this point, so that the people might at least be
shown some results within this province in which their
interest was so great, Lasker and Miquel took the
matter in hand.   Rejecting all the provisions of a positive nature to be found in the long Government bill,
they selected only four negative ones for their new
bill, by which, however, all the most oppressive restrictions were removed : —

The guilds shall not be allowed to prevent a non-
member from exercising his trade. . . . . .

No person shall be prohibited from carrying on more

than one trade at one and the same time . . . . nor from hiring journeymen apprentices at his own discretion ; nor from engaging as laborer with any employer without distinction as to trade. . . . .

No distinction of town or State with regard to the pursuit of a trade shall henceforth be allowed.

To this Delbrück declared that the Federal Council had as yet not been enabled to arrive at a decision with regard to the newly proposed measure; personally he did not hesitate to say that he could see no objection to it; that he, moreover, understood the bill not to be antagonistic to that of the Government, but to be offered merely as a temporary arrangement, which, with the adoption of the more comprehensive bill, would, as a matter of course, be abrogated.

The authors of the bill confirmed this view, withdrew an objectionable paragraph, and, for the sake of insuring the adoption of the essential features, rejected with decision every attempt to amend, whether proceeding from the Left or the Right. Thus their effort was crowned by success in the Reichstag, and they could also feel assured that their motion would receive the sanction of the Federal Council.

By these three laws regarding imprisonment for debt, co-operative associations, and this first advance toward freedom in industrial pursuits, new avenues were opened to a broader field of labor and intercourse, the fruits of which would be reaped by all within the limits of the Confederation.

Finally, to the credit of this session must be mentioned that the harmonious action of the Federal Council and Reichstag gave to the German people at this time the advantages of the metric and decimal systems of measures and weights, whereby an impetus was also given to the reform of the German system of coinage so hopelessly confused. To this must be added, that with equal unanimity of purpose the Federal organs adopted the Prussian law by which but a short time previously the public gambling-houses had been ordered to be closed on December 31st, 1872, and made it applicable to all the territory of the Confederation.

Taking all this into consideration, together with that which had been accomplished in the spring, as has been related, we can readily understand that notwithstanding the sterility of the Customs Parliament, notwithstanding the political quarrel in the Reichstag and the disaffection in the annexed provinces, which made itself felt in many ways, the King had good reason for the warm words of commendation with which, in his speech from the throne, he closed the session, expressing his thanks for the past fatiguing and successful labors, as well as his appreciation of the great significance of the results achieved. For, party contentions, like the discontent in the land, would pass away; but the emancipating laws would remain, bringing with them ever-increasing blessings, by which the entire life of the people in business and intercourse, in labor and enjoyment, would be raised to a higher level of development.

In truth, although a generation has as yet not passed

away, the old life during the days of national disunion has been forgotten, and existence in the national Confederation and Empire has been accepted as the natural order of things ; of course, always with the proviso, which every independent man reserves to himself, — that he is privileged to find quite as much to criticise and quarrel about upon the now fruitful field as he once did upon that which was so sterile.

CHAPTER II.

FLUCTUATIONS IN FRENCH POLITICS.

I. THE RISE OF LIBERALISM.

IN Germany, through its great results in war, the Government had gained sufficient power to keep the movements of the political parties within bounds. At the same time, through the national significance of its triumphs, it had won the hearts of the nation as well, or at least the great majority of those in North Germany. Confident of this, it could without anxiety recognize and extend the rights of the people, and yield to the representative body of the Confederation a strong and influential position. To be sure, the onward movement would continue; new and greater demands would be made; an enduring balance of power was, however, assured for some time to come.

In France matters stood differently. To understand this last phase of the Second Empire, together with the causes which led to the great war, it will be well to take a rapid survey of the previous events.

The Empire was the product of political and social revolution. In view of the threatening danger of further overthrow and communistic tyranny, every one in

France who was numbered among the proprietary or earning classes — and to these belonged the great mass of the peasantry — welcomed with acclamation the rescuing *coup d'état* of Louis Napoleon, notwithstanding its many deeds of blood, and accepted without remonstrance the dictatorship fatal to political liberty which sprang from it.

Every one was content that order and peace had again been restored to the land, and rejoiced that property was once more secure, that industrial and commercial development was again possible, and that in consequence every kind of material enjoyment was increased.

So much the greater, however, was the bitter resentment which filled the hearts of the parties vanquished for the time.   He who had violated his oath on December 2d was in their eyes an outlaw against whom every true patriot should use every weapon at his command.

At first Napoleon could afford to look with disdain upon the exhibition of these violent passions.   He was popular with the clergy, the army, and the peasantry. The great discernment displayed by his administration had achieved important results upon the economic field; but that which probably served him best was, that during the first seven years of his reign his foreign policy had been conducted with so much energy and insight that France suddenly found herself once more the leader in European affairs.   Nowhere has such a sovereign ever been deposed, but least of all in France.

Yet here, as everywhere, the transforming hand of

time was at work, and with permanence of power the
empire witnessed a rapidly progressive change in the
foundation upon which it rested.   The dread of the red
spectre had converted the intelligence of France, as it
had its property-holders, to the *coup d'état*.   However,
as with the effective administration of government the
danger of revolution grew more and more remote, the
question whether this dictatorial power were still necessary was agitated in ever-widening political circles.
Ever since 1815 France and Paris had been uncon-
strainedly extolled as the source of all political freedom
upon the European Continent; and now, instead of the
great principles of 1789, there was in reality the omnipotence of a most arbitrary police system, the repression
of the right of association and of the freedom of the
press, whilst the elections to the popular representative
body, although based upon the principle of universal
suffrage, were conducted under the domineering direction of the State officials.

Shame and anger at this were felt by the best elements of the population, — by the men who were still
public-spirited, and still inspired by an ideal.   Should
this tendency continue, the Emperor would soon stand
surrounded only by a company of office-seekers, deserted by all save his soldiers and the peasantry, entirely
estranged from the intellectual life of the nation.

It was the ablest of his advisers of that time, his
half-brother Morny, who, as in the *coup d'état* he had
been the foremost actor, so now was the first to perceive
that a change must be wrought in the internal policy:

the absolute empire must be transformed into a liberal one. It was, of course, not the intention that on some fine day the Emperor should lay all his sovereign rights at the feet of the representatives of the people ; by no means, for the power of final decision was to remain his under any consideration. In truth, he possessed such an abundance of prerogatives that without in the least endangering the stability of his crown, he could relinquish a great number of individual ones to the delighted parliament and people, who, it was hoped, would be duly appreciative.

In 1860 an experiment was made by conferring upon the Legislative Body, as the French call their representative chamber, the right to reply to the Emperor's speech from the throne at the opening of the session, by an address to be discussed in that assembly ; at the same time the official publication of all the transactions of the assembly was inaugurated. But what should the next step be ?

It was evident that the solution of the problem required a man of marked prominence in the parliament, one actuated at once by liberal and monarchical, in fact, by Bonapartist ideas, and who, holding firmly to his principles, would yet be dexterous in the manipulation of given conditions. Such a phœnix it was, however, difficult to find. The strong Majority of the representative body was not at all liberal and quite as little intellectual ; the slender Opposition, well-endowed, but most decidedly republican in its views. Yet it was in just this group that Morny's discerning

eye descried the man whom he sought in the representative of a thoroughly democratic district of Paris,
Émile Ollivier.   He was the son of a much-persecuted
Republican of the days of 1848, the pupil and favorite
of the great tribune of the people, Ledru-Rollin, then
in exile.   Ollivier was therefore a man who of all men
might naturally be supposed to be bound to the republican cause; he, however, did not allow himself to be
restrained by the memories of the past.   He was in
the prime of life, ambitious and self-appreciative; of
an excitable temperament, and exceedingly vain.   His
desire was not to revolutionize, but to rule ; not to
pull down, but to build up.   He had discovered how
largely the promises of his republican friends were
made up of sounding and empty phrases, and how
little true freedom could be expected from the in-
tolerant Jacobin school from whose principles he had
long been at heart an apostate.

Thus Morny found him when, in 1864, he laid before
him the draft of a Government bill in favor of labor
coalitions heretofore so strenuously prohibited, solicit-
ing him to be its champion in the House.   He declared
this to be merely the first step in the direction of
liberalism toward which the Government had set its
face, gladly willing in the new course before it to
give ear to Ollivier's counsel.   The pleader had struck
the right chord.   Ollivier could not resist the picture
of France organized according to his liberal principles,
and, as he hoped, governed under his ascendency.
How little would it matter then whether in name

France were monarchy or republic. No more was necessary: Ollivier was won.

Robespierre's biographer, Hamel, assures us that Ollivier was rewarded for his treason to the sacred cause of the republic by an annual income of 30,000 francs. I cannot gainsay this; but justice demands that this allusion should be accompanied by the statement that his liberal principles in their essential features were never to be bought either with gold or with the prospect of power.

Unhesitatingly he entered upon his task. Should the liberal empire, or, in other words, the constitutional monarchy under Napoleon III., gradually become a reality, it would in the first place be necessary to raise the standard of the new cause in the parliament itself, in the midst of the monarchical and republican absolutists. Success attended this effort in so far as that in the debate upon the address of 1865, a group of 61 members (out of 280) was induced to vote for a motion protesting the nation's utter loyalty to the Bonaparte dynasty, and entreating the Emperor to vouchsafe to his devoted people a further advance toward political freedom. The motion, assailed by both the Right and the Left, was defeated; but the "third party," by which it had been made, was established, and favorable circumstances combined to promote its progress.

First of all, through an uninterrupted succession of mistakes and failures in its foreign policy, the prestige of the absolute empire had suffered greatly since 1859.

The Opposition, constituted of a variety of elements, made a point of holding up to the gaze of the ambitious and easily irritated populace the loss of power which France had sustained through Napoleon's toleration of the growth of German and Italian unity without securing compensation for himself in a corresponding enlargement of his own kingdom. In these reproaches the ultimate aim of the Opposition was by no means to incite to an early war of conquest, which was dreaded more than it was desired; its purpose was to testify to the inefficiency of the personal government, and to spread parliamentary tendencies among the people.

The nature of these attacks was such as must necessarily cause Napoleon great anxiety; a Bonaparte could ill afford the continued sneer that under him France had been degraded to the rank of a third-rate Power. Against his own will, therefore, he found himself forced to strive for acquisition abroad, and to endeavor to place a check upon the growth of his neighbors. This he did by seeking powerful alliances, and by endeavoring to put his own military forces into an ever higher state of readiness. This naturally rendered the assurance of European peace impossible, although the French people, like every other, earnestly desired it.

No one, moreover, wished for it more eagerly than did the Emperor himself. By nature he was a man of peace and not of war. He loved to meditate, to plan, to dream; to make the decision requisite for action was always difficult for him, and rapid decision, such

as warfare demands, was simply impossible to him.
And finally, by his nearer view of the horrors of the
battlefield in 1859, his nerves had received a serious
shock, making the thought of more bloodshed abomi-
nable to him.

This was his state when he received the blow which
for his future career was the decisive one. In the
year 1865 he suffered the first attack of a serious
kidney and bladder malady, after which, with longer
or shorter intervals of remission, no year passed without a return of these attacks with ever-increasing severity, at times complicated with lancinating gout
pains, and precluding all hope of ultimate recovery.
When enduring these agonizing pains the Emperor's
physical and mental powers forsook him; his only
wish was for utter repose. After the sufferer had been
relieved, he pondered the future with gloomy forebod-
ing; not his own alone, but that of his young son as
well. In August, 1866, just arisen from a bed of suffering, he summed up the situation in the words: " A
fundamental change has become necessary, — the in-
auguration of an entirely new plan of action in our
foreign and internal policy."

He began the first by giving the cold shoulder to
conquered Austria, and by making the notorious proposal of alliance to victorious Prussia, according to
which he should receive Luxemburg at once and Belgium later, South Germany to fall to the share of
Prussia. The third member of this alliance, he hoped,
would be Italy; thus without the shedding of a single

drop of blood, the name of Napoleon would be restored to all its former glory.

We have seen how the negotiations with Prussia were delayed. In December the Emperor was seized with the suspicion that Prussia would not only decline the alliance, but in open opposition would block his way to Luxemburg. He gave orders to the Minister of War under any circumstances to undertake a reorganization of the army, by which its strength would be doubled. Soon after this, in January, 1867, the plan of a Prussian alliance suffered final shipwreck, and the attempted agreement with Italy fared no better. "I have not an ally in Europe," said Napoleon to his Ministers; "my reliance must therefore be upon my people alone." As a consequence, he was resolved to turn his face toward liberalism, to win the gratitude of his people by liberal concessions, and upon this firm foundation to rest his throne and his dynasty's succession to it.

This decision was far from an easy one for him; unnumbered times, probably, his hope gave way to fear, and fear to hope. He knew full well with what bitter malignity the Republicans, Socialists, and Radicals pursued the name of Bonaparte, as he also knew how large a proportion of the townspeople these formed. The only wise plan was, therefore, to proceed slowly and by degrees upon his newly adopted course of liberal concession. In consequence, however, the great mass of his constitutionally inclined subjects might be seized with impatience, and use every conceded liberty as a weapon to enforce the restriction of imperial power.

As for himself, he longed for the time when he could transfer a part of the burden and responsibility to other shoulders, and, ensconced behind a responsible Ministry, view in safety the combat without. But would these Ministers always, with discerning glance and honest endeavor, act in the interest of his crown and his son? Would the parliament always permit this? Would it not, perhaps, after all, be safest to keep the rudder in his own hands as heretofore? How long, however, would the grasp, enfeebled by age and illness, be able to control it? Was not haste necessary in the provision of a substitute, or at least of assistance?

He had already discussed the question with the most eminent of his advisers, Rouher, who at this time filled the office of Minister of State. As such, it was his duty to represent in the Chambers all the bills of the Government, as well as its entire policy; thereby his position far transcended in power that of his colleagues, who, without solidarity among themselves, were merely the obedient secretaries of the Emperor.

At Napoleon's first allusion to liberalism and popularity with the people, Rouher opposed the idea most vigorously, saying he had no wish to meddle with such dangerous things. Napoleon, however, who was not thus to be deterred, put himself in personal communication with Ollivier, and disclosed to him the concessions which he intended to make to liberalism.

Ollivier expressed his great joy at these tendencies,

but regarded the privileges to be granted as insufficient to make a decided impression. Above all else he emphasized the importance of an unqualified and openly announced peace policy, which was synonymous with sanctioning the complete achievement of German and Italian unity; for thus alone could the army reform, already begun and so generally disapproved, become unnecessary, whereby he believed the Emperor would win so great popularity that without the slightest apprehension for the safety of his crown he could inaugurate an entirely liberal and parliamentary government. Napoleon passed over this allusion to a decrease of the military force in silence, for it was the time when the Luxemburg negotiations were daily growing more critically dubious.

When immediately afterward he offered Ollivier a cabinet portfolio, the latter, not wishing to serve under Rouher, refused it with the courtly phrase that he hoped to serve the Emperor better as an independent deputy than he could as Minister. Napoleon consented. Ollivier's clever and dazzling discourse had won for him the entire sympathy of the Emperor, who was wont to cling with an enduring tenacity to such impressions, which, however, were not always based upon a reliable knowledge of human nature. After a short time he wrote Ollivier that he had adopted into his programme certain points which Ollivier had recommended; but that this must be the limit of his concessions, since it would be impossible for him to go beyond.

On January 19th this programme was published in the form of a letter to the Minister of State. It contained the following declarations: —

By the address introduced in 1860 the results expected had not been realized, wherefore, in its stead, every member of the two Chambers would be granted the privilege, when adequately supported by the Chamber, of interpellating the Government.

When advantageous to the discussion of certain questions the Emperor would, in addition to the Minister of State, commission the Minister of the department concerned to represent the Government in the Parliament.

By the enactment of a new press law the discretionary power of the police authorities over the press would be restrained, and the jurisdiction over offences against this law would be assigned to the courts of justice.

By another law the right to assemble and unite in associations would be regulated.

" Thus," concluded the Emperor, " at length I crown with completion the structure raised at the will of the nation."

This reveals to us at a glance that, as eager as Napoleon was to be liberal and popular, the anxiety which the relinquishment of even the smallest part of his power caused him was quite as great. The possibility that in individual cases the Minister of a department would be allowed to confer directly with the Chamber was rather too slight an approach to the responsibility of the Ministry desired by the Liberals, and as yet the degree of freedom which would arise from the promised legislation regarding the press and the right of assembly was left wholly undecided until the enactment of the law. It was, however, in just this connection that Napoleon was destined to make his first unpleasant experience with liberalism.

Until this promised law should be issued, the Government regarded the press as still subject to the regulations heretofore in force. In the country at large, however, it was believed that after the manifesto of January 19th, the former arbitrary control of the press police would, even if not wholly suppressed, be at least restricted within narrow and fixed limits. As a consequence, every one wrote and published as his inclination prompted, and of course the hot-headed and radically inclined were the first to take advantage of the opportunity, and to abuse it. Of rejoicing and gratitude there was no thought. The liberty granted seemed but to have added to the numbers of the enemy, or at least to have brought to light those who heretofore had been concealed.

After such an experience it was no difficult task for Rouher to obtain the Emperor's consent to the use of severe measures to repress these proceedings. This resulted after a few months in an open rupture between Napoleon and Ollivier. The latter, who was little disposed to allow himself to be put off with liberal promises only, assailed the Minister of State in a famous speech on July 12th, 1867, in which he accused him of being inimical to the good cause, an enemy of all liberal aspirations; the manner in which he utilized his high position to repress these was intolerable; even greater than the power of a major-domo or of a grand vizier was the irresponsible control which he exercised as a sort of vice-emperor.

Napoleon looked upon this as an affront to himself, and sent the Minister the grand cross of the Legion of Honor, accompanied by a most gracious letter. His personal intercourse with Ollivier was thus interrupted; and the latter again devoted his entire energy to the interests of the Opposition, allowing no opportunity to pass unimproved which he could utilize in conjunction with Thiers and the Left to demand a Ministry responsible to the parliament, believing this to be the quintessence and guaranty of all political freedom.

To all the politically active advocates of liberalism this principle in its various shades and gradations did in fact constitute an important article of faith, which their newspapers and associations constantly sought to impress upon their adherents. But the great mass of the peasants in the country and the industrial population of the cities, ever since the alarm of 1848, had turned their backs upon political contentions, and under the " personal government " were enjoying their growing prosperity. Now, it was just within this province of material welfare that since 1866 they felt the depressing effect upon their credit and speculations caused by the uncertainty of European peace.

We have seen how earnestly in January, 1867.

Ollivier presented this to the Emperor. "If by sanctioning German unity you make peace assured, you
will achieve so great popularity that you can grant the
most comprehensive political rights without incurring
the slightest risk to your crown," he had urged.

In the fall of 1867 Rouher confirmed this opinion,
although in a directly contrary application. "Procure peace for yourself," said he, "and let the reorganization of the army drop, whereby you will
occasion such popular rejoicing that without the least
apprehension you can recall the dangerous privileges
conferred on January 19th." Afterward, however,
the Minister felt himself constrained to qualify his
remarks by the explanation that for the present the
achievement of this desirable result would have to
be postponed, since it would hardly be wise to let
the Prussians have South Germany, and then to dis-
arm, both because of the agreement arrived at with
Austria at Salzburg, and, above all else, because the
army must not be offended. And so he came to the
conclusion that, after all, the present attitude would
have to be maintained, and liberty of the press as well
as the reorganization of the army be permitted.

Consequently Niel's army reform became the principal subject of the parliamentary struggles of the
winter 1867-1868. As we have seen, the townsfolk
and peasants were incensed by the heavier military
burden for which they saw no need, and the mere
announcement of which sufficed to disturb confidence
in the continuation of peace. Of this the orators and

writers of the Opposition eagerly took advantage, pointing to the dissatisfaction and distrust which had at last taken possession of the peasants and shop-keepers, heretofore the sturdy friends of the Emperor.

" You know of no reason for these tremendous preparations for war. The fact is, everybody desires peace just as do you. It is the Emperor alone who wants war. After marring French reputation in Europe by his foolish policy, through which he has even forfeited the love of his people, he now hopes by foreign conquest to renew his popularity at home, and to re-dye his faded royal purple in the blood of France. Do you wish to prevent this and to retain the blessings of peace? We know one means only by which this can be done, and at the coming election you will hold it in your hands. The Ministers must be made subject to the assembly which represents the people; they must no longer be subservient to the caprice of the Emperor, but to the will of the nation."

Such was the appeal by which, as early as 1868, the assurance of European peace through a responsible Ministry was made the watchword for the elections to take place in the following year. An eloquent aphorism uttered by Ollivier at this time found responsive hearers in every part of the country: " Freedom and peace, or war and despotism ! "

II. ATTEMPT TO FORM A TRIPLE ALLIANCE.

Opposed to these excited masses the vindicators of the former unrestricted empire formed a minority which was less formidable because of its numbers than on account of the influential position of its members. Here, as in the Opposition, there were moderate and radical elements, each of which were influenced by a combination of diversified motives. Until now they had shared in the splendor and benefits of the empire; upon them had been conferred the high positions at court, in the army, in the administration, etc.; they had reason to fear that the further development of the system inaugurated on January 19th would lead to the appointment of new men in their places. Many were oppressed by the greater dread that the decrees of January 19th would in themselves suffice to bring about not only a change of the Ministry in the constitutional sense, but would reopen the abyss of social revolution hastily closed in 1851.

It cannot be denied that in the year 1868 the radical parties furnished reason sufficient to create such an impression. After the appearance of the laws regarding the press and the right of assembly, there was general indignation felt at the Draconic penalties imposed for their every violation, even the least, as also that the jurisdiction over these offences was assigned to the correctional tribunals instead of to those in which the trial would be by jury. However, evincing no fear of prosecution in these courts, the Opposition

availed itself of the newly acquired weapons to make
a violent onslaught upon the Government which had
conferred them. Soon the respectable organs of the
political leaders were joined in their warfare by such
infamous and slanderous sheets as Rochefort's *La
Lanterne*, Ulbrich's *La Cloche*, and similar papers,
occasioning press-trials interminable in their number.
In the larger cities, evidences of wide-spread ferment
appeared; not unfrequently the public peace was disturbed by small riots. There could be no doubt that
new associations were constantly being formed, deriv-
ing both firm support and the requisite centralization
from the London International Association.

The conservative Bonapartists maintained universal
suffrage in itself unaccompanied by freedom of the
press and the right of assembly, to be inoffensive,
as had been demonstrated by past experience; now,
however, provided with these means of attack, they
prophesied it would speedily become the all-powerful
means of driving all the conservative elements out of
the representative assembly, and then all would be in
readiness to deal the death-blow to the monarchy, to
religion, and to the right to hold property. The Emperor had himself torn down the barriers on January
19th, and it was now impossible to retrieve the fatal
step. Thus, they declared, the empire was already
tottering to its fall. Where, indeed, could saving
power still be found?

Some of the most zealous converts to this view
established a club in Arcadia Street, from which they

derived the nickname of Arcadians. In the first place, through their organs they proclaimed their determined opposition to all liberal aspirations, and their intention vigorously to uphold the empire as the bulwark standing in defence of order, justice, and prosperity. They did not stop at this, however. With regard to the future they could see but one way of salvation for the dynasty; this had been indicated by the Opposition itself. Incessantly its leaders proclaimed to the people that the Emperor was ambitious for war, that through brilliant victories he might restore the glory of his House. It was this very war-policy which the Arcadians daily suggested and urged. " Either peace and revolution, or military renown and order," was their device. Nevertheless, with a due consideration of the spirit abroad in the land, they were most careful not to unfold their war banner in public. Only too well, however, did they know the vacillating and excitable French temperament; any sudden step taken by Bismarck might be regarded as an insult to the nation's honor, and thus without a moment's warning the torch might be set to the warlike passions of the people.

It was just this possibility which was so great a source of anxiety to the Emperor, so thoroughly averse to war. The Arcadians, however, did all in their power to bring it about. Their newspapers published everything conceivable which might incite or promote hatred of Prussia and Italy. Above all else they made it their business to keep in circulation the most exasperating reports about Bismarck, representing him to be the omnipresent instigator of mischief and disturber of the peace. He was supposed to bribe the press of Vienna, Budapest, and South Germany; to have supplied Garibaldi's red-bloused volunteers with money and arms; to hire the champions of the revolution in Roumania and Spain, and to be in touch with the Russian Panslavists; to have in his employ aristocratic ladies of the highest social circles in Paris, that through them the seeds of discontent might there be sown. There was no promise which he was not accused of having broken, nor treaty which he had not violated. He was a man of genius and daring they admitted, but a statesman without conscience, neither to be relied upon nor trusted. Ever since the defeat of Austria he was believed to be engaged in laying mines whose explosion would demolish French ascendency, in which he recognized the only barrier to his schemes of inordinate ambition. France must be on her guard!

In the Emperor's immediate circle this party was no less zealously active. Empress Eugénie was beautiful, clever, and fond of enjoyment — not at all bloodthirsty nor eager for war; but her ailing and aging husband caused her many anxious moments, as with each day she realized more and more that her youthful son's succession to the throne was far from assured, so long as the name of Napoleon remained unadorned by the laurels of fresh victories to brighten the splendor of its glorious inheritance. With a large part of the clergy every invective against Protestant Prussia and

Victor Emmanuel, the despoiler of the Church, found hearty response. That the great majority of the corps of officers looked forward with eagerness to revenge for Sadowa was but a matter of course.

As we are aware, the highest government authorities by no means shared this ardent desire for war. Napoleon, Rouher, and Niel realized too fully their country's isolated position in Europe, the inadequacy of its new military preparations, and the substantial strength of its North German rival. Not only annoying, however, but most dangerous as well, was this double concert incessantly being dinned into their ears by friend and foe alike. The Left developed the theme, "You have destroyed French pre-eminence;" whilst from the Right came the wonderfully harmonious refrain, "You must restore the glory and honor of France!" Nothing suggested itself more quickly, therefore, than the question, "Are there no peaceable means by which the French nation's thirst for glory may be satisfied, and yet no blood be shed?"

It was at this time that the Customs Union was reorganized, and early in 1868 it was decided to convene the first Customs Parliament. This suggested to the Government at Paris that as Prussia through its connection with the Customs Union had even before 1866 attained a position of pre-eminence among the German States, so France might enter into a similar relationship with Luxemburg and Belgium, perhaps also with Holland and Switzerland. To this end customs and railroad treaties might serve as a beginning; and, if all went well, these might lead to military conventions and treaties of alliance, offensive and defensive.

This picture appeared so alluring to the Emperor of France, that, without a closer examination into the difficulties which might present themselves, he undertook the first step toward the realization of his pleasing fancy. Early in March, 1868, his cousin, Prince Jerome Napoleon, made a tour to Berlin, ostensibly for the purpose of enjoying the beauties of the Mark Brandenburg, travelling as a private gentleman. He was received with utmost courtesy and friendliness in Berlin, where he discussed the French plan with Bismarck. Since then Bismarck has stated that in allusion to the proposals of August, 1866, the Prince dropped a remark suggesting that should the French hopes be realized, Prussia, too, might find her Belgium.

That Bismarck expressed no opinion either with regard to this intimation or to any other part of the French disclosures is certain. Immediately afterward the English Ambassador at Berlin, Lord Loftus, received the following communication: "Although we have no information with regard to what Bismarck said to the Prince, there can be no doubt that the latter returned to Paris without a new French province in his pocket." At the same time a confidential communication was sent from London to the Cabinet of the Tuileries declaring that a military convention, or even a customs union with France, was rendered impossible for Belgium by that country's neutrality as guaranteed by the European Powers.

As we have seen, Napoleon's attention was fully occupied during the summer of 1868 by the German and Oriental occurrences, and consequently for the time allowed the Belgian interest to rest.   Hardly, however, had he been relieved of these anxieties, when late in the fall he determined to approach the subject in a most inoffensive manner, placing his hopes upon the sympathy of the Belgian Ultramontanes, and their exasperation with the liberal Frère-Orban Ministry.   He induced the French Eastern Railway Company to open negotiations with the management of one Dutch and two Belgian railways for the purchase of these roads, promising to reimburse it for the expense which this would entail as well as that the Government would guarantee to it a reasonable rate of interest.

Allured by a temptingly generous offer, the Belgian companies signed a preliminary agreement in December, 1868, by which the French Government was given possession and control of direct lines to Brussels and Rotterdam.   Hardly, however, had this become known in Brussels, when a feeling of uneasiness spread through the land, and the cry went up that this was the first step toward the incorporation of Belgium with the French Empire.   On December 11th the matter was taken up by the Second Chamber, when the Minister, Frère-Orban, declared that the surrender of a Belgian railway to a foreign company was invalid without the sanction of the Government; and this consent the Government would never give.   In reliance upon the powerful support of France, the railway companies denied the Government's right to interfere with their profitable transaction, and concluded the final negotiations with the Eastern Railway Company on January 31st, 1869.

Immediately the patriotic indignation of the people broke forth on all sides; party differences were forgotten in the impulse given to the national sentiment, and the Minister, quickly resolved, hesitated not a moment to give unmistakable expression to the Government's authority and the people's love of independence. On February 10th he submitted to the Second Chamber the draft of a law making an abalienation, such as was involved in the sale of the railways, dependent upon the consent of the Government. Ten days later the projected law received the almost unanimous approval of both Chambers, and on the 23d it was published, thus invalidating the contracts of sale.

Paris was both highly surprised and incensed at this inconsiderate interference on the part of Frère-Orban, whose declaration of December 11th had been wholly disregarded, the contracts concluded on January 31st being looked upon as terminating the matter. Foremost among the clamorers was the press of the Arcadians, who now hoped that the seeds for a great war had been sown. As was their laudable usage, they announced as a fully authenticated fact that the Belgian Government, actuated by a most friendly spirit at the beginning, had been influenced to its final hostile attitude by pressure brought to bear upon it by Bismarck in the hope that France would be offended, that this would lead to discord, and provide

Prussia with a convenient excuse to make war upon France.

This malicious invention was emphatically denied by all concerned, nor could its originators substantiate their assertions by so much as a grain of evidence. This but heightened the French indignation, that little Belgium should have the audacity to oppose itself to a plan made by mighty France. Such an attitude must be regarded as an open insult to French honor, for which unconditional satisfaction must be rendered; the least amends which could be made would be the immediate sanction of the transactions which had been put in question.

Napoleon, too, was sorely perplexed and personally offended. His intention had been so inoffensive, — the purchase of a railway involving no infringement upon the sovereign authority of the State ; and yet the patriotic indignation which this had aroused created an uproar echoed first in France, and then re-echoed in every part of Europe. "The action of the Belgian Government is a slap in my face," said he.

At this juncture fuel was added to the fire by reports from Germany regarding French diplomacy which, in his irritated condition, exasperated Napoleon to a much greater degree than their actual purport warranted. It was rumored that Prussia had entered an agreement with France according to which no modification in the organization of Germany should be undertaken during the next three years. Napoleon of course knew that the report was wholly unfounded;

still, it added to his annoyance that Bismarck should hasten to assure the South German Courts that the rumor was utterly groundless, and that France and Prussia had not had negotiations of any kind upon the subject.

Still worse was the effect of a report from Karlsruhe to the effect that Baden and Prussia were negotiating a treaty with regard to military freedom of migration, which meant that in future any citizen of Baden could fulfil his military obligations in North Germany, and that, *vice versa*, every North German could serve his term in a Baden regiment. This, to be sure, would in no way affect the State rights of the grand duchy; still, it would constitute another step in the direction of German unity, and this, too, at that most sensitive point along the long Alsace frontier, where there was daily talk of Prussian preparations and spies by which the people were kept in constant excitement. This latest news was received at a time when Belgium's attitude under English protection was felt to be an insult to French honor. To what violent eruptions of the internal ferment might this not lead, or what complications might it not produce! A peaceful measure of skilful diplomacy had been intended, and at the very first step France found herself upon ground glowing with fervor for war. It behooved her to look about for protection and support.

The French Minister at Brussels, La Gueronnière, an ardent chauvinist and enemy of Prussia, who looked upon Bismarck as a shallow-head, a restless politician without fixedness of purpose, outlined the French opinions as follows: " The Emperor is more peaceably inclined than are his Ministers, and they are more so than the people; the people, too, prefer peace to war, but are easily provoked through their sense of national honor. If Bismarck continues his uncertain policy in German affairs, he may bring about a terrible outbreak despite the general desire for peace."

It was this apprehension which drove Napoleon to wholly unexpected action. He summoned Metternich and Vitzthum to the Tuileries, and referring to their proposition for a general disarmament, declared this to be less feasible at the present moment than ever before. He could suggest something better to them; namely, a triple alliance, France, Austria, and Italy. Negotiations with regard to it would have to be carried on with Rouher; not a soul must know of it, not even Lavalette, who usually enjoyed the confidence of the Emperor, and who had recently been made Minister of Foreign Affairs, but most assuredly not that idle gossiper, Gramont, the French Ambassador at Vienna.[1]

In a few days Rouher submitted to them the draft of the proposed treaty of alliance. It stated that the three Powers combined for the purpose of placing a check upon Prussia's immoderate desire for conquest, and of re-establishing Austria's former position in Germany. If Rouher supposed that this proposition would act as an irresistible magnet upon Austria, he was soon to be undeceived. Vitzthum at once declared

[1] Beust, Vol. II., p. 341. Also unpublished memoirs.

that in view of Austria's present internal conditions and Beust's principles as he knew them, there could be no thought of such a design. Metternich unhesitatingly confirmed this opinion, but requested Vitzthum to outline a draft which would express the Austrian view, to which Vitzthum consented.

His production began with the words: " The three Powers, being resolved to follow the same line of policy both in the Orient and the Occident, have concluded a defensive alliance." The subsequent Articles expressed in general terms the intention of the three Powers to give one another effective mutual support; to this there was one carefully stated exception, — in case France should be induced to make war upon Prussia, Austria reserved to herself the liberty to remain neutral during the continuance of such a war.

This by no means fulfilled the French desire. Decided objections were, however, at the time to little purpose; to begin with, for the simple but all-sufficient reason that Beust, speedily acquainted with the matter, and alarmed by Rouher's original proposition, refrained from giving instructions to the Austrian representatives. Actual negotiations could not be opened, therefore, and the matter was allowed to rest at a number of conferences in which these gentlemen came to a preliminary agreement upon Vitzthum's draft, modified somewhat in its details. In March, 1869, Vitzthum received permission to take the writing to Vienna in person, that it might receive a more careful examination.

There a decision was soon reached. For, although Rouher's offensive and defensive alliance had been little to Beust's mind, Vitzthum's proposal of joint action with regard to every question which might arise was exactly to his purpose, since it would act as a restraint upon over-hasty action in Paris, and would allow Austria, in case of extremity, to reassume her attitude of neutrality; otherwise, however, it would establish an effective friendly relation between Paris and Vienna. It received Emperor Francis Joseph's approval also, and early in April, 1869, Vitzthum returned to Paris to open formal negotiations with regard to the triple alliance.

At the same time Napoleon reopened the discussions with Italy which, having proved so fruitless, had been gradually dropped during the past year. For the time, the military *attaché* of the Italian embassy at Paris, Count Vimercati, served as agent between the Emperor and Victor Emmanuel; very soon, however, the Ambassador, Nigra himself, and General Menabrea in Florence, became participants in the negotiations, the latter only in his official capacity as the King's Adjutant-General, and without the knowledge of the Ministry of which at the time he was president.

With such good news from Vienna, and in reliance upon the stanch support of Europe, Rouher, to whom Napoleon had also intrusted the negotiations with Belgium, determined to read this recalcitrant little neighbor a sharp lecture upon its unseemly behavior. As usual his intentions were far from warlike, but he believed that by assuming a high and mighty tone he would overawe the negotiator, no other than Frère-Orban himself, who on April 22d had come to Paris to manifest his good will. Rouher informed him that first of all Belgium must recognize the contracts of sale to the Eastern Railway Company; in that event any clause which might be regarded as endangering Belgian independence would be gladly expunged.

With great decision Frère-Orban declined consent to this standpoint. " The mere existence of the contracts imperils our independence," he cried; " they are and will remain annulled! We will, however, gladly make just amends to the Eastern Railway Company by way of special concessions to facilitate intercourse between the two countries." In the further course of the conferences he submitted proposals of this nature; Rouher, however, declared nothing would be considered until Belgium should first have sanctioned the contracts of sale.

In private all manner of influence was brought to bear upon Frère-Orban, from threats to blandest cajolery. It was represented to him how far better Belgium's position would be should its isolated neutrality be replaced by close relations with France by means of a customs union or military convention. Frère, however, remained inflexibly firm: Belgium was quite content with its condition of neutrality and desired nothing better, was his reply.

On April 19th he made a last proposal to Rouher regarding indemnification to be rendered to the Eastern Railway Company; Rouher, however, was not to be moved, and persisted in his demand that the contracts of sale be first recognized. In this he was upheld by Napoleon; Frère-Orban would weaken before long, thought they. He, however, although abandoning all hope of an amicable adjustment, had no thought of surrender, but prepared for his return to Brussels, there to await whether and how France would take active measures.

This attitude of firm intrepidity availed. Napoleon and Rouher made the discovery that they had not only misjudged the Belgian Government but the French people as well. To satisfy the French national pride they had grasped at the idea of a commercial union with Belgium, only to find that not only was the existing commercial treaty with that country already far too liberal to suit the stronger party representative of French industrial interests, but that the resulting Belgian competition was exceedingly distasteful to them, and that, far from desiring complete amalgamation with Belgium, they would have preferred entire separation, the precise opposite of that which Napoleon proposed to bring about.

When, therefore, the tone of the conferences with Frère-Orban grew more and more harsh, and on all sides there was talk of warlike measures to be taken against those impolite Belgians, the great manufacturers threw the weight of their influence upon the side of the Liberal Opposition, and joined them in their party cry of " Peace abroad and a responsible Ministry at home ! " The entire independent press declared that

Belgium had done no more than any other Government would have done under similar circumstances. Should Prussia attempt to purchase an important railway in Alsace, would France permit it? The Radical journals were of the opinion that the whole affair was simply a subterfuge, and that it was not so much the Belgian railways upon which the Government had a design as it was the liberal Constitution of Belgium at which its action was aimed.

With the Powers the prospects for Napoleon's plans were no more hopeful than they were in his own country. The negotiations regarding the triple alliance developed unexpected difficulties. In England public opinion was rampant against any attempt to tamper with Belgian neutrality as established under European guaranty. Napoleon's friend, Lord Clarendon, was now Minister of Foreign Affairs; and he carefully avoided even the approach to a threat, so that retreat might not be made impossible for the Emperor. No one, however, had the least thought that England would stand passively by and allow violence to be done Belgium. And finally came the momentous question: In case of a rupture, what would Prussia do? To which of the contending Powers would it extend its sympathy?

To begin with, it was Bismarck's opinion that the railway transaction must not be allowed to lead to a rupture. What Prussia could do to discourage warlike inclinations on either side should be done. England, at that time so discreetly careful to avoid all action, must not be allowed to imagine that it could entangle Prussia in the conflict and then remain inactively in the background. Neither should France flatter itself that in fear of a French war Prussia would submit to the least injury to its interests.

I will at this point quote from a letter, the copy of which lies before me. It was written by Bismarck at this time; and in it his attitude toward France, not only with respect to the Belgian question, but during the entire period from 1866 to 1870, is distinctly portrayed.

"Above all," he wrote, "we must not give Paris the impression that we fear an encounter. We do not wish to overestimate our power, nor do we desire war; nevertheless, after careful examination of our strength as well as that of the enemy we must eventually face, it is our conviction that we are a match for France, and that, although recognizing the issue to lie in the hands of a higher power, from our human standpoint the chances of victory are with us. War in itself is always an evil; but that it would be a greater calamity for us than for France, that we have more reason to avoid it than has France, is a view which we cannot understand. It is this consciousness, united with a true love of peace, that actuates our whole bearing toward France; it is due to this, too, that we do not ascribe greater importance to the varying phases of opinion even in the leading political circles of France, nor to the occasional manifestation of hostile velleities."

Owing to this love of peace and reliance upon conscious strength, Prussia's course in connection with the Belgian question was a most simple one, — complete silence. The King remained inaccessible. Bismarck, approached by all the ambassadors, gave pointless and evasive replies, such as, we hope that peace will be maintained ; or, we must await results, and allow our action to be controlled by circumstances.

Beyond doubt this was the policy most conducive to the preservation of peace. His silence placed a damper upon each party's ardor for war without giving either cause for complaint, and ultimately brought Prussia general commendation for the beneficial influence exerted by its attitude.

After all this, Napoleon could no longer be in doubt. He felt constrained to sound a retreat, painful as this was to him. He had hoped for a diplomatic triumph, and lo, he had suffered another defeat! When in Paris it was said that the Emperor succeeded in nothing nowadays, he was compelled to submit to it. He gave orders that Frère-Orban's latest proposition, which had been rejected, should again be laid before him. He now discovered that in its essential features it was excellently adapted to serve as a basis for the technical consideration of the railway interests by a joint commission. The Belgian statesman was then summoned to an audience with the Emperor, and was acquainted with the new turn affairs had taken.

It was the Marquis Lavalette who upon this occasion discussed the matter with him, the harshness of

tone adopted by the Minister of State in his conferences with Frère-Orban having made his further
participation in the negotiations impossible after the
Emperor had decided to yield.

On April 27th the two agreed upon a protocol in
which the contracts of sale made on January 31st
were renounced, and it was arranged that a joint commission, to be appointed fourteen days later, should be
charged with the duty of deciding upon an equitable
indemnity to be rendered the Eastern Railway Company, and upon practical facilitation of railway intercourse between the two countries, their action to
be based upon the memorial submitted by Frère-
Orban.

This ended the political controversy which in its
beginning had flashed up so ominously. We have no
further interest in the labors of the joint commission
upon the technicalities involved; they were complicated and tedious, and were not concluded until July
10th. They did not, however, in any way affect the
peaceful relations re-established by the protocol of
April 27th.

The affair was, however, furnished with a remarkable
after-play by Count Beust.[1] The slow progress made
by the negotiations regarding the triple alliance evidently prompted him to the desire to do Napoleon a
friendly service in another line; and so, obviously as
yet unacquainted with the decision reached on the

---

[1] Compare the transactions of the Austro-Hungarian Delegations in
the year 1869.

27th, he undertook to give Belgium advice by means of a despatch sent on May 1st, the contents of which he communicated at the same time to several of the other Courts. In it he fervently and impressively commended to the Belgians unreserved submission to France, since otherwise their commercial treaty with that country, so greatly to their advantage, would be annulled, inflicting a fatal blow to their industries; their misgivings regarding the French demands he declared to be unfounded; in Austria there were a number of railways conducted under foreign management, from which the State had never suffered disadvantage; the German Customs Union was in itself sufficient evidence that smaller States could enter into such relations with a larger one without surrendering any part of their independence; a customs union between France and Belgium offered the best means of relieving the present strained relations.

Lord Clarendon expressed indignation at the servility to the unauthorized pretensions of France which this tone evinced, a criticism in which the other Courts fully concurred. Napoleon himself moreover gave Beust small thanks for his belated interference. The Emperor had determined to yield; and the more clearly Beust demonstrated the groundlessness of Belgium's resistance, the less could be concealed the weakness of the French policy displayed in the retreat.

Meanwhile, undisturbed by the varying course of the Belgian affair, the secret negotiations regarding the triple alliance of France, Austria, and Italy had been continued.[1] In so far as the compact between France and Austria was concerned, Beust and Rouher arrived at an agreement without encountering any special difficulty, after the latter had submissively accepted the Austrian principle of no offensive, but only a defensive, alliance. The following three Articles typify the character of the draft as it left their hands : —

The three Powers combine in a defensive alliance for the purpose of maintaining peace in Europe . . . . .

All questions which may arise shall be decided by joint diplomatic action . . . . . .

Austria reserves the liberty to remain neutral in case France feels compelled to declare war.[2]

Beust relied upon the hope that these stipulations would remove the danger of a sudden determination on the part of Napoleon, without the previous concurrence of his allies, to make war upon Germany.

The question was now whether Italy could be induced to agree to the conditions of the draft, and here wearisome difficulties arose.

King Victor Emmanuel, to be sure, unlike Beust, was untroubled by the fear of being forced into a position of entire dependence upon the will of France should Napoleon be the victor in a war with Prussia, although

---

[1] I have not seen the documents which resulted from these negotiations, and therefore cannot vouch for accuracy in the wording of the several drafts and proposed modifications, although I can unreservedly attest to the correctness of their sense, as well as of the general course of the negotiations, as based upon information derived from highly authentic sources. The ultimate result, as is well known, was made public in Beust's Memoirs.

[2] Beust, II., 369.

such a possibility was in reality much greater for him
than for Austria. The King, however, in so far as
this was concerned, relied upon his personal relations
of friendship with Napoleon, in addition to which he
by no means felt as certain of Prussia's overwhelming
defeat in a war with France as did Beust. Therefore,
far from being repelled by the prospect of participating
in a great war as the ally of France, this proved rather
alluring to him ; since he hoped in some way to make it
subserve his great aim in life, — the possession of Rome.

In his own country there were but few who shared
this view. In his Cabinet the majority of the Ministers
were filled with deep distrust of Napoleon and an un-
disguised desire for peace. Since the day at Mentana
the hatred which the greater number of the people felt
for everything French had steadily grown more intense ;
all the liberal and radical parties pronounced an alliance with France to be an abomination. Mazzini's
agents spread the doctrine that through his ignominious
subjection to Napoleon's behests the King had forfeited
his right to the crown; he must therefore be deposed,
when the triumphant republic could purge Italian soil
of the taint of the French soldiery.

Although the King did not really fear revolution,
he realized a French alliance to be a game of high
stakes for him, which, should Rome after all not be
won, might prove highly disastrous to him politically.
He therefore replied to the proposal of a triple alliance
by referring to his propositions of 1868, and desired,
as then, that the renewal of the September convention

as construed by Italy should constitute the primary condition; namely, that Italy would guarantee the Pope's security against violence of any kind; France, however, in recognition of the principle of non-intervention, must agree to remove the French troops (never to return) from Roman territory.

But Rouher, in remembrance of his thrice uttered "Never" of 1867, and the burst of applause with which it was greeted in the Chamber, declared that this demand could not possibly be conceded; whereas Beust, at that time engaged in bitter controversy with the Curia over the rights of the Church in Austria, would only too gladly have complied with Italy's wish. On the other hand, when during the further examination of Italy's stipulations that one regarding the acquisition of the Italian Tyrol was reached, Rouher made no objections; whereas Beust would not listen to it for a moment, and Menabrea consequently restricted his demand to the extension of the Italian frontier to the Isonzo, and although this was not so peremptorily refused as was the former proposition, it nevertheless found no place in the treaty. How, indeed, could it be insisted upon, when according to the Italian proposals of 1868 this acquisition was not to be realized until after the close of a successful war, whereas the purpose of the draft under discussion was, as explicitly stated, the preservation of peace.

Another of the clauses Menabrea himself proposed should be eliminated, — the one regarding the combined influence of the three Powers upon the next papal election, a suggestion which the other two Powers, in reflection upon the thorny nature of the subject, gladly accepted.

Upon all other questions arising in the mutual discussion complete harmony prevailed. And so a final result would have been attained had not the Roman enigma again and again defied solution. The Austrians took courage to try their fortune once more with the perplexing problem. Could they but prevail upon Napoleon to renew the September treaty, which was synonymous with a recall of his troops from Rome, Italy would, after the alliance under consideration had been concluded, no longer need to demand the explicit recognition of the principle of non-intervention as essential to its future security. For should Napoleon after its conclusion propose, for one reason or another, to send a garrison to Rome, this step, according to Article II. of the treaty draft, must depend upon the decision reached through a joint consultation between the three Powers, in which Austria as well as Italy would decidedly oppose every forcible measure.

In fact, Menabrea, quite as favorably disposed toward France as toward the Pope, did allow himself to be persuaded to further negotiations on this basis, and restricted his demands to a withdrawal of the French troops from Rome, as conditional upon Italy's agreement neither to attack the Pope nor to suffer him to be attacked. But even with regard to this Napoleon had misgivings. He was willing formally to agree to the withdrawal of his troops from Roman territory as

soon as practicable, but forthwith to designate a date
for the evacuation he did not deem advisable. He
promised to remove his troops as soon as the Pope's
safety should be assured, but more than this he would
not do.

Rouher and Vitzthum importuned the Italians to content themselves with the imperial word; and toward
the end of May, after much writing back and forth,
Vimercati brought the Italian consent from Florence.
Vitzthum announced this with exultation to Beust:
"The only real difficulty was Rome, and this we have
conquered by patience." On the 4th of June he returned to Brussels satisfied with his achievement.

Thus the triple alliance was agreed upon by the diplomats, and the documents were now ready to be presented to the sovereigns for their signatures.

The production, however, did not fully meet Napoleon's expectations. The thought that through this
alliance one hundred million Catholics would be ruled
as by one will he felt to be a most imposing one, an
utterance which reveals to us the light in which he
had viewed himself throughout the long years of his
protectorate over Rome. The firm association of these
millions in time of peace was without doubt a cause
for rejoicing; unfortunately, however, its efficacy in
days of trial, when it was most needed, was rendered
problematic to a dangerous degree by the reservations
made by the two Powers.

As early as the following June this fact was clearly
shown. After learning the opinion of the other Min-

isters, Menabrea had not the courage to reveal to them
the contents of the treaty draft, and so the King's
sanction had to be deferred to some future day. When
this was announced to Napoleon he laid the thus in-
complete document aside, without the least feeling of
annoyance, until such time as his action should be required. During the past few weeks more urgent cares
arising close at hand had claimed his attention; on
May 23d the general elections for the Legislative
Body had taken place, and by their result a momentous verdict upon the absolute *régime* of 1852 had
been pronounced. Should Napoleon remain firm in
his desire to be relieved from his anxious cares, the
men were now at hand who would willingly assume
the weary ruler's burden.

III. TRIUMPH OF THE LIBERAL TENDENCIES.

The programme which Ollivier had once submitted
to the Emperor had included the demand that the
organs of State authority should no longer, as heretofore, influence the elections in favor of candidates put
forward by the Government. But the more critical
the situation grew for the absolute power, the more
generally and emphatically the demand for a responsible Ministry was made, the firmer grew Rouher's determination to resort, as heretofore, to every means at
his disposal to secure a majority favorable to the Government. Prefects, curates, and gendarmes all received
strict orders and unlimited power to influence the

voters by means of persuasion, intimidation, and cor-
ruption. In many places the people were more than
willing to respond to these methods. It was quite as
often the wish of the people which fixed the price
of a loyal election as it was the offer made by the pre-
fect; here, the construction of a new street; there,
the direction which a railway should take; still elsewhere, the support given the erection of a church, and
so on.[1]

The candidates of the Opposition did not refrain
from holding out similar allurements; the manufacturer was promised protective duties; the laborer was
made hopeful of an increase in his scanty means of
support; and to every one were portrayed the blessings
to be realized through peace, liberty, and a responsible Ministry.

The voters who lived at a distance from the polls
had but to choose between the elegant carriages in
which either party was anxious to convey them to the
place of voting; arrived at this, they were sumptuously
regaled both before and after casting their votes, and
in the .evening were driven home in a hilarious frame
of mind. And so, thanks to the right of universal
suffrage, in a large part of France, the 23d of May,
1869, was transformed into a gala day upon which the
sovereign people sold their votes for the highest price
possible; here for greater liberty, there for security

---

[1] To-day such proceedings are not confined to France alone. At that
time, however, they were looked upon in Germany as a sign of political
and moral rottenness in French conditions.

and order, but everywhere for the preservation of peace.

The result showed that the absolute government and the Arcadians had bid too low. The old Majority which had always been so submissive to the Government began to dwindle. The large cities had evinced their radical or even republican tendencies. Ollivier failed to be re-elected from Paris, but regained a seat in the House through the votes of a country district in the South; Thiers and Jules Favre managed to hold their own against Rochefort's associates only as the result of a supplementary election. For several days after the elections there were riotous republican demonstrations in the streets in defiance of the police, having finally to be suppressed by the military.

At first the reports from all over the country indicated the success of 199 candidates favored by the Ministry; as soon, however, as the Chamber convened, this number was considerably reduced, so that the moderately liberal Middle Party (which counted Ollivier among its leaders) was now found to control 130 votes, to which would be added the 40 voices of the Left upon every liberal motion, thus insuring to it a majority. An inquiry with regard to how the votes cast were divided brought to light the fact that the Government had lost over a million adherents since 1863, and that the Opposition had gained in round numbers one and a half million.

That the days of the unrestricted government of 1852 were numbered was therefore declared. Rouher was, however, not yet willing to concede the game lost, and held the wavering Emperor firm. Above all, time must be gained to determine upon the course to be pursued with regard to the future; the Chamber was therefore convened for the 28th of June, although in extraordinary session only, its sole duty being the verification of powers of the newly elected deputies, the drafts for the budget being as yet not quite ready.

The Liberals, urged on by the current of public opinion, were impatient of delay and postponement. The Middle Party announced an interpellation indorsed by 116 members, which it desired to present immediately after the organization of the Chamber, and in which the necessity of a responsible Ministry was emphatically set forth as constituting, together with further parliamentary rights, the surest means of securing to the country a greater share in the direction of its affairs.

A few weeks passed in the verification of powers of the deputies, a sufficient time for Napoleon to accommodate himself to circumstances ; although unwilling to yield fully, he had decided to show a spirit of concession, in the hope of procuring more advantageous conditions. Hardly had the Chamber organized when an imperial message was received forestalling the transaction regarding the threatened interpellation. In it the Emperor announced his intention to recommend to the Senate, which alone had the right to modify the Constitution, that the Legislative Body be granted greater freedom of action with respect to

proposing and examining amendments, the privilege
of electing its committees, as well as the right to vote
the budget by headings. In so far as the Ministers
were concerned, however, only that Article of the
Constitution was to be abrogated according to which
they were disqualified from becoming members of
either Chamber. No allusion whatever was made to
their responsibility.

Naturally enough, the Chamber offered no opposition
to the extension of its privileges, but the displeasure
which was felt at the total disregard of the chief demand was by no means concealed. Many members of
the Right felt an additional provocation, jealousy of the
great power exercised by the present "vice-emperor,"
the Minister of State, Rouher, a feeling which, as was
no secret, was shared by more than one of the other
Ministers. This feeling was so general that the President of the House, Schneider, a great manufacturer,
sought an audience with the Emperor to assure him
that matters could not continue as at present; the
Chamber and the entire country alike demanded that
the Minister of State should be replaced by a responsible council of Ministers.

In painful indecision the Emperor struggled with
his conflicting desires. Rouher's advice was, "Give
me the authority, and I will drive all these bickerers
out of the House, and simply restore the Constitution
of 1852." This was, however, too directly opposed to
the Emperor's views. They were always the same old
questions by which he was tortured, first by the one

side and then by the other. He longed to be relieved
of the troubles, cares, and suffering associated with the
supreme power, and yet the prospect of its diminution
gave him a sense of personal humiliation. Would a
parliamentary Ministry be always both inclined and
able to defend his son's succession against the attempts
of the Republicans? This, to be sure, was exceedingly
doubtful. But with his unfortunate bodily condition,
how long would he still possess the physical and mental
power to hold the reins of government in his own
grasp? In short, he resolved upon the second course.
On August 2d the Senate should be convened, not
only to extend the parliamentary privileges as promised,
but to enact the amendments necessary to the formation of a responsible Ministry as well.

This implied a fundamental transformation of affairs,
and much labor in arranging for all the changes required by the new conditions. To obtain the time
needed for this it was decided to prorogue the Chamber
for an indefinite time, greatly to the dissatisfaction of
the Radicals.

On July 17th the office of Secretary of State was
abolished by an imperial decree (Rouher was nominated to the Presidency of the Senate, an imposing but
empty dignity), and by another, a modification of the
Ministry was ordained. Five of its members retained
their positions, two deputies were intrusted with tho
Departments of Public Instruction and Agriculture,
and that of Justice passed into the hands of a Liberal.
To the surprise of every one, Lavalette resigned the

Foreign Office, exchanging positions with the Ambassador at London, Prince Latour d'Auvergne, a pupil and sympathizer of Drouyn de Lhuys, an unmistakable evidence that Napoleon was far from pleased with Italy's attitude.

Throughout the entire country the impatient Liberals in round terms denounced the new Cabinet as reactionary. In reality, however, most of them felt convinced ·that the present arrangement was but a transitory one, and offered no opposition to the institution of a parliamentary Ministry in the near future, but rather looked forward with eagerness to the day when Ollivier, the present leader and acknowledged head of the Middle Party, should be called to take charge.

And so the draft for a *senatus consultum* was at last completed, bearing the traces of the varying influences and mental conflicts which the Emperor had undergone; and on August 2d it was submitted to the Senate for legislative action.

Upon first sight it seemed thoroughly impregnated with constitutional principles. The rights conferred upon the Legislative Body even exceeded the measure of expectation which the message of July 12th had suggested; there were the additional privileges of making its own rules and electing its own committees; of proposing new laws, of voting the budget of expenditure by headings, and of interpellating the Government. On the other hand, there remained unchanged the prohibition of the right to take action upon an Article of the Constitution, since aside from a general vote of the people the Senate still retained the sole right to amend the Constitution.

The position of the Ministers was then defined: they were to be wholly dependent upon the Emperor; in council they were to be presided over by him; they were to be responsible and liable to arraignment only upon accusation by the Senate; they were privileged to become members of either the Senate or Legislative Body, and were to have the right to appear in these assemblies, and ask to be heard there, at any time.

Thus, that much advocated principle, the responsibility of the Ministry, was at last to be a reality. Since, however, the Articles of the Constitution by which the Emperor was made responsible to the French people remained in force, the Ministers' constitutional independence of the Emperor, and their dependence upon the parliament, could have but little significance.

Nevertheless, he who remembered the consequences to political conditions by which the concessions made on January 19th were followed might very willingly overlook the vagueness and incompleteness of the present achievement in the belief that the representative assembly would in the end, nevertheless, have sufficient power to enforce its wishes in connection with every question of importance.

Meanwhile, before the Senate had completed its task, an event occurred which excluded the thought of everything else from the minds of all. The Emperor, who during the preceding summer had again been quite ill, and obliged to spend several weeks in retirement at

Fontainebleau, suffered another attack of the malady on August 12th, which now developed so rapidly and seriously that toward the end of the month the physicians feared his early dissolution. Immediately an exceeding alarm spread through the whole country, and the Socialists and Anarchists were jubilant; a terrible panic played havoc with the exchanges; gloomy forebodings made all hearts heavy.

The two most prominent members of the Cabinet, Forcade, Minister of the Interior, and Magne, of Finance, were engaged in bitter contentions; the Minister of War, Marshal Niel, had died on August 14th, and Lebœuf, a general of no great ability, had taken his place. In the midst of a constitutional crisis the country was without a representative assembly, without a head, and practically without a Government.

The Senate made great haste, therefore, to arrive at a decision regarding the draft submitted to it. The report of the Committee to which it had been referred for immediate consideration contained only a few suggested amendments in favor of the rights of the Senate. The deliberation in the *plenum* continued from the 1st to the 6th of September. In connection with it a great sensation was created by Prince Napoleon, who in a vigorous speech demanded an effective responsibility of the Ministers, and equal power for the Legislative Body with that of the Senate in any modification of the Constitution.

Everybody recognized in this a bid for the throne in opposition to the claims of the Empress and her son in

the event of the Emperor's death. The Senate, however, gave the Prince a support of only ten voices ; all
the others were in favor of enacting the *senatus consultum* as it had been submitted to that body.

Meanwhile the Emperor's condition gradually improved, so that on September 10th he could be removed to Paris from his sick-chamber at St. Cloud.
On the same day the *senatus consultum* was published
in the official gazette, and thus became a part of the
Constitution. Still, Napoleon's state of health remained
so critical and his exhaustion so great that a previously
planned celebration at the Camp of Châlons had to be
abandoned ; and soon afterward the convening of the
Chamber had to be postponed until the end of November,
by which a storm of indignation was raised among the
Radicals. Before that time there could, of course, be no
thought of undertaking a reconstruction of the Ministry.

In addition to all this, the momentous and long-dis-
cussed matter of the triple alliance came to a decision
in September.

We have seen how, on account of the unfavorable
form which the Roman clause had taken, Minister
Menabrea had for a time refrained from laying the
draft of the treaty before his colleagues. When at
length he did so, it at once became apparent that his
solicitude had not been without cause. The Ministerial Council declared an alliance of arms against the
associate of 1866 to be impossible. Victory thus won
would lead to an unlimited preponderance of French
power. The Council offered no objections to a defen-

sive alliance in which hostility to the results of 1866 and to German unity should find no place, and insisted upon the further stipulation that the French troops should be withdrawn from Rome, and that with regard to that city France should recognize the principle of non-intervention.[1]

During the last days of August, Menabrea addressed a request to Vienna asking Austria to influence Napoleon to remove his troops from Rome at an early day, thus making it possible for Italy to sign the treaty of alliance.   To this Beust gladly consented, and again sent Vitzthum to Paris.   By this time, however, Napoleon's illness had become so serious that the Count could not obtain an interview.   Since, owing to his well-known disinclination to Italy, there could be no hope of accomplishing anything through the Minister of Foreign Affairs, Latour, Vitzthum returned to Vienna with his mission unaccomplished.   This was followed by the Italian declaration, that since Austria had reserved the liberty to remain neutral in case of a war, so Italy must make the condition to refrain from participation in war until after Rome had been evacuated; otherwise no objection was raised against the treaty of alliance.

After his recovery Napoleon discussed the subject with Lavalette and Latour.   Lavalette, who, as we know, was in general so well disposed to Italy, was nevertheless of the opinion that by such an alliance France would find herself in a peculiar position.   "We

[1] Compare Guiccioli, "Quintino Sella," I. 242.

would," said he, " renounce all right to independent
decision in our diplomacy; and in return for this, we
should, in the event of war, when the alliance would
be of greatest value, be left in the lurch by our two
allies. That would be a most one-sided bargain." Latour, to whom any nearer approach to Italy was detest-
able, fully agreed with Lavalette.

This view remained undisputed by the Emperor also.
He recognized, moreover, that the conditions which
had acted as an incentive to his proposal of alliance
in April had materially changed since then. He had
become convinced that Prussia's attitude in the Belgian railway controversy had been one of strict neutrality. The convention between North Germany and
Baden, regarding military freedom of migration, had
in the meantime gone into effect; clearly the political
position of the grand duchy had in no way been affected by it. Bismarck maintained inflexibly the standpoint he had announced on September 7th, 1867 : The
South German States have the right at any time to
declare their intention to join the Northern Confederation; Prussia, however, will make no effort to induce
them to such a step.

Napoleon's conclusion, therefore, was : Since 1868
the outlook has improved; it does not appear to be Prussia's intention to precipitate matters; if German unity
is gradually effected, the French people will become
accustomed to the idea, and, looking upon it as the
inevitable consequence of a national development, will
not be exasperated by it to the point of war.

With so peaceful a prospect before him, Napoleon did not feel impelled to conclude a treaty offering so few inducements. His severe attack of illness had left him exhausted in body and mind, and the thought of inaugurating a complete change in his foreign policy had lost the charm it once had for him. He longed for rest; soon he would have responsible Ministers; he would leave it to them to determine what it was best to do. He wrote Emperor Francis Joseph that he had indefinitely postponed signing the treaty; nevertheless, should Austria be attacked, he would render assistance, even though not bound to do so by treaty. Francis Joseph in his reply expressed his thanks, and added, that the reopening of the negotiations would be left wholly to Napoleon's judgment. The Emperor allowed the matter to rest at that, but very soon afterwards said to Count Vimercati, that after all that had occurred he could not possibly reopen the discussions concerning the triple alliance ; Austria must be the one to do so.

And so the only result of the long-extended negotiations was the promise which the three sovereigns gave one another by letter, that no one of them would enter into alliance with any of the Powers without first informing the other two of the intention, a promise, moreover, which Francis Joseph and Napoleon had exchanged verbally as early as 1867.

Whereas the attempt to bring about a firm association of France and Austria had thus proved futile, success attended the effort made soon afterwards by the Prussian Government to effect a change in its relations to Vienna, proving of greatest moment in its consequences.

Since 1866 intercourse between the two capitals had been restricted to official communications, not always of a pleasant nature. Only recently, after the termination of the Belgian railway transaction, Beust, irritated by the fiasco made by his despatch of May 1st, in contrast to the general commendation accorded Prussia for its attitude of silent reserve, had sent a letter [1] to Dresden on July 8th in which he complained that the Saxon view of the despatch of May 1st had been influenced by another Power to the disparagement of Austria. This gave rise to a diplomatic correspondence between the three Cabinets, in which Beust, as was to be expected from the nature of the subject, did not add to his laurels. The official press of Berlin and Vienna then took up the battle, until finally Prussia, which, despite all the recent friction, was still actuated by the desire to re-establish the old friendship with Austria, put an end to the quarrel by a most unexpected step.

It was at this time that the Egyptian Khedive, Ismaïl, invited all the potentates of Europe to be present at the formal opening of the Suez Canal. Emperor Francis Joseph accepted; Napoleon, owing to his state of health, declined, but sent his Empress, who gladly went in his stead. In Berlin the Crown Prince sought the King's permission to take the interesting

[1] Published in the Austrian Red Book. Prussia was not mentioned by name, but was unmistakably indicated.

journey, which suggested the thought of going by way of Vienna, should it be found, upon inquiry at the Hofburg, that an official visit from the Crown Prince would be welcome to the Imperial Court.

An affirmative reply was at once received, and on October 7th the Crown Prince arrived in Vienna. His reception left nothing to be desired. The Emperor, wearing the Prussian uniform, awaited the Crown Prince at the railway station; in the Hofburg, much to his surprise, he was received by the Empress, whom he had supposed at Ischl; no distinction of honor was omitted.

"After the events of 1866," wrote the Crown Prince, "every Austrian must have found it hard to look upon a representative of our King; no one, however, allowed me to feel this. The Emperor was unchanged in his demeanor to me, and one who knows his manner as well as I do could not for a moment be in doubt that his welcome was a sincere one."

The archdukes, too, were most cordial, especially Archduke Albert, who, being best versed in such matters, expressed his appreciation of the manner in which the Prince had fulfilled his duty as a soldier, which, he said, every one was compelled to recognize. The Liberal Minister, Giskra, gave expression to the pleasure which the visit afforded him as being indicative of a return to relations of friendship; the consequences of the visit would gradually make themselves felt. Count Beust, too, he remarked, no longer harbored thoughts of revenge, but had concluded to let bygones be bygones.

In fact, Beust defended himself vigorously against Bismarck's accusation that he influenced the press against Prussia, but closed with the remark, that, in so far as the South German situation was concerned, he was not at all opposed to its further development; however, as Minister of Austria, it was his first duty to advance the interests of the Austrian crownlands, and that therefore he must watch the development of the South German question with a jealous eye, that he might guard against anything by which their welfare might be threatened.[1]

This declaration, together with the general conditions prevailing at that time, is a sufficient explanation of the fact that Emperor Francis Joseph carefully excluded every topic of political interest from his conversation with the Prince, either in Vienna or later in Egypt. The Emperor's attitude for the future had, however, been quite correctly forecast by Giskra's utterance. The first eventful step toward a reconciliation between the two former rivals had thus been taken, and with it a greater prospect of established peace for Europe had been opened.

[1] In the Delegations of August, 1869, Beust had in fact repeated his declaration of March, 1867, namely, that the treaties of alliance, defensive and offensive, between Prussia and the South German States, were a violation of the Treaty of Prague.

CHAPTER III.

COSMOPOLITAN ASPIRATIONS.

THE prodigious advance toward realization of German unity which the year 1866 had witnessed was by no means allowed to halt there, but was carried onward through the united efforts of the Liberal and National parties. Although their ideas did not wholly coincide, they sprang from a common fountain-head; and this, despite many differences and frequent friction, always made a return to united and fruitful labor possible.

The endeavor of the Liberals was to secure greatest freedom for all individuals in the incalculable multiplicity and variety in which nature produces them. In recognition of this principle they held that every person should have the right to free development and a full realization of himself, unrestrained by foreign and unfavorable influences, in so far as this was compatible with a state of order in the community.

Prompted by wholly the same spirit, the National Party demanded that the German people as a whole should be allowed the freedom fully to develop the aspirations common to the individuals, and should be protected against the domination or influence of elements contrary to their nature and inimical to their independence.

The surprising power with which these tendencies had asserted themselves upon German soil in the very heart of Europe had not failed to produce a corresponding reaction in more than one direction. The adversaries were by no means united, but, on the contrary, were divided by bitter enmity, their ultimate aims being as widely sundered as are brief human happiness and eternal blessedness. But in their antagonism to German unity they met upon common ground in their devotion to one fundamental, negative doctrine, the rejection of all individual liberty and national independence.

All men are equal, for in them all the chief qualities of human nature find repetition. The minor traits in which the individuals differ are comparatively of little importance, and give no one a claim to particular rights. When a man whom nature has especially favored seeks to raise himself above his fellow-men, it becomes the duty of the community, in the name of reason and the love of humanity, to crush this arrogance, and restore equality in every respect.

It was upon this principle that the social-democratic State was developed which in 1793 showed the world how completely individual liberty can be suppressed, and the confines of nations be obliterated.

The same end, though by a wholly different route, is reached by the clerical mode of reasoning. All men are equal, for they are all sick with sin, which is dragging them to everlasting destruction; it therefore behooves them, one and all, king as well as beggar, children of the North as well as of the South, to seek salvation by submission in their inward convictions and outward actions to the ordinances of the one holy physician.

For both of these movements the year 1868 was an epoch-making one.

I. COMMUNISTIC MOVEMENT.

Poverty and misery have existed upon our earth at all times, and will continue to do so as long as nature produces not only strong and clever men, but weak and stupid ones as well. No less has there ever been a lack of endeavor, both by theory and by force, to transform poverty into prosperity, or, as it is expressed nowadays, to solve the social question.

In olden times it was the condition of the peasantry which in this respect claimed the attention of the nations. Since the last century the mammoth manufacturing establishments, performing their labor largely by machinery, have brought together great numbers of laborers at certain centres, resulting not only in colossal production, but in an enormous amount of misery as well, in consequence of which a new impetus has been given the endeavor to solve the social question.

In Germany, where this industrial development did not assume proportions of significance until after the Customs Union had been formed, there were comparatively few writers before 1848 who devoted them-

selves to the study of the workingman's condition;
and these received but little response from the public.
Chief among them were Friedrich Engels and Karl
Marx. In the March revolution the Republican Party
became thoroughly impregnated with socialistic elements of a most radical kind, wherefore, after the triumph of the reaction the Socialists found themselves
pursued with twofold severity, and to a great extent
sought refuge in foreign lands. Marx, after much
wandering about, finally made London his headquar-
ters.

The consequence was, that in Germany within the
province of economics the individualistic and free-trade
views had the field to themselves once more. Predominant above all other demands were heard those
for freedom to hold property and to transact business;
freedom to combine and to compete. It was firmly believed that the unrestricted activity of these agencies
would lead not only to greatest possible production,
but to the most equitable distribution of wealth as
well; at the same time the State authority was warned
to withhold its hand from direct interference with these
matters.

The working-classes received the fair-sounding promises contained in these axioms with more of suspicion
than of confidence. Marked success, however, had attended the efforts made in their behalf by Schulze-
Delitzsch, when, as has been related in connection
with the transactions of the Reichstag of 1867, in a
truly helpful spirit of philanthropy, he not only urged

them to help themselves, but furnished through his co-operative associations at once credit, cheaper raw materials, and a market. At the same time he made the earliest suggestions regarding liberty both for employer and employed to combine in coalitions. Schulze, however, was not allowed to continue long undisturbed in his well-intentioned activity. Since 1863 he was made the object of constant hostile attacks by Ferdinand Lassalle, a Hebrew bourgeois like Marx, from whose writings Schulze had adopted certain socialistic views. Lassalle was a clever, eloquent writer of exceeding self-conceit, who said of himself that every line he wrote was equipped with all the erudition of the nineteenth century. In fact, his addresses and writings bespeak an extent of reading which in a measure justifies his proud assertion; quite as evident, however, is the fact that the nineteenth century makes much greater demands for unprejudiced conception of premises and correctness of deduction than Lassalle ever evinced.

In so far as his character is concerned, I will confine myself to the statement that after his death his co-workers expressed very different opinions regarding it. In the year 1869, at the Congress of Internationals held at Basel, Liebknecht paid him the tribute of pronouncing him to have been a man of great ability and energy of purpose, and above all else, highly honorable, which was more than could be said of his successors. In contrast to this, Bernhard Becker, who took his place as President of the German Working-

men's Association, in a special pamphlet published in
1868, portrayed him as a man given over to the pleasures of life, and who came to his death through a dis-
graceful love affair.

Lassalle not only antagonized Schulze, but together
with him the whole Party of Progress. His earliest
weapon of attack was Ricardo's iron law of wages,
according to which competition and the constant
growth of the population always keep the laborer's
wages at the minimum required for the mere necessaries of life. Therefore, it was argued, the economy
which Schulze advised the workingmen to practise was
to them an impossible virtue ; no wage-earner could
accumulate property. To advise the laborer to rely
upon self-help was futile ; it was the duty of the State
to furnish the necessary aid.

To this end Lassalle proposed that the State should
advance to each working-men's society the capital required for the establishment of a factory, to be conducted by the workingmen collectively and upon their
own responsibility. He hoped that these companies
would soon be enabled from the proceeds of the factories to repay the State the sum advanced, together
with a reasonable interest.

The German working-men eagerly grasped at this
suggestion of aid to be rendered by the State ; many
thousands were won over by the new hope held out to
them, turned their backs upon Schulze-Delitzsch, and
combined in societies which were to lead to the organization of productive associations with State aid. How-

ever, even when the necessary capital could be raised, the practical execution of the plan proved successful only in very rare instances. In the case of all factories requiring a complicated industrial technique, the republican administration by the working-men evinced itself to be impracticable. In the instances in which their management proved efficient because of the less complicated conditions, and the success of the establishment made the employment of additional laborers necessary, the thought failed to suggest itself to the founders that these new co-laborers should be admitted into their association. They regarded themselves as the owners, backslid to the odious capitalist system, and simply employed the new laborers as wage-earners. When these made complaint, they received the conclusive reply: "We have devoted ten years of thought and labor to accumulate a capital; you have not shared the labor, why should you now participate in its fruits?"

The argument was unanswerable, and was a blow felt by the entire social-democratic system.

Lassalle never openly advocated abolition of private property. In his writings upon jurisprudence he confines himself to an attempt to establish with a great show of historical learning and dialectic skill that the historic foundations upon which rest our notions regarding property and the principle of inheritance have wholly disappeared, and that these ideas owe their existence at the present day wholly to the arbitrary decree of the law, wherefore they can at any moment be legally abolished by the enactment of new laws, and, as he explicitly states, without rendering indemnification of any kind to the erstwhile property-owners.

Any outwardly visible effect these writings seem not to have had, and as contributions to scientific literature they have received but slight recognition.

On August 31st, 1864, Lassalle died of a wound received in a duel; a few weeks later a much more able successor stepped into the place thus left vacant. On the 28th of September, Marx took part in the organization of an International Working-men's Association in London, although the original suggestion came from Paris. At the time, the originators of the plan had little thought either of politics or revolution in connection with it; soon, however, Marx, who had long made it his purpose to impart an international character to the entire labor movement, and as early as 1848 had closed a fiercely revolutionary manifesto with the words: "Proletarians of all nations, combine!" soon influenced his associates to adopt his programme. Although not their president, he became the general secretary of the association for all its affairs in Germany.

No other one of the managers could compare with him in point of information and capability to work, in boundless fanaticism and native executive ability; and very soon Marx became the life and soul of the "International" so highly esteemed by the working-men, and hated and feared quite as much by all other parties.

His aims he had long before proclaimed in a number

of shorter writings. In 1867 he began the publication of a ponderous work entitled " Capital." In this it is his purpose, by tracing the history of the rise and consolidation of English capital since the 16th century, and by portraying in conjunction with this the present wretched condition of the English laborer, to exhibit to its full extent the enormity and intolerableness of this state of affairs. At the same time he attempts to demonstrate scientifically, that, by the existing social and economic order, the laborer is hopelessly condemned to be the exploited slave of the capitalist, who holds sole control of the means necessary to labor; this he declares to be so inevitable a consequence of the system that even the merciful capitalist is forced to exploit the labor of his workmen. There is no remedy for this, he holds, other than the annihilation of the entire system, by compelling the parasitic capitalists to surrender the materials and instruments of labor indispensable to the management of a factory, such as land, buildings, machinery, raw materials, money, etc., into the hands of the productive workers. Consequently all private competing capital should be transformed into a united collective capital. Since such a revolution in affairs can of course be accomplished only by force, the laborers of all countries are advised to organize in firm unions under the direction of the International.

He seeks further to prove such a social revolution to be both justifiable and inevitable by a theory regarding values and wages again borrowed from the English political-economist, Ricardo. Its leading features must be briefly outlined here, since it continued to be the creed of the Social-democratic Party of Germany.

According to it, human labor creates the exchange or purchase-value of a commodity, provided this satisfies a want of the community, in other words that it serves a purpose useful to the community. " A bee," says Marx,[1] " in the construction of its cell puts many an architect to shame, but that which from the outset distinguishes the poorest architect from the best bee is that he has constructed his work mentally before he builds it with materials. At the end of the process of labor, a result appears which at its beginning existed as an image in the brain of the workman. He therefore not only transforms natural materials, but with them realizes the purpose which he knows, which determines the nature and method of his labor, and to which his will must be subordinated."

The effect of labor conducted according to such a plan is, to quote Marx, that the worker, through the use of his brain, nerves, and muscle, imparts to the materials employed a value not previously theirs ; he creates a surplus value.

This may be well exemplified by a trivial illustration. A tailor purchases cloth for 35 marks, and incurs a further expense of 5 marks ; in twelve hours he produces a coat of a fashionable cut, and sells it for 60 marks ; by his labor, therefore, the value of the cloth has been increased by 20 marks. This the purchaser recognized in paying the price; the tailor received the

[1] Vol. I., p. 142.

amount of the surplus value because he produced it, and therefore earned it.

Further, however, the new style of coat meets with so great approbation, that, to fill all the orders he receives, the tailor employs ten wage-earners. According to the iron law of wages he hires them at a rate corresponding to the minimum of expense required for existence in his locality; we will assume, 5 marks. He provides them with material and implements, gives them the necessary instructions, and then lies down on his sofa to see that they carry them out. In the evening the ten coats are finished, and on the next day they are delivered and paid for. And now, how stands the account?

Receipts, 600 marks; expenditure for cloth and other necessaries, 400 marks; gain, or surplus value, 200 marks. Of this each wage-earner receives 5 marks; all of them together, 50. This leaves 150 marks for the employer, who performed no labor, — thirty times as much as any one laborer, and ten times as much as they all receive.

He has the money with which to purchase materials at a low price as occasion may offer; laborers he can, according to the iron law of wages, procure at any time at the lowest possible price. Human labor, which creates all surplus value, falls, as a consequence of the always greater supply than demand, far below the actual value of that which it produces.

In the place of the little tailoring workshop, let us now substitute a great factory with several hundred employees; with machinery which in every hour produces tenfold, perhaps a hundred-fold, that which can be made by hand. It will then be realized how, by appropriating the product of his workmen's labor, though performing none himself, the manufacturer becomes with rapid strides a millionnaire, whereas the daily exploited wage-earners, with their meagre daily wages, can never be more, notwithstanding all their exertion, than poor wretches looking forward with eagerness to the emancipating revolution.

It will be at once perceived that this theory rests upon a twofold foundation : the iron law of wages, and the doctrine of the origin of surplus value. Should either be proved fallacious, the whole structure falls to the ground. Both, however, are false, — contrary to truth and contrary to experience.

The iron law of wages is a scientific abstraction, the answer to a theoretically circumscribed question : Presupposing that the immediate advantage of the two contracting parties decides the point, what will be the rate of wages?

In reality, however, the question seldom arises so free from modification ; usually, numerous other influences are brought to bear upon it. A compassionate employer seeks to alleviate the wretchedness of his workmen, and nevertheless is able to meet the ever-menacing competition. Every far-sighted employer knows that his own interests are better served by healthy and contented workmen than by miserable and resentful ones.

Moreover, the measure of the law of wages — the minimum of expenditure necessary for existence — is in its amount constantly subject to change. At a time of growing and general prosperity, there is a relative increase in the demands made by the people in all stations of life, and public opinion compels every employer to better the condition of his workmen in a corresponding degree.

To these considerations must be added another, which has become an important factor since the day when freedom to form coalitions was achieved, and the right of assembly established, — the workmen's greater power of resistance. Very soon thereafter their income had become so much larger that they could save and accumulate. They are at present enabled to meet the demand made upon them by innumerable strikes and boycotts; they pay into the treasuries of their local or trades unions as well as into the treasury of the general Communist Union their regular dues, sufficing to provide the salaries of numerous officials and editors, as well as compensation for their representatives in the Reichstag, though paid in violation of the law. The party itself has in consequence repudiated the iron law of wages. How, indeed, could it uphold it, and at the same time demand contributions from its members belonging to the laboring class?

The second question, who among those engaged in a large manufacturing establishment is the real producer of surplus value, it seems to me is peremptorily answered by the very illustration cited by Marx; and it is to be regretted that in the statement of details Marx forgot to draw the conclusion. Labor, he declares, creates new values when it serves a useful purpose, the idea of which exists in the brain of the workman before he begins his labor; "which he knows, which determines the nature and method of his labor, and to which his will must be subordinated." This is in itself a sufficient answer to the question. He who has preconceived the manufacturing process in its entirety, who determines upon and provides the necessary means of production, who assumes the entire risk of the undertaking, who in the process of production subordinates his own will and the activity of his employees to the demand of the great purpose to be accomplished — he is not to be found among the laborers attending to the machinery according to instruction, but in him alone by whom the enterprise was undertaken — the factory owner, the capitalist.

Marx's assertion, that he is the parasite who without effort on his own part pockets the surplus value produced by his workmen, is a subversion of the truth. The manufacturer by his intellectual labor, unremitted during the entire process of production, is in reality the creator of the surplus value which therefore justly belongs to him alone. The operatives have no greater influence upon it than have the machines which they manipulate according to his instructions, without understanding or needing to understand the connection or purpose of the various stages of the process.

Upon this point the scholarly Marx, who was never a wage-earner himself, exhibits a strange want of appreciation of intellectual as compared with manual labor, a tendency which ever since that day has been steadily

growing in the Communistic Party. Notwithstanding
the many years of wearisome preparation by which intellectual power can alone be gained, notwithstanding
the incalculably great achievements which under proper
direction it can render, he concedes to it no higher
merit than that which he attributes to the generally
meanly regarded exertions of the day-laborer.

The adequate remuneration of the intellectual producer lies in his greater appreciation of the production
itself, has recently been said by a wiseacre. This is all
of a piece with the utterance heard in the Reichstag in
connection with the dotations to our military leaders in
recognition of their services. " Every soldier imperils
his life for his country; what more can a general do? "
He can do that which every soldier can by no means
do, lead our armies to victory, and save our country

That the fallacious reasoning of the communistic
theory should secure a lasting hold upon the minds of
millions of people might appear strange did we not
remember that the arguments are clothed in the ob-
scure language of philosophy, unintelligible to the half
or wholly uneducated public to whom it appears most
impressive, and to whom, moreover, the conclusions
drawn are perfectly intelligible, since they appeal not
to the understanding, but to the strongest passions of
those to whom they are addressed.

Besides his literary labors, Marx undertook the institution of an effective propaganda immediately after
the organization of the International. A general council, having its seat at London, exercised a general con-

trol over the affairs of the association; and a general
secretary was appointed, to have special charge of its
interests in each country, where a central committee
served as the directing authority for the district groups
or sections of the several societies. At a congress to
be held at Geneva in 1866, reports were to be given
upon the progress so far made, and the permanent organization of the association was then to be completed.

To Germany, Marx sent in 1865 one of his ablest
disciples and most ardent admirers, Liebknecht, whose
acquaintance we have made in the German Reichstag.
Arrived there, he found it necessary, first of all, to famil-
iarize himself with a most confused state of affairs.

After Lassalle's death, the societies over which he
had exercised a dictatorial sway had either been wholly
discontinued or were engaged in bitter contention.
The one party recognized as leader the Countess Hatzfeld, a once beautiful, and now wholly emancipated
lady, very rich, crafty, and imperious. The other had
fallen under the domination of the son of a Frankfort
patrician, Von Schweitzer, a man of profligate habits,
but equipped with a fine intellect and great will-power.
Ostracized by his own class of society because of his
ill fame, he had, in the hope of finding a new spice of
life, grasped the reins of government over one group
of socialist societies, which he held with a firm hand,
guiding its affairs to most excellent results.

The warfare which Lassalle had begun against the
Berlin Progressists, Von Schweitzer now pursued with
fresh vigor. When, in imitation of the English ex-

ample, this party undertook the organization of trades-unions, under the direction of Dr. Hirsch, for the purpose of establishing a fund to be used in maintaining strikes, a course by which they hoped to make Progressists of the workmen, Schweitzer immediately did likewise, after which the Progressist and Socialist trades-unions were unceasingly engaged in a lively quarrel.

Suddenly, however, appeared an acrimonious manifesto issued by the Hatzfeld group; in it Schweitzer and Hirsch were criticised in an equally rancorous tone of enmity, and strikes in general were condemned as a folly, working ruin to the participants. Thus there was strife everywhere; one after another the societies disbanded, and only by strenuous exertions did Schweitzer succeed in holding his together.

In this confusion new labor unions were organized in Saxony and Thüringen; and, by keeping aloof from these dissensions, they gradually became more numerous, added greatly to their membership, and in politics either associated themselves with the Progressists or entered the arena as a democratic People's Party.

In these circles Bebel, an honest artisan and self-made man, gradually rose to a position commanding respect and influence; in 1865 he was elected to the presidency of a working-men's society of Leipzig, and in 1867 became chairman of a committee charged with the affairs of an association composed of these recently organized societies. He was at the time a member of the constituting Reichstag, and as such denied

being a Socialist, claiming to belong to the People's
Party. If he was not already a Socialist, he was
about to become a Communist.

As early as 1865 he and Liebknecht had become
fast friends, and the latter had initiated him into the
doctrines of his prophet, Marx. In 1868 the annual
meeting of the German working-men's societies was in
session at Nürnberg, from the 5th to the 7th of September. More than one hundred and twenty societies were
represented by delegates. As President of the principal
society, that of Leipzig, Bebel moved that the assembly
adopt as its own the approved programme of the International as accepted by the Geneva Congress. After
a long and excited discussion, the motion was carried
by sixty-eight voices against forty-eight; whereupon
the minority protested, and left the hall to constitute
themselves an independent German organization upon
the basis of the old programme.

In the new programme adopted by the majority, the
words "abolition of private property" were carefully
avoided. The communistic doctrine was, however,
clearly indicated; in the first place, by the words
"identification with the aspirations of the International,
since the emancipation of the working-men can be
achieved only by the combined endeavor of the workers
of all lands;" and further by the declaration that the
working-men's economic dependence upon the monopo-
lists of the instruments of labor is the foundation of
their servitude in all its forms, the source of their social
wretchedness, their mental degradation, and political

dependence. This assertion was again simply a discreet circumlocution of Marx's demand, that the capitalists should be forced to surrender the means of labor, — and what is not to be classed among these? — to the associated craftsmen, and meant nothing less than that all private property should revert to the community. In contradistinction to the course pursued by the seceding minority, by the Lassalle societies, and by the Progressist trades-unions, from all of which political aims were excluded, their activity being directed solely toward promoting the material welfare of the workingman with reference to the existing social order, the majority now declared further: Political activity is indispensable to the economic emancipation of the working-men; the social question is inseparable from the political question, and can be solved only in a democratic State.

Thus it was that cosmopolitan communism was for the first time in Germany proclaimed to be the political creed of a large association. The effect was soon found to be by no means an insignificant one. Bebel and Liebknecht called a general congress of the Social-democratic working-men's societies of Germany to meet at Eisenach on August 7th of the next year. At this assembly, there appeared, besides their own adherents, the representatives of the Lassalle societies, who, although greatly in the minority, yet numbered one hundred and ten delegates, whereas the Communists sent two hundred and sixty-two, nominally the representatives of 150,000 working-men.

New dissension, however, quickly arose, and the Lassalle representation again withdrew, the two parties
continuing their deliberations in separate halls.   The
promising outlook which the Nürnberg programme had
opened to the working-men had evidently proved a
magnet of great attraction.   Nevertheless, Liebknecht
did not even yet deem it advisable to come to the front
openly, partly because of the excessive power unfortunately still exercised by the police, partly for fear of
repelling some of the less resolute among his associates.
The programme of this assembly, therefore, began with
the declaration: The Social-democratic Party in Germany is in favor of a State ruled by the people.

Thus the designation of tne party as communistic,
and the word republic as the name of the desired form
of government, were discreetly avoided.   When during
the course of the debate an outspoken delegate moved
the use of the word republic, this was at once rejected
as inopportune.

It was then further resolved, tnat the existing political and social systems were highly unjust, that they
were to be indefatigably combated, and that every form
of class-supremacy ought to be destroyed.   To this
was joined the declaration in which at Nürnberg the
abolition of private property had been cloaked, namely,
that all the instruments of labor should be surrendered
into the hands of the workers.   It appeared, however,
with some of its rough edges smoothed away, thus:
The economic dependence of the working-man upon the
capitalist is the origin of his servitude in all its forms :

therefore the Social-democratic Party devotes its activity to securing to every worker a full share in the products of labor; it seeks to accomplish this through the downfall of the present system of production (the wage system).

At this point, which was the decisive one, it appeared how wise had been the course pursued out of consideration for the possibly irresolute members of the party. For the clause as it had been proposed, the assembly now substituted the words: The present system of production must be superseded by that of cooperative labor. Liebknecht consoled himself with the reflection that in this form the communistic principle was embodied full as well, which was quite true.

Political freedom was then declared to be inseparable from social freedom, and with respect to the existing conditions it was especially desired that all men over twenty years of age be given the right to vote for every representative assembly; that direct legislation by the people be introduced; that a system of defence by the people take the place of the standing army; that education in the public schools be compulsory and free to all; and that all indirect taxes be discontinued, and a single, progressive income tax be levied (an inheritance duty was added by the assembly).

It was also emphasized and resolved, that it was most expedient that the party should be united in its organization; that it should be constituted under the direction of a committee of five; and that final decision upon the more important resolutions of a congress be reached through a vote of all the members.

The party then announced itself to be a branch of the International, but with the distinct reservation: " In so far as this is not in conflict with the law of the land." Liebknecht was designated as editor of their party organ, *Der Volksstaat*, for which every member was expected to subscribe, or else contribute a groschen a week for party purposes. To avoid financial irregularities, a special committee to control the money affairs was appointed.

As resolved at this meeting, the next general assembly of the Social-democratic Party was held at Stuttgart from the 4th to the 7th of June, 1870. Again the Lassalle delegates appeared, and again to no purpose; they were too few to assume control, and so disappeared from the scene. Bebel and Liebknecht found a support of seventy four delegates, representing a hundred and eleven localities, or 15,398 members. The membership had therefore fallen off greatly since 1869: many of the lukewarm had probably dropped out, whilst others may have been unwilling to pay regular fees.

At all events, in this assembly the forethought and discretion which had marked the previous meetings were cast to the winds. It was felt to be a circle of friends, and caution was, therefore, no longer necessary. The leaders now advised the party to seek representation in both Reichstag and Customs Parliament, in the hope that at times the scales might be turned in favor of less undesirable legislation ; always, however, to agitate the party views, and upon every occasion to expose the transactions of both these assemblies as idle and a mere farce.

It was then resolved, that since in agriculture as in manufacturing, production is most profitable when conducted upon a large scale, in consequence of which the great land-owners would soon crowd out the smaller farmers, forcing them into the position of wage-earners, and since the soil to be tilled is the original source of all the means of production, therefore, all agricultural lands should be transformed into common property, and this be leased to agricultural companies, which should be placed under obligation to cultivate the land to best advantage by accepted scientific methods, and to divide the proceeds among the associated laborers according to a contract to be agreed upon.

In this resolution the congress openly avowed the communistic doctrine to be its programme. If Bebel and Liebknecht really thought that such a proposal would win the farmers for their cause, they simply showed how little idea they had of the true conditions and views prevailing among the peasants. The more recent counter-proposal made by Herr von Vollmar (to divide the large estates among the farm-hands) proves him to be a better posted and therefore more dangerous demagogue.

By danger in this connection I do not refer simply to the imperilling of existing social conditions, but far more to the danger incurred by the thousands who as

yet put faith in the words of the communist leaders,
and allow themselves to become enlisted in the ranks
of those who in the class conflict are arrayed against
capital. Should I be called upon to indicate the way
in which the solution of the social question may be approached, it would be the very reverse of an association
of laborers for the purpose of entering the class conflict. For, as class against class, there is no antagonism between capital and labor; their interests are one.
Capital is but the fruit of past labor, and proficient
workers are constantly stepping into the ranks of the
capitalists.

At the time of which I write, such aspirations on the
part of the working-men had, for more than a decade,
been furthered with ever-increasing devotion by the
citizens as a body, their incentive to this by no means
being fear of Lassalle or Marx, but only their own
liberal inclinations; especially was this true since the
achievements of 1866. It was not an assembly of
craftsmen who, in the Cathedral of St. Paul, and later
in the North German Confederation, procured for the
people the right of universal suffrage; again, it was the
citizens in general who since 1867 were seeking to
obtain for the working-men the right of coalition; and
yet again it was the " bourgeoisie " as represented in
the Federal Government and representative body, to
whom the laws regarding liberty of immigration, freedom from pass-restrictions, greater industrial liberty,
and freedom in contracting marriage, owed their being.

It was Schulze-Delitzsch, so bitterly reviled by the Socialists, who had called into existence the co-operative associations and people's banks, which during the foregoing year had increased in number from thirteen hundred to two thousand, and the capital advanced by them to members from sixty-seven to one hundred and eleven millions. Numerous building associations were endeavoring to place healthy habitations within the reach of the laborers, and the administration of public instruction was everywhere ordering the erection of well-lighted and spacious public school buildings ; city communities were establishing schools to improve the education of workmen, that through increased knowledge their advancement might be facilitated ; savings banks were being instituted in which the poor man could place the smallest sum at interest, and in which in Germany hundreds of millions were soon deposited.

Public opinion among the property-holding classes was incessantly directed to like humanitarian designs, endeavoring to discover existing defects, and reminding the citizens of the obligations incurred by ownership. As yet the declaration of war made by the Communists, was not allowed to interfere in the least with these philanthropic aspirations, partly in the belief that revolution is best prevented by removing just causes of complaint, partly in the vain hope that wholly unrestricted freedom of discussion would lead the malcontents to discover the fallacy of their programme themselves. The chief reason was, however, that with our firmly established institutions there was little belief in any real danger from communism.

However, should this ever seriously menace our country, which God forbid, the outcome would be in Germany as in 1851 it was in France, — the nation would welcome with acclamation the dictator who under suspension of political freedom would furnish protection against Communist domination.

II. CLERICAL ASPIRATIONS.

After the development of Ultramontanism in the Catholic Church from 1814 to 1840, as has been related,[1] this tendency continued to assert itself more and more in Germany as it did in every other part of Europe. In Prussia, under Frederick William IV., it encountered little to impede its progress. The State's controlling power over the Church, which was so antagonized by the Ultramontanes, was exceedingly distasteful to the King also. In the Catholic communion he beheld a sister church, of whose firmness of doctrine and mighty influence he was inclined to be envious, although with a feeling of admiration and not of malice.

It was this already powerful influence for which the achievements of 1848 opened new paths to power. The persecution which the Friends of Light and German Catholics had suffered at the hands of the State authorities who were entirely in sympathy with the

[1] Vol. I., p. 93.

orthodox confession, had filled the Liberals of the Protestant faith with indignation; and, with a short-sightedness incomprehensible to us, they yielded to this feeling sufficiently to restrict in every direction the State's sovereign power over the Church, that religious freedom might be secured; whereupon they soon discovered that it had been for the so-called liberty of the Church for which they had been working; namely, for the unfettering of a temporal power which regarded the annihilation of every dissenting opinion to be its highest duty.

To be sure, when the liberal majority of the Representative Assembly adopted among the other Prussian fundamental rights the clause: The recognized churches shall be free to conduct their internal affairs according to their own judgment, the intention was not to ascribe to them complete sovereignty. It was understood as a matter of course that ecclesiastical administration should, notwithstanding the independence of the Church as a corporate body, conform to the restrictions of the general laws of the State, just as was expected of communities of citizens, or of science and its teachings, to which the Constitution also guaranteed freedom.

However, the authority upon which within this province everything depended was inclined to yield to the Catholic bishops the greatest possible extension of the right granted. The King practically allowed every form of control which, during the past century and from 1814 to 1840, the State had undisputedly exercised over the Church, to fall into desuetude. In the direction of the public schools by the clergy, and the separation of the gymnasiums according to the faith professed, he now beheld no more than the just fulfilment of a provision of the Constitution. He relinquished every kind of influence he had heretofore exerted upon the nomination, transfer, and removal of parish priests, whereby the arbitrary authority of the bishops was allowed full sway. He desisted from every kind of inspection and oversight over religious orders or corporations, in consequence of which Jesuit communities and institutions more than all others were soon spread like a network through all North Germany. Finally the State gave up all participation in the administration of church property also; the body of directors to whom the Church assigned that duty was responsible neither to the community nor to the State authorities, but only to the bishop and his court of accounts.

In fact, with the sole exception of the continued existence of that wicked Protestant heresy, no wish of Rome was at that time left unfulfilled in Prussia. The bishops especially were well content, were most graciously disposed toward the Government, and took care to avoid all doctrinal disputes. Thus, even after a change of sovereigns, the Government of William I. found no cause to interfere with the existing condition of affairs.

The clerical movement which was so triumphant here was developed in like manner in all the countries of Europe ; everywhere, as its immediate aim, the emancipation of the Church from the dominion of the State was kept in view, and, to gain strength for the combat all stood firmly gathered about the common centre of the universal Church, the Holy See at Rome. The storms of revolution had played havoc with the principles of the proud Gallican national Church as well as with the demands of the three Rhenish Electors as put forth at the convention of Ems. It was the boast of Rome that never before had the Pope rejoiced in so undivided and submissive an episcopate as during the present century. The clergy, from the lowest to the highest order, gave evidence of no other spirit than that of zealous submission to the commands of the representative of Christ.

So great and general adulation could not fail of its effect upon him who was its object, the head of the Church; although it inspired him with no new ideas, it increased his ardent desire to witness the realization of his aspirations.

Pope Pius IX. (Mastai Ferretti) was by nature a man of vivid imagination and extreme self-consciousness, his nervous system was so highly wrought that in his youth he had suffered from epileptic attacks. Owing to the limitation of his acquirements his intellectual horizon was necessarily a circumscribed one; and through his susceptible temperament he was greatly influenced in outward matters by the impressions of the moment, which made him unsteady of purpose in his political relations. So much the greater, however, was his inflexibility in matters of conviction. Spiritually he was strongly inclined to mysticism, a tendency which it is said first asserted itself whilst he was still very young. At a later period he claimed to be the recipient of Divine revelation, and to be in spiritual communication with the Holy Virgin, manifestations which he experienced to the end of his days. Every year found him more absorbed in religious meditation, and with higher ideals of what the authority of the Church should be in the world, and the authority of the Pope within the Church. His convictions were not based upon scientific evidence, but upon spiritual revelation, and were therefore proof against every doubt.

Later, when he himself occupied the pontifical chair, and his exile in Gaeta, whither he had fled before the Roman revolution, had terminated in his restoration to the throne through the combined intervention of the Catholic Powers of Europe, it became the desire of his heart to add new lustre to the name of his heavenly queen whose protection he had implored in the days of adversity.

With this intention he convened a numerous council of bishops, and laid before them for their consideration a solemn decree, in which an old question, controverted between the Dominicans on the one side and the Franciscans and Jesuits on the other, was decided in favor of the latter. It proclaimed to the world that the Pope, by the authority of Christ and the apostles Peter and Paul, as well as by the authority vested in himself, declared and decreed the immaculate conception of the Blessed Virgin to be a doctrine taught of God, and therefore binding as an article of belief on the acceptance of all the faithful. This was followed by the customary threat of punishment made against every one who should dare to think otherwise.

When several of the bishops gave utterance to a few timidly expressed doubts, they were silenced by the answer: Should the Pope make this declaration simply upon his own authority, it would still be a manifestation of the sovereign power of the Holy See over the Church, as well as of the infallibility with which Christ has clothed his representative. This ended the deliberation, and on December 8th the new dogma of the Catholic Church was solemnly proclaimed.

It was not long before the Pope enjoyed a new triumph of wide significance, which he accepted as a gracious reward from the hands of his heavenly queen for the homage he had rendered her. In 1855. Emperor Francis Joseph allowed himself to be persuaded by Bishop Rauscher to conclude a concordat, in which he formally recognized the canon law in its integrity to be the established ecclesiastical law in all the lands subject to him, — the very law which asserts the power of the papacy over states and sovereigns, together with the right to depose the latter under certain conditions. In addition, the concordat invested the bishops with sovereign authority over the clergy, the schools and literature; it placed under their independent administration a fortune of two hundred million florins; it provided for the institution of a large number of Jesuit schools, and for severe restrictions upon the rights of Jews and Protestants.

Urgently and with gratifying success the Vienna diplomats then commended a like course to the Protestant Courts at Stuttgart, Karlsruhe and Darmstadt, that from the vantage ground of equally excellent concordats they might withstand the re-awakened aspirations of Prussian ambition. In Vienna, moreover, there was at this time great hope that as Prussia through the Customs Union had linked Germany's material welfare to her own, so its intellectual interests' might become identified with Austria through her ecclesiastical policy.

In all this the Roman Curia beheld prospects of wide extended conquests, greater than any made during the last generation.

What the future really held in store, however, was a radical change in affairs. That great national movement was begun, first in Italy and then in Germany, by which after a struggle of ten years Italy was brought, a united State, including two-thirds of the papal territory, under the sceptre of Victor Emmanuel, and by which in Germany was achieved the founding of the North German Confederation under William I.; in both countries Austrian supremacy came to an end.

To the Curia all this was of course most odious. That two nations, heretofore so divided, should stand forth in the vigor of newly born Great Powers, was in itself an infraction of the principle upheld ever since the 13th century; namely, that all extensive realms should be dismembered that the mitred priest might rule over all. Moreover, although the national principle had been led to victory by the arms of two Kings, it nevertheless owed its birth to the Liberal parties, and it was therefore to be assumed that from the first day of their existence these two new political creations would be dominated by liberal ideas. And finally the sub-Alpine robber had even dared to extend his hand toward the territory of the Church, and only through the protection of a French occupation had the patrimony of St. Peter, together with its capital, been preserved to the Pope.

Pius IX. was not the man to accept such proceedings with meekness; but instead, at the earliest stirring of the adverse elements he grasped his weapons of defence, and with every degree of danger the energy of his resistance grew apace. In Italy he excommunicated the usurpers of the Romagna in the spring of 1860, and the conquerors of Urbino and the Marches in the following December. Through the obstinacy with which he adhered to his demand to be restored to full power, he made the *rôle* of protector so irksome to Emperor Napoleon that in 1864 the latter concluded the convention of September 15th, in which he agreed to recall his troops from Rome, and Victor Emmanuel in return gave his promise both to respect and protect Rome and the papal territory.

In this the Pope beheld an open menace to Rome, and therefore daily expected its occupation by the Italians, never loth to break either their word or their faith. On December 8th, 1864, the day celebrated as the anniversary of the immaculate conception, he made a formal declaration of war against modern culture and politics, in the form of a consistorial address to the cardinals, which then found its way as an encyclical to every part of the world, accompanied by a list or syllabus of eighty pernicious errors. Among these were religious liberty, freedom of the press, freedom in matters of philosophical research, the education of children by the laity, the exclusion of the Church from all dominion over temporal affairs, the *placetum regium*, the assertion that Roman Pontiffs and Œcumenical Councils have exceeded their authority, and have usurped the rights of princes, as also the opinion that the Church has not the right to avail herself of force, or has any direct or indirect temporal power in general, and that the abolition of the temporal power of which the Apostolic See is possessed would contribute to the liberty and prosperity of the Church, etc., etc.

This document left no possibility of doubt that the Church claimed entire independence from the control of the State in matters ecclesiastical, and beyond this, demanded obedience from the State in temporal affairs as well as in spiritual.

When on February 25th, 1865, a great Roman jubilee was proclaimed, this decree again referred to the circular and the syllabus which as the ordinance of the visible head of the Church must be received as the voice of God.

Upon a representation made by the French Minister, Drouyn de Lhuys, that the continued occupation of Rome by the French troops was rendered difficult by the difference in the policy of the two Governments, in that they were not actuated by like ideas or principles, Cardinal Secretary of State Antonelli replied on November 19th, that if the Minister referred to the principles which lay at the root of the social transformation, — for example, liberty of conscience and of worship, and other like exemptions from restraint, — the Holy See had frequently condemned these errors, and it was therefore the duty of every good Catholic to subordinate his judgment upon such questions to the judgment of him whom God had set above the people, to be their guide and teacher, not alone in matters spiritual, but in whatever belongs to the sphere of morals and the right.

Of what prescription emanating from the State could it, indeed, be said that it did not affect either morals or the right, directly or indirectly, and therefore would not come under the deciding influence of the Pope?

In so far as Germany was concerned, it was but to be expected that as soon as the old rivalry between Prussia and Austria should again break forth, the Roman Curia would with greatest energy take sides with its ally, Austria, and seek to advance the interests of that country. In this respect, the Pope's chief reliance was placed upon the Jesuits, who, ever since the doctrine of the immaculate conception had been established, basked in his favor, wielding an influence over him to the exclusion of all others, and, whilst commending his every thought, insinuated their own ideas into his mind. They were, therefore, quite ready to foment an active agitation against Prussia and in favor of the greater Germany.

As a beginning to this, such newspapers of Rome, Italy, France, and Austria as were subject to their influence, as well as those of like sympathies in South Germany and even in Prussia, opened a cross-fire of adverse criticism upon the Bismarck Ministry, and thus during the conflict-period became valiant allies of the Liberals otherwise so odious to them.

The Prussian bishops having been exempted by William IV. from supervision by the State, and being alienated from the Jesuits by mutual aversion, kept discreetly aloof; so much the more did the lower clergy, assistant curates, vicars, and chaplains, smarting under the oppression of their utter dependence upon the bishops, join with great ardor in the Jesuit agitation, the object of which was to do honor to the Pope and to assail Prussia's policy. Now, ever since 1848, there existed in Germany a number of Catholic societies which during the ensuing years of peace with the Church had fallen into a state of calm inactivity. These were now to be quickened, their number increased, their organization strengthened, and the annual general assembly was to be re-enforced by a central committee to serve as the organizing medium for the discontented lower clergy.

Outside of Prussia the storm of Ultramontane displeasure was, in Baden, directed against the liberal Roggenbach Ministry because of its vigorous defence of the State's sovereign power over the Church in its

outward relations, as well as of the State's unqualified
right to control the schools. In Darmstadt the clerically inclined Minister Dalwigk, hand in hand with
the ambitious Bishop Ketteler, was waging fierce war
against the liberal Majority in the Second Chamber.
How greatly this general agitation strengthened the
hopeful courage of both Rome and Vienna it is not
necessary to say. In the latter it reached its climax
in the assertion, claimed to be based upon reliable
information from Prussia, that not a Catholic among
the Prussian soldiers would fire upon the Catholic
emperor's troops.

But, as we know, each and all of them did fire, and
Königgrätz opened a new era for Germany. In no respect, however, did this deprive the Catholic Church
in Germany of its liberty. Nevertheless, the Vatican
could not forgive King William the deadly sin of having allied himself with Victor Emmanuel. Nor was
this the end of the vexation. Not only had Austria
been vanquished by Prussian arms, but, that internal
harmony might be restored, it had yielded to the per-
suasions of liberalism, and had bestowed upon itself
a Constitution which was not only at variance with its
concordat, but was directly opposed to the declarations
of the syllabus. For it granted liberty of worship to
all confessions of faith, and freedom of the press to all
citizens, and by special laws did away with the controlling influence of the clergy upon the right of contracting marriage, and upon the direction of the schools.

This blow from the hand of a secular ally incensed

the Pope beyond endurance. In another allocution, issued on June 22d, 1868, he condemned the Austrian Constitution, and its accompanying fundamental laws, as productions of unspeakable infamy and abomination, declared them invalid now and forever, and instructed the Austrian bishops to do all in their power to prevent them from being carried into effect.

If the circular and syllabus of 1864 had indicated a complete revulsion in the Pope's feelings, and his reconversion to all the assumptions of his mediæval predecessors, this, his latest address, proclaimed his actual pretensions to supremacy over all State authority. The more cautiously inclined of his adherents sought to soften matters by the explanation that all this was not meant as harshly as it sounded; that the Pope should denounce a law by which a one-sided modification of the legal status of the Church was decreed could hardly cause surprise; the severity of expression was wholly due to the traditional official language of the Roman Church.

The reply suggests itself, that he who feels entitled to employ such official expressions by their use makes pretensions to sovereignty and supremacy, or else he cuts a ridiculous figure, and that Pius IX. was such neither his friends nor his foes will maintain.

By way of digression, how, in connection with this address, appears the oft repeated assertion that the possession of the Papal States is necessary to the Pope's ecclesiastical independence? If in 1867 Austrian dominion had still prevailed in Italy, and that of the

Pope in the States of the Church, at this declaration of hostility an Austrian army would have invaded the papal territory. Would that have contributed to the independence of the Church?

As it was, divested of his sovereignty over the Papal States the Pope *was* free ; and, ready as ever to assume the initiative in combat, he now decided to take the step he had long pondered, and which he intended should lead to the complete and valid sanction of the standpoint which he had adopted. On June 29th, 1868, he convoked an Œcumenical Council, an assembly of all the Catholic bishops of the world, to meet in the Vatican on the 8th of December, 1869, the day of his favorite festival, the immaculate conception of the Virgin.

The bull said nothing of the questions to be deliberated upon by the council, or rather, it said too much, namely, that the council was called to remove all the wicked prejudices of this sinful age. But the *Civiltà Cattolica*, the special organ of the Pope, founded and endowed by Pius himself, and edited by two Jesuits under the daily supervision of the Pope, created a profound sensation by an exhaustive discussion of the famous bull issued by Boniface VIII. in 1302, according to which all kings and princes derive their sovereign power from the Pope, and must exercise it at his behest upon penalty of being deposed. This decree had been corroborated by a council convened in the 16th century, and it was now doubtlessly intended that the action of the proposed council should give it additional sanction.

The excitement which these articles produced was intense; soon after their appearance they were officially disclaimed, but this only added to the surprise which the secrecy whereby in Rome the assiduous preparation of the propositions to be laid before the Council continued to be surrounded. Nevertheless, it gradually became known that the Council was called for the special purpose of defining the infallibility of the Pope as regards " whatever belongs to faith and morals, or the primacy and teaching authority of Peter," as also that the discipline and welfare of the Church would be discussed. Further it was rumored that the tenets of the syllabus were to be transformed into positive dogmas; and it was also discovered that a special committee was employed upon politico-ecclesiastical questions, hence, with the relations of church and State.

These reports were regarded as of so grave importance that the Bavarian Premier, Prince Hohenlohe, was induced to address a circular note to the Powers on April 9th, 1869, in which he invited them to consider whether it were not advisable by a conference of the European Powers to determine upon some combined plan of action whereby the Court at Rome would be relieved of all uncertainty regarding the attitude which they would assume toward the Council.

However, the existing political situation was not favorable to such a course of action. Of the Catholic Powers, of whom it would naturally be expected that they would take the lead, France, as having reassumed the *rôle* of protector of Rome, stood first; here the

outward and internal crises were so all-absorbing that
there was no inclination to arrive at a decision as yet
regarding the Council.   The relations of Austria to the
Curia, and those of Italy and Spain as well, were of
so strained a nature that the effect of representations
made to the Pope by these Governments would most
likely have been to stimulate him to more extreme
action.   It was therefore decided to await events.

Rumor said that many bishops of different countries
would dissent to the papal proposition; among the
more educated classes of the Catholic world signs of
opposition were also perceptible; in May an address
against infallibility was sent from Coblenz to the
Bishop of Trier; prompted by a like spirit, a large
number of noted scholars and their enthusiastic disciples gathered about the foremost theologian of Catholic Germany, Dr. Döllinger of Munich, who had ere
now experienced the papal displeasure; members of
the faculty at Bonn and Breslau had similar experiences.   There was, therefore, after all, a possibility that
the ecclesiastical endeavor would suffice to dispel the
threatening storm and that intervention by the Governments would not be necessary.

However, to have assumed this to be the probability
at this early stage would have been rash indeed.   The
announcement of the Council was followed by redoubled
activity on the part of the Jesuits in France and Germany.   Numberless pamphlets, newspaper articles, and
society resolutions proclaimed the fact that all faithful
Catholics had long been convinced of the Pope's infalli-

bility; that the Council was not about to establish a
new dogma, but simply to acknowledge a truth which
even now dwelt in the hearts of all; without entering
into a prolonged debate, the bishops would sanction
the doctrine of infallibility by acclamation; and should
an obstinate one be found among them the entire clergy
of his diocese would rise as one man against him. Even
the more moderate Ultramontane newspapers of the
Rhine district, and which in the beginning had dared
to be doubtful of the infallibility, were in the end
carried along with the current, and violently attacked
the signers of the Coblenz address. The general assembly of the Catholic societies in its latest resolutions
outdid all it had heretofore done — which is saying a
good deal — in the way of zealous adulation of the
Pope, and of vehement threats against his adversaries.
At all events, there was no opposition evinced by the
great mass of the common people. The following
words of Deputy Jörg, which appeared in the *Historisch-
politischen Blätter* of the day, although written with
especial reference to conditions in Bavaria, were beyond doubt aptly descriptive of the general situation
as well: "Between us and the Liberals a social warfare is waged, a warfare in which the people are
arrayed against the bourgeoisie and their official representatives."

By this general agitation the majority of the German bishops were placed in a grave predicament.
They well knew what papal infallibility meant, and
could not therefore conscientiously vote for it. For

years, however, in their struggle against the State's
right to superior authority, they had been so utterly
subservient to the Pope, that to assume an attitude of
opposition now did violence to their feelings. Moreover, it mattered little what stand they might take in
Rome ; in the present state of excitement their action
would be sure to meet with disapproval at home, which,
if coming from the learned profession, would be annoying, but coming from the Jesuits would be dangerous.
In the end they decided to pour oil upon the troubled
waters by issuing a joint pastoral letter. In it they
assured their people that all rumors which had caused
them anxiety regarding the Council's possible action
were groundless. The Council would establish no new
dogma ; its deliberations would be carried on in entire
freedom, and, far from causing a division into parties,
would, under the guidance of the Holy Spirit, and in
mutual love, result in wise decisions.

That the contents of the letter were not born of a
spirit of prophecy its authors were soon to discover.
As early as October, this was clearly indicated by the
explicit declaration which appeared in the *Civiltà Cattolica*, stating that the bishops were not called to Rome
to make decisions according to the opinion of the majority, but only to give their formal sanction to that
upon which the infallible Pontiff had already resolved.

CHAPTER IV.

PARLIAMENTARY CONFLICTS.

RESULTS ACHIEVED BY THE GOVERNMENT.

THE course of our narrative has brought us to that period when during the years whose events we are following the activity of the State within the sphere of home politics claimed the attention of the leading statesman to a greater degree than did questions of foreign policy. The social and ecclesiastical aspirations with which we have become familiar did not for the present occupy much of Bismarck's time, not because he failed to recognize in their evidences the earliest intimation of a possible danger menacing the future, but because at the time there was either no possibility of effective intervention on his part, or else the occasion for it was wanting.

The Socialists of that day were as yet rendered impotent through their division into four groups, each of which had but a small membership. Their time being wholly occupied by bitter contention with one another and with the Party of Progress, they made little trouble for the Government.

With regard to the Œcumenical Council, concerning

which Bismarck was by no means free from anxiety, his hands were tied so long as the Catholic Courts maintained their attitude oₗ extreme reserve.

That which now demanded his thought was not a subject of so theoretic a nature, but a very prosaic and very real difficulty, the present financial exigency of Prussia and of the North German Confederation.

In the speech from the throne with which the Prussian Assembly was opened on November 4th, 1868, the King discussed in the first place the existing deficit, then the reforms to be undertaken in the Constitutions of the provinces and districts in favor of a greater degree of self-government, and lastly the prospect of enduring peace in Europe.

There was a close connection between these three subjects. Provincial self-administration required that each of the provinces should receive a considerable endowment, such as had already been granted to Hanover and Electoral Hesse; and yet this would not be followed by a corresponding reduction in the expenditure of the State. Confidence in European peace, which the Luxemburg affair had so seriously shaken, had not as yet been restored; the French army reforms, the constant allusions made by that country to the Treaty of Prague, and later, the strained relations in the Orient, and the anxiety with regard to Belgium, had not allowed the equilibrium in the world of great industrial and commercial enterprises to be regained; the stagnation in business was growing more serious with every day. We have observed how in France this condition of affairs produced a political revulsion of great magnitude; in Germany its effects were felt in the decrease of State receipts.

On November 6th the Minister of Finance, Von der Heydt, submitted the budget for 1869, accompanied by a memorial in which he called attention to a deficit of 5,200,000 thalers. He stated, that although the balance between expenditures and receipts had not been disturbed in 1866, still, by the interruption which the war had caused in industrial pursuits, together with the anxiety occasioned by the rumors of new wars, the after effects had been extended into the next year. This condition had been aggravated by the poor harvest of 1867, which had resulted in actual famine in East Prussia, requiring heavy sacrifices on the part of the State. The Federal treasury had also suffered a considerable diminution in its receipts, a loss for which the Customs Parliament had refused to provide, making it necessary that the *pro rata* contributions of the confederated States should be increased. The Government had, however, not yet relinquished the hope that an early revival of business would bring relief, and believed that the present ebb in the finances was but a temporary condition. It therefore proposed that the deficit be covered by a sale of a part of the State's property, especially of Cöln-Minden Railroad stock.

In the absence of a better plan, Bismarck and Roon had both consented to this proposal as an expedient, although their hearts were filled with indignation that matters had been allowed to come to such a pass; for in their opinion, to draw upon the capital to meet current expenditures was, if continued, a ruinous violation of the first principles of any wise economy, whether public or private.

The deputies, on the other hand, breathed a sigh of relief at this prospect of covering the deficit without adding to the burden of their constituents either by increased taxes or by the necessary interest upon a public debt. Minister Von der Heydt had reason to rejoice at this, so much the more so, since the parliamentary horizon in general wore a most threatening aspect. From the annexed provinces came reports of complaint and disaffection which in Electoral Hesse and Hanover had found expression in the formation of a society advocating the re-admission of Austria into the German Confederation, together with equal rights for all the allied Governments, which was synonymous with the re-establishment of the Federal Constitution of 1815.

In the House itself a bitter feeling of resentment prevailed against Count Eulenburg because of his slowness and feudal tendencies in matters of administrative reform, in consequence of which he was subjected to some very unpleasant experiences in connection with several items of the estimates submitted by him. The rigid orthodoxy of the Minister of Education and Public Worship, Mühler, as well as his exaggerated economy in the plans for the public schools, had roused an indignant spirit of protest; whereas a number of desired appropriations were refused Eulenburg, Mühler was criticised for having placed his estimates so low.

During the debate upon the budget, the Minister of Justice, Leonhardt, raised a tremendous storm by declaring in plain terms that in defiance of the House he intended to make a certain outlay to which the House had refused its sanction; he was, however, finally induced to agree upon a compromise. Great, however, was the approbation with which the House received a bill providing new regulations to govern mortgage transactions in Prussia, which he submitted, together with an able exposition of the need of a uniform system of national law for all Germany, at the same time expressing the hope that when the bill just submitted should have become a Prussian law it would be adopted, not only by the North German Confederation, but by the States south of the Main as well.

The other transactions, dealing with questions of special Prussian interest, do not concern our narrative. One motion, jointly made by Free Conservatives and National Liberals, must, however, be mentioned. It was proposed that the Reichstag and the Prussian Representative Assembly should be so far identified that the Prussian members of the Reichstag should constitute the Prussian Assembly. Bismarck opposed the plan on the ground that the King would thereby lose his right to dissolve the Assembly, since the Reichstag would not submit to a partial dissolution, and for the further reason that the Prussian Upper House could find no place under the Federal Constitution; and finally, because the number of Prussian citizens willing to accept the office of deputy would grow appreciably smaller if this implied a twofold duty making a double demand upon their time. Hereupon the motion was abandoned.

Immediately after the budget was passed, the session closed on March 6th, 1869.

Two days before, on March 4th, 1869, King William had opened the session of the Reichstag with a speech from the throne, in which he submitted to the consideration of this assembly a long array of treaties and bills, at the same time utilizing the occasion to repeat the advice he had given the Prussian Assembly urging the necessity of providing for the deficiency in the Federal chest, so that a reduction in the *pro rata* contributions might become possible. In conclusion he said that the happy solution of the Oriental question had made peace in Europe assured, the Governments being wholly disinclined to disturb it and the enemies of order lacking the power to do so.

It became evident from the first that the financial question would form the central point of all interest and action, and would be the decisive one in determining the character of German politics. That we may arrive at this all-absorbing subject with as little delay as possible, we will take but a rapid survey of the most important legislative achievements of the session.

A number of postal treaties, as well as several conventions for the protection of literary property, were sanctioned by the Reichstag without calling forth criticism of any kind; but the treaty establishing military freedom of migration between Baden and the North German Confederation aroused great patriotic enthusiasm, to which Bennigsen gave eloquent expression.

A most conscientious and thorough consideration, partly in the whole House, partly in committees, was given to a number of bills for the promotion of freedom and security within the province of economics. Of these the most important ones, those dealing with the regulation of trade and industry, remained a subject of discussion throughout the entire session. With regard to the general principles underlying them there was but one mind, the furtherance of freedom in industrial pursuits; numberless practical details suggested themselves, however, and gave rise to many amendments and corresponding changes in the text of the bill. The Federal Council recognized the merit of many of these, and submitted to the others. The result was a production so excellent that it still forms the basis of our present industrial system.

The purpose of another bill was to protect the laboring classes against a baneful practice which at this time was working wide-spread mischief; it was induced by the right which every creditor had of securing himself against the loss of a loan made to a laborer by attaching the wages due the debtor or to become due in the future, thus throwing the responsibility upon the employer. The consequence was an unwholesome and usurious credit, which the laborer would have found it impossible to obtain except for the security rendered by the attachment on his wages, and of which many a careless one took advantage to his own ruin. As an example, a large factory was cited, among the employees of which 1,600 cases of attachment on wages had occurred within a year. In the Dartmund district, there had been 10,000 like instances within the same period. The bill became a law by the large vote which the Reichstag cast in its favor.

It had been intended to supplement the law establishing freedom of migration by another enactment fixing the conditions necessary to the acquirement of a legal residence by which public relief could be claimed. The Prussian Government had submitted such an one to the Federal Council, based like its predecessor upon the principle of greatest freedom in intercourse; but it met with so much opposition from several of the Middle States that it was abandoned, and never reached the Reichstag.

A better fate was in store for a bill which provided that the tribunals of every State belonging to the Confederation should, upon requisition made by a tribunal of any other one of the confederated States, render legal aid such as could be demanded were the applying tribunal and the one addressed within the limits of the same State. The first section, that concerning aid in civil suit, encountered no opposition, and was quickly accepted; with regard to criminal prosecution, however, it was questioned whether it were not better to postpone action until after the appearance of the promised Federal penal code. Doubts were also ex-

pressed regarding compulsory evidence, and the surrender of a person accused of having trespassed the
law in the State making requisition, but who was a citizen of the one to which application was being made.
These difficulties did not, however, prove insurmountable, and the bill became a law.

In the foregoing year, there had been talk of adopting as a part of the law of the North German Confederation the German commercial law and the statute
laws concerning bills of exchange which had originated in the time of the old Confederation, thus making
them binding upon all the confederated States. This
was now done, furnishing an opportunity for the Government of Saxony to propose the establishment of a
Federal Superior Court of Commerce at Leipzig. Although Hamburg made the counter proposal that a
general Federal Supreme Court should be established,
the Reichstag complied with Saxony's request as recommended by the Federal Council.

A greater contrariety of opinion appeared in connection with a bill which the Federal Council had regarded as hardly more than a mere matter of form, —
a law regulating the elections for the Reichstag according to the principles of the Constitution. It will be remembered that in this respect slight irregularities had
occurred in several of the States during the recent elections. Regarding most of the amendments to which
the debate gave rise, an agreement was soon reached;
but the clause by which members of the army and navy
were excluded from the privilege of voting caused a
vigorous clash of opinions.

Lasker, Waldeck, and Bebel, in unusual combination, declared that in view of the universal obligation to serve, in other words, with a citizen army such as was that of North Germany, it was most pernicious to exclude for years its members, the young and able men of the nation, from the most highly prized privilege of the people. To be sure, said they, the Government was doing all in its power to render the army entirely distinct from the people; nevertheless, the principle that a free nation and its army should be one remained true.

To this, General Steinmetz retorted by way of a question, asking whether the gentlemen advocated an army of disputants who while under arms might form themselves into parties, and make it possible for ambitious generals to issue pronunciamentos after the Spanish fashion. It was finally decided that the clause should read: All members of the army or navy are debarred from the privilege of voting as long as they are in active service.

During the very first days of the session Lasker again presented his motion for the inviolability of deputies, or their exemption from prosecution in consequence of utterances made in the exercise of their functions, a privilege to which the Prussian Upper House had remained inflexibly adverse. In connection with it he now expressed the hope that Bismarck, in fulfilment of the promise he had given during the session of the past year, would further its sanction by the Federal Council.

In reply, Bismarck declared that he was fully in sympathy with the principle which the motion embodied, as also that in his opinion this was a matter within the jurisdiction of the Reichstag, but added that, whereas upon questions of great practical importance he always sought to throw the full weight of Prussia's influence with the Federal Council into the scale, yet it was his practice upon all other occasions to adhere strictly to his principle upon all questions of less moment fully to respect the independence of the several States. Such a question he considered the one now before the House to be, since in consequence of past events the prosecution of a deputy for the cause indicated had been practically rendered impossible.

To this the retort was made, "You are quite willing, then, to see Prussia dominated by the smaller States?" With imperious calmness Bismarck replied, "My action in the Federal Council must be determined wholly by my own judgment; by this course I have so far been successful in promoting the stability of our union, which was by no means always an easy task. I cannot allow myself to be influenced through the opinions of others to forsake my principles." Lasker's motion was then adopted by a vote of 140 voices against 51. The Federal Council, however, refused to sanction it.

Another motion made by Lasker in conjunction with Miquel had no better fate. Its design was to extend the jurisdiction of the Confederation, as defined in Article IV. of the Constitution, to the entire domain of civil law, as well as to legal procedure inclusive of the organization of the courts.

That in any extensive country uniformity in the department of the law is of benefit, and gives increased security both to the public and the interpreters of the law, as also that in a Federal State it has its political advantages, no one will dispute. In the present debate the objections of a technical character, which this question also did not fail to suggest, receded before the greater interest which centred about the more radical objection, that since herein a modification of the Constitution without the required unanimous consent of all the Governments was involved, it was a matter beyond the jurisdiction of the Confederation. This was an argument which had been put forward as early as 1867 in connection with the deliberation upon the Constitution, but had been disregarded by both the Reichstag and the Federal Council.

This motion also was adopted by the Reichstag, and rejected by the Federal Council.

Two motions of a contentious nature, originating in the desire for parliamentary power, are still to be mentioned; by the first of these, presented by Waldeck, it was proposed to substitute for the clause of the Constitution by which deputies were prohibited from receiving compensation of any kind for their services in the Reichstag, one granting allowances to the members. No new arguments for or against were brought forward; and though the motion was carried by a vote of 109 against 94 voices in its first reading, in the second it was lost by 110 voices against and only 100 in favor. Whether its advocates had deserted it, or its adversaries had increased in number, I cannot say.

A most brilliant and interesting parliamentary encounter took place on April 16th, induced by a motion made by Twesten and Count Münster with the support of eighty-one sympathizers gathered from the ranks of all the various parties. Its theme was an old one often disputed, — a demand for responsible Ministers at the head of the Federal Departments of Foreign Affairs, of War, of the Navy, of Justice, of Finance, and of Commerce. The gentlemen who introduced the motion protested most earnestly that it was not meant as a vote of want of confidence in the Chancellor, but quite the contrary; the intention was to lighten the labor which was now required of him, and which far exceeded anything that human strength could render. They proposed, therefore, to divide it among several independent departments; thus more firmly established order and greater system in the conduct of the affairs of the State would be secured, and the present uncertainty regarding parliamentary influence upon the action of the Government would be removed.

Since the proposed plan designated neither the degree of responsibility to be assumed, nor the manner of enforcing it by legal measures, Bismarck did not find it a difficult task to prove its total inconsistency with the Federal Constitution and with the prerogatives of the allied sovereigns, as well as to demonstrate the advantages of the present system. It was one of his red-letter days. His speech upon this occasion, occupying several hours, is one of his most brilliant parliamentary achievements, both for richness of original thought and for versatility of style, leaving no tone untouched in the scale of argument, from the most impassioned and bold polemic to the most subtle but always good-natured irony. It is a masterpiece of which an abstract can give no idea, and which to be appreciated must be read.

Despite the fact that Bismarck had deprived the advocates of the motion of all hope that it would be successful in the Federal Council, it was nevertheless passed by the House, although by but a small majority (111 against 100 voices).

The lively interest which the majority had shown in the subject was due in the first place to their wish to diminish the influence of the Federal Council upon the Federal Government, and it was chiefly against this that Bismarck's attack had been directed. It was, however, also prompted by the old desire of the majority to acquire a controlling influence upon the Government through the parliament. There was doubtlessly in connection with it less thought of the few cases in which a Minister's breach of trust would make proceedings advisable, than there was of the practice to which the institution of a responsible Ministry had led in other constitutional States, namely, that of compelling an unpopular Minister to retire AT ONCE by a vote of want of confidence. Of the dark side which this system presents in the consequent instability of the

Government, Prussia had at this time seen as little as it had of the possibility of getting rid of an obnoxious Minister even without legal responsibility by means of PERSISTENT parliamentary opposition. It was not long before such an instance occurred.

Three days previously, on April 13th, the Federal Council had submitted the budget for 1870 to the Reichstag, and the spirit with which it was there received was not improved by the unqualified rejection which the Twesten-Münster motion had met in the Federal Council. To be sure, the estimates for the Federal expenditures offered little opportunity for criticism; five-sixths of the entire amount were comprised in the army budget, which by the provision of the Constitution was not subject to criticism by the House until 1871. That the much-discussed loan for the navy had been increased from ten to seventeen millions roused no opposition; and the first appearance of the Foreign Office in connection with the Federal estimates was rather an occasion for congratulation than otherwise, wherefore its individual items were not called into question. The estimated expenditures for the other departments fared equally well.

A much less pleasing prospect was revealed by the chapter of estimated receipts. In consequence of the reduced postal rates the revenue from this source had fallen off greatly, and there was but little hope that this condition would be modified by an increase in the postal business. A number of reductions in customs rates had been followed by a similar result. In fact, the second reading of the budget showed the expenditures of the Confederation to exceed its independent revenue by twenty-five million thalers, or by two and one half millions more than for the current year 1869. This increase for 1870 would therefore have to be met by correspondingly larger *pro rata* contributions required of the individual States.

This brings us to the source of all the dissatisfaction. Prussia, whose proportionate share according to the number of its inhabitants was four-fifths of this sum, a round twenty millions therefore, had a growing deficit to face at home, and was consequently neither able nor inclined to furnish so large a contribution. As we have seen, the Prussian Minister of Finance, Von der Heydt, had avoided the difficulty in connection with the Prussian budget for 1869 by the sale of a part of the State's active capital, in the hope that the long delayed revival of business would soon set in, and would then quickly supply the deficiency, whereas, owing to the strained relations prevailing in Europe during the year 1868, quite the contrary of this was true. The closed account of the actual receipts and expenditures for 1868, as presented, showed that the current fiscal year had been begun with a larger deficit than had been anticipated; that in the business world better times were as yet not at hand; that Prussia had diminished its active capital by seven millions, and was confronted by a probable deficit of between ten and eleven millions in its accounts for 1870.

The Prussian Ministry had rejected the proposed repetition of the expedient resorted to in 1868 quite as emphatically as it had refused to meet the exigency by a loan, its action being based upon the principle that in a well-conducted system of economy ordinary expenditures are provided for by ordinary receipts. But in so far as a defrayment by additional taxation was concerned, it was believed in Prussia that the direct taxes could not possibly be increased; it was therefore determined in the Federal Council, that about one-half of the amount of the necessary *pro rata* contributions should be raised through indirect taxes, which, to become lawful, required in part the sanction of the Reichstag, in part that of the Customs Parliament.

Consequently, in connection with the first reading of the Federal budget, President Delbrück at once proposed three new means of adding to the revenue, — stamps on bills of exchange, withdrawal of the franking privileges, and, what was most important of all, a higher tax on brandy. A fortnight later a Federal delegate made the rather timid announcement, that yet four other propositions were receiving their final revision in the Federal Council, — a very low tax on beer, a most modest one on illuminating-gas, a tax on certificates of sale required in stock transactions, and an increase of ten per cent in the tariff of railway charges for journeys of more than three miles. Finally, that the entire field of its financial activity might lie fully revealed to the critical eye of the representative body, notice was given that the Customs Parliament also would be called upon to give its consent to higher taxation, — besides the duty on petroleum refused in the last session, a higher tax on beet-root sugar. All these revelations were then concluded, again after the lapse of a few weeks, by a memorial submitted by Minister von der Heydt, and containing an explicit statement of Prussia's financial dilemma, offered in proof of the necessity for all these demands.

The conclusive argument which these figures presented by no means improved the Minister's position in the eyes of the Assembly. The consequences of the mistake he had made in seeking escape from the difficulty of 1868 through the sacrifice of a part of the interest-bearing capital of the State, which was in itself an unwise measure, had now to be faced. As diligently as his subordinates had worked ever since it had become evident that the hope of better times was a vain one, much time had nevertheless been lost; therefore, instead of being able to present a comprehensive, well-devised plan of action at the beginning of the session, one inadequate and supplementary device after another in the shape of new taxes, the necessity for which failed to be shown, was now brought forward, with intermissions of weeks between. And all this was done toward the latter half of the session, as though it were intended to make a thorough examination by the Reichstag impossible.

Lasker did not hesitate to rise to the very personal criticism that a man who in two years had reduced the Prussian finances from a condition of prosperity to this pass was not fitted to conduct the affairs of

a great State. The most unfortunate circumstance
for the Minister was that in 1868 he had supported his
plan by the claim that the deficit was of a transitory
nature, and that there was every reason to believe it
would soon disappear. The arguments which he had
then offered in evidence of this were now repeated to
him as being still entirely pertinent. Such a deficit
has, in fact, frequently arisen in the Prussian finances
without being followed by any serious consequences,
a surplus soon appearing in its place.

"And for a cause so transitory you expect us to
sanction a long list of taxes, which, unlike it, will be
permanent," asked the orators of the National Liberal
Party, "so that long after the deficit has disappeared,
the people will still be staggering under this additional
burden, although the Government will be rolling in
wealth?" (In Prussia no tax can be abated or reduced
without the consent of the Government.) "It will be
our privilege to discuss the army budget for 1871,"
said Lasker, "and I am by no means disposed to consent to all these taxes to-day; for so we shall place our
opponents in the position to say to us two years hence,
'There is no reason why the military expenditures
should not continue as at present; the means with
which to defray them are at hand.'" And that was
the burden of every speech made on the Liberal side, —
no more taxes to continue for an indefinite time.

"You are willing, then, that a question of constitu-
tionality shall again arise in Prussia?" remarked Bismarck; "that again an extension of parliamentary

power be made the condition to procuring needed
funds for the State? Evidently the centre of gravity
of Prussian State authority is not located to your
liking; you would move it a few points nearer the
reach of the parliament. This might be made matter
for a bargain between us; I have no scruples which
would restrain me from coming to terms with you.
Never, however, by such a barter as this. If you per-
sist in making a modification of constitutional privileges
the price of higher taxation, you will force the Government to renounce the increase in revenue, and to
get rid of the deficit through a reduction of expenditures by incurring only such as are legally and absolutely necessary, forcing it not only to postpone
everything that is not immediately needed, but to leave
undone much that would promote the best interests
of our country."

In reply to the criticism that this was a threat, he
said that it was simply the expression of that which the
Constitution imposed as a duty; he could hardly assume that a representative assembly would prefer to see
him spend money which had not been duly appropriated.

Nothing could have been more pleasing to the majority of the House than the intelligence that by a reduction of expenditure all necessity for additional revenue
would be obviated, and every one knew full well what
that great item of expenditure was of which above all
others they wished to be rid. Upon this point also,
Lasker's intimation found repeated echo on the Left.

The present condition is not to be endured, it was

said; our oppressive military system is fatal to culture, prosperity, and liberty; moreover, it is wholly unnecessary; for the nations, prompted both by their natural inclinations and by regard for their interests, advocate peace, whilst in every speech from the throne his Majesty reiterates how little disposed are the Governments to disturb it. Why, then, do we maintain this colossal soldiery? Why this waste of money and ability? Prussia was the first to put its army upon such a footing; it should be the first to reduce it, or at least to propose to the other Cabinets a general disarmament.

"There is but one way," said Löwe in concluding a vigorous speech, "by which we can return to a well-ordered financial condition, and that is by economy in our army budget." It was on the 22d of May, 1869, that a truly conscientious politician indulged in these dangerous illusions, and by their utterance won the applause of the Reichstag.

To heighten the disfavor with which Von der Heydt's proposals for increased taxes were received, there was the disapprobation with which the majority regarded indirect taxes in general, as being an unjustly imposed addition to the burden of the poorer classes. In the Reichstag this opinion found its strongest expression in the utterances of Becker (Dortmund), a fearless revolutionist in 1848, an honest Democrat ever since. As was consistent with his earnest nature, he had passed from a sphere of diversified activity and well-grounded study through the stage of speculative theorizing, and had arrived at a thoroughly practical comprehension of public affairs. In the present connection, however, he allowed his humanitarian sympathies to lead him into exaggerations and contradictions; he spoke of all taxes on articles of consumption in the same tone, as though taxes on the necessaries of life and those on superfluous articles of luxury were alike reprehensible; whereas those proposed by the Minister all belonged to the latter class. Becker, however, condemned them all, because he believed the poor man felt their pressure more than did the rich man. " I shall vote against every tax," he exclaimed, " which adds to the cost of labor and to the difficulty of intercourse." This added difficulty is, however, encountered by the rich as well as by the poor, and it is not possible that a tax which enhances the price of labor, therefore raises wages, can be especially oppressive to the laborer.

Be this as it may, Becker succeeded in convincing the assembly. After a long-continued debate, all the lucrative tax projects were rejected on June 1st, the tax on brandy by a nearly unanimous vote, the one side hesitating to add to the price of the glass of schnapps which warms the poor man, the other fearing that the proposed tax would cause the ruin of the small distilleries, and would therefore be fatal to the prosperity of the rural middle class. Both, however, were as yet not inclined to extricate the Governments from their financial embarrassment, that these might for a while continue to realize their dependence upon the parliament.

On the field upon which had been fought the battle
for higher taxation there now remained amid the ruins
of all the other propositions only two as yet unscathed,
because, forsooth, they had been reserved for the action
of the Customs Parliament, — the reintroduction of the
duty on petroleum, and a slight increase in the duty
on imported sugar, besides a corresponding tax upon
domestic beet-root sugar.

The first measure which was submitted to the Customs Parliament after the opening of the session on
June 3d was the promised law making general reforms
in the administration of customs affairs with a view to
facilitating commerce; after this came the bill regarding the tax on sugar which the advocates of free trade
had suggested in 1868; and finally the bill dealing
with a comprehensive tariff reform. In this a reduction of the duties upon a variety of iron manufactures
and of the duty on rice appeared; and between these,
as a compensation for the loss of revenue to which
these would lead, figured the duty on petroleum. The
bill was accompanied by the positive statement that the
tariff propositions were inseparable; that is, the entire
tariff reform was conditional upon the sanction of the
duty on petroleum.

In consideration of the fact that the advocates of
free trade were in the majority in the Parliament, the
Governments had made their already liberal offer still
more so by supplementing the reduction on pig iron
proposed in the previous bill by correspondingly lower
duties on the various forms of manufactured iron, hop-

ing in this way at last to procure the consent of the
Parliament to the duty on petroleum. The prospect
for a definitive result was, however, not at all encouraging. The free-trade majority was by no means of one
mind. The conservative landowners of East Prussia
who in 1868 had voted for the duty on petroleum were
now delighted at the prospect of a less restricted importation of iron manufactures, picturing to themselves
the happy consequences which would ensue for their
agricultural interests. The same regard, however,
would have prompted them readily to forgive the Governments had they omitted from the list of reductions
that on rice.

Influenced by wholly different motives, an uncompro-
misingly free-trade group insisted upon the reduced
duty on rice, and in opposition to the judgment of the
Governments demanded a still further reduction of that
on pig iron. The group of sugar manufacturers also
had their interests to guard; they made their consent
to the tax on beet-root sugar conditional upon a higher
duty on the imported article, and the assurance of a
legally established export premium for the product of
their factories. And finally, by far the greater number
of the party, although they would gladly have seen the
tariff reform enacted, nevertheless hoped to compel
the Governments to content themselves with the duty
on sugar as sufficient compensation for the tariff reductions. For they were fully resolved to reject the duty
on petroleum; at the same time, they were most solici-
tous that the Governments should be protected against

the sin of wilfulness and the dangers besetting too
great riches.

As with the majority, so it was with the minority;
the protectionists were no more harmonious than were
their opponents. The sole object of the German
brothers from the South was, as it had been during the
previous session, to prevent any fruit from being produced upon this Prussian soil. The South German
National Liberals, who had now constituted themselves
an individual fraction as "the bridge over the Main,"
nevertheless remained united with the Opposition in
hostility either to the duty on petroleum or to certain
provisions of the revised tariff schedule. As for the
others, the representatives of the iron industry were
unreservedly for the rejection of the entire bill, whereas
a more moderate group would have qualified the rejection by a resolution promising consent to the reduction
of the duties on iron in the next session, provided the
Governments would, in the meantime, procure correspondingly advantageous conditions in England and
France for the German manufactures.

When the varying influences which these conflicting
interests brought to bear upon the debate are taken
into consideration, it will not be difficult to realize how
party combinations changed again and again. However, to record these here would not be to our purpose.
After the bill regulating customs affairs had been accepted almost without change, the first reading of the
tariff-reform bill resulted in the following decisions: a
reduction of the duties upon iron manufactures, but

none on pig iron, was passed by a vote of 130 against
104 voices; the lower duty on rice was also approved,
despite the opposition of the conservative element; the
duty on petroleum was rejected by a vote of 155
against 93 voices, Lasker having delivered a most
acrimonious speech against it; after which, with quite
as much energy, he defended the cause of the sugar
interests as represented in the higher protective duty
and the correspondingly increased tax on beet-sugar.
When this had been adopted, he moved that the rates
on sugar should go into effect simultaneously with the
new tariff law.   President Delbrück, however, in the
name of the Governments, at once protested against
the association of these two laws between which there
was not the slightest connection, and announced at the
same time that the Governments would accept the
amendments which the proposed sugar law had received.

At the beginning of the final deliberation upon the
tariff, Bismarck again commended the duty on petroleum to the favorable consideration of the House, and
reiterated the declaration that a tariff reform apart
from a duty on petroleum would not receive the sanction of the Presidium.   That this announcement would
not effect a change in the decisions arrived at in the
second reading was, however, quite evident from the
beginning; and the duty on petroleum was rejected by
157 voices against 110.

Neither did the Parliament alter its decision with
regard to the sugar law; although it was in this connec-

tion that the Government won its only victory of the entire session, Lasker's motion to associate it with the tariff reform being lost.

The Government then withdrew the tariff-reform bill, and the Parliament was closed on June 22d.

The session of the Reichstag was concluded on the same day. The King on this occasion expressed his appreciation of the effective legislative activity of the House, as well as his regret that an agreement had not been reached with regard to the finances. No action making possible a reduction in the *pro rata* contributions devolving upon the several States having been taken, the question of finance must now be solved in the several Representative Assemblies, the emergency having to be provided for either by curtailing expenditures or by increasing such taxes as were subject to local control.

What this implied was revealed when, three months later, the winter session of the Prussian Assembly was opened on October 6th, 1869. In the speech from the throne, it was announced that the year 1870 would be entered upon with a deficit of five and one-half millions, in consequence of which the income, class, flour, and slaughter taxes would have to be raised twenty-five per cent; a great reduction of expenditure in nearly all the departments was reported; it was proposed that the thirteen millions worth of treasury notes issued during the foregoing year should be covered by a definite loan; and, finally, two important bills were submitted, which, having been long looked for and much desired, would, it was hoped, cheer the spirits of the assembly; they were a law introducing a new system of district regulations in the six eastern provinces, placing these on a basis of self-government, and the general education law of which the Constitution had given promise.

That the Government had at length taken the initiative in these important matters was gratefully recognized by the House; although the impression which the contents of the two bills, when heard, made upon the majority was of a doubtful if not wholly unfavorable nature. If such was the reception accorded these bills, what might not be expected for the propositions of the Minister of Finance? What he heard of the spirit manifested by the deputies robbed Herr von der Heydt of all hope. It was to no avail that Otto Camphausen advised him to strike at the root of the evil by means of a radical reform; he did not believe that such a measure could be carried out, even should the House consent to it. On October 25th he tendered his resignation; and on the 26th it was accepted, Otto Camphausen, at the time President of the Institute of Maritime Commerce, being nominated as his successor.

It was on the same day, the 26th, that the House appointed the 29th as the day for the opening discussion on the budget. After a few other matters on the order of the day had been disposed of, the new Minister of Finance addressed the House, both to introduce himself, and to present the difficulty of the position by which he found himself suddenly forced to assume the responsibility for the budget, although his knowledge of the preparatory work and preliminary deliberations was wholly inadequate. It was therefore impossible for him, he said, to present the financial situation from *his* point of view; and he must, therefore, beg permission to postpone his exposition of the chief point in dispute, namely, the amount of the deficit and the best way to get rid of it, until such a time as he should be better acquainted with the subject.

" A general intimation," he continued, " I think I may allow myself even to-day; the intimation that in my opinion a correct financial policy requires that greater liberty of action be allowed the State with regard to the deficit; it should have the privilege to set aside larger sums for this purpose in years of prosperity, and smaller ones during less favorable times." (Cries of " Very good!" from more than one part of the House.) " When I realize through a closer examination of the budget before me that it closes with a deficit of five and one-half millions, but at the same time applies, as the law demands it should, eight and one-half millions toward the liquidation of debts of longer standing, I must acknowledge that our financial estimates are such as might arouse the envy of most of the other countries of Europe."

A lively expression of approval ran through the House. As though by a magic touch darkness were turned into light, so the deficit seemed suddenly to vanish and give place to a surplus, and instead of violent conflict appeared the prospect of internal peace.

To be sure, the goal was still far distant, and misgivings, doubts, and differences of opinion would not be wanting; still, the way seemed once more clear, and he who was the leader upon it impressed all as being an able financier in whom full trust could be placed. " Even his intimation of the manner in which he means to set about his great task was masterly," said Löwe. The House complied with his request, and deferred the debate until the Minister should have had time to formulate his system of action.

On November 4th, after Camphausen's plan had been approved by the King and his Ministers, the first preliminary deliberation upon the budget was begun. Before following its course, report must first be made upon a motion introduced by Virchow, with the support of the entire Party of Progress, on October 21st, a few days preceding Camphausen's nomination. It was directed against Von der Heydt's proposed increase in taxes, a song to the old tune of relief for the overburdened people through reduction of the military expenditures. So large an army, it was declared, was especially unnecessary, since this constant state of readiness for war was not brought about by the jealous disposition of the people, but only by the attitude of the Cabinets; through diplomatic negotiations a general disarmament might therefore be rendered possible.

Lasker sought to prevent action upon this motion by the counter motion to pass to the order of the day, assigning as the reason for this proceeding that the Federal army budget was legally fixed until the close

of 1871, that the conviction of the Prussian people
and their representatives with regard to the necessity
of lightening the military burden was too evident to be
doubted, and that therefore in 1872 the then newly
elected Reichstag would certainly take up this question,
and finally that diplomatic negotiations upon the subject of general disarmament would at present be much
more likely to lead to discord than to an agreement.

Lasker's action was not prompted by any doubt of
the final rejection of Virchow's motion, but by the wish
that through his motion the disapprobation of the military burden which it voiced might find a record as being
the sentiment of the House.

The decision of the House was that a general discussion of Camphausen's plan should be followed by one
on Virchow's and Lasker's motions.

Accordingly Camphausen developed his theory of
action. A full exposition of this and its advantages,
together with the objections and doubts raised against
it, would lead us too deeply into the technicalities of
finance; we must content ourselves with an outline of
the controlling thought.

Since 1820 Prussia possessed a sinking-fund into
which the law required the State to pay annually a sum
amounting to one per cent of all government loans,
together with the interest accruing upon these sums;
the fund grew steadily under this accumulation of
interest upon interest, until, with the additional one per
cent on all these loans, it had in thirty-eight years become sufficient to repay them. This was an excellent

system so long as there was a surplus; when, however, the State found itself confronted by a deficit in its accounts, this necessity of paying interest compelled it to raise a new loan to pay the old ones, a scheme evidently both absurd and improvident.

Since within recent years Prussia had contracted many new and large government loans, its annual payments into the sinking-fund now amounted to eight and two-thirds millions, besides which a deficit of five and one-half millions had arisen in its exchequer. Camphausen proposed to relieve the State of one-half of its obligations to the sinking-fund by transforming one-half of the State debt, two hundred and twenty-three millions, bearing interest partly at four and one-half, partly at four per cent, into a perpetual loan, with a uniform rate of interest at four and one-half per cent.[1] To induce the creditors to consent to this conversion, a premium of not more than one per cent was to be offered. Camphausen hoped that these favorable conditions would influence by far the greater number of creditors to accept the new arrangement; for those who refused to do so, matters were to continue as heretofore.

The Minister then explained, that, owing to its release from these compulsory payments upon 223,000,-000, the State would be enabled to save four and a half millions annually; it would therefore not need

---

[1] It was not deemed advisable to place the rate of interest lower, since 4½ % paper was quoted at 97. Should a lower rate of interest be offered, the risk would be incurred for the future that many debtors would demand the payment of the debt at its face value.

the higher taxes, and could cover the remaining deficit by the amount to be realized upon certain domains long destined to be sold.

In the discussion which ensued, and which at once entered minutely into the details of the plan, this was assailed by scarcely so much as a single adverse criticism; on the contrary, one of its keenest opponents, E. Richter, declared that if the principle underlying the measure were admitted to be correct, its application could not have been more ably or carefully worked out.

But what of the principle itself? It soon appeared that the first favorable impression made upon a part of the Opposition on October 29th had been replaced by a feeling of uneasiness. They had hoped by refusing the Government new sources of needed revenue, or at least by restricting these as much as possible, to compel it to make certain concessions dear to their hearts, such as an extension of their parliamentary privileges, or a reduction in the yearly levy of recruits, or perhaps limiting the term of military service to two years. All these pleasing anticipations, which were to be realized through the success of their strategic plan, would vanish into empty air should Camphausen succeed in permanently relieving the financial crisis. Should his plan of action be adopted, the future would not fail to provide occasions enough when the Prussian Assembly would be called upon to sanction new loans or taxes to meet further demands of the State; but, according to all human foresight, a deficit, that is, an insufficiency of means wherewith to meet the expenditure required by existing institutions, would not arise for many years to come.

By means of the old system, the extinguishment of the debt was gradually accomplished; but the amount of money at the disposal of the Government for the defrayment of yearly expenditures was diminished, although the financial condition of the State was steadily improved. The reverse of this would be the case should Camphausen's plan be put into practice; then the State would continue to carry its burden of debt undiminished, but the sum annually to be expended by the Government would for a time be increased by three and a half millions, and later, through the consolidation of the entire debt, would for the indefinite future be eight and a half millions larger than at present, without so much as being mentioned in the yearly budget. " By doing away with the sinking-fund," said one orator, "we shall give the Government liberty equivalent to the privilege of contracting a loan of three and a half millions annually without the need of parliamentary sanction."

That this was not to be tolerated Virchow doubted not for a moment; he therefore opposed Camphausen's plan, as he had Von der Heydt's, by his motion to reduce the deficit by curtailing army expenditures; to force the Government to adopt this course, no other way out of its dilemma should be left open to it.

When Lasker confronted him with the Article of the Constitution by which the military expenditures were fixed until 1872, he replied that this need not be regarded as an insurmountable obstacle if only the Governments would manifest a spirit of willingness to concede to the wish of the people and their representatives. In the heat of the discussion he declared further that this Article had moreover been so negligently worded that its text permitted of two constructions: the one, that in 1872 the Reichstag could diminish the expenditure for the army at its pleasure; the other, that even after 1871 the present estimate would continue in force until such time as the Governments should consent to its change.

This was, in fact, quite true, and exactly expressed the intention of the Governments; but Virchow could not have allowed a remark more fatal to the hopes of the Opposition to escape him. His hostility to the demands necessary for the maintenance of an army adequate to the country's safety was a widespread distemper of the time, a remainder of the conflict of former days. His confidence in the peaceful disposition of the French people only seven months before the declaration of war was also shared by many others in those days. It is, however, not to the credit of the great naturalist that he allowed this opinion to lead him to make the general statement that this condition of constant readiness for war was not necessitated by the mutual jealousy of the nations, but by the attitude of the Cabinets toward one another. For since 1813 this century has not witnessed a Cabinet war; that is, a conflict into which the hesitating ruler was not swept by the current of a strong popular sentiment, or at the close of which (with the single exception of 1866) his people did not express to him their gratitude for his defence of the national idea.

It became more and more evident as the discussion progressed that the game was a hopeless one for the Opposition. They were advocating a motion which, even if adopted, could not at the time be put into practice, but which would leave the finances in a very unsettled condition for the present, with prospects of serious conflicts ahead. To this the Government opposed a plan by which a system in itself fallacious would be abandoned, the deficit which had dragged on from year to year would be got rid of, and harmony would be restored between the factors of legislation. There could be little doubt regarding a choice of such alternatives, especially since a large part of the House shared neither Virchow's confidence in the continuance of peace, nor Lasker's opinion that a reduction of the military burden was necessary.

And so, on November 5th, Lasker's motion to pass to the order of the day was promptly rejected, and 215 voices against 99 spoke their disapproval of Virchow's motion as well.

After a bill embodying the completed plan of the Minister of Finance had on November 16th been submitted to the House, and then referred to the Committee on the Budget, it was on December 13th reported back to the House, with a recommendation in favor of its adoption approved by the voices of 17 against 13

of the members of the Committee. At the close of the
very animated debate which followed, the House, rejecting all amendments involving any important or
fundamental changes, approved the bill by 242 against
128 voices.

It was a turning-point of great consequence in the
German political situation of the day. This was realized so much the more since neither the friends nor the
foes of the new law had any thought of how soon a
tremendous rush of conflict would sweep the German
nation on to a complete transformation of its political
existence.

For the present the effect produced by the relief of
Prussia's financial difficulty, as evinced by the changed
relations between the Government and the representatives of the people, was less perceptible in the Prussian
House of Deputies than in the Reichstag. For in the
Prussian Assembly there was a fundamental difference
of opinion not only upon matters of finance, but with
regard to affairs of legislation as well; among the
latter may be mentioned Eulenburg's proposed system of
provincial self-government, and Mühler's education law,
both of which failed to be enacted during the session.

In the Reichstag, on the contrary, with the disap-
pearance of the Prussian deficit and the reaction upon
the Federal economy, all cause for dissension was removed, so that the Federal budget for 1871 was
quickly and harmoniously determined. With regard
to Federal legislation, moreover, there was from the
outset, under the leadership of Bismarck and Delbrück,

perfect concord of action between the Federal Council and the Reichstag Majority. Their endeavors were directed toward the attainment of the same general ends, although naturally this by no means excluded the possibility of a difference of opinion — at times slight, at times very decided — upon individual points.

Now, after the financial difficulty had been surmounted, the Reichstag, on February 14th, 1870, entered upon a session which promised to be rich in much-desired results.

At the very beginning of the session the speech from the throne announced a bill of utmost importance, the just-completed draft of a uniform penal code for the States of the North German Confederation. To this was added a law to protect the rights of authors. Then there were the drafts of four laws which may be characterized as supplementary of the recently enacted laws regarding freedom of migration and the regulation of trade and business. These were followed by a treaty with Baden, according to which the tribunals of this State and those of the North German Confederation were to render each other mutual legal aid; it corresponded to the law of this nature which, during the past year, had been enacted for all the States of the Confederation. Finally there was a bill to supply the defects in the law on weights and measures, intended to lead to the establishment of uniformity within this sphere throughout the States of North and South Germany.

" The entirety of the treaties, by which the North

and the South of Germany are linked together," the King continued, "forms a safeguard for the security and welfare of our common German fatherland, and affords those reliable guaranties which are inherent in the strong and firmly established organization of the North German Confederation. The confidence which our South German allies place in these guaranties rests upon complete reciprocity. The sentiment of national unity, the mutually pledged word of German princes, the community of our common country's highest interests, impart to our relations with South Germany a solidity wholly independent of the ever-changing waves of political passions."

The speech concluded with an expression of confidence that peace would continue undisturbed, since everywhere, among the Governments as well as among the nations, the conviction was daily gaining ground that each political community is entitled to the right independently to foster its own welfare, and that each country regards its armed force as a protection to its own independence, not as a means of assailing that of others.

This speech surely afforded no one an opportunity to read between its lines an urgent desire for the union of the South Germans with the Northern Confederation. On the contrary, despite the attacks to which the Minister, Prince Hohenlohe,[1] had been subjected at the hands of the clerically inclined foes of Prussia, the King's utterances were only such as expressed confident

---

[1] The retirement of the Prince did, in fact, follow a few weeks later.

satisfaction with the aspect of Germany's political relations. The treaties are to be relied upon, he said; the
interests of our common country are secure; no one of
our neighbors has any thought of interfering with our
internal affairs, nor is the least trace of hostility
evident.

A proposal for mutual disarmament made by the
French Minister, Daru had, notwithstanding Bismarck's
repellent attitude, in no way disturbed the relations
between the two countries; in short, King William saw
no occasion to change the policy heretofore pursued by
Germany, but rather every reason to continue upon the
carefully selected and well-tried course of the past.

In connection with the debate upon Virchow's motion in the House of Deputies, Lasker had spoken
words of warning against diplomatic negotiations regarding disarmament; but at the same time had emphatically declared that Germany need ask neither leave nor
license of the other Powers with respect to the policy
it might choose to pursue in furthering its internal
interests, — a valiant stand to take, but one which was
hardly to be expected of a deputy who almost in the
same breath advocated a reduction of the army.

His eagerness to welcome Baden into the Confederation continued unabated, however. Through his opposition an address in reply to the speech from the throne
was defeated because it did not, as he wished, express a
desire for Baden's admission into the Confederation.
On February 24th, 1870, in connection with the deliberation upon the Baden treaty providing for mutual

legal aid, he moved that the Reichstag sanction the treaty, and at the same time express its appreciation of the national aspirations which the Baden Government and people had manifested, declaring further that the Reichstag regarded these as indicative of national unity, and with gratification recognized their object to be an early union with the established Confederation.

The motion was a failure, even with respect to its form; it should have been addressed to the Government of the North German Confederation, for it was manifestly not within the province of the Reichstag to commend or advise a foreign State. Why this particular time rather than 1869 or 1871 was selected by the originator of the motion remained undisclosed; surely every occasion for it was wanting. It is, moreover, an unpardonable indiscretion to give a momentous question, involving serious consequences, the notoriety of a parliamentary debate without the Minister's previous knowledge, unless, indeed, the intention is to force him to retire.

Lasker, however, quite upon his own responsibility, commended the national policy of Baden, the State ever ready to unite with the Confederation. " With whom lies the blame for its continued exclusion ? " he asked. " I can find it only with Prussia. This is a question into which regard for the opinions of foreign Powers should not enter. France and Austria are fully occupied by their own internal affairs ; the former to so great a degree that the very existence of the dynasty is at stake." (Which, we interpolate, is the very reason why a party growing stronger with every day is incessantly urging to war.)   " This," he continued, " cannot therefore be the reason by which Bismarck is deterred.   You have heard his declaration, that an appeal to fear finds no response in German hearts ; what, then, is the solution of this enigma? "

The motion was a most unpleasant surprise to Bismarck.   He, too, regarded combination with the Southern States as the ultimate aim of his endeavor; he did not, however, wish to see it consummated until such time as both Governments and people, wholly uninfluenced from abroad, should desire it and welcome it with gladness.   But this was still far in the future, and for this reason the speech from the throne had sought to emphasize the fact that even under present conditions the security of the common fatherland was well established.

Bismarck hoped that when the time should be ripe for the much-desired step, all the Southern States would stand forth together to claim the new relationship.   Alone, he might perhaps be willing to admit Bavaria; Baden, however, less than any one of the others, for, as a glance at the map will reveal, its long and narrow extent would greatly add to the difficulties of defence for Prussia, whilst by its admission Bavaria and Würtemberg would be delivered over to Austrian influence, and France would be given a pretext for war.

This was all true beyond a doubt, but was of a nature not well adapted to public explanation.   Bismarck,

in his reply, took the standpoint that it was to the
interest of German unity that the nationally inclined
Baden, as the pioneer of the national idea, should be
allowed to remain undisturbed in its relations to the
South, rather than be encouraged to sever them by
union with the North. The skill with which he developed this argument was quite wonderful. The consequence was, that Lasker withdrew his motion on the
ground that through its discussion his purpose had
already been accomplished. The treaty regarding mutual legal aid was, of course, sanctioned.

The transactions which are now to be reported are
those concerning the bills announced in the speech
from the throne, the new penal code, and the four proposed laws supplementary of those already enacted regarding freedom of migration. Their discussion dealt
with legal details of so technical a character, involving many complicated and much-controverted questions,
that only a jurist of widest information and experience could give an accurate account of them. I shall
therefore attempt no more than to indicate the general
purpose of the several bills, together with the pre-
dominating influences which entered into the deliberations and shaped the final result.

After a brief debate, several of the bills of minor
importance were accepted wholly unaltered in their essential features. The bill which in this session again
fared the hardest was the one regarding the conditions
requisite to a settlement; and again, as in 1869, it was
at the hands of the Federal Council that it received

its harshest treatment. The end, which in this connection also the Prussian Government kept steadfastly
in view, was to procure for the citizens of the Confederation the highest possible degree of liberty and
freedom from legal complications in their movements
in all the States subject to its jurisdiction; the Government had, therefore, made the provisions of the proposed law applicable to all the States alike. To this,
Saxony, Hesse, Mecklenburg, and a number of the
smaller States objected, claiming that exception should
be made in favor of their peculiar institutions. This
led to a lively altercation between the respective Federal delegates, which was carried even into the Reichstag; here, however, the majority took hold, and in
full sympathy with the Prussian standpoint went even
so far as to strengthen and extend the provisions so
distasteful to the opponents of the bill. The result
was, that with mournful resignation Hesse and Saxony
consented to a compromise, thus making the enactment of the law possible.

As was natural, much greater importance attached
to the discussion of the penal code. In these debates,
which were continued throughout the entire session,
the loftiest heights of philosophical or theological specu-
lation upon the lawful authority of the State to punish
alternated with minute consideration of the measure of
penalty represented by a fine of a given sum of money,
or by imprisonment for a certain number of days for
slight offences.

The reform now undertaken had been awaited with

growing impatience; for, viewed from the standpoint of humane liberalism, the law heretofore in force, and especially that of Prussia, was regarded as much too rigorous and inflexible. Although it was wholly in this spirit that the Committee of the Federal Council in charge of the draft had constructed it, the special debate soon revealed that the expectations and demands far exceeded that which the draft realized. A motion wholly doing away with the death penalty induced a most violent and protracted debate, which, despite Bismarck's energetic opposition, ended in its adoption. And so it went on. All kinds of penalties were made lighter; the judges were allowed greater liberty to use their own discretion in imposing them; many mitigating circumstances were allowed; for all political offences, the motives of which were not dishonorable, penal servitude in a house of correction was replaced by imprisonment, or confinement in a fortress; disregard of official orders was made punishable only upon the one condition that convincing proof had been given the judge, that the order violated was one within the jurisdiction of the authority by whom it had been issued.

Among the ablest advocates of these views, as also in connection with the reform laws of a later date, Lasker figured most prominently. The subject was one within his own particular province, and therefore brought into play all his versatile talents. He was a jurist of unusual keenness and assiduity, a highly educated and philosophical idealist, an enthusiast for the cause of humanity. One of his most intimate friends has portrayed him most excellently in the words, " He was a man of law and justice." His entire activity was prompted by the desire to obtain for every fellow-man the protection of the law against arbitrary power and error; for every one unjustly accused, efficient defence and due exoneration; for every minority, the right to just consideration. To this end he sought not only to make the law the foundation of the State, but the judge upon all points the deciding authority of the State. Even Bamberger admits that for the fulfilment of duties such as Lasker would have assigned to judges, they had need to be ideally perfect men, such as existed in Lasker's imagination, but not elsewhere.[1]

It cannot be denied also that his ardor to vindicate the unjustly accused led him to slight the equally grave obligation to endeavor as earnestly to bring the guilty criminal to justice, so that honest citizens may have protection for person and property. We find the explanation for this in the fact that he was an idealist of extremest kind; although he by no means despised the maintenance of order in the community, yet nearer his heart lay the thought of personal freedom, although it is patent that without the proper restriction of the latter no degree of order is conceivable. To realize these ideals was the sole ambition of his life; outward show and material pleasures were never objects of pursuit to him. As is usual with thoroughly devoted idealists, in his plans he took into consideration human judgment and insight more than he did the passions of

---

[1] Bamberger, "Charakteristiken," p. 101.

men, his enthusiasm rendering him incapable of seeing men and conditions in their true light, and of acting accordingly, an ability which is, however, most essential to the practical statesman. Still, when all is said, his weaknesses were but such as were inseparable from his strength, and consistent with the moral purity and pre-eminent nobility of his nature.

The special debate upon the penal code was closed on April 8th, 1870, and the final deliberation upon it was not in order until after the session of the Customs Parliament had been opened on the 21st.

Aside from a few matters of minor importance, this assembly found a most simple task awaiting it, — an altered and it was hoped, improved tariff reform; again a long list of reduced or wholly abated customs duties; and to supply the resulting deficiency in the customs revenue, an increase, this time not in the unpopular coal-oil duty, but in that on coffee, which would yield a half million more of revenue than had been expected to accrue from the coal-oil duty proposed in 1869.

At first the prospects seemed very dubious. The several groups having special interests at heart continued to thwart one another by motions and counter-motions as during the foregoing session when we made their acquaintance. One group favored the retention of the protective duty upon cotton goods, and another that on iron manufactures, whereas a third blustered in favor of a still greater reduction of the duties on iron, whilst still another reopened the dispute regarding the duty on rice. For the higher duty on coffee a minority only

was won, although the Government had again made
the entire tariff reform conditional upon the sanction
of this duty.

The members of the South German faction rubbed
their hands in glee. "For a third time," said they,
"this Customs Parliament will prove itself a sterile
institution; this is the last session of the present legislative period, and as yet nothing has been accomplished.
Perhaps next year we shall be spared the trouble of
elections for this Prussian creation."

It was, however, just this attitude which led to a
strong reaction. All the Conservatives and National
Liberals to be found in the various groups united to
declare that the German name should not thus be
sullied, the national idea should receive no such rebuff,
the old dismemberment of the fatherland should not be
renewed. Herr von Patow, an Old Liberal, took the
matter in hand, and after consultations which occupied
several days, brought about a compromise between all
the groups with the exception of the South German
faction and the "German" Party of Progress. The
protectionists were mollified by the retention of the
higher duties on cotton goods, the free-trade deputies
were won by a reduction of the duty on pig iron and
rice; and the Governments were granted the desired
higher rate on coffee, thus obtaining an increase of
revenue although but a small one. Such was the decision reached on May 6th by a vote of 186 voices
against 84, and by which the Customs Parliament was
after all given a happy issue.

On May 9th the Reichstag resumed its labors, which were at once directed toward the removal of an evil of long standing, the Elbe duties, a Government bill to that effect being passed without delay. On the 13th the law for the protection of literary property was approved. The draft of a bill providing government aid for the St. Gothard Railway submitted at this time will be referred to later.

On the 21st the final deliberation upon the penal code was begun. The Minister of Justice announced that the Federal Council had as far as possible accepted the amendments proposed; with regard to the most important point in controversy, that of the death penalty, it had been decided to retain it only in punishment of murder, and attempts upon the life of the head of the Confederation or upon that of a ruling prince.

Fortunately for the code, Bismarck returned to Berlin on that day, after a sojourn of several weeks at Varzin on account of serious illness.

On the 23d a compromise motion was introduced by Planck and associates to the effect that the death penalty should at least not be reintroduced in Saxony and Oldenburg where it had been abolished. To this Bismarck immediately replied that for the sake of furthering the national object the Governments had made many concessions against their better judgment; there was, however, ONE which they would not make even for this purpose, and that was the sacrifice of the principle of national unity itself. "I should be untrue to all my past endeavor," said he, " should I now favor an act establishing two different codes of law for North Germany, two different classes of North Germans, — the select few of Saxony and Oldenburg, a sort of higher-culture class who no longer need the executioner's axe for their evil-doers, and the *profanum vulgus* of twenty-seven millions who have not as yet attained to this superior grade of culture.

"The declared purpose of our present task is to place all North Germans upon an equal footing before the law; to establish an inequality would, therefore, be a political impossibility. Our hands have been raised against peculiar rights, against special institutions, against the prejudices of individual Governments and individual races; at times, in realization of the worthiness of our ultimate aim, we have been hard, or at least severe; but we have never lost sight of our national object, and to its inspiration was due our strength, our courage, our power to act as we have. The moment we lose this inspiration we shall no longer be justified in being unyielding and in crushing with an iron heel the obstacles which obstruct our progress toward the restoration of the German nation's strength and glory." (Enthusiastic shouts of "Bravo!" followed by the cry of "Oho!" from the Social-democrats. Renewed and deafening applause).

It was a powerful and masterly speech, the worthy supplement and companion of the one against Lasker's motion for the admission of Baden. The one was a warning uttered against over-hasty action by which the way leading to the national goal might be blocked;

the other was an appeal not to allow sectional sympathies to impede the onward march toward the object pursued. That no one had at this point expected such a clarion-call to rally to the cause of German unity made it none the less effective, whereas a repeated refutation of the arguments against the death penalty would most likely have fallen flat.

The Minister of Justice then officially announced what Bismarck's speech had already made clear, that the Governments would sanction the penal code only upon condition that the death penalty be agreed upon.

There were, nevertheless, many and long speeches still to be heard; but when on May 25th the final vote was taken, the Federal Council's amendment was accepted by 128 voices against 107.

Thus harmony had been fully restored; and when on May 26th, with the end of the session and of the legislative period as well, the King had occasion in his speech from the throne to review with gratitude the glorious results achieved during the four sessions since 1867, he had but words of praise and appreciation for the vast amount of work accomplished in so short a time, as represented by the new institutions, treaties, and laws, by the organization of the army, the founding of a navy as yet still in process of formation, by the well-regulated administration of the Federal finances.

His closing words were: " These achievements within the province of public welfare and culture, of liberty and order, made possible only by faithful and incessant labor, are evidences which give assurance abroad as well as at home that the strength of the German nation, as promoted by the North German Confederation in perfecting its interior arrangements and establishing its national union with the States of South Germany as provided by treaty, is not a menace to the general peace, but a powerful agency in its favor. The respect and confidence which this course has won for us among foreign peoples and Governments are additional influences in the same direction.

" Should we, in God's providence, be the instruments by which the German nation will achieve the position among the nations of the world to which it is entitled and peculiarly fitted through its historic significance, its strength and its peaceable disposition, Germany will not forget the share which this Reichstag had in the work, and for which, again, I thank you." [1]

[1] Despite the facts related in this chapter, a number of French historians have asserted that Bismarck incited the war against France to extricate himself from the difficulties and embarrassment of his position at home. How little thought of war there really was in Germany at this time is shown by the circumstance that during the latter half of June the King was seeking refreshment from the baths at Ems, Bismarck was at Varzin recuperating from the nervous strain of the winter, Moltke was in Silesia, Roon was rusticating in Brandenburg, Camphausen was visiting his relations in the Rhine Proinvces.

CHAPTER V.

CLERICAL TENDENCIES IN THE FRENCH GOVERNMENT.

WHEN Napoleon abolished the office of Minister of State, and nominated Rouher to the Presidency of the Senate, he took the first irretrievable step in the transition to constitutional government. That each advance toward its realization should be hesitatingly undertaken, and carried out with much vacillation, was not only consistent with his character, but lay also in the nature of the matter in hand. He longed to be relieved of anxiety, yet every renunciation of personal power filled him with misgivings. He wished to see his dynasty permanently established, but where in the France of that day was permanence in anything to be found?

As a consequence, he submitted the draft of the *senatus consultum* to the Senate, but nominated for the administration of State affairs a milk-and-water Ministry of docile officials. Then came his severe attack of illness, and the exhausted condition in which he returned to official life forbade all further delay.

His personal liking for Ollivier had not suffered through his recent difference with the leader of the

Liberals; and as early as October he reopened correspondence with him, in which the formation of a responsible Ministry under Ollivier's direction was now discussed without reserve. Notwithstanding the goodwill brought to the task by both parties, many difficulties nevertheless arose.

The Emperor was willing to subscribe to the principle of the Ministry's dependence upon the majority in the representative assembly, but stipulated that only conservative and reliable Bonapartists should be nominated to it. In contradistinction to this, Ollivier felt impelled by all the power of past and present influence to desire a numerous and strong representation of the moderately liberal elements in the Ministry; he had turned his back upon the republic; he felt constrained therefore to proclaim in loudest tones his adherence to the principles of liberalism.

The first question to be decided was whether any of the present Ministers should continue in office. Against the Ministers of War, of the Navy, and of the Imperial House, Ollivier had no objections; but to the Minister of the Interior, who was entirely in sympathy with Rouher, he was decidedly opposed, although he was willing to place upon his list the present Minister of Finance, Magne, because of his technical skill and pliable politics. The Emperor's offer of the portfolio of Foreign Affairs was in turn declined by each of its last two heads; by Prince Latour because Ollivier had announced his programme for this department to be the unconditional preservation of peace, from which Latour drew the conclusion that South Germany would be yielded to Prussia, and Rome to Italy. Although this would have troubled Lavalette but little, he, it appears, had not sufficient confidence in the practical ability of the new leader to dare to take the leap into the dark with him without which a constitutional government could hardly be achieved under a Napoleon.

That by far the greater number of cabinet positions would fall to the share of the third party was, as matters had developed, but to be expected. In the consultations on this point, it soon became evident that the party was by no means a unit, but, on the contrary, was composed of a number of very different elements, of which it was exceedingly doubtful whether they would remain united in the future. About one-fourth of its members made much more extreme demands with regard to the reforms to be inaugurated by the new Government than did Ollivier and the great majority of the party; as a consequence, the former gradually constituted themselves a minority (later called the Left Centre), in distinction from the majority (later, the Right Centre). Napoleon would have preferred to confine his cabinet nominations to members of this majority. Ollivier, however, directed his attention to the fact that a much larger number of talented and capable men were to be found on the other side; and to insure to the Cabinet a strong position, their leaders should not be excluded from it. But when he addressed these gentlemen, his offer was not only received without any great show of gratitude, but, to his surprise, most exacting demands were made the condition to acceptance. The very first of these, that aside from the Ministers of War, of the Navy, and of the Imperial House, none of the present members of the Cabinet were to remain in office, placed Ollivier in a painfully embarrassing position with respect to the Minister of Finance.   Concerning the future reforms, there were also many conflicting opinions which failed to be harmonized; at all events, nothing was accomplished in this quarter.

The next attempt was to make a list of the possibilities in the Right Centre; these candidates, however, had no prospect of commanding a majority in the Legislative Body except in absolute dependence upon the Right, an utterly impossible position for Ollivier.

. The Emperor was beginning to weary of these endless consultations back and forth.   His own mind was fully made up; and the Empress, whose insight into affairs of State had inspired him with a high regard for her opinion, quite agreed with him.   After his recovery she had taken the trip to Egypt; and in one of her letters from the Nile she advised him to pursue undeterred the course upon which he had entered, that the world might see that his action was not the result of passing influences, but of unalterable conviction.

He was of the same opinion, and urged speedy ac tion; since, although he was for the present free from suffering, his physical condition could not be relied upon from one day to the next.   It was at this time that he drew up the draft of a decree arranging for the regency in the event of his death; it provided that the

Empress should assume this responsibility, and in case she were absent from the country at the time of his death, Prince Napoleon was named as regent until her return. He did this at a time when he expected the Empress to return in four weeks, — an evidence of how precarious he felt his condition to be.

This, moreover, fully explains his readiness to concede to Ollivier's proposal. When on November 29th the interrupted session of the Chambers was resumed, the speech from the throne was an echo of Ollivier's views. In it reaction and revolution were alike repudiated, and freedom based upon order was proclaimed. "For order I will answer," said the Emperor. "Aid me, gentlemen, to establish liberty." He then announced a great number of reforms and improvements to be inaugurated, called attention to the larger revenue arising from indirect taxes as an unmistakable evidence of a corresponding advance in the prosperity of the French people, and closed with a brilliant tribute to the nineteenth century. To live in it he deemed a high privilege; for it was an age in which sovereigns and nations alike were earnest advocates of peace, in which slavery had been suppressed in America and in Russia the serfs had been liberated, in which from the assembled bishops at Rome a work of beneficence and wisdom only was expected, and in which the fruits of advancing civilization were everywhere visible.

It was an eloquent speech, abounding in pleasing phrases, but from which binding and decided promises were carefully excluded.

During the next few weeks, which the Legislative Body devoted to the verification of disputed election returns, Ollivier renewed his negotiations with the Left Centre, and brought them to an issue by adopting a number of desired reforms and by agreeing upon a compromise Ministry in which, besides the present Ministers of the Imperial House, of War, and of the Navy, there were to be eight deputies, chosen equally from the Right and Left Centre; from the former, Ollivier (Justice), Talhouet (Public Works), Louvet (Commerce), Richard (Fine Arts); from the latter Count Daru (Foreign Affairs), Buffet (Finance), Chevandier de Valdrome (Interior), Segris (Public Instruction).

The more important departments, those directly affecting and affected by politics, had, as we see, been captured by the Left Centre.

The Emperor now accepted the tendered resignations of the present Ministers, and invited Deputy Ollivier to name persons who would in association with himself form a homogeneous Ministry, faithfully representing the Majority of the Legislative Body, and resolved to carry out the spirit of the *senatus consultum* of September 8th.

On January 2d, 1870, the nomination of the gentlemen named above was made public. The liberal empire had at last received its responsible Ministry, and Ollivier had now to show whether he could suit the action to the word.

That the first condition requisite to the existence of the new Cabinet, the support of a majority in the

Chamber, would be forthcoming was assured from the
outset.   Together, the Right and Left Centre numbered about one-half of all the representatives ; and
since the Right was composed throughout of declared
adherents of the Government, the Ministry could rely
upon most of these as well, if for no other reason than
simply because it *was* the Ministry.   To be sure, the
former Arcadians, who now as a group of from thirty
to forty constituted the Extreme Right, took no pains
to conceal their thorough disapproval of the liberalism
and the peace policy of the Cabinet.   When after an
utterance to that effect Ollivier asked them to give
their distrust definite expression, the reply was, "We
are biding our time."

Still more decidedly and quickly came the direct
declaration of war from the opposite side of the House.
Here hatred was rife against the deserter from their
camp, their former associate, Ollivier, the man of the
flexible conscience, as Gambetta once called him during
a passionate scene which took place amid utmost tumult
in the House.

Attacks of this nature would not have been dangerous to the Ministry had it been in a position to give its
proclaimed liberal tendency, which the country had
hailed with such jubilant eagerness, immediate and
practical expression through the introduction of reforms of various kinds.   Some steps in this direction
were taken : several extremely unpopular officials were
dismissed, old Ledru-Rollin was given permission to
return to his native land, and the police were directed

to allow the newspaper press somewhat greater lib-erty.

The programmes of both the Right and Left Centre gave promise of many and excellent reform laws: one to regulate anew the affairs of the communities; a system of general decentralization in the administration of the communes, cantons, and departments; the abrogation of some especially oppressive police regulations; a revised electoral law; certain economic reforms; and a parliamentary inquiry into the relative merits of protection and free-trade. All this had a very inviting sound; but no part of it had as yet assumed definite shape, nor had any more detailed information with regard to the import of the promised laws been given.

And so one week after another was lost in petty skirmishes, interpellations, and motions. On the Left all hearts were set upon two points in particular, with respect to which the two programmes of the Centre unfortunately differed. The first of these concerned the electoral reform, in connection with which the Left claimed that since the members of the Chamber just entered upon its activity had been elected under the pressure of the absolute *régime*, the Chamber ought now to be dissolved, and replaced by an assembly elected under the new conditions of liberty. Naturally the majority was little inclined to so suicidal a step, and the Ministry held to the parliamentary principle that a Chamber whose majority is in sympathy with the Government is never dissolved.

The second demand put forth by the Left was of a

still more radical nature.   According to the Constitution
of 1852, the Legislative Body had no share in legislation involving a modification of the Constitution;
such laws could only be enacted by the Senate at the
suggestion of the Emperor.   The Left now proposed
that the right to determine upon a Constitution or any
one of its Articles should no longer belong to a Senate
nominated by the Emperor, but solely to the Chamber
elected by the sovereign people.   The result to which
this might lead was obvious, — a radically inclined majority could at any time, in perfect conformity with the
law, abolish the empire.

In the Ministry the opinion prevailed that the Senate
should be deprived of this exclusive right, and in its
stead should be given the privilege of participating n
every kind of legislation.   However, when the members of this privileged body were sounded with regard
to such a change, they would not hear of it; and the
Emperor, too, thought the time not yet ripe for this
step.

Thus day after day found nothing accomplished.   At
last, on February 22d, Jules Favre arose in the name
of the Left to present an interpellation.   He expatiated
upon the country's earnest desire for a free press, the
right of assembly, the responsibility of all State officials, a reduction of the military burden, and greater
opportunities for superior instruction for the masses.
" In view of these demands," he asked in conclusion,
" what policy does the Cabinet propose to pursue ?
What is its programme ? "

It was Count Daru who upon this occasion undertook the reply in an exact and exhaustive statement
regarding the two programmes of the Centre, giving full
assurance of the Ministry's constitutional independence,
and the complete harmony of its members. His effort
was rewarded by a vote of 232 voices against 18 upon
a motion to pass to the order of the day, thus indicating the full confidence of the House in the Government.

Unfortunately, however, on the very next day the
scene was entirely changed. On February 23d the
principle of Government candidatures for the parliament elections was made the subject of a further interpellation. The Minister of the Interior, Chevandier de
Valdrome, replied : " The institution of a parliamentary Ministry necessarily involves discontinuance of the
practice of putting forward official candidates ; however, in making this admission the Government by no
means implies that it is inclined to relinquish the right
which every Government may justly claim of informing
the public which of the candidates it regards as its
friends and which as its enemies." (Enthusiastic applause ; demonstrations of disapproval on the Left.)

The spirit of animosity displayed in connection with
so simple a question as this gave evidence of how this
long-continued abuse under Rouher's administration had
exasperated men and biased their judgment.

Ollivier now arose to reiterate the declaration made
by his colleague with regard to the Government's right,
after which he however allowed himself to be carried

away by the thought of the past, and by the impulse of his own speech. " This right," he cried, " is indisputable; but just as unquestionably should it be the ambition of a liberal Ministry never to resort to it. The influence of the Ministry upon the country should be such that it can commit the defence of the Government wholly into the hands of the voters. Our counsel to the people therefore is: 'Do not become dependent upon our guardianship; exert your own power in defence of yourselves and of us. The strong Government is not that which protects its friends, but the one which is defended and supported by them."

Now it was the Left which was delighted; but so much the more did the Right give vent to its wrath. " How shall we understand the speeches of yesterday?" asked Granier de Cassagnac on February 24th. " Which of the two Ministers voiced the opinion of the Cabinet? "

Without a moment's hesitation Ollivier replied, " The import of the two speeches is identical, and precisely that which I gave you to understand yesterday; the Government will put forward no candidates should an election occur during its continuance, but will preserve an attitude of utter neutrality." No more radical a position could have been taken. According to this stand the Government could not so much as declare itself to be Whig or Tory; as a preliminary to the elections it could not even announce the bills it hoped to carry in the new House; but, in passive neutrality, it would have to await the commands which the representatives of the sovereign people would be pleased to impose upon it. Such a course would be unwise, even in a democratic republic; in a constitutional monarchy it would be a transgression of the first principle of the Constitution.

For Ollivier, however, it earned his first and last tribute of applause from the Left, whereas by far the larger half of the Right voted against him. Two days later the members of the Right organized a club in declared opposition to the Government, under the leadership of the former Minister of the Interior, Forcade de la Roquette, ably assisted by a gay Court cavalier, Baron David, and by a former pupil and disciple of Ollivier's, Clement Duvernois, a young man as ambitious as he was gifted, who had expected an appointment to the Cabinet of January 2d, and through his disappointment had been transformed into an open antagonist of his former master.

Owing to the great esteem with which the members of this group were regarded in the highest circles, their open desertion of the Ministry did not tend to lessen the difficulties besetting it in its home policy.

Meanwhile, Count Daru was guiding the foreign affairs of France with a firm and skilful hand. He was a veteran parliamentarian, who had retired from public life twenty years before the era of the Napoleonic dictatorship, and now, after the last elections, had made his reappearance in the Legislative Body as a liberal member. He was very much in earnest with respect to his party's peace programme, and quite as much so with regard to the Ministry's responsibility. The Emperor, fully as desirous to maintain peace as was his Minister, was quite willing to yield upon both points.

Prince Latour had sent General Fleury, the intimate confidant of Napoleon, to St. Petersburg with the general commission to arouse sympathy for France in the Emperor Alexander, which might perhaps lead to combined action in the Orient; his special charge, however, was to recall to the Czar's mind the unsettled North-Schleswig question, as well as the unfulfilled Article (V.) of the Treaty of Prague. Bismarck had resented this with considerable sharpness, as being an inexcusable interference; whereupon Count Daru had cautioned General Fleury to be most circumspect. "The new Minister," wrote a companion of General Fleury to a friend in Paris, "has bound us hand and foot; for great results we can therefore no longer hope. From Emperor Napoleon we hear not a word; he seems to have fallen into apathy, and to leave everything to the Minister."

This attitude was still more marked in connection with another step by which Daru intended to convince Europe that peace was indeed assured. We remember how decidedly Napoleon had rejected the plan suggested by Vitzthum, and submitted to him by Rouher in the fall of 1868, according to which the Emperor should propose mutual disarmament to the King of Prussia. He had at that time, in view of the Prussian military system, pronounced any such idea to be a self-delusion; an opinion in which Baron Stoffel, the French military *attaché* at Berlin, had fully agreed, saying: "As long as universal obligation to military duty continues in force in Prussia, disarmament is not possible in that country."

Now Count Daru, in the name of the Ministry, advocated the selfsame step, and the Emperor raised no objections. On February 1st, 1870, Count Daru requested the good offices of England to transmit such a proposal to the Prussian Government. Bismarck replied that the idea was so entirely opposed to the Prussian military organization that he did not so much as trust himself to suggest it to the King. But Daru was not so easily discouraged; a fortnight later, to remove all doubt regarding the sincerity of his purpose, he made the announcement in Berlin, through Lord Clarendon, that the French Government on its part was ready to reduce the levy of recruits for the present year from 100,000 to 90,000 men. In reply, Bismarck regretted that even this could not influence him to a change of opinion.

For the European situation and the general peace it mattered little whether these two Powers, keeping jealous watch over each other, diminished their armed force in equal proportion or not; and so this fruitless correspondence attracted little attention abroad.

Much greater was the impression made by the news of Lasker's motion of February 24th, advocating Baden's admission into the North German Confederation, and Bismarck's manner of disposing of it; for, although he had for the present disapproved of such a step, he

had utilized the occasion again to hold up German
unity as the ideal to be realized by the future. " It
is his intention, therefore, to overstep the Treaty of
Prague upon the very first occasion which may present
itself," was the angry comment of Paris ; and with
increased energy the Arcadians, who beheld in Ollivier's renunciation of official influence upon the elections
a new peril to the Empire, now urged the Court, the
army, and the press to pick up the gauntlet thrown
down by Prussia, and to restore the now tarnished fame
of the dynasty to its former splendor by a brilliant
exploit at arms.

It was at this time that Archduke Albrecht, returning
from a pleasure trip into Southern France, spent a few
weeks in Paris.[1] He was most cordially received by
the French officers, and was given every opportunity
to study the military arrangements and resources of
France.   One day he said to the Emperor, " It seems
the situation is again becoming more strained, as though,
perhaps, our two States might be forced into war.
Would it not be advisable to come to an understanding
with regard to our joint preparations ? "   Napoleon was
little disposed to discuss the political question, under
what conditions he would consider a conflict to be unavoidable, and so eagerly took up the military topic.
" Should we feel compelled to resort to war, what military operations would you suggest ? " he asked.

[1] What follows is based upon the authority of unprinted memoirs, as
well as upon the statements of Prince Napoleon and Generals Lebrun
and Jarras.

In reply, the Duke sketched out a plan of campaign.
The main body of the French army, leaving Strasburg,
would as rapidly as possible move upon Stuttgart; an
Italian army of one hundred thousand men would advance toward Munich; an Austrian division from Bo-
hemia would press forward into Bavaria; thus the
South of Germany would be severed from the North.
Meanwhile, the remainder of the French troops, following the Saar, would be distributed through the Rhine-
lands, and a French fleet manned by Danish troops
would make a landing on the Baltic coast.

Napoleon listened in silence, and then asked for a
written statement of what he had heard. The Archduke added that his plan presupposed the existence of
the triple alliance discussed during the past year; he
regarded it to be his duty to tell the Emperor that
judging from all he had seen while in France he believed that without an ally the French army, even
should it include ALL the troops now stationed in Al-
geria, would be too weak to undertake a war against
Germany. Napoleon himself was not free from this
apprehension, but, without entering into a further discussion of the plan, told the Duke that he would ere
long send an adjutant to Vienna with all the latest
army estimates, from which he hoped the Duke would
receive a better impression of the French forces.

Napoleon, on his part, evidently did not consider the
situation to be as precarious as did the Archduke; for
he laid away the plan of campaign without discussing
it with any one, or submitting it to his general staff;

nor, for the present, was anything further said about sending an adjutant to Vienna after the Duke's departure thither.

Napoleon's Ministers, however, despite their love of peace, upon which their programme laid so much stress, were more sensitive than was their Emperor. When the first reports of the Berlin occurrence were received in Paris, Daru, in the presence of several diplomats, expressed surprise that Bismarck, in his reply to Lasker's motion, had not referred to the Treaty of Prague, by which the admission of Baden was prohibited. This found its way into the newspapers; and Bismarck, always determined not to allow the slightest foreign interference in German affairs to pass unreproved, ordered a reproduction of the Article in the *Nord Deutsche Allgemeine Zeitung*, accompanied by a short comment, stating that the Federal Chancellor had certainly not mentioned the Treaty of Prague in this connection, nor did he deem it at all necessary to do so, since the stipulations of the treaty did not cover the case of Baden's admission into the North German Confederation.[1]

Napoleon and Daru allowed this to pass unnoticed. But the more impressionable Ollivier, who in connection with these transactions had discovered to how great a degree the incessant endeavors of recent years to stir up enmity against Prussia had succeeded in implanting in the hearts of the French townsmen and peasants, as a rival to their love of peace, a bitter

[1] Berlin *Times* correspondent, March 9th.

hatred of Prussia, now feared that any new provocation might lead to serious consequences. He therefore summoned a correspondent of the *Kölnische Zeitung*
to an interview, intending through this medium to
impart a timely warning to the German nation. He
told the correspondent that he regarded the fostering
of friendly relations between France and Germany as
a matter of supreme importance, and that immediately
after his accession to office he had instructed General
Fleury to let the North-Schleswig question rest. He
and his colleagues, he declared, were by no means
averse to a combination between South and North Germany; but he felt compelled to say that a large part
of the French nation was most unpleasantly affected
by the new conditions across the Rhine, and that this
element might prove strong enough to force the Emperor to resist any further Prussian aggrandizement.
Only in case union between the two sections of Germany should result from a wholly spontaneous desire
on the part of the South could the Ministry see any
prospect of its consummation without entailing warlike
intervention. The German Liberals, he believed, could
not be too cautious in this respect.

Bismarck did not think that this explanation called
for public comment, and thus the controversy to which
Lasker's speech had given rise subsided without being
followed by any immediately harmful consequences. It
cannot be doubted, however, that it had re-aroused suspicion in Paris, and had led to instructions to Benedetti, enjoining him to be exceedingly watchful, orders.

which were not calculated to improve the relations between the Ambassador and Bismarck.

At this juncture the attention of the French Government was diverted from German affairs by nearer anxieties, growing more absorbing with every day.

Since December 8th, 1869, the Œcumenical Council was holding its sessions in the Vatican. Its deliberations were of a nature to affect the whole world, more or less; but no other Government was at one and the same time so directly responsible for the assembly, and yet so impotent to influence its proceedings, as was that of France.

Napoleon's peculiar position with regard to it was this: it lay within his power at any moment to put an end to its deliberations; but he had no other means whereby to influence, even in the slightest degree, the action about to be taken. Should he recall the French troops from Rome, the Council would be immediately dissolved; [1] therefore, by continuing his protection, he shared with the Pope the responsibility for its decisions, as little as he approved their import in so far as this could be anticipated.

The attitude which the Pope had maintained for the past twenty years gave little encouragement to the hope that action regarded as politically dangerous might be prevented. He did, in fact, continue the course he had resolved upon, wholly undeterred by

[1] The Pope would not have exposed the assembly of bishops to the tender mercies of Garibaldi's volunteers, nor allowed them to remain under the protection of the "sub-Alpine robber."

the Emperor's repeated remonstrances. He was fully aware that fear of the French clergy and their influence upon the elections for the Chamber would prevent the Emperor from recalling his troops, and maintained that in protecting the Holy Chair, and rendering reverent service to him who occupied it, Napoleon, as a Catholic ruler, did no more than fulfil the demands of duty.

We know how in 1867 Napoleon sacrificed the contemplated triple alliance to considerations of this nature. Nevertheless, the more decidedly the Jesuit principle of the supremacy of church over State was now asserted in Rome with a view to its practical enforcement, the power thus gained to be concentrated in the hands of the Pope, the more unalterable grew Napoleon's determination to meet the appearance of such tendencies in the Council with advice, warning, and protest addressed to the Pope, and to uphold the liberties of the Gallican Church as established by the concordat.

To this effect Prince Latour had instructed the French representative at Rome, Monsieur de Banneville, and immediately after the formation of the liberal Ministry, Count Daru had reissued the orders of his predecessor. Very soon, however, it became evident that Ollivier, the Minister of Justice, to whose department, according to French usage, belonged all matters affecting the church, took an entirely different view of the Roman question than did the Minister of Foreign Affairs.

Both men were sincere Catholics, and both belonged to the circle of Count Montalembert's intimate friends. Strange as it may seem, the Count was at this time ardently advocating Ollivier's election to the French Academy against that of Lamartine. Now, it so happened that in furthering his wish to see the church emancipated from the control of the State, which was ofttimes formal and self-interested, Montalembert had done more than any other Frenchman to arouse widespread enthusiasm in France for the supremacy of the church in general, and of the Papacy in particular.

When, however, it became the proclaimed endeavor of the Jesuit order to turn the tables, and make the States subject to the command of the church, and this in turn to the unrestrained influence of the Pope, then Montalembert's experience was like that of Döllinger, his German fellow-combatant in the long struggle for the liberty of the church. He recognized in this movement the beginning of the suppression of all liberty, incomparably more dangerous than was the inconvenience arising from the *jus circa sacra* in the hands of the State; therefore, with an ardent protest, he turned against it.

Wholly different was Ollivier's attitude. Surely, according to his view of it, he was not clerically inclined; no one, he declared, could justly accuse him of that. The incentive of his every action, controlling his entire being, was freedom, — freedom of the State in its sphere, freedom of the church in hers, and a liberal and kindly agreement between the two in regard to their common affairs. The insignificant point upon which everything hinged, however, namely, as to what constituted these " common affairs," Ollivier did not deem it necessary to explain, regarding it as all-sufficient if with respect to the question in hand the right solution were found.

As every one knew, the Council was called for the special purpose of defining the infallibility of the Pope ; and this, Ollivier doubted not, was a matter wholly within the province of the church, one regarding which the State had not the least right to interfere, or by its action to deprive the assembly of holy fathers of perfect freedom in their decisions. Utter passivity in this connection was, he held, the unmistakable duty of the State.

But as yet the Council was not dealing with the question of infallibility, and the Government could therefore postpone all action ; this it was the more willing to do, since the French bishops in Rome were quite as far from harmonious as were the Ministers in Paris. The leader of the minority was Archbishop Darboy of Paris, heretofore Napoleon's trusted adviser in all ecclesiastical affairs. The majority were unquestioning adherents of the Pope, in which they enjoyed the full sympathy of the lower clergy, vicars and parish priests, by far the larger number of whom were uncompromising Ultramontanes.

Now, toward the middle of February, 1870, it became generally known that the Pope had laid before the Council the draft of a decree, a so-called schema, in which the church reasserted her claim to a control of

the State and civil society in general in very mediæval
style. The excitement it produced throughout Europe
was intense. This was a measure of which Ollivier
could not assert that it concerned the church alone;
nevertheless, his admiration for the imposing picture
suggested by this proposed spiritual empire of the world,
together with his disinclination to enter into a controversy with him who wore its crown and dispensed its
blessings, remained unshaken.

It was on the ground of momentary inexpediency
that Ollivier now opposed a forcible note, in which, with
the Emperor's approval, obtained on the 20th of February, Daru defended the rights of the modern State
against the pretensions put forth in the schema, and
announced that a personal representative of his Majesty
the Emperor would be sent to Rome, in his name to
present to the Council the claims made by France.
Until the days of Pius IX. this had been the undisputed privilege of every Catholic sovereign. Ollivier,
who would have preferred the preservation of complete
silence, had his way in so far, at least, that the note
underwent a total revision in the Council of Ministers;
the announcement of an imperial representative to be
sent to Rome was wholly omitted, and every demand
was qualified, and deprived of all character, the whole
being fittingly closed with a respectful request for information regarding the action taken upon the schema.

As might have been expected, so extreme and devout
humility received a corresponding reply, in which, under
date of March 19th, the Curia peremptorily upheld every

paragraph of the schema, demanding that to the church be conceded the control of every State arrangement affecting "whatever belongs to faith and morals." (It would be difficult indeed to find one that did not do so.)

Again Count Daru's indignation was roused by this new evidence of papal arrogance. He proposed, again with Napoleon's consent, that France should make vigorous protest against the proposed subjection of the State to the church ; further, that this should be made known to the world at large and to the Council, and be then communicated to the other Courts, with a request for their support.

Ollivier heard all this with deep anxiety, believing that if France assumed this tone, the haughty pontiff would resort to a still loftier one, and an open rupture would become unavoidable. This would naturally be followed by a severance of diplomatic relations, which would result in the recall of the French troops, and finally in the dissolution of the Council. This calamity Ollivier intended to avert at any cost. He flattered himself with the thought that to him, the Liberal, would be ascribed the world-renowned deed of having made it possible for the Council to complete its deliberations. He did not, to be sure, succeed in preventing a reply to the uncivil note received from the Curia, but carried his point in so far that a memorial expressing Daru's view was, like his despatch of an earlier date, greatly modified and softened in its form, and was then, on April 10th, forwarded to the Pope with expressions of deepest reverence, together with the request that its contents be made known to the Council. That the Pope would meet this with a refusal couched in friendliest terms, Ollivier knew full well before it was sent.

Although Daru's memorial received the support of several of the Powers, — Austria, Prussia, and Bavaria, — the Pope was not to be moved. " As Abbot Mastai I believed in the Pope's infallibility; as Pope Mastai I FEEL IT," said he. Cardinal Antonelli explained to the French representative that the memorial could not possibly be officially presented to the Council, and added, " Nor will I trouble your Government with a refutation of its contents. You have, however, no cause for alarm; in theory we are zealous and aggressive as were Gregory VII. and Innocent III., in practice we are lenient and long-suffering; and especially will a State like France, between whom and us there exists the tie of a concordat, experience no change in our relations so far as we are concerned."

It was evident that this second rebuff left no further opportunity open for negotiations. The only choice now left to the Governments was either to submit in silence, or to take extreme measures, demand the suspension of the Council, or compel its dissolution. There was but one way in which the latter could be accomplished, and France alone controlled it, — the recall of the French brigade now garrisoned in the Papal States, thus leaving Rome at the mercy of the Italians.

Again Ollivier, in opposition to Daru, won the majority of the Ministry over to his policy of inactivity; and upon his representation that the recall of the troops was incompatible with the national honor, and that the longest possible duration of friendly relations with the Pope was an irremissible duty, the Emperor also yielded, and allowed the Ministry to follow the course determined upon.

All thought of harmony between Ollivier and Daru was now at an end. A new complication soon arose through which the crisis was precipitated.

The applause which the Left had accorded the Ministry on February 24th for its stand against official influence upon the elections as declared by Ollivier soon died away, whereas the Arcadian aversion to Ollivier's liberalism was more openly displayed with each succeeding day.

The worst feature of the internal situation was the Government's utter sterility in all the provinces of legislation and administration. In January the Ministry had veritably deluged the people with promises of new laws and reforms, but month after month passed in inactivity: numerous committees were at work upon the preparation of bills, but actual results there were none ; and so public opinion with regard to the Ministry was constantly changing. March began as February had ended ; scarcely a day passed without an urgent interpellation or important motion from the Left ; tremendous battles of words were daily fought, often with vehement bitterness, the attack being not infrequently directed against Ollivier, who met it with haughty defiance.

Now came a repetition of the demand for the dissolution of the Chamber; the mayors, it was moved, should no longer be nominated as heretofore by the Government, but be elected by universal suffrage; the Senate's constituent power was again assailed, and its transfer to the popular Chamber demanded. Indeed, there seemed to be no limit to the possibilities of democratic motions. This led the Government, I cannot say whether at Napoleon's or Ollivier's instance, to the resolution as quickly as possible to reach a definitive decision upon such questions at least as affected the Constitution, that an end might be made of this uncertainty regarding public opinion.

On March 9th Ollivier announced to the Senate that the Government would ere long submit to its consideration the draft of a decree making all needful modification in the Constitution. This course had the approval of the Emperor. Count Daru, however, declared that the Constitution of 1852 had been sanctioned by the voice of the people, or in the speech of ancient Rome, by a plebiscitum of eight million suffrages. According to the provisions of this Constitution, amendments to its several Articles could be enacted by the Senate at the instance of the Emperor; but a fundamental revision, such as was now contemplated, could become valid only through ratification by the people by means of a plebiscitum, as had been the case with the original compact. To this, however, the Emperor offered unyielding resistance;[1] perhaps because after the elec-

---

[1] Ollivier, " L'Église et l'État," II., 225.

tions of 1869 the risk appeared too great to him, although Daru assured him that according to the reports
of the prefects a plebiscitum would awaken great popular enthusiasm, especially so since its purpose was
a direct fulfilment of that which had been desired in
1869, the transformation of the empire into a liberal
monarchy.

As in either case the first requisite to action was an
expression of opinion from the Senate, which was by no
means favorably inclined to the matter, it was at once
suggested that the president of that body, the former
Minister of State, Rouher, be invited to participate in
these preliminary conferences. It was the first occasion
upon which the once powerful statesman found himself
associated with his successful rival in the discharge of
a joint official duty. As may be supposed, Rouher was
by no means disposed to make difficulties for Daru in
connection with the plebiscitum, but, on the contrary,
recognized in it a means by which a more conservative
direction might be given the policy of the Ministry,
which with every day appeared more doubtful to him;
but especially did he hope that through it the empire
might regain its former position of strength.

He had long interviews with the Emperor, and later
with the Empress also. It is said that the Prime Minister, Ollivier, had been known to sit a long time waiting in the anteroom while Rouher was conferring with
royalty. The representations made upon these occasions by the former Minister probably revolved about
the following thoughts: Since the enactment in 1868

of the laws concerning the press and the right of assembly, the implacable Republicans have continued their revolutionary incitement with renewed zeal; the Ministry of January 2d has caused the announcement of a number of prospective laws, all of which are destined to promote individual liberty at the expense of the Government's means of exercising power; this naturally increases the danger inherent in a wholly unrestrained Republican party intent upon overthrow, and by which the permanence of the dynasty may ultimately be jeopardized. Under these circumstances, it is the opinion of the Extreme Right, the prestige of the Emperor and certainty with regard to the succession can be restored only by the triumphs of a great war; when the absence of a strong alliance and the enemy's thorough preparation for war are taken into consideration, this must, however, be regarded as a most dangerous remedy; whereas (in Rouher's estimation), a judiciously managed plebiscitum will be quite as effective. As yet, in by far the larger part of the country, sentiments of peace and contentment prevail, so that there can be no doubt that the plebiscitum will result favorably. And what possible argument will then be left to these Democrats who are constantly speaking in the name of the people, if the people, by the direct vote of many millions, proclaim their desire to uphold and fortify the empire?

At all events, Rouher succeeded in convincing the Emperor and Empress. On March 22d a letter was published, addressed to Ollivier, in which Napoleon expressed his approval of the Prime Minister's views, and requested him in association with his colleagues to prepare the draft of a *senatus consultum*, firmly fixing the dispositions of the Constitution and dividing this form of legislation from the ordinary.

As early as March 28th, Ollivier submitted the completed draft to the Senate, together with a report remarkable for its display of erudition and rhetorical ability. It was said of it in Paris that never before had an invitation to political suicide been couched in so elegant a speech. For, if the provisions of the Draft were enacted, the Senate, in which heretofore had been vested the exclusive right of amending the Constitution, would now exercise this power for the last time, and for the purpose of renouncing it forever. Henceforward the new Constitution could be amended only by means of a plebiscitum authorized by the Emperor, in precisely the same manner as that in which the new constitutional pact was now to receive the sanction necessary to its validity. According to its provisions the Emperor, as chief of the State, retained all his former prerogatives, — the chief command of the armed force of the country, the appointment of public officials, the nomination and direction of the Ministry, the right to declare war and conclude peace; he remained responsible to the nation, and could at any time appeal to its decision. The members of the Senate were, as heretofore, to be nominated by the Emperor; their number was, however, to be increased. The legislative power was to extend to all subjects except such as, according to the decree, were directly reserved for control by the Constitution. A number of especially obnoxious Articles of the former Constitution were revoked, and upon the Legislative Body was bestowed the privilege of receiving petitions.

The publication of the Draft aroused deep and general interest. The first impression was, that the autocratic Constitution of 1852 was now to be replaced by a liberal one based upon the modern two-chamber system, and definitely establishing all that which in 1860 and 1869 had been granted the people in the form of rights.

A closer inspection, however, gave rise to grave misgivings. What possible value could attach to the Ministry's responsibility to the representative body as compared with the Emperor's direct responsibility to the nation, and the power of its plebiscita? It would be of little consequence how decided a stand the two Chambers might take against pernicious demands made by the Emperor; for should he re-enforce these by the omnipotence of a plebiscitum, would not any opposition which the Chambers might offer prove utterly futile? The final opinion was therefore: hereby the significance of the parliament becomes a mere semblance; all real power will lie in the authority which the Emperor can at any time reassume by sanction of a plebiscitum.

That the introduction of the plebiscitum was not calculated to enhance the renown of the parliament no one will deny. On the other hand, it will be as readily conceded that the occasions would be exceedingly rare upon which this course would be adopted; only indeed at such critical moments as would otherwise be met by a *coup d'état*, or end in revolution; for in connection with a situation of less gravity, the risk incurred by the Emperor through such a proceeding would be entirely too great, out of all proportion to that which might be gained. In the future, as had been the case in the past, in the ordinary course of events, decades would probably pass before an appeal to the plebiscitum, whereby the authority of the Chambers might suffer, would be even so much as suggested.

We cannot therefore feel that Ollivier was wrong in declaring that the plebiscitum would inaugurate the transition from the absolute to the constitutional empire, and lay the foundation for the rule of liberty in France; that otherwise, however, it would lead to no innovations.

As circumscribed as the effect of this plebiscitum proved in reality to be, it was nevertheless a disposition by the sovereign people through the medium of universal suffrage; and therefore to oppose it was but an awkward beginning for the republican Left, whose orators upon other occasions could not say enough in glorification of the people's sovereignty and the right of universal suffrage. They, however, had as little doubt that the plebiscitum would result favorably to the Emperor as had Rouher and Daru; and, quite like their Jacobin predecessors of 1793, their love for the republic was greater than their regard for the idolized sovereignty of

the people. It would be difficult to find severer criticism, or more acrimonious derision of the right of universal suffrage, than was indulged in upon this occasion
by the orators of the republican Left. Whereas at all
other times they delighted to pose in the parliament as
the truest representatives of the exalted people, and as
the special champions of the right of universal suffrage,
they now spoke of the sovereign citizens as though they
were mere voting cattle, without judgment or will of
their own, because, forsooth, their action in connection
with a plebiscitum was not through the medium of the
parliament, but in utter dependence upon themselves.

"The plebiscitum," declared Grévy, "calls upon
every citizen to cast his vote individually, without the
opportunity of previous consultation with his associates,
or of adding to the proposition, or modifying it by
amendments. By such a procedure the will of the
people cannot be asserted; every appeal made by the
Emperor becomes a command." Now, no one will be
disposed to defend this inability to amend as an advantage of the system; neither, however, can it be made
the ground for disputing that the plebiscitum is in the
nature of an expression of the popular will. The assertion made at the time, that the plebiscitum affords
no opportunity for consultation between the several
political parties, or between the members of a party, was
a departure from the exact truth; these opportunities
were no more restricted in connection with a plebiscitum than with an election for the Legislative Body, and
we can see no reason why the people's power of judg-

ment should be less in the one than in the other instance. If this ability is not sufficient for the demands of a plebiscitum, then universal suffrage in general is a folly.

The exasperation of the Left was increased by the realization that the discussion of the Constitution or a plebiscitum was wholly without the province of the parliament. To be sure, a new Constitution was about to be enacted; but for the present the old one was still in force, and according to its provisions all power to act upon constitutional questions was reserved to the Emperor and the Senate. The Left Centre also complained so bitterly of this complete exclusion of the popular Chamber from the discussion of this important matter, that Ollivier sought and obtained the Emperor's consent to reply to an interpellation regarding it, presented by the Left, whereby all the floodgates of oratory were thrown wide open on April 4th and 5th.

After an exceedingly animated debate, three motions to pass to the order of the day were before the assembly; one by the Left, together with a direct rejection of the Senate's Draft on the ground of its being opposed to the principles of 1789; a second one by the Left' Centre, expressing appreciation of the reforms contemplated in the draft, to which, however, should be added the provision that henceforward no plebiscitum whose text had not previously been examined and approved by the two Chambers should be submitted to the people; a third, expressing entire confidence in the Government. After the first two of these had been rejected,

the third one was approved by 225 voices against 34
of the Left, the Left Centre having voted in favor
of the motion.

The triumph of the Ministry was complete; the
decision was made; no further discussion of the momentous question was possible in the Legislative Body,
and on April 13th, at the suggestion of Ollivier, the
Chamber adjourned until after the vote upon the plebiscitum should have been cast, since the deputies
wished to be among their constituents while the great
conflict was being waged.

This put an end to a ministerial crisis as well;
whereas the practical Prime Minister, Ollivier, saw
no objection to the institution of the plebiscitum either
for the present or for the future, the Minister of
Finance, Buffet, was, on principle, opposed to the plebiscitum in every respect. Count Daru, although he
had himself been the originator of the one now proposed, believed that in the future an appeal to the
plebiscitum should be allowed only in case the draft
of the plebiscitum had been approved by the two
Chambers. Both these gentlemen retired from the
Cabinet on April 14th; and in a few days their example
was followed by a third member, Marquis Talhouet.
Ollivier deferred filling the places thus left vacant
until after the decision of the plebiscitum. In the
interim, he himself assumed the administration of the
Department of Foreign Affairs; the Minister of Public
Instruction, Segris, that of Finance; and the Minister
of Fine Arts, Richard, that of Public Instruction.

Thus relieved of any further consideration for the three most powerful of his colleagues, Ollivier threw himself ardently into the agitation for the plebiscitum. He had promised to purge the elections for deputies of all official influence; the matter now before the public he regarded as of an entirely different nature, declaring that in connection with it there was but one official candidate, and that candidate was Liberty; to achieve it every patriotic citizen ought to use every influence at his command. He therefore charged all officials of his own department, as well as those of the interior administration, prefects, under-prefects, mayors, and police officers, to be "consumingly" active; in fact, he instigated an official agitation of such magnitude that it might have been the envy of Rouher.

It very soon appeared who the actual official candidate of the plebiscitum was. On April 20th the Senate approved the draft of the Constitution as submitted to it; and on the same day the Left published a manifesto which was no less than an out-and-out declaration of war against the empire in any form, and called upon the people to end the conflict in victory for themselves by answering "No" to the plebiscitum. "The 2d of December," it said, "brought the French nation under the yoke of one man; in the elections of 1869 the voice of the people declared against this personal *regimé*, and demanded in its place the government of the people by the people. It is now represented to you that through the decree of the Senate such a Government is to be established, and you are expected to recognize this by voting for the plebiscitum. You will, however, refuse to do this; for you are too well aware that the promised reform is a mere chimera. You have not forgotten that all the misery and outrage of the past eighteen years were brought upon you by two plebiscita. You will therefore not allow yourselves to be duped a third time, for you realize that only in a FREE DEMOCRACY can the liberty of the people and the nation's sovereignty be enduringly established."

Nothing could be more plainly spoken; should the plebiscitum result in a "No," the republic would be proclaimed.

The suspense was soon over.

On April 23d an imperial decree formulated the plebiscitum as follows:

The French people approve the liberal reforms which the Emperor, with the co-operation of the great bodies of State, has wrought in the Constitution since 1860, and sanction the Senate decree of April 20th, 1870.

Together with it appeared an imperial proclamation addressed to the people, which, after a retrospective glance at the restoration of the empire by the voice of the people, culminated in the appeal:

Give me now a fresh proof of confidence. In bringing to the urn an affirmative vote you will dispel the menacing danger of revolution, you will establish order and liberty upon a firm foundation, and render the TRANSMISSION OF THE CROWN TO MY SON MORE EASY.

A circular note addressed by the Ministers to all officials was of like tenor:

In 1852 the Emperor appealed to the people for power to restore order; in 1870 he appeals for power to establish liberty. The question which your vote will decide is not whether the empire shall continue, but only whether or not it shall undergo a liberal transformation. We must seek to give our country the prospect of a tranquil future, so that upon the throne as in the humblest cottage THE SON MAY FOL-LOW HIS FATHER IN PEACE.

Here, then, the purpose of the plebiscitum was boldly acknowledged to be the permanence of the hereditary monarchy, even without the expedient of war; and, as the sugar coating to sweeten the pill, it was accompanied by an extension of political freedom. The " one official candidate" was in reality the heir to the throne, the Prince Imperial.

From the Pyrenees to the Ardennes, France now became the scene of stirring activity. Manifestos and newspaper articles, central and local party committees, travelling preachers and government agent, — all these became factors that worked together or against one another with daily increasing energy.

A most anxious hour was passed on the afternoon of May 8th, when for a time the official reports had a dubious sound; and no one dared to admit even to himself what the full extent of the consequences of defeat might be. Soon, however, the sky brightened; and when in the evening the voting was at last over, the result showed how correct had been the judgment of Rouher and Daru. The plebiscitum had been approved by seven million suffrages, and rejected by only one and a half millions; an overwhelming majority had therefore spoken in favor of the new Constitution, and at the same time in favor of the hereditary monarchy. Notwithstanding all that could be said of the undue influence exerted by prefects, magistrates, and by the clergy, divided even upon this question, so tremendous a majority could not have been secured through artificial devices; it bespoke a mighty current of public opinion that had asserted itself at the polls. There was much to be criticised in the eighteen years during which Napoleon III. had reigned, but the result of the plebiscitum was an irresistibly convincing evidence of the Emperor's present popularity.

The opponents laid great stress upon the fact, that, of the three hundred thousand votes cast by the army, over forty thousand had been in the negative; which to our mind is but another instance in proof of the rule that to obey and not to vote is the business of the armed force.

Similarly it was emphasized, that in by far the greater number of large cities, which are generally regarded more as the centres of culture than are the villages, the majority had been on the negative side.

Despite these criticisms, the fact remained that the impression made by the event upon friend and foe alike was tremendous. It was generally believed that the Napoleonic Empire had taken a new lease of life, and was unassailable at least for twenty years to come. That the impetuous spirit of the Opposition had been broken, both the Chamber and the press gave evidence.

During the days of greatest agitation against the plebiscitum, the Left had divided, forming a close and an open fraction, as they were styled, one group even yet implacable, the other evincing a spirit of concession toward the expressed will of the people. The Left Centre had not only lost all influence with the Ministry, but was for the present completely disorganized in consequence of the difference of opinion existing among its leaders; there had been no party decision with regard to the plebiscitum, every member having been left wholly free to act. All sections of the Right had been united in their zealous exertions for the plebiscitum; even the Arcadians had for the time forgotten their distrust of the Ministry. Ollivier could now proceed unhindered to the re-formation of the Ministry.

His first effort was to restore the interrupted relations to the Left Centre. Since Segris remained permanently in charge of the Department of Finance, that of Public Instruction was assigned to Deputy Mege, one of the Vice-Presidents of the Legislative Body, and a party associate of Segris. To the position at the head of the Department of Public Works, left vacant by Talhouet, Deputy Plichon was nominated, who, being a moderate Liberal of decidedly clerical predilections, was well fitted to be a support to Ollivier in more than one respect. And finally, on May 15th, to every one's surprise, the portfolio of Foreign Affairs

was offered to Agénor de Gramont, Duke of Guiche
and Prince of Bidache, who for the past nine years had
been the representative of France at Vienna.

It was well known that the Emperor had no very
high regard for the ability of the new Minister of
Foreign Affairs; and among the people, too, the general opinion was not flattering to him. That Napoleon
suggested his nomination is not at all likely. Had
the Emperor really cherished plans of war at the time,
he would nevertheless hardly have selected for so important a post the man whom in 1869 he had excluded
from participation in the consultations regarding the
triple alliance, a preparatory step to war, because of
his inefficiency. If, on the other hand, Napoleon was
anxious to preserve peaceful relations with Prussia,
Gramont's advancement is still more inexplicable; for
the Duke's hatred of Prussia was quite as notorious
as was his indiscretion. We must therefore conclude
that Napoleon, being now a constitutional monarch,
accepted him in the belief that a gentleman of so in-
ferior mental calibre would make a Minister easily to
be managed, forgetting, however, that shallow-headed
individuals have not infrequently been also hard and
hot-headed, and with these qualities have carried the
wise but undecided along with them.

And who may it have been. by whom the Emperor
was persuaded to this nomination ?

Certain information with regard to this point I have
none ; the following facts may, however, throw some
light upon the question.

After Daru's retirement on April 14th, Ollivier had, as has been told, temporarily assumed the direction of foreign affairs. With evident pride he himself relates that a telegram was at once sent to the Vatican reading: " Daru dismissed; succeeded by Ollivier; the Council is free to act." Ollivier then withheld the French memorial from presentation to the Council, and a little later instructed Monsieur de Banneville in no way to discuss the Council, either with the Pope or with Antonelli. Meanwhile, the French troops were not recalled, and the States of the Church continued to be protected against an Italian attack. Thus the Pope and the Council were shielded against interruption, and the proclamation of papal infallibility was placed beyond the possibility of doubt.

Aside from the Roman affair, Ollivier searched the documents of the Foreign Office for general information regarding the immediate past; and, as he expressed himself later, the records of the negotiations concerning Luxemburg and the Treaty of Prague filled him with deep patriotic indignation at the repelling haughtiness of Bismarck and the cowardly weakness of the French Ministers. He tells us that then and there he made a vow, that, although he would by no means precipitate a war from a sense of injured national pride, he would, however, despite his love of peace and his German sympathies, conduct diplomatic negotiations with Prussia in a very different tone and with different results than had the Messieurs de Moustier and de Lavalette.

It is more than likely, therefore, that in Daru's place he desired a colleague who was disposed to protect the Council and the Papal States, and at the same time to conduct negotiations with Prussia with fitting firmness and spirit. Having these two qualities, it mattered little whether the new Minister possessed more or less information or talent, since the Prime Minister felt that out of his own superabundance he could supply any deficiency in this respect which might be found in his colleague in charge of the Foreign Office. From this point of view we can readily understand that Gramont must have been just the man for Ollivier; for in his tendencies he was thoroughly clerical, and it would have been difficult to find in all Europe any one more eager for an opportunity to strike at Prussia, and, above all else, at Bismarck.

To estimate the achievements of the great German statesman according to his principles and methods of action was wholly beyond Gramont's capacity. He saw in them no more than the triumphs of a successful course of disregard for the impositions and restrictions of the ordinary sense of duty and honor. In 1866 the story was told in Paris, that upon being informed of Gramont's enmity, Bismarck had given the terse reply: "He is the greatest blockhead in Europe." Incensed at this, Gramont had exclaimed to Count Mensdorf, "I will revenge France!" Moreover, the saying was often heard in Paris, that although Gramont was not actually a native of Gascony, still he was born just across its boundary.

His imaginative faculty was excitable and creative to a high degree; every impression produced by a strong emotion assumed the form of an imagined experience, an event of the reality of which, owing to the weakness of his memory and the dulness of his perception, he remained immutably convinced until the next excitement drove the old fantasy out of his mind, only to replace it by some freshly imagined fable. Moreover, once having in this way assumed a position, he was proof against all argument, the irritation caused by its refutation simply urging him on. He was as little open to conviction as was Ollivier, although for a wholly different reason. With Ollivier, this was to be found in the vanity of the successful orator and advocate, which prevented him from recognizing the truth in the arguments of others; whereas, with the dialectic of the virtuoso, he succeeded in persuading himself of the correctness of the most erroneous views. With Gramont it was merely the näive haughtiness of the aristocrat of circumscribed education, who in his opinions is undisturbed by any annoying consciousness of the rest of the world.

When he condescended to assume the arduous duties of a responsible Minister he declared himself wholly in sympathy with Ollivier's views: no offensive war, but energetic resentment of every affront.

Perhaps there remained this distinction, that in any difficulty which might arise Ollivier would resort to the sword with regret, whereas Gramont would do so with inward satisfaction. And herein Gramont would have found no scarcity of powerful sympathizers. His thorough antipathy to Prussia made him quite as welcome to the Minister of War and to the army as to the clergy who hoped for new *Gesta Dei per Francos* against Prussia and Italy. To the Arcadians he was also most acceptable; for, despite the plebiscitum, they still firmly believed that through Ollivier's liberal measures the monarchy would in a short time be rendered defenceless against the Republicans unless the dynasty should acquire renewed prestige through brilliant success in war.

And herein lay an indication of the change which the situation had undergone. The influence of the plebiscitum had been toward a peace policy; the crisis in the Ministry which it had induced had furthered the opposite tendencies. Daru had owed his nomination not to Ollivier alone, but to the wish of the Left Centre which was distinctly a peace party; for Gramont, the Extreme Right, a war party, had been active.

However, as yet Ollivier's interim administration still continued; since Gramont, before assuming his duties on June 1st, had returned to Vienna to make his adieus in person. Meanwhile France gave no sign of an intended departure from its present policy; European affairs had settled into a deep calm; in no direction did an occasion present itself for a characteristic assertion of French diplomacy.

About the middle of June, public opinion in Paris gave evidence of considerable agitation when it became known that the North German Confederation contemplated participating in a treaty concluded between Switzerland and Italy on October 15th, 1869. The Swiss Government had furnished twenty million and the Italian forty-five million francs toward the construction of a railway over the St. Gothard; and North Germany now held out the prospect of twenty millions more, which decided the choice of the St. Gothard as the point at which the railway should cross the Alps, a matter which until then had not been fully settled in Switzerland.

To contribute so large a sum of money toward a foreign railway, the nearest station of which was six hundred kilometres distant from the frontier of the Confederation, was certainly not an every day occurrence; and to induce the Reichstag to consent to the appropriation of the sum, Bismarck characterized the undertaking as one of great significance to Germany, not only from a commercial point of view, but from a political one as well; a significance which was so generally understood, and had been so frequently discussed, that he felt any further explanation to be unnecessary. His meaning was simply this, that at present Germany was dependent upon either the Austrian or the French Alpine railways in its intercourse with Italy, which would therefore be seriously interfered with in the event of a quarrel between these Great Powers. Being under the control of Switzerland, which was always neutral, there would be no such uncertainty in connection with the proposed St. Gothard railway, whereby security in our Italian relations would be greatly promoted.

It would seem that no transaction could be less
provocative of criticism than was this one ; however,
suspicion and dislike of Prussia having been once
aroused in Paris by Thiers and his associates, the circumstance that Bismarck had declared the St. Gothard
railway to be advantageous to Germany was sufficient
to create uneasiness there.   It was regarded as an evidence of malice that Prussia had deprived France of
this opportunity of profit; to be sure, Switzerland had,
in 1865, applied first to the French Government for
pecuniary aid, which had, however, been refused.   The
Government was now reproached with this by the
orators of the Left.   The disadvantage of competition
which the St. Gothard road would force upon the
French railways was pictured in vivid colors; but
above all else, the opportunities it afforded the Prussian love of conquest were presented to the hearers
in every possible and impossible aspect.   " By means
of it," exclaimed Keratry, " Prussia can in one night
transport an army from Mainz to Venice, whilst we
remain shut in between the Rhine and the Alps."

Hereupon the Minister of War informed him that
Prussia would require four days to move twenty-five
thousand men from Mainz to Verona, whereas France
could in the same time transport a whole army from
Lyons to Verona; and that, moreover, in such an
emergency it would be an easy matter to destroy the
Baden road at several points.   Gramont, too, spoke to
the same effect, declaring that there could be no doubt
that Switzerland would maintain its customary neu-

trality with regard to the St. Gothard road, and would not allow it to be used for the transportation of troops. The representations of the Ministers were so convincing, that when Gramont again arose to reply to renewed expressions of apprehension from Deputy Ferry, the Chamber saved him the trouble of further explanation by a vote to close the debate.

This was an instance when the endeavor of the French Government was wholly in the interest of peace. Before the week ended another event occurred which, although creating much less stir, was of a nature well calculated to influence the initiated few not to depart from this course.

As long as Daru was Minister of Foreign Affairs, Napoleon maintained as complete silence with respect to Archduke Albert's plan of campaign, discreetly locked away in his chest, as he did with regard to the Prince's remarks, as carefully preserved in his memory. When, on May 15th, Gramont was nominated to the Ministry, and Ollivier remained temporarily in charge of foreign affairs, the Emperor hoped as heretofore to be able to avoid war, especially since at the time neither Germany nor Italy gave the slightest indication of an offensive policy. Still, ever since 1866, he believed peace to be uncertain from one day to the next, and was therefore constantly employed with thoughts of how, in case a complication should arise, he might promote his prospects of victory. He was of course fully aware that he had no formal alliance with any Power to rely upon; the negotiations of the past

year had, however, given him hope that both Austria
and Italy would render him friendly assistance should
France be compelled to undertake a great war. He
now, on May 19th, submitted the Archduke's plan of
campaign to the examination of a council of the highest officers. After carefully performing their task,
these gentlemen came to the conclusion that the mobilization of the Austrian troops would require at least
six weeks, that of the Italian army a still longer time;
it was deemed unadvisable to expose the main army of
the French for so long a time in an isolated position far
from home.[1] A new plan was therefore worked out
and one of the officers, General Lebrun, a personal
friend of the Emperor, was sent on June 6th upon a
confidential mission, devoid of any political significance, to Vienna, there to discuss the matter with the
Archduke.

But even this led to no definite decision; the Archduke rejected the French plan, and agreed with Lebrun
upon a third one only in so far that it remained subject
to further revision. Before the General's departure
the Archduke urged him to seek to obtain a private
audience with Emperor Francis Joseph, notwithstanding the fact that the General was neither accredited
nor empowered by his Government. Lebrun consented,
although not without misgivings, and was most graciously received. He told the Emperor of his commission to the Archduke; without entering into a

---

[1] "Souvenirs du Général Jarras," p. 47. "Mission du Général Lebrun," in *Figaro* of January 19th, 1887.

discussion of the plan of the campaign, the Emperor remarked that he wished to employ this opportunity to make a frank declaration, namely, that under no consideration could he bind himself to declare war against Prussia simultaneously with France should a conflict between these two countries become unavoidable. He then referred to the difference of sympathies and opinions existing among the various races under his dominion; his German subjects would resist to the utmost a declaration of war against North Germany.

The plan of campaign, he said, appeared to him to be a most practicable one; he felt, however, that he could not too urgently beg the Emperor Napoleon not to rely upon any false hopes of Austrian assistance.

The prospect of an alliance had not, therefore, been held out by even so much as a verbal promise. Again, as in January, 1867, Napoleon had reason to exclaim, "I have not a friend in the world!" Austria was firmly determined upon neutrality; Ollivier's Roman policy had rendered an Italian alliance highly improbable. The situation was surely one to place a damper upon any warlike spirit which might arise in Paris.

It was not surprising, therefore, that on June 30th, in connection with the deliberations upon the army budget for 1871, the Minister of War should, in view of the unclouded prospect of peace, declare himself content with a levy of ninety thousand recruits instead of the usual one hundred thousand. When later, in the same connection, Glais-Bizoin advocated the discontinuance of the great standing armies, and Thiers in reply argued their existence to be the surest means of preserving peace, exclaiming, "Do we wish to promote peace? Then we must first of all be very peaceable, and secondly be very strong," Ollivier arose to say, "I wish to state that the Government entertains no fears whatever that peace will be disturbed, for never has it been more certain than at present. Look in whatsoever direction we will, no question is encountered which is at all likely to prove dangerous. Upon all the Cabinets of Europe the conviction has forced itself that treaties must be respected, especially those two upon which the peace of Europe chiefly rests, the Treaty of Paris of 1856, securing peace for the Orient, and the Treaty of Prague, securing peace for Germany."

This final allusion to a treaty upon which, as was notorious, the contracting parties placed two entirely different constructions indicated that the love of peace was after all but conditional. The subject was not pursued further, however.

In the English Parliament also it was announced at this time that in foreign affairs a dead calm prevailed.

The day after Ollivier's declaration, on July 1st, the Emperor was again laid upon a bed of suffering by a renewed attack of his ailment. Here was an additional reason why hostile intentions were not to be expected of the French Government.

BOOK XXIV.

ORIGIN OF THE FRENCH WAR.

BOOK XXII.

OR, THE SPANISH-AMERICAN WAR.

ORIGIN OF THE FRENCH WAR.

WHEN amidst the profound tranquillity prevailing throughout Europe in the spring of 1870, a quarrel suddenly arose by which within twelve days two great nations were precipitated into a war of unparalleled results and colossal sacrifices, the world demanded to know upon whom rested the responsibility for this tremendous disturbance, bringing unexampled renown to the one side, and fearful disaster to the other. Opinions differed in sharp contrast; and even now, after a lapse of twenty years, are not agreed.

In France it is to this day the general belief that Bismarck, excellently prepared for war and hard pressed by difficulties at home, wished to entice Emperor Napoleon into a declaration of war; that through an intrigue of long preparation he systematically offended the French nation's self-respect; and that the Emperor, although aware of the inadequacy of his military preparations, allowed himself, with deplorable stupidity, to be led into the well-devised trap.

In Germany, from the outset, the conviction has prevailed that the *casus belli* declared in Paris was no more than a threadbare excuse to grasp the sword, seek revenge for Sadowa, and throw the German nation back into the old state of dismemberment.

More recently, however, it has been claimed that evidence has been discovered establishing the fact that for two years Napoleon was engaged in attempts to bring about a great European coalition for the purpose of an attack upon Prussia; but that, fortunately for Germany, on the eve of its consummation he was carried away by impulse to declare war. That by this newly made discovery Napoleon's attitude, just before the declaration of war, is placed in a false light, our narrative has demonstrated.

On both sides there are those, as need hardly be mentioned, whose judgment is calmer and whose research is more careful, and who therefore represent in varying degree views that are more moderate.

Under these circumstances my readers will, I trust, forgive me if, supported by valuable and hitherto unpublished material gathered from manifold sources, I seek to relate the events of those twelve days most accurately and correctly, and consequently with an attention to detail not elsewhere permitted to my narrative.

CHAPTER I.

THE HOHENZOLLERN CANDIDACY.

In Spain the revolution of September, 1869, was followed by a period of great uncertainty and agitation. The victors had established a provisional government, at the head of which were Marshal Serrano as Regent, and Marshal Prim as Minister of War and President of the Ministry.   Both men were monarchists, their view being the prevailing one also in the constituent Cortez convened in February, 1869.   The duty next at hand was, therefore, to find a royal race to supply the place of the dethroned dynasty.

All such plans were, however, vehemently and bitterly opposed by four different parties, who, fortunately for the Government, pursued one another quite as relentlessly as they did the present head of the State. Of these factions the largest and most daring one was that of the Republicans, who at various points and without any attempt at concealment were preparing the country for another uprising.

There were also the adherents of the dethroned queen, Isabella, who were endeavoring to combine for the purpose of reinstating either the Queen or her son,

Alfonso.   As yet these were few in number, but enjoyed a most decided advantage in possessing Napoleon's declared favor.   In the Basque Provinces the remnants of the old Carlist Party were bestirring themselves, although without meeting with any marked response from the people, who were weary of war. And finally there was the circle of friendly admirers surrounding Queen Isabella's brother-in-law, the Duke of Montpensier, the youngest son of Louis Philippe. In January, 1868, Prim had opened negotiations with him, holding out prospects of the throne to him if he would espouse the cause of the revolution.   Prim had, however, turned from him in disgust when the Duke's extreme discretion induced him to keep out of sight on the battle-field of Alcolea.[1]

In the tumult of this party conflict, a memorial with regard to the candidates likely to appear in connection with the coming choice of ruler was published by an influential member of the Liberal Party, Salazar y Mazarredo,[2] State Councillor and Deputy.   In it he demonstrated that neither Bourbon nor Orleans could be thought of in connection with the throne; that the difference of creed must inevitably debar an English prince, even should he bring with him Gibraltar as dower; or a Prussian, and were it even the famous

---

[1] This, as well as what follows, is according to Salazar's memorial of October 23d, 1869.

[2] Gramont in his books and Chaudordy in his deposition insinuate that Salazar was influenced to this action by Prussia, but there has not been so much as an attempt to prove this intimation. With regard to the manner in which the candidacy originated, Chaudordy offers a number of data, not one of which is confirmed.

military hero, Prince Frederick Charles. He then suggested in the first place the name of Ferdinand, titular
King of Portugal, who had been Prince Consort to
Maria da Gloria when she was the reigning queen of
that country; the second place he accorded to the
Prince's son-in-law, the Hereditary Prince Leopold of
Hohenzollern-Sigmaringen, in whom, he claimed, all
the qualities most desirable were combined, — firmness,
prudence, integrity; a man of thirty-five, hence in the
prime of life, happily wedded and blessed with children; not Ultramontane[1] in his inclinations, and yet
an orthodox Catholic.

The proposals put forward by the memorial soon
found their way into a number of newspapers, and, as
can be readily imagined, were discussed with much interest.[2] Toward the end of March, 1869, the French
Ambassador at Berlin, Count Benedetti, learned that
his former Spanish colleague, Rancès, lately transferred

[1] New Catholic was the expression in Spain.

[2] Lauser (*Spanische Geschichte*, I., 219) claims to have learned from
the Spanish diplomat Marcoartu, that in March, 1869, the candidacy of
Prince Leopold had been suggested to Napoleon for consideration by a
relative of the Emperor; that the Empress had, however, opposed it,
her former friendship for the House of Hohenzollern having been transformed into enmity by the failure of one of her matrimonial projects,
through a refusal on the part of the Prince of Roumania. Marcoartu's
account is, however, rendered highly improbable by the entries in the
diary of King Charles of Roumania, made during his sojourn in Paris
in the fall of 1869, as well as by those regarding the manner in which
Napoleon received the announcement of his intended marriage; as also
by letters of Madame Cornu, and by certain remarks made by the Empress in conversation with the Roumanian *chargé d'affaires* at Constan-
tinople. (*Deutsche Revue*, November, 1893.) Every word of the diary
testifies to the unbroken relations of intimate friendship between Napoleon and the Hohenzollerns.

to Vienna, had recently spent five days in Berlin, and had during that time had two long interviews with Bismarck.   Forthwith the suspicion was aroused in the Ambassador that the subject of discussion must have been the elevation of Prince Leopold to the Spanish throne.   Bismarck being at the time in Varzin, Benedetti made inquiry of the Undersecretary of State, Von Thile, from whom he received the reply, as he reported on March 31st, 1869, that Von Thile had heard absolutely nothing of such intentions; and that he could, moreover, assure the Ambassador upon his word of honor that Rancès had not so much as alluded to such a possibility, but on the contrary, had referred to the Duke of Montpensier as the probable candidate for the throne.

Every word of Thile's statement conformed entirely to the truth.   Bismarck himself could have given the Ambassador no other information; for as yet not a word from Madrid regarding the future occupant of the Spanish throne had been received, either by the Prussian Government or by Prince Leopold.

The Spanish Ministry was composed of members of the Liberal Union and of the Progressist Party; Prim was a Progressist, Deputy Salazar a Unionist.   Prim, like Salazar, would have preferred a Portuguese candidate to all others, but failing to procure such a one, would have sought an Italian Prince, and not a Hohenzollern.   Accordingly, on April 4th, 1869, he induced the Ministry to offer the crown to King Ferdinand, and upon his instant and not very gracious refusal on the

6th, to extend a like invitation to the King of Italy for his second son, Amadeo, Duke of Aosta. Here, too, the answer was unhesitatingly given that the House of Savoy was not so rich in princes that it could resign one of them to Spain.

Prim was seriously annoyed. In view of Napoleon's endeavors for the restoration of Isabella, he had every reason to assume that neither an Austrian nor a Bavarian prince would accept the dangerous gift. But where else could he find a Catholic prince? Only through the pressure of necessity, therefore, was he induced to act upon Salazar's second proposal, and allow an inquiry to be made of Prince Charles Anthony at Düsseldorf as to whether Prince Leopold would consider an offer of the Spanish crown.

The answer was a direct refusal; the Prince, King William, and Bismarck were all of the same mind with regard to it.[1]

Meanwhile Count Benedetti had been summoned to Paris to participate in a consultation of some kind. Upon this occasion he told the Emperor of his interview with Thile, adding, however, that Thile was not always intrusted with Bismarck's secrets, and that it was therefore his intention before long to approach the Minister himself with regard to the matter. Napoleon approved of this, and explained to him that the elevation of Montpensier, being anti-dynastic, would be an affront to himself alone, and that he could therefore suffer it; whereas, on the other hand, the Hohen-

[1] Compare Benedetti, " Ma Mission," pp. 307 and 331.

zollern candidacy, being anti-national, would not be
tolerated by the people; it must therefore be prevented. (This, we observe, was not the expression of
his personal view, but of a popular opinion.) Accordingly the Minister's instructions to the Ambassador were to interview Bismarck upon the subject,
but to regulate his own conversation in such a manner
as would avoid any appearance of a wish on the part
of France to enter into negotiations with regard to
the matter.

After his return to Berlin, Benedetti reported on
May 11th that Bismarck had not shown himself at all
averse to a discussion of the subject, and had at once
declared that in view of the very uncertain condition
of affairs in Spain, the King would most assuredly
not advise the Prince to accept the crown should the
Cortes proffer it to him; and that Prince Anthony, as
he, Bismarck, knew with certainty, quite agreed with
the King.

" If full reliance were to be placed on his word,"
wrote Benedetti, " we might feel re-assured; but past
experience leads me to believe that he has not fully
disclosed his mind to me. I therefore remarked to
him that the Prince could not, of course, comply with
the wish of the Cortes without the King's consent, and
that the Prince's decision must therefore be such as
the King might command. Bismarck ACKNOWLEDGED
THIS TO BE THE CASE; but instead of assuring me that
THE KING WAS FULLY DETERMINED UNDER ANY CIR-
CUMSTANCES to insist upon the Prince's refusal, he re-

turned to his former position, reiterating that the perils by which the new sovereign would find himself surrounded were such that the King would surely advise the Prince against the step. 'Moreover,' he added, who knows whether the offer will ever be made? 'Whether so ambitious a man as Prim will not in the end prefer to keep the highest place for himself?' Before leaving the subject, I impressed upon him the fact, that, although the Emperor's Government was inclined to be most circumspect in its observation of events in Spain, nevertheless their further development would never cease to be a matter of supreme interest to it. Bismarck, however, did not go beyond his previous statement. He took pains to avoid the direct declaration that the King would IN NO EVENT allow the Prince to accept, although Thile had given me this assurance on his word of honor. We can but conclude, therefore, that Bismarck intends to reserve to the King full freedom of action for any future event. To put the question to him directly, and thus force him to a reply which might lead to serious consequences, I did not deem advisable, owing to my instructions to observe extreme caution."

Here we have an excellent example of how a suspicious mind can, from absolutely nothing, draw inferences which are so self-deluding that the actual facts appear wholly distorted; not infrequently the seeds of terrible catastrophes are thus sown.

Benedetti, in this connection, refers to his report of March 31st as representing Thile to have pledged his word that the King would never consent to the candidacy of the Prince; whereas in reality the report speaks of Thile's word as having been given merely in assurance of the fact that he had not had the least intimation of the matter. Further, Benedetti represents Bismarck as having conceded that the Prince in his decision would be entirely subject to the King's command; whereas we know from what we learned of the provisions of the Hohenzollern family compact in connection with the Roumanian question [1] that Bismarck COULD not have said this; he may have said that the Prince WOULD not accept without the King's consent, but surely not that he COULD not. And finally, Benedetti had not given Bismarck the slightest intimation that Napoleon was decidedly opposed to the Hohenzollern candidacy, but had deemed it sufficient to allude to the fact, of which everyone was aware, that France was greatly interested in the Spanish throne question. To him it seemed but a matter of course that Prussia must engage NEVER to entertain a view differing from the present one; consequently he regarded it as a serious ground for suspicion that Bismarck, into whose mind the possibility of such a demand did not enter, should persistently confine his statements to the present phase of the case, and not include all possible conditions which the future might bring about.

And yet Benedetti was a man inclined to peace; to him it would have been cause for rejoicing had France unconditionally accepted the consummation of German

[1] Vol. VI., p. 417.

unity.[1]   He did not dream that by his endeavors to draw from Prussia a promise that the candidacy would be positively forbidden, both for the present and the future, he had suggested a fateful thought in Paris; one which would prove the cause of frightful bloodshed and of a conflict most disastrous to his country.

After the occurrence of these conversations reported by Benedetti, several months passed during which the Hohenzollerns heard not a word regarding the Spanish question.   At Madrid the Cortes completed the Constitution on June 1st, and then reinvested Serrano with authority to conduct the regency.   This, however, was by no means conducive to a more tranquil state of affairs in the country; but, on the contrary, both Carlists and Republicans now endeavored with redoubled energy to gain the upper hand.   In July the Carlist pretender himself appeared on the scene of action in the Basque Provinces, and succeeded in the organization of armed troops at several points. The Government, however, took such vigorous steps to suppress the attempt, that order was restored within a few weeks, and the pretender, in great trepidation, fled to France.

The energy and extent of the Republican agitation, on the other hand, were such as to give the provisional administration sufficient cause to be anxious to find an occupant for the vacant throne as speedily as possible. In this predicament Prim yielded to Salazar's enthu-

[1] Compare, in " Ma Mission en Prusse," the exhaustive report of January 5th, 1868, particularly on p. 265.

siastic representations, and gave him permission to go
to Germany, there to present the Spanish offer to
Prince Leopold in person, and to assure him that if
he were at all inclined to respond to the call he could
feel assured of a large majority in the Cortes. At
the same time Prim gave Salazar a letter of introduction to a German acquaintance in Munich,[1] who was
in a position to put him in communication with the
Prince of Hohenzollern.

About the middle of September, preserving the deepest secrecy, Salazar hastened to Munich, and upon his
arrival there was announced by the Munich acquaintance to the Prince, then sojourning at Castle Weinburg
in Switzerland. The Prince having signified his willingness to receive him, Salazar hastened to the village
nearest the castle, and there awaited the evening, when,
in the darkness of night, he made his way to the castle,
and gained admission without having been recognized
by any one.

He was received with utmost courtesy, but without
the slightest sign of enthusiasm. The Prince evinced
little inclination to the idea, and the Hereditary Prince
unhesitatingly declined the offer. But Salazar did not
allow himself to be so easily discouraged. He pictured
the excellency of the conditions which awaited the
Prince in Spain; although he admitted that the attitude of the Republicans was sufficiently dangerous to

[1] That which immediately follows was learned through a conversation held many years ago with the acquaintance to whom reference is
made.

make an early decision advisable, since all might be lost by long-continued hesitation. He asked to be told the obstacles which were in the way, and under what conditions a favorable answer might be expected. This led to a further discussion, in which the closing words of the Prince were to this effect: When the Spanish Government can lay before me convincing evidence that Emperor Napoleon and King William both regard my son's accession to the throne of Spain with favor, and not until then, can I give the subject serious consideration.

This was the only reply that Salazar could take back with him to Spain.

It is again characteristic of the relation of the Hohenzollern House to the Crown of Prussia, that Prince Anthony upon this occasion left the inquiry to be made of King William to the Spanish Government; whereas any true prince of Prussia would, without doubt, have hastened at once to inform the sovereign head of his family of what had occurred. No less significant, on the other hand, is the fact that, as Prince Leopold told an English newspaper correspondent a year later,[1] when Emperor Napoleon was informed of what had transpired, he raised no objections at the time, and still less did he give any intimation that the question might develop into a cause for war.

Napoleon's conduct upon this occasion can be readily understood; for the negotiations had remained wholly

[1] "War Diary of William Russell," German translation by Von Schlesinger, p. 28.

without result, and in the event of a future offer, acceptance had been made conditional upon Napoleon's
approval.   There was therefore no occasion for a hasty
protest, which, if presented at this juncture, might mar
the cordial relations which for years had existed between the Emperor and the Prince, and might also
give rise to unnecessary negotiations with Spain.

When Salazar reported the result of his mission at
Madrid, Prim at once pronounced it to be a politely
framed, but none the less positive, refusal, and therefore, still actuated by his earliest preference, induced
the Ministry to make a new application to Victor Emmanuel, this time asking his sanction to the candidacy
of his young nephew, Thomas, Duke of Genoa, for the
Spanish throne.   But here, too, difficulties did not fail
to present themselves without delay.   Although the
Republican agitation, which just at this time culminated in open revolt, was completely subdued within
a week, and order and quiet were restored throughout
the country with a firm hand, yet the question of a
choice of king effected a new division of parties.   In
opposition to Prim's advocacy of an Italian candidate,
Salazar, on October 23d, issued a revised form of his
appeal to the country to place upon the throne the
Hereditary Prince of Hohenzollern ; and, could he have
vouched for acceptance, he would doubtlessly have
found ready response among his friends of the Liberal
Union.   Since, as matters stood, this was not possible,
the prospects of a third candidate grew brighter, those
of the Duke of Montpensier who, although he had

avoided exposing himself to the bullets at Alcolea, now came forward with alacrity to recognize the new Constitution, and encourage his adherents to advocate his election among the members of the Cortes.

For Prim this was all highly vexatious. He had broken so completely with Montpensier that the latter's accession to the throne meant political annihilation for him. Meanwhile in Florence the prospects for his plans took on an unexpectedly favorable aspect. Victor Emmanuel evinced a much greater inclination to the election of his nephew than he had shown for that of his son. What was most auspicious, however, was that Napoleon, who in the interest of the deposed Isabella had expressed himself as opposed to the Duke of Aosta, had by this time recognized the hopelessness of her cause; and, being averse to both Montpensier and Hohenzollern, now used his influence in Florence with great effect in favor of the youthful Thomas, so that Prim for the time found his endeavor furthered by the mighty support of France.

Upon his opponents in the Cortes who were members of the Union all this made no impression whatever; for they rather resented the idea of having a king forced upon them by a foreign Power; and for this very reason a considerable number of them advocated the choice of Montpensier. All of them, however, opposed that of the Duke of Genoa, on the ground that he was still a minor, and Spain in its present crisis needed above all else a strong man at the helm of State. In this they found an unexpected ally in the widowed mother of

the young Duke, a lady of sense and decision, who refused with unwavering firmness to yield her son to so
perilous an adventure. King Victor Emmanuel hesitated
for some time; when, however, it became evident that
the Duke's popularity with the Cortes was waning, he
finally declared, on December 31st, 1867, that his action
could not be contrary to the wish of the Duke's mother,
and that he must therefore decline Prim's offer with
thanks.

And so matters still stood as they had at the outset,
a vacant throne and a kingdom without a king. Party
dissension made the election of a native of the country
impossible; and yet with offended pride the sons of
Spain were compelled to behold the once world-subdu-
ing crown of Spain disdained by foreign princes.

The firm union of the Progressists and Unionists,
wherein the present Government found its chief support, had been severely shaken by the conflict caused
by the latest attempt to procure a king; and to Prim's
discomfiture he now beheld the seeds sown by the
friends of Montpensier, the candidate most distasteful
to him, spring up in every direction. He realized that
there was nothing so desirable as a return to combined
action between the two liberal parties. It was this
which now disposed Prim to lend a more willing ear to
Salazar's representations than he had during the past
year. Salazar urged upon the Marshal that the Hohenzollern refusal had not been an unqualified one, and
that the Prince had expected the Spanish Government
to obtain the consent of Napoleon and King William.

To be sure, Salazar was obliged to admit that it was to be feared Napoleon would not suffer a Hohenzollern to ascend the Spanish throne.

But at this point it became evident that Prim's regard for Napoleon had been impaired through the fruitlessness of French influence in Florence. " What objection can the Emperor have to the Prince of Hohenzollern?" he asked. " Our original choice was not a Prussian prince. Were we not compelled to endure the most cruel derision from the Paris press when our first efforts proved futile? We have been unfortunate everywhere; and, as every one knows, the Duke of Montpensier or the republic will also encounter Napoleon's veto. Shall this be reason sufficient to condemn the September achievements to a never-ending state of incompleteness? What has France to fear from a Prussian prince upon the throne of Spain?" [1]

Prim believed that although Napoleon would receive the announcement ungraciously he would in the end, nevertheless, prefer the Prince of Hohenzollern, with whom he was upon terms of personal friendship, to the Duke of Montpensier as head of the Spanish Government.

The result of the consultation was that in February,[2] with Serrano's consent, Salazar was again sent to Germany to reopen the negotiations with the Hohenzollerns, which had been suspended in the fall. He took

[1] As stated in Salazar's preface to the third issue of his pamphlet, July 8th, 1870.

[2] " *Vers le mois de mars,*" says Gramont in " La France et la Prusse," p. 21.

with him a personal letter to King William, which he was commissioned to deliver into the King's hands if possible,[1] and another of like tenor to Bismarck;[2] the object of both being, of course, to discover the views of the recipients with regard to an eventual candidacy of the Prince of Hohenzollern, and, if possible, to incline them in its favor. Both letters contained an earnest request that profoundest secrecy be preserved, to the end that the undertaking might not be frustrated by hostile party intrigues.[3]

From beginning to end the overture was of an unofficial character;[4] neither the Spanish Minister of Foreign Affairs, nor any member of either of the two embassies, had taken part in the transaction or had any knowledge of it.[5] From the outset King William was determined on his part, also, to treat the matter not as

[1] The King's statement to Benedetti. Benedetti, "Ma Mission en Prusse," p. 331. Benedetti misunderstood these remarks made by the King, believing him to refer to the later negotiations conducted in June, which is utterly impossible, since it is an established fact that no Spanish agent either sought or obtained an audience with the King at Ems. In fact, the King knew nothing of the negotiations carried on behind his back until after their conclusion, and, therefore, could not have given Bismarck information regarding "divers incidents," since he knew of none such. Nor did Bismarck receive his first information regarding the issue of the negotiations through an official announcement made to him by the King, but from a gentleman accompanying Salazar. It is highly important that this fact should be definitely established, since the consequences of Benedetti's error were so grave.

[2] Gramont, at the place mentioned.

[3] As stated by Bismarck to the Federal Council, according to Hahn, "Deutsche Politik," 1867–1870, p. 354. To be found in other publications also.

[4] According to the same statement.

[5] As stated by Prim. according to Benedetti, p. 419. As stated by Rascon, according to Gramont, pp. 19, 365.

an affair of State, but as one of family interest alone. Consequently he refused Salazar an audience ; neither the Ministry at home nor the Prussian embassy at Madrid received instructions from him to give the subject consideration.[1] As head of the family he called the Hohenzollern magnates together to a family consultation, to determine upon the course to pursue should the Spanish crown be actually offered to Prince Leopold.

As had often been the case theretofore upon occasions of less moment, and has been since, the King invited the most trusted of his advisers, Count Bismarck, to be present at these discussions. During their progress the disinclination which Prince Leopold had frequently manifested since 1869 evidently remained unchanged. The King's attitude was as we learned it to have been in 1866 and again in the spring of 1869. It conformed in every respect to the prescriptions of the Hohenzollern family compact. The King allowed the Prince full liberty to decide for himself; if, however, he desired advice, the King's counsel was decidedly against the undertaking, unless, indeed, the Prince felt a strong inward calling to assume the responsibility.[2]

Under these circumstances the matter would have been very quickly disposed of had not Bismarck ex-

[1] Benedetti, p. 333.

[2] Compare the communications of Baron Werther made immediately after his return from Ems to the French Minister, according to Hahn (in the publication to which reference has been made), p. 318; also the statement to be found in a letter written by Wilmowski, " Deutsche Revue," January, 1894, p. 5.

pressed an entirely different view. Regarding the motives which actuated him I am enabled to give a somewhat explicit account. Among them hostility to France, or the wish to utilize the occasion as a means of goading France on to an over-hasty declaration of war, had no place whatever. In this assembly, gathered for consultation, there was even less thought than had Marshal Prim that the candidacy of the Prince would call forth a decided protest from Napoleon, much less provoke him to designs of war (an inference which had evidently been drawn from the Emperor's attitude in connection with the Roumanian choice of sovereign, and from his silence with respect to the communication received by him from Weinburg in September).

In discussing the candidacy, the question whether France would oppose it, and the attitude to be assumed in that event, was not so much as suggested. Bismarck was of the opinion that, owing to Napoleon's dislike for Montpensier, as well as to the relations existing between the Emperor and Prince Charles Anthony, it would not be difficult for Prince Leopold, immediately after his election, to obtain a personal interview with Napoleon in Paris, and come to an understanding with him in perfect harmony and uninterrupted friendship. This, he believed, would be quite possible if the Prince, in conformity to the demands of his new position, would forget his German origin, and become wholly a Spaniard.[1]

---

[1] Just after the battle of Sedan, when in the darkness of night Bismarck was riding to his quarters accompanied by a. Prussian general,

This supposition having been once assumed, Bismarck could point out many advantages, although, in truth, not very great ones, which, owing to the similarity of interests between the two countries, would arise to Prussia should a prince friendly to that country rule at Madrid. Further, he was of the opinion that although the contemplated step would have been an utterly reckless one in 1869, when the waves of revolution were running high in Spain, yet now, after the rebellion had been twice suppressed, and the Government had acquired strength upon which reliance could be placed, there was much to be hoped from the accession of an able monarch. Moreover, before irretrievably deciding the question, the stability of conditions in Spain could be ascertained.

Whenever Bismarck advocated a point with earnestness and persistence he was wont, as the world well knows, to make a deep impression upon his hearers. Upon this occasion, however, before the discussions were concluded he was attacked by a tedious indisposition, which compelled him to seek rest at Varzin, where he grew so seriously ill that he was forbidden to take any thought of political affairs for a long time.

During his absence the favorable aspect of the Span-

---

the conversation fell upon the origin of the war, and Bismarck related the events of the candidacy. In this connection he used the expression, "It would have required of the Prince that he should turn Spaniard, and forget his German origin." He was not aware that the Prince and several officers were riding directly behind him; to his surprise the Prince called out, "Pardon me! A Spaniard I would willingly have become, but never would I have forgotten that I am a German."

ish offer found no representative in the family council; both the King and the Hereditary Prince remained unshaken in their disinclination to the project; and early in May a telegram addressed to Marshal Prim was sent to the Prussian legation at Madrid,[1] definitely stating it to be the Prince's intention to decline the offer, should it be made him. The King believed that this matter, so annoying to him, was now disposed of definitively.

Upon his return to Berlin toward the end of May, Bismarck could not alter the situation; but to Prim, who had insisted upon an expression of opinion from him also, he wrote a consoling letter, in which he spoke encouragingly of the Prince's candidacy at some future time, saying it was an excellent idea, one which ought not to be relinquished, but regarding which it would be wise to conduct negotiations with the Prince himself, and not with the Prussian Government.[2]

Notwithstanding these hopeful possibilities, the still vacant throne placed the Spanish Government in an exceedingly embarrassing position for the moment. The factions which had been subdued took courage afresh; after the second refusal had been received from the

---

[1] As stated in Prim's speech to the Cortes in the sitting of June 11th. The date given was learned through word of mouth from Bernhardi, at that time military attaché to the Prussian legation at Madrid.

[2] Gramont, "La France et la Prusse," at the place mentioned. "Passé et Présent," p. 88. Chaudordy also refers to this letter; its text, as he quotes it, does not, however, agree with Gramont's statement in detail, although the general tenor of the two is identical. A third letter of like purport is to be found in Bl. Jerrold's "Life of Napoleon III.," Vol. IV., p. 456, although its authority is not mentioned.

Prince of Hohenzollern, the adherents of the Duke of Montpensier among the Unionists rapidly increased in number, and the great majority of the deputies, weary of this fruitless detention, were importunate in their desire to return to their homes; and yet should the assembly adjourn before this question of an occupant for the throne had been settled, a deep gloom threatened to fall upon the future of the country.

Prim knew not whither to turn for another and happily more willing candidate. The situation grew desperate; and so he came to the hardly less desperate determination to make a fourth attempt to secure the same candidate, despite the discouraging replies he had received to all the confidential inquiries he had set afoot. He decided to open the new negotiations, not with the Prussian Government, but with the Hohenzollerns themselves, who by this time had left Berlin, and were in South Germany. Though success had not been possible WITH the knowledge of King William, Prim still hoped to gain his object behind the King's back. For that there was such a possibility Salazar, who was aware of the position accorded to the Hohenzollern princes by their family compact, had informed him; and he therefore knew that from a legal point of view the Prince could accept, even should the King refuse his consent.

This time the intention was not to inquire of Prince Leopold what his attitude would be IF the crown were offered him, but to proffer it under the condition of certainty as guaranteed by the confirming action of the

Cortes. This required first of all that the election should be placed beyond doubt in the Cortes. To this end Marshal Prim effected the enactment of a resolution by that body making an absolute majority, not of the members present, but of the whole number of deputies, namely 273 votes, necessary to a choice. This was the death-knell of Montpensier's candidacy; there was not the remotest prospect that he could command so large a number.

No rival now stood in the way of the Hohenzollern candidacy; and Prim, again with the full approval of Serrano, found it no difficult task to persuade the principal leaders of the two great parties to consent to it. They, too, were requested to maintain complete silence with regard to it, but most of those who were initiated into the secret kept it but illy. On June 11th Prim addressed the Cortes at length upon the throne question, for the double purpose of allaying the impatience of the deputies, and of eliciting from them an expression of consent to the plans he entertained.

After referring to the refusals received from the titular King of Portugal and the Dukes of Aosta and Genoa, he continued: " You now probably expect, gentlemen, that I am about to propose the name of a new candidate with whom I have opened negotiations in the name of the Spanish Government. This, however, is not my intention, since it would not only be highly indiscreet, but would most likely lead to complications; and, aside from this, I have given my word in promise of silence. You, gentlemen, will undoubtedly approve of my reticence. (Cries of Yes, yes!) The candidate whom I have in mind would, unquestionably, meet the requirements of Spain : he is of royal lineage (*sic*), a Catholic, and of age. But fate decreed that upon this page of our history also should be recorded an unsuccessful attempt to procure a King. With as great courtesy as good will, I have been apprised that the Prince cannot at the present moment accept the crown. The Government has therefore thought it advisable to turn to the Cortes, and make this assembly the arbiter of the question. Fortune has not favored the Government in its negotiations ; we are not in a position to present to you the name of a candidate, at least not to-day. But shall we be able to do so to-morrow, or the next day? That is the very point upon which I can give you no definite information. I can only assure you that the Government and the monarchically inclined members of this assembly are actuated by one and the same spirit, and that the Government has not been deprived of all prospect of finding a King. Without designating a definite time or date, the Government will continue to pursue the matter with both caution and reserve until it shall be enabled to present to you the name of a candidate who shall be one to compel public opinion in his favor."

He concluded with the remark, that although the prolongation of the interim was doubtlessly an evil, yet the Government held control of the means wherewith to ward off any dangers which might be induced by it.

Thus, as we have seen, he mentioned no name; and yet there could hardly have been a doubt with regard to this point among his hearers. Salazar's pamphlets and Prim's conferences with the party leaders had made the name of Hohenzollern famous; all the world felt certain that Prince Leopold was the candidate who had declined. So said the reports which the correspondents of the *Times* and *Daily News* sent to London; such was the opinion of the Italian Ambassador, Cerutti, as expressed to the Madrid academician, Lauser; so, later, Herr von Bernhardi assured me with the remark that at the Prussian legation, ever since the appearance of Salazar's first pamphlet, the entire proceeding was looked upon as a rash venture on the part of Prim.

Who this future candidate was to whom Prim referred, every one except the initiated few was left to decide for himself; whether it was again the Prince of Hohenzollern, or a Bavarian or an Austrian Prince, the speech in no way indicated. Of two persons we can assume with certainty that they had no thought of a renewed overture to be made the Prince of Hohenzollern, — King William, who was aware that the offer had been thrice declined; and Emperor Napoleon, who now knew of at least two refusals, and who had also been assured that without his consent the offer would not so much as receive consideration from the Hohenzollerns.

However, on June 14th, only three days after his speech to the Cortes, Prim sent Salazar, now fully provided with all the requisite credentials of his Govern-

ment, to Sigmaringen.   Arrived there, Salazar found
the mood of both father and son greatly changed in
favor of Spain.   Through what influence, I cannot say.
Soon thereafter it was rumored in Berlin that Prince
Charles Anthony had come to the conclusion that the
position of King of Spain was after all more desirable
than that of a Prussian staff-officer.   Perhaps Bismarck's arguments presented during the March conferences, although at that time without apparent effect
upon the Prince, had upon longer reflection made acceptance of the crown appear in the light of a patriotic
duty.   However that may be,. he now met Salazar's
urgent appeal with the single condition that the election to the Spanish throne should be deferred for three
months.[1]   The events now to be related show, however,
that he did not insist upon this condition.   At any
rate, on June 20th he decided, and, without previously
consulting the King, gave the Spanish envoy his promise to accept.

On the same day the King arrived at Ems to enjoy
the baths as was his wont.   He was accompanied only
by a number of adjutants and Legation Counsellor
Abeken.   It was here that King William received the
communication from the Prince (a simple act of courtesy, as Salazar styled it), stating that, owing to the
promptings of an inward calling, he had accepted the
proffer of the Spanish crown, and now begged the King
for an expression of approval.   The King was com-

[1] The King's statement to Benedetti.   "Ma Mission en Prusse," p.
356.

pletely taken aback, and did not seek to hide his annoyance from the Prince in his autograph reply, in which he declared, however, that he could not oppose a step which the Prince might decide upon in response to an inward calling.[1]

Thus, at last, the object so persistently pursued by Spain seemed to be attained; and Prim hoped to be able in a few days to ask the Cortes to elect their King, when a wholly unexpected event in Madrid put an end to all these anticipations. The longing which the deputies felt for hearth and home entirely overpowered their political scruples; and on the 24th of June the assembly, which by this time had dwindled to one hundred and thirty members present, resolved to adjourn until the 1st of November.

More definite information regarding the motives which led to this step, so astonishing at this juncture, I am not enabled to give. Rothan [2] tells us that a despatch in faulty cipher gave the French Ambassador premature information of the secret. This does not, however, explain how such a despatch could bring about the adjournment of the Cortes; although it is perfectly evident that by this step the Cortes made it

[1] Compare, in addition to the statements by Werther and Wilmowski to which reference has been made, Salazar's preface to his pamphlet of July 8th, and an article in the *Kreuzzeitung* of July 14th. Thiers, after claiming to have received his information from persons filling some of the highest places in Europe, says, that in answer to the Prince's letter, the King made the significant reply that Leopold was free to accept or refuse, but that he, the King, could not protect him against the consequences of his undertaking. "Enquête Parlamentaire, Dépositions," I., p. 6.

[2] "L'Allemagne et l'Italie," p. 3.

impossible to keep the candidacy a secret until the time
of the election, since, before this could now take place,
the Cortes would have to be convened in extraordinary
session by a public manifesto.

On the afternoon of July 2d the Ministers discussed
the situation with the President of the Cortes; and later
in the evening Prim gave an audience to the French
representative, Baron Mercier de Lostande, for the purpose of preparing him in as discreet a manner as possible
for the momentous intelligence.   The remarks made by
the Ambassador upon hearing the announcement were
of a most threatening character, whereupon Prim assured
him that his first choice, from first to last, had been a
Portuguese, and, failing that, one of Italian extraction,
in consequence of which it had been with great difficulty that he had kept Montpensier and the republic
in check.   "But," said he, "the danger grew more
menacing with every day, when at last a candidate was
suggested to us in whom were combined all the qualities desirable in a Spanish sovereign.   It is our only
hope; I cannot reject it.   How will the Emperor receive it?"

First of all Mercier declared that in his official capacity he could make no reply, since as yet his only
instructions were to preserve an attitude of extreme
reserve.   He could, therefore, only express his personal opinion, which was that the Spanish Government
could not have determined upon a more hazardous and
dangerous step.   "With the existing feeling against
Prussia," he continued, "the accession of a Prussian

prince to the throne of Spain cannot fail to make a tremendous impression in France. The nation will look
upon it as an intentional provocation, and a Napoleon
cannot remain insensible to that." Like Napoleon himself in his conversation with Benedetti in the spring
of 1869, Mercier now spoke not of the Emperor's personal view, but of a national current of public opinion
which he could not resist.

It was in vain that Prim tried to persuade Mercier
that this first impression would, upon maturer consideration, gradually wear away. " Not at all," was the
reply; " for this first feeling is one of those which a
national Government will always share, for it springs
from the very heart of the nation."

Thus beset, Prim gave utterance to a word which
was destined to be quite as fateful as Benedetti's report
of May 11th, 1869. " My chief consolation," said he,
" is that this candidacy is not one which I suggested,
nor did I even solicit it; it was put into my hands.
There was a time when, just as I told the Cortes, I
thought it would disappoint us as had the others; then,
unexpectedly, it was presented to me all cut and dry,
and in our predicament I cannot refuse it."

The candidacy had, as we know, been presented to
him by Salazar and the Liberal Union; and he had
consented to it only when forced to do so by necessity,
after repeated refusals had been received from both
Lisbon and Florence. Mercier, however, gathered a
very different meaning from his words. " Ah," cried
he, " I have for some time observed that Herr von Bis-

marck seeks to meddle in your affairs; and you must admit that, did he not expect great gain, he would not venture so high a stake."

Here Prim interrupted him.   "You are entirely mistaken," said he ; "the idea originated here.   I have never discussed politics either with Herr von Bernhardi or with Herr von Canitz " (the North German Ambassador).

"And the Prussian squadron whose arrival in Spanish waters has just been announced to you?" asked Mercier.

"I have had no such information," declared Prim; "so much is certain, however; if we let this opportunity escape us, Montpensier or the republic, that I hate as I do perdition, will triumph over us."

"Very well; then let it be Montpensier."

"What!   Am I to understand that the Emperor prefers Montpensier to a Hohenzollern?"

"He has not said so, but I have no doubt of it; for the Emperor is first of all a Frenchman."

On the following morning Mercier first sent a short telegram and then a full report of this conversation to Paris.   As yet he did not consider the matter as decided beyond recall.   He closed his report with the remark that the rumor of an accepted German candidacy was general in town; a deputy had told him that in all probability the Cortes would be convened in extraordinary session during August.   It was therefore his intention to continue to make every possible endeavor to influence Prim against it.

However, as early as July 4th, the Council of Ministers, presided over by the Regent, Serrano, decided formally to recognize the Hereditary Prince Leopold of Hohenzollern as the candidate of the Government, and to convene the Cortes for July 20th for the purpose of electing a King.

Now, at the close of these long protracted negotiations, it will be profitable to take a brief survey of their most important features.

He who originated and first advocated the Hohenzollern candidacy was not a Prussian, but the Spanish State Councillor, Salazar. For Gramont's assertion that he was doubtlessly acting at the suggestion of Prussia, that he was in fact a Prussian agent, no proof has been so much as attempted, much less established.

Prince Leopold in no way endeavored to secure for himself the Spanish crown, but, on the contrary, thrice refused the offer made him from Madrid, and accepted it only in response to a fourth solicitation.

According to the Hohenzollern family compact he was entirely free to decide this matter according to his own judgment; he did not require the King's permission either to accept or to refuse. This is not gainsayed by the fact that the King's opinion had great weight with him.

Of the first inquiry made in the spring of 1869, and of the refusal which was its reply, the King was fully informed; he approved the latter, and discussed it confidentially with Bismarck. Of the second offer received at Weinburg, and its provisional refusal, Prince Charles

Anthony informed the Emperor Napoleon; but King William and Bismarck did not learn of it until later.

The third offer, made in the spring of 1870, was in the form of letters addressed by Marshal Prim to King William and Bismarck; these, as the writer expressly stated, were private communications, wholly unofficial in their character, and were accompanied by the request that they be regarded as strictly confidential. Hereupon the King called a Hohenzollern family council to discuss the question, and to these conferences Bismarck was invited. The result was, that the offer was declined by both the King and the Prince, after which Bismarck addressed a private letter to Prim, in which he declared the candidacy to be in itself an excellent idea, but that it must not be negotiated with the Prussian Government.

This was followed by a fourth offer in June, made by the Spanish Government and addressed directly to the Prince, wholly without the knowledge of the King; it was accepted by the Prince without previously consulting the King, although he had long been fully aware of the King's disapproval of this step.

Such were the facts in which French suspicion claimed to discover a carefully prepared Prussian, or rather Bismarckian, intrigue, by which it was intended so to offend the honor of France that the Government would be provoked into a premature declaration of war.

CHAPTER II.

THE WITHDRAWAL OF PRINCE LEOPOLD.

On July 3d two telegrams were received at the Paris Foreign Office; one was from Mercier, reading: The Hohenzollern affair has reached an advanced stage, if, indeed, it is not already decided; Prim is my authority. The other one was sent by the (incorrectly informed) Havas Agency, and was to this effect: The Government has decided to offer the Spanish crown to Prince Leopold of Hohenzollern; a Spanish deputation is on its way to Germany for that purpose.

Mercier's telegram indicates that the " Hohenzollern affair " was a matter with which Minister Gramont was fully acquainted.[1] Now, as we know, in March, 1869, Emperor Napoleon had himself advised Count Benedetti that the French nation would not suffer this choice, and it must therefore be prevented. Mercier, as we are aware, knew this to be the Emperor's wish, but had not received the corresponding instructions to interfere with the election, but, on the contrary, had been directed

---

[1] That this was the case is also revealed by an expression used by Mercier in his report; he says that Prim opened the conversation with the remark that he had an unwelcome communication to make; after which the report continues, " And I knew at once to what he alluded."

to maintain an attitude of absolute reserve. We naturally ask why was this the case? Was it because after
the crown had been twice refused it was believed that
it could not possibly be accepted without Napoleon's
consent, and that the consequently unnecessary and unpleasant negotiations with Spain in regard to it might
therefore be avoided? Or was it because in secret
Gramont cherished a desire at variance with that of his
Emperor, intending to permit the choice of Prince Leopold because he knew the French nation would not endure it, and hoped it would prove a means of rousing
the masses out of their peace-loving lethargy? Who
can tell?

Upon one point there can, however, be no doubt;
namely, that instantaneously with its reception Gramont's interpretation of the intelligence received was
unalterably fixed. He assumed, as a matter of course,
that the candidacy was of Prussian origin, — a comprehensive intrigue devised by Bismarck, with the ultimate
aim of re-establishing the world-empire of Charles V.
That there was not the least evidence in support of this
theory was a fact of which he was superlatively uncon-
scious; in his excited imagination rose the wildest
fantasies, which, owing to the weakness of his power of
discernment, were no sooner conceived than they appeared to him as actual experiences. "One FEELS
INTUITIVELY," he wrote in one of his circular despatches, "that this is a project of the unscrupulous
Berlin policy, and not of the gallant Spanish nation,
with which we are dealing."

In this, as he assumed, Prussian plan to place upon the Spanish throne a Prussian prince he beheld an injury to the vital interests of France, a menace to its position of power maintained for more than a century; it was, therefore, a deadly insult to the honor and dignity of the nation, for which Prussia must give France complete and public satisfaction. I do not mean to say that Gramont was already fully resolved to render a conflict with Prussia unavoidable; for, to begin with, he was so thoroughly convinced that the French army was invincible, and was so regarded by the world in general, that he did not for a moment suppose it possible that either King William or Bismarck would dare maintain an attitude of defiance should France signify her displeasure by any serious threat of war; but, on the contrary, he fully expected that Prussia would forthwith be cowed into penitent submission to the commands imposed by the bold and spirited diplomacy of France. However, should matters after all turn out differently, should Bismarck be rash enough to offer resistance, then, to be sure, France would be compelled to let the thunder of her cannons reverberate through Germany.

Unhesitatingly he set about his task. Immediately upon the receipt of the two telegrams on July 3d he directed the French *chargé d'affaires* at Berlin, Le Sourd, Benedetti being on leave of absence, to interrogate the Prussian Government regarding the candidacy. "We have been informed," he wrote, "that an offer of the Spanish crown has been made the Prince of Hohenzollern through a deputation sent to Germany by Marshal Prim, and that the Prince has accepted it. We can but feel surprised that a Prussian prince should aspire to the crown of Spain. We should be glad to learn that the Berlin Cabinet has had no part in this intrigue ; should the reverse of this be true, my only comment at present is, that the impression here would be a most unfavorable one ; let your words be to this effect."

This despatch was sent before Gramont had received Mercier's report. He did not, therefore, at the time, know that the Prince had accepted, but took this for granted, just as he had that the Prince had striven to secure the crown of Spain.

His second official step of that day, taken like the first one in ignorance of the true state of affairs, was a still greater blunder. The excitement which the Havas telegram created in Paris was already intense. Gramont hastened to stimulate it to a perfect storm of indignation by means of two official announcements published in *Le Constitutionel* of the 4th. The first of these made known to the public the contents of the Havas telegram, and was accompanied by the comment that as yet it had not been ascertained whether the event were merely the result of a personal intrigue on the part of Prim, or whether the undertaking had been approved or desired by the Spanish people. " Should the latter be the case," it was said in conclusion, " it would have that claim upon our consideration that the will of a nation controlling its own destiny may expect.

But even then we could not repress a feeling of surprise that the SCEPTRE OF CHARLES V. SHOULD BE INTRUSTED TO A PRUSSIAN PRINCE, the grandson of a Princess Murat, whose name can have no other than unhappy associations for Spain."

There can be no doubt regarding the official nature of this article, since it gave an exact outline of the programme followed by the Government immediately afterward, — we respect the will of Spain, but through pressure brought to bear upon Prussia we mean to prevent it from being put into effect.' It is somewhat surprising that the Minister of a Bonaparte should seek to make Prince Leopold distasteful to the Spanish people by referring to his relationship to the House of Bonaparte.

A second article from the same pen suggested the question of how this Prussian candidacy had originated, and at the same time directed attention to the rumors current in the French press during 1868, although these had been promptly contradicted in Berlin, namely, that the thought of deposing Queen Isabella had been suggested to the leaders of the Spanish malcontents by Bismarck, and that in the September revolution they had received aid in the form of large sums of money from him. According to the same authority, Bismarck's next step had been to suggest the name of the unpopular Duke of Montpensier for the candidacy, that upon his defeat he might propose that of the Prussian prince, etc. The writer closed with the questions: "How much of truth is there in these rumors? Does to-day's occurrence form but a link in the chain of those events which are the talk of all Europe?"

The tremendous effect produced by this double signal we shall soon learn.

Hardly had it been sounded abroad through all France by *Le Constitutionel* when Gramont received Le Sourd's telegraphic reply from Berlin. Bismarck being still at Varzin, the *chargé d'affaires* had addressed his inquiry to Herr von Thile, and had been given the plain and brief reply that the Prussian Government knew absolutely nothing of this affair; in fact, it had no existence so far as the Government was concerned (no information could therefore be furnished with regard to any negotiations which the Spanish Government might have conducted with the Prince of Hohenzollern).[1] Le Sourd's despatch closes with the extraordinary comment that Thile had not directly asserted that the Government had no knowledge of the negotiations and their issue. It would seem that this had been clearly enough indicated, for he who is totally ignorant of a matter can have no knowledge of the negotiations which have taken place in regard to it.

Thus Gramont had received confirmation of that which on the foregoing day he had claimed it would give him pleasure to learn. It would appear that, did he not wish to be regarded as a disturber of the peace, the course to pursue now lay plainly before him, — a

[1] The parenthetical clause does not form a part of Le Sourd's despatch; it is, however, to be found in Bismarck's report made to the Federal Council on July 16th.

statement that he was satisfied with Thile's official assurance that the Prussian Cabinet had not been a party
to the negotiations, followed by a courteous but decided
declaration that the candidacy was incompatible with
French interests, and under existing circumstances
would tend to excite public opinion in France to a
dangerous degree; joined to this, the wish that the
Prussian Government, regarding whose influence at the
Court of Sigmaringen there could be no question, would
act as mediator, or would express itself in favor of
allowing the matter to be decided by a concert of the
Great Powers.

With opinions such as we know were held by both
the King and the Prince, this would have put an end
to the Prince's candidacy.

However, that which Gramont had on the day before referred to as information which would be highly
welcome, namely, a declaration by Thile that Prussia
had not participated in the negotiations regarding the
candidacy, he now denounced as a well-planned lie,
a derisive reply, the attempt of a detected plotter to
hide his duplicity, and to circumvent those who would
expose it. He regarded it as beneath his dignity to
continue the correspondence he had begun with the
Prussian Cabinet; instead, he now sent the King, who
was seeking health from the baths at Ems, a threatening message. When the Prussian Ambassador, Baron
Werther, whose acquaintance with the Minister dated
from the old Vienna times, took leave of him before
his departure for Ems, the Duke urgently requested

him to present the danger of the situation to his sovereign; for never, he declared, would France tolerate
that a condition of affairs prejudicial to her safety
should take place just beyond her borders.

On July 5th, the note of alarm which had been
sounded by *Le Constitutionel* was echoed with increased force and with many variations by the Paris
newspaper press. Moderate sheets such as *Le Temps*
and *Le Siècle* represented, that, should a Prussian Prince
be placed upon the throne at Madrid, France would be
thrown back into a position even worse than had been
hers during the days of Charles V. In a more violent
tone *Le Rappel* declared, "The Hohenzollerns evidently aspire to an empire of the world such as that
of Charles V.; not content with the conquest of Germany, they hope to subjugate Europe. It is to the
everlasting shame of our times that such a plan could
be so much as devised, let alone attempted."

During all this ado Gramont received the intelligence from Madrid that the Cortes had been convened
for July 20th for the purpose of electing a King; his
anxiety increased, for now there remained only fourteen days in which to prevent the present choice, before an accomplished fact would confront him.[1] Haste
was advisable, therefore, and the assumption of a high
and mighty tone, that an immediate check might be
placed upon this Prussian arrogance. That Mercier's

---

[1] In 1831 the Brussels Congress decided upon the choice of the Duke
de Nemours for the throne of Belgium; this did not, however, deter
Louis Philippe from refusing his consent to the election.

report of the 3d now came to hand, in which he read
the confirmation of Thile's declaration in Prim's statement that the candidacy had not been suggested by
Bismarck, but had originated in Spain, made no impression whatever upon him. In this, too, Gramont
beheld only a hypocritical concealment of the truth;
and he told his colleagues that Mercier had stated that
the candidacy had been suggested to the Spaniards
from abroad.

In the Chamber, also, a violent spirit of exasperation
was now asserting itself. Several members of the Left
Centre, under the leadership of a Monsieur Cochéry,
presented an interpellation. As was to be expected,
lack of information did not deter Gramont from making
a reply. It did not occur to him to await Werther's
communication from Ems regarding King William's
intentions; by no means. His one thought was to
thwart Bismarck's covert plotting by opposing to it
the peremptory will of France, which was now to be
voiced in the Chamber as it had already been proclaimed through the press. He found momentary encouragement in the general disfavor with which the
Hohenzollern candidacy was regarded abroad; the confident assertion made by France had everywhere given
the impression that the candidacy had been devised by
Bismarck.

In Germany people scoffed at the absurd excitement
stirred up in Paris by the anticipation of great disadvantage to be incurred by France because a petty
German prince was to sit upon the tottering throne of

Spain. This, however, also suggested the question of what benefit Prussia could expect to reap; and not a few were vexed that for so slight a cause the peace of Europe should be endangered. Especially did the Swabian Republicans and the Bavarian Ultramontanes rejoice that in this, Bismarck had at last made a fiasco; and they cheered their French partisans on by hearty acclamation.

The Great Powers of Europe, although hardly approving the violence of the commotion raised by France, still, without exception, cautioned the Berlin authorities to be considerate of the not wholly unjustifiable irritation in France.

A statesman of truly peaceful inclinations would have concluded from this condition of affairs that little difficulty would be encountered in the endeavor through diplomatic action to prevent the undesirable candidacy; above all else he would have been careful not to forfeit the general good will abroad by rash and offensive measures.[1]   But with Gramont there was little likelihood of so much forethought. He, on the contrary, reasoned: All the Powers are on our side; I must, therefore, make the most of this opportunity to resent the attempted insult on the part of Prussia.

---

[1] Gramont holds that such a course was made impossible to him by Prussia's declaration that it could not enter into negotiations with regard to the matter. That Thile's reply to Le Sourd does not imply this, is patent; and, in truth, Gramont bases his claim chiefly upon statements made by the Prussian Ambassador at London, withholding the fact that these were the result of instructions received from Bismarck as late as July 8th.

As early as the 6th of July the Council of Ministers, presided over by the Emperor, determined upon the official reply to be made to the Cochéry interpellation. With regard to the course which these deliberations took, there are several conflicting accounts, the leading features of which will be briefly mentioned here.

Gramont, in his testimony before the parliamentary Investigation Committee in 1872, stated that his draft of the reply did not contain the last sentence making the threat of war, but that this was added by the Council, and that he read the reply thus framed, word for word, to the Chamber.[1] According to this statement, it would appear that it was he, more than the other members of the Council of State, who was disposed to proceed in a peaceable manner. After the disastrous issue of the war he wrote an imposing volume, the purpose of which is to show that he preserved this attitude throughout the entire crisis.

This narration was supplemented after Napoleon had been deposed by an anonymous publication, according to which the reply, as formulated by the Ministers, was of a pacific tone throughout, but at the last moment was transformed into a war manifesto by the imperious intervention of the Emperor at the decisive point.

The incredibility of this story is palpable. It was quite the fashion in Paris, after the fall of the Empire, to lay all the cause of disaster at Napoleon's door. If the bellicose final clause really was added by the Council of Ministers, this does not by any means signify

[1] " Dépositions," I., 90, 91.

that it was done àt Napoleon's command. Such a step
would have been entirely inconsistent with the Emperor's brooding, undecided character, which made him
averse to any sudden action, and is, moreover, rendered
highly improbable by the fact that at the time he was
suffering from a renewed attack of his malady, by
which, as has been mentioned in a former connection,
his craving for rest was always increased, and his powers of judgment and of will were paralyzed.[1] Is it at
all likely that in this condition he should, by an imperative order, have spurred his resisting Ministers on to
what was equivalent to a declaration of war?

There is, moreover, no want of positive evidence to
the contrary.

Thiers, who at this time was upon terms of intimate
friendship with Ollivier, assures us [2] that Ollivier was
decidedly inclined to peace, as was also the Emperor,
who at this period had lost much of his will power, and
was, in general, vacillating in his opinions and slow of
decision.

Of a still more positive nature is the evidence given
by the Minister of War, Lebœuf, before the Investigation Committee.   What could have been more welcome
to this unhappy man at the close of the fatal year 1871,

[1] According to the testimony of Madame Carette (II., 123), a consultation of the ablest physicians, Ricord, Faurel, See, Nelaton, and Corvi-
sart, took place on July 2d.

The " Papiers de la Famille Impériale," II., 59, contain an opinion by
Professor See, dated July 3d, 1870, according to which Napoleon was
suffering from gout, hemorrhoids, and a serious bladder malady of five
years' standing.

[2] " Dépositions," I., 8.

as well as to his hearers, than to be able to prove that
the fallen Emperor had been the originator of this ill-
fated war?

Lebœuf, however, declares: [1] "In the Council of
Ministers opinions were divided with regard to the
reply; several members, although otherwise approving
the contents of the draft, criticised the form as being too
harsh. Permit me to say, that the Emperor also was of
this opinion. In consequence, many of the expressions
were modified. But upon our arrival in the Chamber
we found great agitation and evidences of an over-
wrought patriotic feeling rife among the deputies. We
allowed ourselves to be carried away by the prevailing
spirit; and the original writing, or at least one which
approximated it, was read from the orator's tribunal.
Whether Gramont had brought two forms with him, or
whether the modified expressions had been written between the lines of the original draft, I cannot say;
neither do I remember whether any part of the modified
form was read. We adopted a version which we regarded as more dignified and more in harmony with
public opinion."

Thus Lebœuf not only testifies to the peaceable inclinations of the Emperor, but to an independent proceeding on the part of Gramont as well, in which he
himself was a participant. The Emperor advocated
moderate expressions; Gramont desired that Prussia
should be humiliated. When at a later sitting of the Investigation Committee he was confronted with Lebœuf's

[1] "Dépositions," I., 46.

version of the matter, without being told who was its authority, and was asked what he had to say to it, he exclaimed in consternation, *"Mon Dieu!* That is a hard question for me!" And then, painfully and in fragments, he disclosed the facts as stated above.

There is no opportunity left us to be in doubt with regard to the inference; it was not the Emperor, but Gramont, who on the 6th of July entailed war upon his country by the speech which upon his own responsibility he made in the name of France.

Before presenting it to my readers, we will cast a glance at the hearers and readers for whom it was intended.

Through the newspapers of the 4th and 5th the country had already been thrown into a state of unusual excitement. Although the French people earnestly desired peace in the interest of their material welfare, nevertheless, through their veins coursed unchanged the old Gallican blood with its easily touched sense of honor and its sensitive vanity. There was scarcely one among all these millions who did not feel the eclipse of Solferino's glory by the greater renown of Sadowa to be a personal affront.

Then came the Opposition's incessantly reiterated charges that Napoleon's short-sighted policy had permitted the consummation of German unity under Prussian leadership to the prejudice of France. This was followed by Marshal Niel's demands for adequate protection against this powerful neighbor, as well as against the grasping covetousness of Prussia, which required that the military burden be doubled.

The tendency of all this was to arouse a constantly
growing dislike of all that was Prussian. So far only
a minority among the Liberals had allowed this to influence them to an openly acknowledged eagerness for
war. But the opinion of the majority also, if put into
words, would have read somewhat after this fashion :
We desire peace, and are rejoiced that since January
our Government has felt itself justified in declaring it
to be assured ; nevertheless, should these arrogant Prussians allow themselves the slightest discourtesy toward
us, the whole French nation will arise as one man, and
crush them to atoms.

And now, one after another, like the alarum of trum-
pets, came the reports that in Spain Prussia had long
been intriguing against France, that now it was openly
extending its hand toward the crown of Charles V.,
that this was but the first step toward inflicting a serious injury and humiliation upon France. It was not
surprising that deep anxiety quickly took possession of
the great mass of the population. The number of those
advocating war grew with every day ; in all the larger
towns the press gave forth violent signals of war.

As a matter of course, excitement ran highest in
Paris, where the influence of the Government, of the
army officers and the prelates, of the political parties
and the press, was most quickly and directly felt. In
the Chamber the Extreme Right, consisting of the
group of Arcadians, believed the object of all their
ardent hopes to be at length attained, a pretext for war
upon Prussia, by which the declining renown of the

dynasty would be raised to unapproachable heights of glory. Since the Government itself was now evidently facing in this direction, they had reason to expect that the ever-submissive Right, and a part of the Right Centre as well, would be with them.

But upon the side of the Liberals also were to be found impetuous men of Monsieur de Kératry's stamp; men who, although free from dynastic considerations, were eager to take up the sword against Prussia without further delay. Of the Left Centre, only a part still clung to the hope that peace might be preserved; and the Extreme Right was quite alone in its resolve to make a determined stand against a war policy.

Such was the assembly in which, on the afternoon of July 6th, Gramont and Ollivier made their appearance to reply to the Cochéry interpellation. All parties were waiting in breathless expectation; the galleries were crowded with diplomats, officers, high officials, and ladies of rank and distinction.

Gramont began. He said it was true that Marshal Prim had offered the Spanish crown to Prince Leopold of Hohenzollern, and that it had been accepted; but the Spanish nation had not yet given its decision. With the details of these negotiations, which had been concealed from the French Government (evidences of excitement in the Chamber), he was still unacquainted; consequently, an exposition of the affair would be to no purpose, and the Government therefore requested that it be deferred to some future day.

All this was perfectly true, and it would seem that

the obvious wisdom of his last remark would have deterred the speaker from attempting that which he himself had declared to be fruitless. He, however, continued: first he did homage to the sovereign will of the Spanish people, whose decision France would always duly respect; this was followed by the wholly untruthful statement that France had refrained from exerting any influence whatever with regard to the former candidates, manifesting neither approval nor disapproval of them.

Then he came to the principal point with the words: "But regard for the rights of a neighboring people does not require us to suffer a foreign Power to place one of its princes upon the throne of Charles V., thereby disturbing the European balance of power [animated applause] to the detriment of the national honor and interests of France. [Renewed applause; continued bravos.] This event, we confidently trust, will, however, not come to pass. We count upon the wisdom of the German and upon the friendship of the Spanish people to prevent it. Should it, nevertheless, befall otherwise, then, made strong through your support and that of the nation [applause], we will know how to do our duty without hesitation and without weakness."

An unexampled storm of tumultuous acclamation greeted these closing words; two objecting voices were quickly silenced. On his way from the orators' tribune to his seat, the Minister received a perfect ovation of applause and congratulations. The entire audience was in a state of intense excitement; there was general clapping of hands, the ladies waved their handkerchiefs, the men shouted hurrah; the uproar was indescribable.

Gramont could, in fact, pride himself upon having achieved the unprecedented. In almost one and the same breath to acknowledge his ignorance of the transaction which had taken place, to make complaint of the secrecy preserved in connection with it, and then, with categoric assurance, to hurl in the face of a foreign Power an open threat of war on account of its supposed attitude, which it had however officially disclaimed — this was in all likelihood a deed without a precedent.

Even in the Chamber the opinion prevailed, to which Crémieux gave unreserved utterance, that it had been the Duke's intention to indicate a *casus belli* against Prussia, so that Ollivier, who could but regard such a proceeding as ill-advised, in order to soften the impression made, intervened with the emphatic declaration that the Government desired peace, but peace consistent with honor. The effect of Gramont's great achievement was, of course, not to be counteracted by such words. The diplomats present were utterly amazed. Is this conduct, they asked, to be regarded as the result of a fixed determination to declare war, or is it to be laid to the inexperience of Ollivier and the incompetence of Gramont? Upon one point, however, there was but one mind among them all; and that was, that any negotiations for the purpose of preserving peace, any attempt at international mediation, had been rendered extremely difficult, if not impossible, by Gramont's offensive threat.

Meanwhile the tumult which Gramont had occasioned in the Chamber was transmitted to all the various parties and classes of the population. The newspapers, irrespective of party, vied with one another in a show of valiant patriotism.[1] " Our country's honor has been saved! " exclaimed the *Gaulois;* "for the first time this Ministry has spoken words worthy of France! Can peace be preserved, it will be well; should it come to war, it will be still better." Another organ of the Left, the *Opinion Nationale*, proclaimed, " If the Government abides by its noble and strong words, it will find the whole country with it. Bismarck oversteps all bounds : if he wants peace, he must retract; for us this is no longer possible." The *Ultramontane Univers* declared that to-day the Ministers had spoken as the deliberate' organs of the entire nation, and his Majesty King William and Herr von Bismarck might as well know it.

And so the same tune was rung through all the various changes ; and if the Extreme Left, the Republicans and the Socialists, did not join in, it was not because of any wish to defend Prussia, but to deride the Government. " What if Monsieur de Gramont is not in possession of Bismarck's secretly preserved documents," asked the *Réveil*, "and Prussia declares that it knows no more of this affair than does France ? What answer can the Cabinet of the Tuileries make to that? In that case would Prussia not be justified in demanding satisfaction, which the French Government, being wholly in the wrong, cannot refuse? "

[1] Compare Giraudeau, " La Vérité sur la Campagne de 1870."

In the position which Gramont had created for himself, such criticisms were like so many lashes goading
him on to speedy action, especially so since above the
noise of applause could even now be discerned individual voices which in their demands went far beyond the
line which he had indicated. "If Prussia to-day withdraws its support of the Prince," said the *Figaro*,
"France has the right to ask still more. After all the
subterfuges which have been made, guaranties must be
required." And forthwith the *Liberté* joined in with
the remark, "Should Spain reject the candidate that
has been forced upon her, France and Europe must
demand of Prussia binding guaranties for the future."

All this insured Gramont against any criticism of
his independent action which the Emperor or his colleagues, less eager for war than was he, might be inclined to make, and stimulated his desire to proceed
upon the course on which he had entered. On the day
after his valiant speech he made a clean breast of it
to Lord Lyons, the English Ambassador, saying, "We
cannot fly in the face of public opinion; considerations
of a diplomatic nature must give way before that which
our internal safety demands. Prince Leopold's accession to the Spanish throne is synonymous with war."

Accordingly, on the 7th of July, he sent another
despatch to Le Sourd at Berlin, the spirit of which was
quite in harmony with his speech of that day, but with
a marked advance in that which was demanded of
Prussia. It was in this connection that the idea by
which his policy was controlled, the keynote of his

entire diplomatic action, was first fully revealed. In
his speech he had made the maintenance of peace dependent chiefly upon the condition that the Prince should
not ascend the Spanish throne. He now indicated
more definitely the manner of its prevention; namely,
that King William should forbid it. For since the
candidacy had implied an affront to the honor of France
for which the King through his sanction of it had
become responsible, France must receive satisfaction
directly from him, — a formal retraction of the insult
offered; the King must therefore command the Prince
to withdraw his acceptance of the crown.

"No one will believe," said Gramont, "that a Prussian prince could accept the Spanish crown without the
approval of the King who is the head of the house.
Now, if the King has authorized the Prince's action,
what becomes of the alleged official ignorance on the
part of the Berlin Cabinet? This is a case in which
the King can either permit or forbid; if he has not
permitted, he can forbid. By doing so he will avoid
grave complications. It is no more than the Emperor
did with regard to Prince Murat's candidacy for the
throne of Naples. A like course now would be convincing evidence that Prussia really desires the bond
of friendship between the two countries to be enduringly strengthened."

And again he did not await Le Sourd's reply, but
supplemented the demand made by a step most surprising in itself. On the evening of the same day, the
7th of July, he sent instructions to Count Benedetti,

then staying at Wildbach, directing him to go to Ems, there to open personal negotiations with King William in addition to those of an official character which were being conducted with Berlin.   In a confidential letter to the Ambassador he wrote: " Thile's evasive reply is not sufficient; you must seek to procure a positive statement.   The only one which will satisfy us is: The King disapproves of the Prince's candidacy, and commands him to withdraw from it.   There is need of haste in regard to this; for in case the answer should not' be satisfactory, we must forestall the enemy, and begin the mobilization of the troops on the day after to-morrow.   Should you succeed in influencing the King to RECALL his consent, we will have achieved a great triumph; if not, war is inevitable."

And so the strategic move preparatory to the two-fold diplomatic onslaught upon Prussia was executed. As is not infrequently the case in connection with Gramont, we remain in doubt as to which in him was greater, the ignorance or the presumption with which he led his country into a fatal conflict.   Without evidence of any kind, he imagined that Bismarck had devised the candidacy, that Prince Leopold was a member of the royal house of Prussia, that he had received the King's consent to accept the offer of the Spanish crown, that the Prussian Government was responsible for the answer which the King determined upon without consultation with his Ministers, and gave after the Prince had signified his willingness to accept.

The actual facts were just the reverse of all these

fantasies. Let us, however, assume that it was all as
true as it really was false, to what inference would it
lead ?   There can be no question that a Power does
not exceed its rights when it opposes an undertaking
which it believes will result to the prejudice of its
national interests. But in the case under consideration every unbiassed person will pronounce the anxiety
evinced by France to have been highly exaggerated,
and the allusion to the empire of Charles V., in connection with the condition of Spain at this time, to
have been simply absurd. Still, every nation is justified in the claim that it is a better judge of its own
interests and that by which they may be injured than
any other one can be ; and no one would be inclined to
criticise France had it sought to protect its interests by
preventing the candidacy in a seemly manner.

As has already been stated, and as later events will
show, success would undoubtedly have attended any
such endeavor. That which imprints upon Gramont's
policy the perpetual stigma of malice, and makes him
responsible for all the consequent calamity, is the
hatred and arrogance which prompted him to declare
the candidacy to be an affront to the honor and dignity
of France, justifying the demand that it be not only
renounced by the Prince, but that the King of Prussia
must give France satisfaction by commanding the withdrawal.   And this he asked of the mighty victor of
Königgrätz !   Although constantly alluding to the sovereignty of the Spanish nation, the indignity offered
Spain by his attitude toward Prussia seems never to
have occurred to him.

If he looked upon a closer connection between Prussia and Spain as an affront to the honor of France, does this not imply that he regarded Spain as exclusively the domain of France? Did he not deny to it the right to form alliances? And surely, although Bismarck hoped that with Prince Leopold upon the Spanish throne friendly relations would be fostered between Spain and Germany, he nevertheless fully realized how wholly improbable it was that the Spanish marshals and Cortes would ever allow their youthful foreign King to form a defensive alliance with Germany. But the mere possibility of such an event appeared to Gramont to be incompatible with French honor. It could not have been proclaimed more plainly that in Paris Spain was considered as vassal to France, and that it was the intention to punish Prussia above all others for having presumed to lay her hand upon that which belonged to France.

So far much has been said of what took place in Paris, and but little of that which meanwhile was going on in Germany. The very good reason for this silence is, that there was little to relate. In the Government circles of Prussia there was, as we are aware, as little thought of a possibility of war toward the middle of June as there was in the rest of the world. The King and the Ministers of the most important departments had left Berlin for their various summer retreats, and were engaged with plans for recreation at the baths, in the country, or upon journeys.

On the 8th of June, Bismarck had returned to Var-

zin to recuperate in the seclusion which his country-
seat afforded, and to invigorate his overtaxed nerves
with Carlsbad water, intending to remain away from
Berlin for six weeks, until the beginning of August.
He, too, had no thought of war.

Since 1866 he had upon several occasions observed,
that if, in case of a difference of opinion, Prussia maintained an attitude of calm intrepidity, the turbulent
waves of French wrath soon subsided. Far from an-
ticipating any real difficulty in connection with the
Spanish affair, he had, as we know, hoped it could
be easily adjusted. He was of course aware of Gramont's hostility, and of the hatred of Prussia cherished
by many of the political parties in France, such as the
Arcadians, Clericals, and Chauvinists;[1] but he also took
into consideration Napoleon's irresolute character and
abhorrence of war; and as late as the 25th of June,
after the King had informed him of the Prince's intention to accept, he made the remark to Herr von
Schlözer, a diplomat with whom he was personally on
terms of friendship, that he rejoiced in the prospect of
a peaceful summer. Accordingly he was completely
taken by surprise when, three days after the Prince's
acceptance had been made public, he found himself
face to face with a *casus belli* uncivilly proclaimed in
Gramont's speech, and when, immediately afterward,
the Paris press began its insolent Witches' Sabbath.

However, without a moment's hesitation, he resolved

---

[1] As stated in a speech delivered in the Reichstag on December 12th,
1874.

upon the attitude now to be assumed. It mattered not whether the candidacy was of great or little value to Prussian interests, whether it was popular or unpopular in Germany and elsewhere in Europe — after the gauntlet had been so insultingly thrown down as it had been by Gramont in the name of France, and before the eyes of all Europe, the Prussian Government could not enter into negotiations with Gramont in regard to the matter until the affront publicly offered had been as publicly retracted. Consequently, immediately on July 8th, instructions of like tenor were received by Thile in Berlin, Solms in Paris, and Bernstorff in London,[1] and which may be summed up as follows : Prussia has had no part whatever in the negotiations carried on without the King's knowledge between Madrid and Sigmaringen ; friendly explanations with regard to them we should not have refused, but Gramont's threats have sealed our lips ; we shall seek no quarrel on this account ; however, should the French attack us, we will defend ourselves, — defend ourselves in a way that will make them smart. On July 10th the Chancellor made a similar announcement to the Federal Council.

Under existing circumstances this position was unassailable ; and Bismarck now calmly waited to see whether French wrath would be discharged in the form of cannon-balls or only in blustering words. For the

---

[1] As learned from the English reports of the statements made by these gentlemen. Compare also Horst Kohl's Bismarck-Regesten, July 7th, 1870.

present he remained in Varzin, and neither he nor the Minister of War gave orders for military precautions of any kind to be taken for the event of war. Nor was Moltke disturbed in his rural retreat by any alarming communication.

The wisdom of this course appeared even more clearly when on July 7th Prussia's explanation received official confirmation through the action of Spain. On that day the Spanish Minister of Foreign Affairs, Sagasta, sent out a circular letter in which he declared most positively that the Serrano Government had been influenced in its selection of a candidate for the throne by no other consideration than the welfare of Spain; that from the moment of his accession to the throne the Prince would be a Spaniard, and a Spaniard only; that in accordance with the democratic Constitution he would thenceforward be subject to the will of the people, by which he would be constrained to observe the strictest neutrality in his foreign policy. With particular emphasis Sagasta stated that in this matter the Government had acted wholly according to its own judgment; and that he who was at its head had been influenced during the course of the negotiations by no national interest abroad, and most certainly not by any foreign interest. The Prince upon whom the choice had fallen was entirely free to control his own action; being related to most of the reigning houses, although excluded from the possibility of succeeding to any throne, his election precluded all thought of intended hostility toward any one of the Powers. His candidacy,

therefore, could in no way affect Spain's friendly relations to the other Powers, and neither could nor
should disturb the relations existing between any of
these.

Entirely in harmony with this was the preface to
Salazar's pamphlet as reissued on July 8th, stating that
the Prince had accepted the offer of the crown without previously informing King William of his intention, and that his letter begging the King to sanction
his undertaking was merely an act of courtesy.

Either owing to this declaration on the part of Spain,
or to Prussia's silent reserve, Gramont now began to
waver in his haughty offensive.   Early on the morning
of July 8th, as he tells us, in consequence of a despatch received from Mercier, he telegraphed instructions to Benedetti, directing him to address himself
directly to Prince Leopold; the intention being to desist
from the demand which it had been designed to make
of King William, and, as the speech of the 6th had
indicated, to be satisfied with the voluntary withdrawal
of the Prince.

Emperor Napoleon entirely approved of this; and it
was doubtlessly at his suggestion that on the afternoon
of the same day Gramont had an interview with Lord
Lyons, during which, although he opened the conversation with the usual violent threats against Prussia, he
suddenly made the conciliatory remark that there was
one possible solution of the difficulty, one which he
asked Lord Lyons to commend most earnestly to the
attention of his Government; namely, that the Prince

of Hohenzollern should of his own free will renounce the Spanish crown. This voluntary withdrawal would be the happiest possible termination of the affair, and he entreated the English Government to exert as strong an influence as possible to this end. Lord Lyons, who had severely criticised Gramont's previous attitude toward Prussia, declared himself gladly willing to comply with this request, and held out encouraging prospects with regard to his Government also.

But the Minister's good intention was not destined to long life. The tone of the Paris press was now more violent than it had yet been; the official sheets vied with the independent ones in the wildest war fanfaronades against Prussia. The allusions were now no longer to the Spanish question alone, but to Prussia's violation of the Treaty of Prague as well; and between these rang out the taunt that despite all the provocation received, Prussia still remained inertly silent. Louder and louder rose the demand that the Ministers should put an end to this trifling. Generals and deputies importuned the Government with equal impatience, and Gramont had not the fortitude to withstand the clamor he himself had occasioned.

"I admit," he relates,[1] "that early on the morning of July 8th, resolved to leave no means of preserving peace untried, I determined to appeal directly to Prince Leopold. But this was a mistake. He had not become a candidate without the concurrence of the King; the candidacy was of Prussian origin, and as such France

[1] "France et Prusse," p. 66.

resented it. The King was responsible for it, and therefore to the King alone could Benedetti address himself. On July 9th I begged the Emperor to give me orders conforming to this view."

He does not tell us what representations he made to the Emperor at the time. The outcome was, that on the afternoon of July 9th he was enabled to telegraph to Benedetti: You are not to enter into any transaction with Prince Leopold; the Emperor does not approve of an appeal to him.

Gramont's intention was, therefore, that the instructions given on July 7th should remain in force; namely, that the King should be asked to cause the Prince to withdraw from the candidacy, which would be equivalent to a recall of the King's sanction of it.[1] The Emperor's idea was, however, an entirely different one. Whether Benedetti addressed himself to the Prince or not was a matter of indifference to him. There were still other ways by which the Prince could be induced to withdraw, and, as Napoleon believed, peace be preserved. He had just received[2] a Berlin telegram from the Havas Agency containing the announcement: The King of Prussia, who, by the way, is not the chief of the elder line of the house of Hohenzollern,[3] advised Prince Leopold against accepting the offer of the Span-

---

[1] "France et Prusse," p. 67.

[2] According to a German translation by Hirth of Diary I. (p. 194), found by Prussian troops among the papers left by Napoleon at St Cloud.

[3] The statement should have been: Who as head of the family has no right to lay his commands upon the Prince with regard to the Spanish matter.

ish crown; since then he has not been again consulted in regard to the project.

From this Napoleon concluded that the King would not oppose the Prince's withdrawal; and he therefore decided, that, instead of acting through Benedetti, he would use his influence directly with the Prince in the interest of peace. Without consulting his Ministers he solicited the King of Belgium in his behalf to represent to the Prince of Hohenzollern that his renunciation of the Spanish crown was the only means of preserving peace to Europe.

Napoleon had no doubt regarding the effect of this step, but fully expected that the Prince would withdraw his acceptance, and that consequently the threatening war-cloud would be dispelled. King Victor Emmanuel, who, notwithstanding his strong inclination to a French alliance, did not at the time consider himself in a position to participate in a conflict, had, immediately after Gramont's fierce speech of the 6th, announced to the Spanish Government that for the sake of obviating the necessity for the Hohenzollern candidacy which was giving so much offence, he was willing to reconsider the offer of the Spanish crown to his son Amadeo, which he had at one time refused.[1] But greatly to his peace of mind, he received a despatch from Napoleon on July 11th, stating that peace was assured.[2]

As creditable as the Emperor's incentive to this step was, the whole proceeding, from begining to end, furnishes an excellent example of what a policy should

---

[1] Massari, II., 372.   [2] Rothan, " L'Allemagne et l'Italie," II., 60.

not be. Here we have a Minister who on July 6th puts forward a demand which he supplements by a new and highly dangerous one on the 7th; he recalls this on the 8th, and renews it on the 9th. Over him is a monarch who never openly opposes this vacillation, but in the end endeavors in secret to defeat the Minister's purpose. Such a Government could not escape shipwreck, even had its opponent possessed only one-tenth of Bismarck's ability.

Hardly less severely will we be inclined to criticise Gramont's next step, by which, on July 9th, he called upon the neutral Great Powers for support against Prussia. His circular letter of that day directed attention to the fact that France made no claim in connection with the Spanish affair which was not based upon the principles of European international law; that in 1831 the son of Louis Philippe had not been permitted to ascend the throne of Belgium, in 1862 the Prince of Leuchtenberg and the English Prince Alfred had had a similar experience in connection with the Greek throne, and in 1860 Napoleon III. had forbidden the candidacy of Prince Murat for the crown of Naples. All this had been in pursuance of the principle that no prince of the reigning dynasty of any one of the Great Powers should acquire a foreign throne without the consent of the other Powers. France now expected to be allowed to benefit by this oft-enforced doctrine.

In this document Gramont, for good reasons, passed in silence over the fact that he not only desired the withdrawal of Prince Leopold in conformity with the precedents cited, but that he made the additional claim which formed the objectionable feature of the demand, that King William should cause him to take this step.

For in that case what reply could he have made if Bismarck had very courteously recognized this principle of international law, and had as politely added the remark that Prince Leopold was not a member of the royal house of Prussia, and with respect to this matter was not subject to the orders of the King?

And further, is it not rather surprising that the Government of Napoleon III. should be the one to insist upon the enforcement of this principle? For had he not in 1859, without asking the consent of the other Powers, used every means at his command to place his Cousin Jerome upon the throne of Tuscany? In 1860, again wholly upon his own responsibility, he had advocated the candidacy of an Austrian archduke for the throne of Mexico; and in 1866, greatly to the discomfiture of England, Austria, and Turkey, he had not only suggested the name of Prince Charles of Hohenzollern, the brother of Prince Leopold, as candidate for the throne of Roumania, but had furthered his election in every way possible. There is no escape from the alternative — if he considered Prince Charles a Prussian prince, he had repudiated the principle to which Gramont now appealed; or, if he had then acted in conformity to the principle, he could not have regarded Prince Charles as a Prussian prince. Why, then, was all this outcry made because of Prince Leopold's acceptance of the Spanish crown?

The answer, to be sure, is not difficult to find. The Roumanian occurrence was distasteful to the other three Powers, but the Spanish one was displeasing to France. There lay the difference.

Meanwhile, on the evening of July 8th, Benedetti had arrived at Ems, not especially delighted with the ticklish task which lay before him; first of all to discover what the King's attitude had been, and what his present intentions were; then to propose to this powerful monarch that he should retract that which he had said. In truth, he could have felt little surprise if, after Werther's announcement of Gramont's demands, the King had refused to grant him an audience at all, asking that the communication be made through the usual official channels; or if he had briefly declared that Prince Leopold was entirely independent in this matter, and that all further explanations must be conditional upon a recall of the unprovoked threats made by Gramont.

The King, probably apprehensive that in view of the lately displayed French arrogance such an attitude might precipitate a rupture, and being himself firmly determined upon the course to pursue, leniently consented to waive formality.

Early on the morning of July 9th Werther called on Benedetti to state that, since the King had felt he had no right to forbid the Prince to accept the Spanish offer, he would hardly be likely to command his withdrawal, or even to advise it. Although Benedetti's hopes of success fell in consequence of this communication, they rose again when the King graciously granted him an audience. The King, to be sure, opened the conversation with a severe criticism of Gramont's speech, which he denounced as a defamation of Prussia's policy, being, in fact, an open challenge. Benedetti, who was most anxious to preserve peace, did all in his power to soften the impression made by the speech, representing its sole purpose to have been to allay the excitement in the Chamber. As conducive to the same end, he then laid his proposal before the King in the most courteous form possible, namely, in that of a wish that the King would advise the Prince to withdraw from the candidacy which had assumed so critical an aspect.

In his reply the King rehearsed the events as we know them, laying especial stress upon the fact that in this matter he had acted wholly in the capacity of head of the family, and not as sovereign, his Government having therefore had no part whatever in the affair; that when Marshal Prim's agent had desired to deliver into his hands a private letter from the Marshal, he had refused him an audience; that, instead of laying the matter before his Ministers, he had discussed it exclusively with the Hohenzollern princes, although he had made Bismarck his confidant;[1] that the Prince had in the end accepted the candidacy without his knowledge; after which he, the King, had been solicited as head

---

[1] As has been told, Benedetti, who had no knowledge of the family council held in March, misunderstood this remark, believing it to refer to the final negotiations in June.

of the family to give his consent; and finally that he had no right to forbid the undertaking. Accordingly, the King declared it would be impossible for him to command the Prince to withdraw, or to anticipate him in any step upon which he might decide voluntarily. He had, moveover, written to the Prince's father at Sigmaringen, the Prince himself being away upon a journey through Switzerland, and as soon as he had received a reply from Prince Charles Anthony he would give the Ambassador his final answer; should the Prince decide to renounce the Spanish crown, this step would meet with his unreserved approval.

According to this statement, the King had evidently made known at Sigmaringen, not that he desired the Prince to decline the offer, but that, as upon the former occasion he had made no objection to the Prince's acceptance, so now he would make none to his withdrawal. Had France desired no more than to remove the objectionable candidacy, this would have been the solution of the crisis. But, as we are aware, Gramont demanded more, — the King's retraction of a permission supposed to have been granted; and, as might have been expected, all Benedetti's attempts to make this proposal appear acceptable to the King were destined to end in failure.

Nevertheless, Benedetti was not at all disheartened by the result of this first interview. Notwithstanding the offence which Gramont's speech had evidently given, the King had consented to a discussion of the matter, during which he had acknowledged that the

Prince had solicited his sanction of the candidacy and had received it, — a point which had been surmised in Paris, but of which heretofore there had been no definite knowledge. And finally the King had explained his Government's attitude by the distinction existing between his own position as sovereign and that of head of the family, a distinction which Benedetti at once assailed by the argument that the King's position as head of the family was his simply by virtue of his sovereignty, — an argument which was in turn sustained by the fact that he had asked the Prime Minister to participate in the deliberation in question.

Upon Gramont these explanations had no other effect than to encourage him in the hope of final triumph in the demand he had made. On the 10th and 11th the Ambassador received from him one telegram after another, all urging him on to action. Get us a decisive answer from the King, we cannot wait; we must have it by to-morrow, the day after will be too late; if the King refuses to command or advise the Prince to withdraw, 300,000 reserves will be called into active service; that the KING SHALL CAUSE the Prince to withdraw is of greater importance to us than the withdrawal itself.

On the 11th Gramont decided to inform the Chamber that as yet he had no definite announcement to make, since the reply, upon which all depended, had not arrived. "All the Cabinets which we have addressed have recognized that we have just cause for complaint," was the remark with which he concluded.

Within certain limits this had been true at the beginning of the controversy; he, however, preserved a discreet silence regarding the change of opinion which had taken place among the Powers since July 6th. With respect to King William, Gramont had no doubt that he had adopted the right course to extort from him the penitent declaration he desired. Immediately after the close of the day's session he telegraphed to Benedetti: Your demands lack firmness; the Prince must receive the King's orders to withdraw from the candidacy by to-morrow at the latest.

Across the Rhine the interview at Ems had produced just the contrary effect; whereas in Gramont it had aroused hopes of victory, it had awakened anxious thoughts in Bismarck. It was not the menacing clatter of French sabres by which it was followed that disquieted him; for, as small as was his belief in any serious intention behind the French threats and talk of mobilization, as great was his faith in the ultimate superiority of Germany's strength, should they be actually carried out. Neither did the Prince's renunciation of the Spanish crown, which had now become highly probable, disturb him. As pleasing as it would have been to him to see the Prince upon the throne of Spain, he nevertheless appreciated the motives which might induce the Prince to withdraw in consequence of the burst of displeasure in Paris. To Prussia it was a matter of small moment. From the outset the Government had declared that it had taken no part in the transaction, but that the Prince, in conducting the negotiations and eventually accepting, had acted wholly upon his own responsibility; if now, with a like freedom from restraint, he decided to renounce the crown, what was this to Prussia?

However, to maintain this standpoint consistently required that the French demand, asking the King to cause the Prince to withdraw, should be rejected most rigidly; every word was to be avoided in which Gramont might behold even so much as the semblance of interference by the King. Otherwise the Prince's renunciation would imply a retreat on the part of the King in consequence of Gramont's threats, whereby Prussia would suffer a serious defeat.

It was this which caused Bismarck anxiety; for he well knew the King's great love of peace, and how urgent an appeal was being made to it at the present time by certain members of the circle surrounding him. Bismarck considered it too friendly an advance that the King had granted the French Ambassador an audience at all, and had not first demanded a retraction of the insults Gramont had cast at Prussia; that he had admitted his acquiescence in the candidacy; that he had mentioned having written to Prince Charles Anthony; that he had promised, in case the Prince should decide to withdraw, to announce to the Ambassador that he had given his consent to this step,— all this appeared most hazardous to Bismarck. How easily, thought he, could a malevolent opponent distort such an announcement into a concession to the advantage of France! And we shall soon see that this was actually done.

Bismarck was quickly resolved. He sent word to the King at Ems that the state of his health had so improved that he was quite able to undertake a journey; he was therefore ready to proceed to Ems at the King's command. The reply, sent on the following day, was that Bismarck should come as soon as possible.[1]

General von Roon, too, found it advisable to leave his country-seat for the city on July 11th, that he might be at hand in case of need. On the evening of the same day he discussed the all-absorbing question of the day with the Ministers who had remained in Berlin; however, in the absence of Bismarck, Camphausen, and Moltke, no decision could, of course, be reached, and of military preparations there was as yet no thought.[2]

In the country at large the affair had, unquestionably, aroused great interest, but of any strong excitement there was no evidence. At first it had not been supposed possible that the choice of a ruler for Spain could lead to a conflict between France and Germany; gradually, however, the proceedings in Paris developed the suspicion that perhaps the Spanish question was being made the pretext for a rupture which had long been resolved upon. Evidently public opinion was not free from the influence of geographical position; in the Rhine Provinces the possibility of war was regarded not without a certain amount of anxiety;

[1] As related by Bismarck. Compare Jules Favre, "Gouvernement de la Défense Nationale," I., p. 177.

[2] According to a report made by Lord Loftus on July 12th.

whereas in the East voices could be heard here and there declaring that it was time to end this dilly-dallying, and reply to these French aspersions with German musket-shot.

Benedetti's second interview with the King, on the morning of July 11th,[1] took much the same course as had the first. The Ambassador was a little more urgent in his representations, but failed to bring forward any new reason justifying Gramont in his demand that the King should take the matter in hand, and command the Prince to withdraw from the candidacy. The King began to show some impatience at this second unseemly attempt to enforce an unjust demand, but did not depart from the position he had previously taken, again declaring that he could do nothing before receiving the expected reply from Sigmaringen.

Hereupon Benedetti besought him to take into consideration the terrific ferment in the French Chambers, by which his Government was being driven to extremity; action could not, he declared, be long deferred with safety.

To this the King replied that he expected the answer within twenty-four hours; to be impatient of so short a delay bespoke a desire on the part of France to precipitate a conflict in any case.

When Benedetti earnestly protested against this construction of his Government's diplomacy, the King

---

[1] On the evening of the 10th Benedetti had exchanged a few words with King William during an accidental meeting on the street, the King informing him that he had not yet heard from Prince Leopold.

again intimated that the answer would in all probability bring the announcement of the Prince's withdrawal, which would then be followed by his own approval of this step.[1] From this Benedetti concluded that the King already knew with certainty that the Prince would withdraw his acceptance; he therefore believed that with the King's expressed consent all cause for war would be removed.

This, however, was by no means Gramont's view of the matter. Although by a telegram sent at noon on the 12th, he declared himself willing to postpone action for a single day, this first despatch was followed by a second one, only one hour later, containing the instructions: Employ all the skill, nay, even cunning, at your command to establish the fact that the Prince's withdrawal was announced or communicated to you, or at least acknowledged BY THE KING or his Government. This is of great moment to us; it is absolutely necessary that the King should himself admit his concurrence, or that this should be manifestly evident from the facts.

Thus, to the very last moment, Gramont persisted in the demand by which war was made inevitable, insisting that the King's approval of the Prince's withdrawal would not suffice, but that the step must be taken as the consequence of the King's express command, or at his instance, that he might stand a penitent sinner before France and the rest of the world. But Gramont's hour of disappointment was at hand.

[1] Lettre particulière, 11 Juli, " Mission," p. 358.

After sending his second despatch he was permitted just one brief hour in which to indulge in his presumptuous hopes.

For the King, as might have been foreseen, was immovable in his determination not to humiliate himself or his country by compliance with the French exactions. He met Gramont's discourteous urgency by the simple tactics of deferring all action on his own part until after the Prince's voluntary withdrawal from the candidacy had been announced in Madrid by the Hohenzollerns themselves. Then the orders which Gramont desired the King to give the Prince would not only be unnecessary, but every occasion for them would be wanting; and, like a soap-bubble when pricked, the Minister's carefully devised cause for war would vanish in air. And this was in fact just what Gramont was about to experience.

This way out of his embarrassing position had been suggested to Prince Charles Anthony from more than one side. We are told that at the instance of Olozaga, Stratt, the Roumanian *chargé d'affaires* at Paris, went to Sigmaringen to ask, in the name of Prince Charles, that the Hereditary Prince renounce the Spanish crown. The appeal made by Emperor Napoleon with the same end in view has been mentioned. Presumably also King William had at least made it known at Sigmaringen that he would not object to the Prince's withdrawal.

This was all-sufficient for Prince Charles Anthony, who had no wish to allow his son's candidacy to oc-

casion a devastating war; and without awaiting the
Prince's return to Sigmaringen he sent the following
despatch at eleven o'clock on the morning of July 12th,
not to King William, but to Marshal Prim at Madrid,
and simultaneously with it one of like tenor to Olozaga,
the Spanish Ambassador at Paris: —

In view of the complications which have arisen in
consequence of my son's candidacy, and by which the
vote of the Spanish people will be deprived of that
freedom which my son believed it would have at the
time he accepted the Spanish crown, I now, in his
name, withdraw his acceptance of the offer.

At the same time he made a like announcement to
the public, although in briefer form, through the pages
of the *Schwäbische Merkur*. To King William he sent
a telegraphic message stating that on the following day
the King would receive detailed information with regard to the matter.

In the course of the afternoon of July 12th the news
of the Prince's withdrawal was carried to every part of
Germany by telegrams and extra sheets. It was received with mixed feelings; no one regretted that the
candidacy, which had at no time been popular, had
been abandoned; and there was rejoicing that, as was
believed, peace was again assured. Nevertheless, with
many people the news left a bitter after-taste; for, in
a matter wholly justifiable, a German prince had retired in consequence of the entirely unjust interference
of France.

On the evening of the same day Bismarck, who had

left Varzin at once upon learning the King's wish, arrived in Berlin, fully intending, despite the fatigue
caused by a hot journey of ten hours, to take the night
train for Ems. Upon hearing the news of the Prince's
withdrawal as received at the Foreign Office, he, however, determined not to undertake the tedious night
journey, since evidently the decision had already been
made at Ems; for, like Napoleon and all Europe, Bismarck believed the matter to be disposed of now.   He
sent a message to King William excusing himself on
the ground of extreme fatigue; and, as the King had
expressed a desire for advice, he requested the Minister
of the Interior, Count Eulenburg, to go to Ems in his
stead.

He himself remained in Berlin, although by no means
with a mind relieved from care, but, on the contrary,
oppressed by anxious thoughts. For now no opportunity remained to resent Gramont's insulting threats
as they deserved; since, after the chief point at issue
had been decided, any subsequent complaint would be
out of place. He was harassed by the fear that the
King might not have found it possible to avoid even
the slightest approach to participation in the step which
the Prince had taken, as well as any communication
regarding it to Benedetti, and thus, through him, to the
French Government. For it was by this course only
that Prussia could escape so much as the semblance of
having suffered a defeat.

Should it have happened otherwise, he was resolved
to have no further share in a policy which he could not

approve. He wrote to his wife advising her not to follow him to Berlin, as in all probability he would return
to Varzin in a few days, but whether he would then
still be Minister was very doubtful. In painful suspense he awaited news from Ems and Paris.[1]

[1] Compare Bismarck's personal report of September 23d, 1888, regarding the diary of Emperor Frederick III. (Published in the *Reichs-
anzeiger* of the 27th.)

CHAPTER III.

NEW CLAIMS MADE BY FRANCE.

To the utmost surprise of every one, Prince Leopold's voluntary withdrawal, far from having a pacifying effect upon Paris, seemed but to add fresh fuel to the fire.

The despatch which Prince Charles Anthony sent to Olozaga was not in cipher; and before delivering it to him for whom it was intended, the telegraph-office at which it was received forwarded a copy of it to Minis- ter Ollivier. Despite the good will which the Minister had so consistently shown toward Germany, the recent agitation had not failed of its effect upon his excitable temperament; and within the last few days he had inveighed as valiantly against Prussia for the supposed insult offered France as had Gramont himself. Still, he had at no time been really eager for war; and now, at sight of the despatch, all his former love of peace reasserted itself. Without a word to his colleagues he hastened to the palace of the Legislative Body; upon his arrival there, he found the halls and corridors crowded with deputies, reporters, and members of the Exchange, all eagerly expectant of important news. Ollivier rushed into their midst with the cry: " Peace, peace! We have triumphed; the Prussian candidate has withdrawn! Peace is once more assured!" He allowed the despatch to be passed from hand to hand, and the greatest tumult soon arose. The speculators hurried to the Exchange, where within a few minutes prices rose from 68 to 70, and millions changed hands.

In the Chamber, however, the Bonapartists and Chauvinists surrounded Ollivier with angry exclamations. Is this, they asked, the satisfaction which was to be required of Prussia, this a triumph over Bismarck? Is peace as the result of this paltry note from Papa Charles Anthony a peace consistent with French honor? What have we to do with Papa Charles Anthony? Or with his precious son, either, for that matter? Our quarrel is with Prussia. What satisfaction has Prussia rendered for the injury done us?

Immediately after the session was opened Clement Duvernois announced his intention to interpellate the Government as follows: We desire information regarding the guaranties which the Cabinet has agreed upon, or expects to agree upon, for the purpose of preventing a repetition of complications with Prussia.

The discussion of the budget, which was the order of the day, proceeded amidst general indifference. Many of the members who were adherents of the Ministry crowded about Thiers, who, at the very first words uttered by Ollivier, had called out to him to make sure of peace this time. They implored the famous orator most earnestly to continue to bring all his influence to bear upon the Government to this end, promising to give him their ablest support. These were the men whose election had been advocated by the Government, all of them peace-loving fathers of families, but at the same time the implicitly obedient servants of the Government.

Ollivier, deeply perplexed, had withdrawn immediately after the first outburst of this storm of indignation to confer with Gramont. For hours Thiers discussed the situation with the Ministers present, and in the end hoped he had converted at least two of them to his opinion. Toward the close of the day's session a member of the Left, Guyot-Montpayroux, declared himself resolved to compel the Ministers to break the silence which implied disrespect for both the Chamber and the country. It was rumored that in opposition to Thiers, he intended to call upon the Government to throw down the gauntlet to Prussia for its infraction of the Treaty of Prague.

Shortly before three o'clock the Duke of Gramont received a call from Baron Werther, who had just returned from Ems. Their conversation had, however, scarcely begun, when the Duke was handed a copy of the Sigmaringen telegram forwarded to him by the Havas agency; at the same time the Spanish Ambassador was announced, who had come to give official information regarding the same despatch. He remained only long enough to congratulate the Minister upon this happy result, and then withdrew.

Gramont was dismayed; [1] he had written Benedetti:

---

[1] Gramont, "La France et la Prusse," p. 114.

That the Prince shall withdraw is not of so much
importance to us as that the King shall cause him to
take this step. Now the Prince of Hohenzollern had
prevented the King's intervention by his voluntary
withdrawal, and far from having ascribed his decision
to a Prussian command, had assigned as its reason the
threats made by France. Gramont had a feeling of
having been outwitted by the King, and defrauded of
his demanded satisfaction.

It was with this end in view, then, that the King
had delayed matters; this was why he had pretended
to await a reply from Sigmaringen which could not
arrive before the next day, — that he might avoid, both
for himself and his Government, every appearance of
having participated in the transaction. On the spot
Gramont became convinced that the King had long
known of the Prince's decision, perhaps had even influenced him to it in private, and certainly had sanctioned
it. What perfidy! To affect ignorance, and ask for
delay until France should have received from Madrid
the announcement of the Prince's withdrawal, determined upon without the least interference on the part
of the King! King William, thought Gramont, could
not have been capable of such an intrigue; this was
but another of Bismarck's diabolical schemes, and must,
therefore, be frustrated at any cost. This time the
King had escaped the clutch of France; by what
device could he be cornered now, and, despite the
Prince's voluntary withdrawal, be forced to make
formal amends to France for the indignity suffered?

As Gramont could find no answer to this question, he took up his interrupted conversation with Werther, hoping that before its close something might be said which would suggest a new pretext for war.[1] "The Prince's withdrawal is a minor consideration," said he ; "for that we should have suffered him to ascend the Spanish throne was simply out of the question. Our real grievance is Prussia's action, — that its King permitted the candidacy without previously asking France for an expression of opinion regarding it."

To this Werther replied that King William had no right to forbid the Prince to accept the Spanish offer ; and then explained that the King, moreover, had not had the least idea that the candidacy of a prince closely related to the imperial house of France would give offence in Paris. These words suggested a sudden thought to Gramont. "If such was the King's belief at the time," said he, "he will now probably have no objection to make this known to the Emperor ; he might, for instance, write him (Gramont at once jotted down a draft of the desired letter), that in sanctioning the candidacy he had no intention to injure the interests or influence of France ; that he now concurred in the Prince's refusal to be a candidate for the crown of Spain, and hoped that henceforward all cause of misunderstanding between his own Government and that of France might be removed."

Gramont requested the Ambassador to lay this proposal before his sovereign at the earliest moment possible.

[1] "France et Prusse," p. 115

Whether it was malice or want of judgment which caused Gramont to overlook the tremendous difference between such a thought entertained by the King on the 21st of June, and its formal expression in a letter addressed to Napoleon after all the late threats of war made by France, is a point which I will not attempt to decide.[1] With great candor he then explained to the Ambassador how the publication of such a letter, or of its substance, would tend to allay the frantic indignation of the French people. At this juncture Ollivier, still under the influence of the recently witnessed scene in the Chamber, entered the room, and added his urgent representations to those of his colleague.

Again it must remain an open question whether it was weakness of insight or of character by which the Ambassador was deterred from resenting the very suggestion of such a humiliating step as the height of insolence. He contented himself with the answer that Gramont's speech of the 6th had done much to make the sending of such a letter more than ordinarily difficult. When the two French Ministers replied to this, that if he would not transmit the new proposal to the King, they would instruct Benedetti to lay it before him, Werther consented to make the desired communication to King William. This official discussion, in which a new *casus belli* had arisen, had lasted little over half an hour.

[1] On the same page ("France et Prusse," 124) on which he cites his draft of the proposed letter to be written by the King, he indulges in an expression of righteous indignation at "Bismarck's lie," by which it had been asserted that he, Gramont, had demanded of the King *une lettre d'excuse.*

Immediately after its conclusion, at four o'clock, Gramont hastened to St. Cloud to discuss this latest phase of the situation with the Emperor. Napoleon, like Ollivier, had hailed the Sigmaringen despatch as the solution of the crisis, perhaps had even looked upon it as the result of his own endeavor, and in an audience just given the representatives of Austria and Italy, had expressed himself as overjoyed that thus the preservation of peace had again become possible.[1] "Write your King," he had said to Vimercati, "that the dispute is ended; there will be no war."[2] Then, however, he had learned of the intended interpellation announced by Duvernois concerning the guaranties which the Government proposed to demand; and when the Duke of Gramont now appeared, he complained to him of the annoyance which this intention caused him, explaining that this required the immediate re-opening of negotiations concerning this highly dangerous subject, whereas ordinary prudence would suggest that any further negotiations should be deferred to as late a day as possible.[3]

At the mention of guaranties a new idea regarding the course of action now to be adopted toward Prussia flashed upon Gramont. "Quite right," he exclaimed; "it will not do to accept Prince Charles Anthony's announcement of his son's withdrawal unless accompanied by fixed guaranties for the future. The motive

---

[1] Duret, "Histoire de Quatre Ans," I., p. 109.

[2] According to a communication sent by Vimercati to Vienna.

[3] Gramont, p. 130.

which led to the proposed interpellation is so fully in harmony with the temper of the majority in the Chamber, as well as with public opinion in general, to which almost the entire press has given vigorous expression, that it will be impossible not to give it due consideration. Do we wish to retain the faintest hope of bringing this affair to a close without bloodshed, we must to a certain extent act in sympathy with the national feeling."

The account which Gramont's book gives of this interview concludes with the words : "I pass in silence over the careful and conscientious deliberation which preceded the final decision of the Government." Certain it is that his object was not as easily attained with Napoleon as with Werther ; for instead of half an hour, as with the Ambassador, the discussion with the Emperor was continued for three hours before Gramont obtained Napoleon's hesitatingly given permission to instruct Benedetti to make the attempt with King William, and lay the proposal before him in the most courteous form of which it admitted. Then he hurried back to Paris, and at seven o'clock telegraphed to Benedetti : Through Olozaga we have been informed of Prince Leopold's withdrawal as announced in his name by Prince Charles Anthony ; to be effectual this step requires that the King of Prussia shall concur in it, promising that this candidacy will not be permitted at some future time ; ask the King at once to give you this assurance, which he cannot refuse if his intentions are truly such as he claims them to be ; make a paraphrase on this despatch such as you can communicate to the King.

Accordingly, on the morning of July 13th, King William would learn of these two latest demands, — a humble letter of apology to be written to Napoleon, and the issue of orders forbidding the Hohenzollern candidacy for the future. Whether the two were to be regarded as inseparable or as an alternative, Gramont in his haste forgot to state.

After the despatch had been sent, the Duke discussed the situation with the English Ambassador. Making no mention of Benedetti's latest announcement, namely, that the King had promised his consent to Prince Leopold's withdrawal, and that this was to be communicated to the French Ambassador on the morrow, the Duke now complained to Lord Lyons: "The manner of this withdrawal places us in a most embarrassing position; public opinion is so exasperated that the Cabinet may be forced to resign to-morrow if this affair is declared to be concluded without satisfaction having been obtained from Prussia. Otherwise," said he, "the Prince's withdrawal removes the original cause for complaint; Spain has no further part in the transaction, and the quarrel, should it come to a quarrel, is now between France and Prussia."

Lord Lyons was utterly and most unpleasantly surprised. "What!" he exclaimed, "you hesitate to accept this simple solution of the crisis, although only a few days ago you declared to the English Government through me that should the Prince decline the crown the situation would be relieved? Should your policy lead to war, the verdict of all Europe will be: 'The responsibility rests with France; without real provocation, but wholly because of over-sensitiveness and a feeling of injured pride, she has rushed into war.' In that case entire Germany will stand by Prussia, and France will incur the censure of the whole world."

Lord Lyons was a far-sighted and experienced statesman, a man of calm judgment, and wholly unprejudiced with respect to the question in controversy. In what he said he expressed no more than that which the facts in the case would lead every unbiassed observer to conclude; namely, the conviction that by making new demands Gramont would entail most terrible disaster upon his country. On Gramont, however, it made no impression. "To-morrow morning," said he, "the matter will be finally considered in a Cabinet Council, and the decision reached will then be announced to the Chambers, and thus to the world."

If the English Ambassador's unreserved criticism had annoyed the Duke, he found ample compensation for this in a letter from the Emperor, which was delivered to him at about ten o'clock. In it Napoleon declared that after maturer reflection upon the subject of their last conversation he had arrived at the following conclusions:—

That since the Sigmaringen despatch had not been addressed to the French Government, it was not to be regarded in the light of an official communication. . . .

That since the withdrawal had been announced by Prince Charles Anthony, it was not binding upon Prince Leopold. . . .

Accordingly, Benedetti must demand a categorical reply, by which King William would pledge himself not to permit the Prince to follow his brother's example, and some day make his appearance in Spain. . . .

So long as such a reply was not forthcoming, military preparations must be continued. . . .

Until this point should be decided, it would be inexpedient to give the Chamber any nearer information.

Every word in this letter is remarkable; in the first place, that the official character of the despatch which the Spanish Ambassador had formally communicated to the French Government should be denied, as well as that the assertion should be made that the declaration it contained was not binding upon Prince Leopold, although it especially stated that it was in his name Prince Charles Anthony made the announcement. Furthermore, the unreasonable apprehension that, despite his father's declaration and the hostility manifested by France, Prince Leopold might suddenly appear in Madrid as had Prince Charles in Bucharest in 1866, although the latter had not been restrained from doing so by a previous withdrawal, and had, moreover, been in every way supported and encouraged by Napoleon. And finally, we are prompted to ask, what had suggested all these strange fancies to Napoleon, who only three days previously had alluded to the Prince's withdrawal as the surest means of preserving peace, and no more than two hours before, in conversation with two ambassadors, had referred to the happiness which the achievement of this event had given him?

Gramont solves this riddle for us.

In his book he cites the Emperor's letter,[1] and adds the comment: "The letter, truth to tell, was no more than a concise recapitulation of that which we had determined upon in the afternoon." Since at the beginning of their conversation Napoleon had advocated just the reverse of these views, Gramont hereby fathers the opinions now expressed by the Emperor. The letter, therefore, testifies not to the warlike spirit of the Emperor, but to the weakness and want of will-power of an ailing man. Gramont, during the course of his discussion with the Emperor, may even have outlined a draft of this defiant writing, just as for Werther he had indicated the text of the letter to be written by King William. However that may be, the assertions made in it are an echo of Gramont's opinion. According to this view of it, Napoleon's consent to the very polite request now to be made of the Prussian King had been finally wrung from him after a struggle of three hours; but it required yet three hours more before the eager advocates of war by whom he was surrounded could induce him to sign the desired writing. Its final clause only, the one directing that for the present no communication concerning the matter should be made to the Chambers, would seem to be the

[1] "France et Prusse," p. 137.

Emperor's own suggestion, since, as we are aware, it was Gramont's intention to take this step on the very next day.

Be that as it may, Gramont had achieved his desire, for now Ollivier also gave his consent. Just before midnight the Duke sent another telegram to Benedetti, followed an hour later by a second one of similar import, from which, however, the direction to make a polite paraphrase on its contents was omitted. Quite in the spirit of the writing received from the Emperor, the despatch briefly and unceremoniously declared: "The communication received by us, but not addressed to us, announcing the Prince's withdrawal, cannot be accepted as a sufficient answer to our just complaints, and still less as a guaranty for the future. To insure us against the possibility that the son may not feel bound by his father's word, or that he will not appear in Spain as did his brother in Roumania, it is absolutely necessary that the King shall promise that he will not permit Prince Leopold to accept the candidacy at some future time."

The despatch closed with the assurance that in making this demand the French Government had no hidden motive, neither did it seek a pretext for war, but desired only that the crisis might be terminated with honor to itself.

Even yet I would hesitate to assert that this assurance was a deliberate falsehood, that Gramont fully intended to make a conflict inevitable. Not that he was at all loath to undertake it, but he still hoped to achieve the desired humiliation of Prussia's king without it. That by which he was inflexibly held to this fatal course, aside from his personal feeling of enmity, was his fear of the patriotic fury to which he himself had roused the populace within the space of one short week. He had set the stone to rolling, and now, an irresistible avalanche, it swept him onward.[1]

The untruthful representations with which he had flooded the country; the assertion that Prussia had striven to place Prince Leopold upon the Spanish throne; that this was an affront to the honor of France for which full and glorious satisfaction must be required of King William, — all this had been gradually absorbed into the very life of the Parisians and throbbed in their veins. With noisy demonstrations they concurred in the criticisms which were showered upon Ollivier for his announcement that peace was again assured; they were enthusiastic over Duvernois' demand that guaranties against Prussia's eagerness for conquest must be insisted upon. Louder and louder rose the cry that the Spanish incident was the last drop by which the cup of French endurance had been filled to overflowing. It mattered little what Papa Charles Anthony might write. France had quite enough of this Prussian presumption; ever since Sadowa this rapacious neighbor was seeking to rob France of its leading position in Europe; it was high time to end all

[1] He admits this himself (Dépositions I., 105), saying: "We were forced to make the demand for guaranties by the pressure of public opinion," etc. "It was, moreover, necessary," he adds, "and in no way an affront to Prussia."

this; to take the step whereby South Germany would be prevented from falling under the Prussian yoke; to rescue the annexed provinces from out of Bismarck's iron clutch; to throw this over-ambitious rival back into the old impotency.

On this warm July night the people gathered in crowds upon the boulevards, and struggled eagerly to get the latest editions of the evening papers, which gave vehement utterance to the war feeling. Seated high upon a cart amidst the crowd, an opera-singer struck up the Marseillaise, which was greeted with wild applause. Wherever soldiers appeared they were hailed as the protectors and avengers of French honor. Organized bands marched through the streets uttering fierce cries of " War, war! Down with Bismarck! Down with Prussia! To Berlin, to Berlin!" The police looked on impassively. As an appreciative eye-witness remarked later, a war was here organized as is a riot ordinarily.

Amidst all this tumult there were, of course, many who did not lose their heads, — quiet citizens and substantial business men, who looked forward with anxiety to the disturbance and injury which even a successful war would cause.[1] But no one dared to stem the tide, and thus incur the suspicion that his was but a lukewarm patriotism. And finally, when early on the 13th the morning papers with few exceptions violently denounced Prussia, and invoked imprecations upon a peace secured on the present basis, scarcely one person

---

[1] So Thiers, an eye-witness, tells us.

in this seething metropolis had any doubt that the heart of the French nation was set upon a war with Prussia, upon revenge for Sadowa, and that any stand which the Ministry might take against this valiant beginning would be utterly useless.

So matters stood when, on the morning of the 13th, the Cabinet met in council at St. Cloud, presided over by the Emperor.[1] Gramont presented the situation thus: After the Prussian king had authorized the Hohenzollern candidacy, which was injurious to the honor and dignity of France, we could not do otherwise than require satisfaction of him, and therefore demanded that he give the Prince orders to withdraw his acceptance of the Spanish crown. He has made compliance with this demand impossible by treacherously delaying his reply until after the Prince had voluntarily renounced the candidacy. After this evidence of perfidy it was advisable to place the future under the safeguard of guaranties. Hence, we asked the King to declare that he will forbid the Prince to renew his attempt to acquire the Spanish crown.

This exposition gave rise to two entirely contrary opinions. The Minister of War, Lebœuf, had little hope that the King would make any such humiliating concession; whatever the issue, there was a probability of war to face, and every reason to take wise precautions. In Prussia the mobilization of the army was being rapidly carried forward, he said; it was a matter

[1] Compare Gramont, p. 148, and Lebœuf's testimony before the Investigation Committee, I., 47.

of life and death for France that the enemy should not be allowed to gain the advantage in this respect. He therefore proposed, with the concurrence of the Minister of the Navy, that the war reserves be called in at once.

In opposition to this view the great majority of the Ministers not only advised against any such measure as being equivalent to a declaration of war, but against Gramont's demand for guaranties as well. They held that all that Gramont had claimed on the 6th had been complied with in that the Prince had withdrawn; hence, the affair was ended.

They were supported in this opinion by a writing received from Lord Lyons during the course of the consultation, in which, in the name of his Government, he most earnestly commended the adoption of this course.

Count Beust had also condemned Gramont's quarrelsome attitude in a most vigorously expressed telegram sent on July 11th, declaring that entire Europe would hold him responsible for all the suffering which the coming war would cause. On the 13th he sent another despatch counselling Gramont to accept as sufficient, and to make the most of the diplomatic triumph which had been achieved in the Prince's withdrawal.

Despite all these warnings, the outcry made by the Arcadians, the newspapers, and the street mobs, impelled Gramont to hold to the unreasonable standpoint that the preservation of French prestige required not only the Prince's withdrawal, but that formal satisfaction be

rendered by Prussia. " In what we ask for the achievement of this end we are as moderate as can be," he explained to his colleagues. " The instructions given the
Ambassador at Berlin were not intended as an ulti-
matum, and should not be regarded as such. Neither
was our demand for guaranties inflexible ; it permitted
of qualification and modification ; nothing, for instance,
was said with regard to any particular form in which
they should be given; the Government is inclined to
come to almost any agreement in this respect."

Gramont's latest telegrams to Benedetti, as we remember, were in a very different tone ; but that the
demand he desired to make might not encounter the
opposition of the Cabinet, he now represented it as an
inoffensive proposal, leaving almost everything open to
further agreement. As is obvious, the action desired by
Lebœuf did not carry out this idea at all ; if the demand for guaranties was of so inoffensive a nature,
where was the necessity for great military preparations
by which the now glowing spark would be fanned into
a blaze ? Realizing this, Gramont felt constrained to
oppose Lebœuf, and thus succeeded in pacifying his
more peaceably inclined colleagues. The result was a
half-way measure ; the demand for guaranties was persisted in, the military preparations were postponed.

Hereupon Lebœuf declared that he must in that
case tender his resignation, in consequence of which
the Emperor directed that the question of mobilization
should be further discussed on the 14th.

At two o'clock the Chamber was awaiting the appearance of the Ministers with illy suppressed impatience. Gramont announced that the Spanish Ambassador had given official notification that the Prince of Hohenzollern had withdrawn his acceptance of the Spanish throne; the negotiations with Prussia, however, which throughout had been directed toward the achievement of this one object, had not yet been concluded; meanwhile it was impossible to give the House a full and detailed explanation of the matter. This intelligence was received by the middle party with feelings of anxiety and disappointment; on the Right, however, Duvernois instantly called attention to his interpellation regarding guaranties; and, in order to deepen the unfavorable impression, Baron David, prompted by his enmity toward the Ministry, added a second interpellation, asking the reason for the Cabinet's dilatoriness in conducting the negotiations with Prussia, through which it was incurring the sneers of the world, endangering the nation's dignity, and destroying the prosperity of the country.

When Gramont protested against this criticism of the Ministry's policy, and asked that the discussion of the two interpellations be deferred until the 15th of July, Monsieur de Keratry called out from his seat on the Left: "By such hesitation you allow Bismarck to make game of you! As a Frenchman, I protest most earnestly against it!" Nevertheless, the desired delay was granted by a large majority.

Minister Gramont breathed again ; this would give him a respite of at least twenty-four hours. He left the hall of assembly to repair to the Senate, there to make the same statement. Hardly had he arrived there when he was handed a despatch from Ems, the contents of which left him little hope of success for the latest negotiations undertaken by Benedetti. In consequence, Gramont was doubly eager in the representations he made to Lord Lyons immediately afterwards, assuring him of his own desire for peace, explaining that so far Prussia had not made even the smallest concession, or offered the least satisfaction, and calling the Ambassador's attention to the moderation which marked the French demands (again he put them in writing) : If the King forbids the Prince ever to reconsider the candidacy the quarrel is at an end. — He desired the Ambassador to report this in London, accompanied by the request that Lord Granville advise Prussia to comply with this demand.

To such strange inversions of the truth did Gramont's blind obstinacy lead him. He, who from the outset had maintained that Prussia had suggested and furthered the candidacy, now insisted that in abandoning it Prussia made no concession, did not retreat from its original position.

Count Benedetti, as we saw, took a different view. King William, in his conversation with the Ambassador on the 9th of July, and again on the 11th, had given him to understand that he fully expected the Prince to withdraw voluntarily, and that his consent to this step would then be given without hesitation. Benedetti flattered himself with the anticipation that thus his task would be brilliantly accomplished.

On the 12th of July the King told him that by a telegram from Sigmaringen he had been notified that the letter expected from Prince Charles Anthony would arrive at Ems on the forenoon of the 13th; as soon as it had been received he would summon the Ambassador, and give him his final answer.

Whether this telegram contained a preliminary announcement of the Prince's withdrawal or not, the nature of the matter in hand required that the King should enter into no definite negotiations with the Ambassador before the letter containing the full statement was at hand.

During the night, from the 12th to the 13th, Benedetti received the despatch which Gramont had sent on the previous evening, instructing him to endeavor at once to induce the King to promise that he would forbid the Prince to re-accept the Spanish crown at some future time. The Ambassador had little heart to do this latest bidding; however, on the morning of the 13th he took a stroll in the Park near the springs, hoping that he might there meet one of the gentlemen of the royal suite, and through his intervention obtain as early an audience as possible with the King. At the end of the promenade that follows the bank of the Lahn, quite near the music pavilion, which as usual was surrounded by a crowd, he suddenly came face to face with the King, who was attended only by an adjutant.

King William turned to the Ambassador with a friendly greeting. "The courier from Sigmaringen has

not yet arrived; but here is good news," said he, hand-
ing Benedetti an extra edition of the *Kölnische Zeitung*
containing the Sigmaringen despatch. " This ends all
your anxiety and trouble," he added cheerily.

After returning the King's salutation, Benedetti
replied that he had already heard of the Prince's withdrawal through a despatch received from his Government during the past night; this had, however, also
contained instructions directing him to request the
King — then followed the new demand for guaranties.

The King was utterly surprised and greatly disturbed by this latest development. He, however, confined himself to the reply that before the arrival of
the Sigmaringen courier he could say no more.

Hereupon Benedetti grew more urgent. " But, your
Majesty, could we not even now discuss the letter hypo-
thetically? *If* the Prince withdraws, will your Majesty authorize me to telegraph my Government that
you give the desired promise? "

" You ask," replied the King, " that I shall bind
myself for all future time and for any event; I cannot
and ought not to undertake such an obligation; I must
reserve the liberty to decide each individual case according to the circumstances. Most assuredly I have
no hidden motive in this connection; the affair has
caused me too much anxiety not to be glad to have
it settled past recall. Nevertheless, I cannot possibly
go as far as you desire."

Still undaunted, Benedetti made a third attempt.
" I can readily understand," said he, " why your Gov-

ernment, or you as sovereign, should hesitate to bind yourself for the future; but your Majesty has assured me that in this matter your action has been simply that of head of the family, and as such it would seem possible that you might comply with our wish without incurring any political disadvantage. I dare to hope, therefore, that your Majesty will graciously authorize me to send the despatch mentioned."

At this unseemly importunity upon the public promenade, the King's patience at length gave way. With impressive dignity he replied, " No; on the contrary, I must repeat what I have already said; I cannot give you the desired authority. I refuse, once for all, to comply with this new and unexpected claim." [1] This ended the conversation; and beckoning to the adjutant, who had stepped a little to one side while the two were conversing, the King continued his walk.

Owing to the articles which had appeared in the Paris newspapers, Benedetti had been an object of general interest to the public of Ems ever since his arrival in town. Consequently this brief discussion, growing more earnest and animated with every word, was observed with eager attention by the people in the immediate vicinity of the King; and the impression received by all was that something unusual must have occurred.

Indeed, this day was destined to bring with it much more that was out of the ordinary.

In the course of the afternoon the King received Werther's report informing him of the French demand

[1] Benedetti, p. 376.

that in an autograph letter to the Emperor Napoleon
he should formally disclaim having had any intention
to injure the honor or influence of France in giving
his consent to the Hohenzollern candidacy. The effect
was such as was to be expected, especially after the
irritation caused by the demand which Benedetti had
presented in the morning. The King was indignant
that such a humiliating act should be expected of him,
and so much the more so in view of the publicity which
it was intended it should have.[1]

Toward one o'clock the letter from Prince Charles
Anthony arrived, containing, as had been anticipated,
the announcement that the Prince had withdrawn his
acceptance of the Spanish crown. In conformity with
what the King had said to Benedetti, the latter should
now have been invited to an audience with the King;
the Ambassador, who in the meantime had received the
more urgent despatches which Gramont had sent during the night, was in fact counting the minutes until
he should be summoned. However, the encounter in
the Park had not failed to affect the King's sentiments
toward Benedetti also. He determined (we shall soon
hear more with regard to this) that the Ambassador
should not receive another audience about this affair;
and that this decision might be placed beyond recall it
was to be made public at once.

The Minister of Finance, Camphausen, who had just
arrived in Ems, concurred most heartily in this step.

---

[1] Benedetti, p. 383. Gramont did not deem it necessary to acquaint
the Ambassador with this second demand.

Soon after two o'clock King William notified Benedetti by one of the adjutants, Count Radziwill, that the letter expected from Prince Charles Anthony had arrived; that it contained the announcement of his son's withdrawal; and that the King now considered the affair as ended.

Nevertheless, Benedetti continued his request for an audience for the purpose of concluding the conversation begun in the morning, making special mention of the latest despatches received from Minister Gramont.

The answer conveyed to him by the adjutant was that the King approved the Prince's withdrawal in the same manner and to the same extent that he had approved his acceptance of the candidacy,[1] and desired that this be communicated to the French Government; but with regard to the guaranties which had been asked for the future, his decision of the morning remained unaltered. This was again the answer which Benedetti received when later, in the evening, he made another attempt to obtain an audience. It was the King's final decision.

Even King William himself probably had no idea how momentous would be the consequences of this step.

We know what were Bismarck's feelings on the even-

---

[1] These are the words used in the report made by the adjutant, whereas Benedetti announced in Paris that the consent had been given *entière et sans réserve*. The expression used by the adjutant unquestionably conforms to the orders received from the King, whose intention it was to convey the idea that he now consented to the withdrawal as once he had to the Prince's acceptance, namely, in his capacity as head of the family and not as sovereign. *Entière et sans réserve* was applicable to it in that case also.

ing of July 12th. During the first hours of the next
morning he still believed that the controversy had been
concluded without satisfaction having been obtained for
Gramont's unprovoked threats, consequently in a manner detrimental to Prussian honor; he entertained serious intentions therefore of retiring from office. Soon,
however, he received news of the change in the situation; first, a communication from the Russian embassy
in Paris,[1] stating that the French Government, not satisfied with the Prince's withdrawal, now made further
complaints against Prussia for the course it had pursued, and intended to put forward new claims against
the Prussian Government.

If this report was true, all Bismarck's apprehensions
of the night before could be cast to the winds. At a
glance he grasped the situation, recognizing how Gramont's customary uncurbed eagerness had led him into
a blunder by which he had become the offender. Now
Germany was again in a position to claim reparation
from the arrogant antagonist from whom such unmer-
ited insults had been suffered during the past week.

In conversation with the English Ambassador, Lord
Augustus Loftus, Bismarck gave full expression to
these sentiments: "If the French Government really
intends to declare itself unsatisfied with the withdrawal
of the Prince, and to put forward new claims, it will
at once become evident to every one that all this ado
over the Spanish throne question was nothing more

[1] According to the entry in the diary of Emperor Frederick, July
13th, 1870.

than an empty pretext, and that the real purpose behind it all was to incite a war of revenge for Sadowa.
Germany, however, is resolved not to allow any affront
or humiliation suffered from France to pass unresented,
but to fight if she is unjustly provoked.   Assuredly we
do not seek war; of that we have given proof, and we
will not now depart from our past course; but we cannot let France gain an advantage over us in the matter
of military preparations." He then enumerated the
measures which to his knowledge had been taken; from
what we learned of the declaration made by Gramont
to Lord Lyons on the 8th, and of that made by Napoleon on the 12th, we know that there were good grounds
for all Bismarck claimed.

"If this continues," said he, "we shall have reason
to ask France for an explanation regarding the purpose
of her military preparations.   Moreover," he declared,
"in view of recent French action our safety demands
that we require guaranties against the danger of being
taken by surprise.   France ought to be required to make
a formal declaration to the other European Powers that
it regards the Spanish question as settled, and consequently makes no further claims.   Should this not be
done, and should France neither recall the threats made
in Gramont's speech, nor give an adequate explanation,
Prussia must demand satisfaction from France.   Under
no other condition can I have further transactions with
the French Ambassador after the utterances which Gramont allowed himself with regard to Prussia, and which
were heard by all Europe."

We see from this how fully Bismarck intended to bring home to her antagonist the indignities offered Prussia by Gramont, — a demand for explanations, for retraction and reparation, for guaranties for the future. Not one had been omitted. The English Ambassador spoke not a word in deprecation, but, on the contrary, made an earnest appeal to his Government to bring the strongest influence possible to bear upon the French Minister in the interest of peace.

As yet, during these midday hours, Bismarck had no intimation of that which meanwhile was taking place at Ems. With impatience the Minister awaited news of how the King had received the communication from Werther disclosing to him the insufferable assumption that he would write the humiliating letter of apology to Napoleon. Until he should be assured upon this point, Bismarck deemed it unadvisable openly to sever diplomatic relations between the two countries. He, however, sent Werther orders to quit Paris at once, directing him to take leave of absence on the pretext of ill health; at the same time he delivered a severe rebuke to the Ambassador for the manner in which he had conducted matters.

That afternoon Roon and Moltke dined with Bismarck. At six o'clock he received Abeken's despatch, sent from Ems at three, informing him of what had occurred up to the time of the first message sent Benedetti through Radziwill. He opened it, hastily scanned its contents, and then read it aloud to his two guests. As frequently as this despatch has appeared in print, I will nevertheless insert it here.

Abeken to Count Bismarck : —

" His Majesty, the King, writes me : ' During an acci-dental encounter with Count Benedetti upon the public promenade he asked me, finally in a most obtrusive manner, to authorize him to telegraph his Government that I would bind myself never to give my consent should the Hohenzollerns at some future time recon-sider the candidacy for the Spanish crown. I refused, somewhat sternly in the end, to comply with his de-mand, saying that I neither could nor would enter into an engagement of this nature *à tout jamais.* I of course told him that I had as yet not received any word ; and since he had already been notified through Paris from Madrid, it must be obvious to him that my Government again had no part in this transaction.'

" Later his Majesty received a letter from the Prince (Charles Anthony). His Majesty having told Count Benedetti that he expected a communication from the Prince, he decided, in consideration of the demand mentioned above, and upon the advice of Count Eulen-burg and myself, not to grant Count Benedetti another audience about this affair, but to notify him by an ad-jutant that the Prince's letter had confirmed the intel-ligence received by Benedetti from Paris, and that his Majesty had no further communication to make to the Ambassador.

" His Majesty leaves it to your decision whether this new demand presented by Benedetti, and our rejection of it, should not be immediately made known to our Ambassador and the press."

The first effect of this despatch upon the two generals was a feeling of deep dejection.

France, then, had not even stopped at the affront of which Werther had given notice, but had added to it this unprecedented and outrageous insolence! Had Gramont forgotten with whom he was dealing? He had himself been willing to concede independence of action to Spain, but had insulted our King because he had done likewise. And opposed to this arrogance there was the good-natured mildness of our monarch. Instead of turning his back upon the Ambassador at the first intimation of such a message, he had deigned to enter into negotiations with him, had tried to justify his own Government, and had asked for advice as to whether it was advisable to grant the Ambassador another audience! What assurance was there that to-morrow Benedetti would not come forward with some new and still more preposterous demand? And all this was to be made known to the world!

But did compliance with the royal order require this after all? The King's directions were that the French demand and its rejection should be made public. But the very nature of the matter in hand forbade the publication of the details mentioned in the despatch; and it was hardly advisable that the exact words of the King should be given to the world, if only for the reason that some quite harmlessly inexact word might thus become liable to contradiction by Benedetti.[1] Moreover, Abe-

---

[1] This did in fact occur; Benedetti's report stated that the King had addressed him (not he the King).

ken's allusion to advice asked by the King before deciding not again to receive the Ambassador was a matter
concerning the Cabinet alone, and easily admitted of
misconstruction in a number of ways. All these considerations determined Bismarck to comply with the
letter of the royal order, and he therefore wrote out
the following despatch: —

After the Royal Government of Spain had officially
announced to the Imperial Government of France that
the Prince of Hohenzollern had withdrawn his acceptance of the Spanish crown, the French Ambassador at
Ems presented a further demand to his Majesty, the
King, asking him for authority to telegraph to Paris
that his Majesty, the King, would bind himself never to
give his consent should the Hohenzollerns at some future time reconsider the candidacy for the Spanish crown.
Hereupon his Majesty refused to grant the French Ambassador another audience about this affair, and notified
him by the adjutant on duty that his Majesty had no
further communication to make to the Ambassador.

This despatch conformed strictly to the King's directions, its wording being exactly that of the despatch
from Ems; and, in the face of the two documents, the
accusation of forgery trumped up by certain French
organs is childish in the extreme.[1]

Nevertheless, in this more concise form, and by the
omission of all particulars and explanations regarding

---

[1] This accusation arose in consequence of comparing Bismarck's telegram, not with the then unpublished original of the despatch, but with
a report made later by Adjutant Radziwill regarding his three commis-
sions.

motives, the impression made by the announcement was
an entirely different one. For the past eight days
France with vociferous threats of war had demanded
the humiliation of the King ; for five days negotiations
with reference to this had been unceasingly in progress ;
now, unaccompanied by explanations of any kind, there
would appear for the eyes of the world the account
of how the German monarch had flatly refused these
demands, declaring the matter to be thus definitely
settled.

Bismarck realized this with inward exultation. More
quickly than the two generals he had recognized at a
glance how all important for the outcome was this order
given by the King. By publishing the refusal its significance would be doubled; by this concise form it would
be made ten times greater. Now it would be for
France to choose whether it would swallow this bitter
dose or carry out its threats.

Bismarck read his despatch to his friends. " That
sounds better," said Roon. " At first it sounded like
the beat of the chamade, now like a fanfare," added
Moltke. Bismarck remarked, " If the despatch to the
embassies is sent out at eleven o'clock it will be received in Paris by midnight, and then these Frenchmen
will see how mistaken their newspapers were when they
declared that Prussia was knocking under. But," he
continued, " assuming that they take offence at this
and strike out, what are our prospects of victory in that
case ? "

" I believe," replied Moltke, " that we are more than

a match for them, always with the reservation that no one can foresee the issue of a great battle." After entering somewhat into the reasons for this, he closed with the remark, emphasizing it by striking his breast as he spoke, " Should it be my privilege to lead our forces in this war, death will be welcome to these old bones as soon as it is over."

The despatch was given to the public at once through the columns of the *Norddeutsche Allgemeine Zeitung*, and at eleven o'clock it was sent to the embassies.

It was a plain statement of facts, the correctness of which could not be disputed. Now, a fact may be indisputable, and yet its publication may be ill advised ; it will, however, be generally conceded that in this case the French Government, which had made its original demand publicly through Gramont's speech of July 6th, bristling with threats of war, and then, after this demand had been complied with, had announced to the Chamber on July 13th that new claims would be put forward, was not in a position to complain, if now Prussia on her part made the public acquainted with the manner in which the discussion at Ems had been terminated. Inseparably associated with this, however, was the fact that the King had declined to give Benedetti further audiences about the matter; although in the absence of the Minister it was a personal favor on the part of the monarch to grant them at all, and after Gramont's speech of July 6th was an evidence of his extreme love of peace.

Nor did Benedetti in any way consider the King's

decision to imply a slight to himself or an affront to his Emperor. Before leaving Ems he read the despatch as published in Berlin, and made no further comment upon it than that its appearance in the press must be attributed to the Prussian Cabinet, since he had given no one the least information regarding the occurrence. He then took formal leave of the King in a short audience which the King had granted for this purpose at Benedetti's request, and which passed without the slightest evidence of any other spirit than one of perfect courteousness on the part of both monarch and ambassador.

In the course of the day, on July 13th, reports of the unfavorable manner in which the discontinuance of the Hohenzollern candidacy had been received in Paris were circulated among the people of Berlin also. If on the preceding day the prospect of continued peace had been greeted with but half-hearted satisfaction, now, at the greater likelihood of war, this feeling was transformed into one of vehement exasperation.

What more do these Parisians want, was asked. Has not the candidacy over which they made so absurd an ado been abandoned? By what right does this Bonaparte assume to dictate to Spain regarding its choice of a king? And now he even seeks a quarrel with us because of it! Let other nations bow submissively before him if they like; if he meddles with us, he will find his day of reckoning. We know him now; to what purpose are further negotiations? Why let that old fox, Benedetti, imbitter our venerable monarch's

stay at Ems? Let us have no more leniency, no ignominious peace! We wish to wrong no one, but neither
will we allow any one to give us orders about our
affairs. If Napoleon is not inclined to respect the
German nation's independence of action, he shall learn
how the German arm wields the sword.

Such were the sentiments which filled all hearts
when, on the evening of the 13th, an extra edition of
the *Norddeutsche Allgemeine Zeitung* made known to
the people by means of the published despatch what
had occurred at Ems. The effect was a tremendous
one; deep from the hearts of the nation rose a single
cry of rejoicing uttered by thousands of voices. At
length, at length, the shadow of dishonor which had
lately fallen upon Prussia's fame was gone; her men
could breathe again, for he who represented all this
boastful arrogance had received a fitting reply, — he
had been shown the door.

On the streets the crowds of excited people surged
back and forth; men embraced one another with tears
of joy; thunderous cheers for King William rent the
air. Meanwhile the despatch had also been posted up
in Ems; on the morning of the 14th it appeared in all
the newspapers, accompanied in every instance by energetic comments, and everywhere calling forth the same
expressions of indignation and satisfaction.

Owing to the prevailing state of intense excitement,
the aroused imagination pictured all that had occurred
in most vivid colors. In Ems the story went the rounds
that at Benedetti's unseemly importunity upon the pub-

lic promenade the King had suddenly turned his back upon him, calling out to the adjutant accompanying him, "Say to the gentleman that I will not answer his demand, neither will I see him again!"

The picture which this scene suggested was reproduced again and again with many variations; in both prose and verse Benedetti's audacity was derided, and King William's manly dignity was extolled. A memorial stone was set up on the spot where the King had repelled the French presumption. The people were prepared for war, and looked forward to it with the confidence inspired by conscious strength.

And now a like flood of national enthusiasm swept in mighty waves over South Germany also; before a musket-shot had been fired, Gramont's audacious proceeding had brought about that which Napoleon had used all his ingenuity to prevent, — the unification of the German nation, the extension of the German Confederation to the Alps. In Baden the people and the Government spoke as with a single voice; in Würtemberg and Bavaria the anti-Prussian Democrats and Ultramontanes suddenly found themselves to be in an alarming minority; through every province rang the enthusiastic call, "To arms!" A few days previously the Bavarian Minister, Count Bray, had remarked to the French representative, "Should it come to war, France will find all Germany a unit."

CHAPTER IV.

THE DECLARATION OF WAR.

SUCH was the pass to which the French Government had brought matters under Gramont's guidance. For the purpose of intimidating the Prussian King into making a humble apology, it had begun operations with a loudly proclaimed threat of war, and had continued them with the accompaniment of constantly increasing demonstrations of hostility in the Chambers, by the press, and by street mobs. Now it had received Germany's reply, a deliberate, irrevocable, publicly spoken No. And was the so hastily threatened war to follow? If so, where could a pretext which sensible people would regard as plausible be found now that the candidacy was a thing of the past? And, on the other hand, if war were not declared, how, after indulging in such boastful denunciations, could France escape derision?

The dilemma was a much too difficult one for the mediocre minds by whom Napoleon was surrounded, and to whom as his parliamentary Ministers he now gave *carte blanche* in matters political. It was but on the day before that Gramont represented the demand for guaranties to be so promising, and compliance with it so probable, that it was deemed unnecessary to call out the reserves.   And yet, before the day ended, came Benedetti's telegram, saying, The King desires me to announce to the French Government that the Prince has withdrawn, and that this meets with his unreserved approval.   The guaranties for the future he, however, refuses most positively, and declines to give me another audience about the matter.

On the morning of July 14th, at nine o'clock, the Cabinet assembled in council, presided over by the Emperor, to discuss the situation as revealed by this latest intelligence.   In the face of war, the ardor for it suffered a sudden collapse.   Gramont assured [1] his colleagues that the King's announcement of the withdrawal accompanied by his approval of this step had been the foremost demand made by France, and had from the outset been considered as the first step toward a peaceful solution of the difficulty ; and further, that if the King had fully resolved not to entertain the proposal of guaranties for the future, this was in itself reason sufficient for declining to grant Benedetti another audience, since any further discussion of the subject would be to no purpose.

According to Gramont's present view of the situation, the prospects for a peaceable issue were not even disturbed by a despatch now received from Le Sourd, stating that the rejection of the French demand had been officially published on the previous evening

---

1 " France et Prusse," pp. 195, 207.

in the *Norddeutsche Allgemeine Zeitung*, although Gramont could not deny that in all probability when this
became known in Paris the popular excitement would
reach a dangerous pitch. Upon these representations
the Council of Ministers did not alter its previous decision that for the present the reserves were not to be
called out.

But hardly had Gramont arrived at the Foreign
Office after the close of the Cabinet meeting, when he
received another calamitous message. Baron Werther
had meanwhile learned of Bismarck's displeasure at the
manner in which he had conducted matters, his orders
being to take leave of absence upon the pretext of ill
health, and before leaving France to notify the French
Minister that, during his absence, Count Solms would
conduct the affairs of the embassy.

In giving these instructions, it was Bismarck's intention, as we know, to avoid the appearance of a formal
severance of diplomatic relations between the two
governments; but owing to the disgrace into which
poor Werther had fallen, he had lost his head completely, and, instead of simply making the communication to Minister Gramont, as he had been directed, his
demeanor in the presence of the Minister was such as
fully to reveal his disturbance of mind. " I am in the
most unfortunate predicament," he said. " I have been
severely reprimanded by my Government because I took
your latest proposal into consideration at all and communicated it to the King. My orders are to leave Paris
at once."

From this Gramont learned that of his two hopeful demands made on July 13th, the second one also had not only been refused even more unceremoniously than had the first, but had not been so much as considered. After this, it seemed hardly possible to him that peace could be preserved. According to the Emperor's direction, another meeting of the Cabinet, presided over by himself, was to be held at noon. On his way thither Gramont's carriage could make its way but slowly through the dense throng of people by which it was surrounded. Cries of: War! War with Prussia! War without longer hesitation! rose upon every side, while menacing fists were thrust into the carriage, and angry threats were uttered against the Minister for his dilatoriness.

Immediately after the opening of the council, Lebœuf, with renewed earnestness, again urged the advisability of mobilization, and again he was opposed by the great majority of the Ministers. "I am convinced," said the Marshal, "that Prussia has already begun preparations; orders have been given for the purchase of horses in Belgium, and a call has been issued to all reserves in foreign lands to return to their country's service." [1]

His assertions could, of course, not be gainsayed by the other Ministers, yet the discussion was prolonged for hours before Lebœuf's colleagues at length acceded to his demand; toward three o'clock in the afternoon

---

[1] His testimony, according to Dépositions I., 47. The latter was certainly an erroneous statement.

he left them to issue orders for the intended preparations.

The Cabinet Council then continued its deliberations; a number of measures were suggested, by which it was hoped that war might be averted and the frantic excitement in Paris be allayed, but not one of them all gave promise of success. But the desire for conciliation entertained by the majority of the Ministers remained unchanged; and especially did Ollivier most eagerly advocate a peace policy, in which he was supported by the Emperor to the full extent of his authority.[1] In the end Napoleon returned to his favorite plan of long ago, the convening of a congress of the Powers.[2] The majority of his hearers gladly acceded to the imperial wish; although Gramont showed much hesitation, and brought forward many adverse arguments, the Cabinet acted upon the Emperor's suggestion, and forthwith a draft of the request to be addressed to the Powers was written out. It contained the proposal: that a congress of all the European Governments should formally and solemnly sanction the principle that hereafter the princes of all Great Powers were to be excluded from the possibility of acquiring a foreign throne.

Finally Gramont also desisted from opposition, and

[1] As stated by Ollivier in conversation with Rothan, "L'Allemagne et l'Italie," I., p. 18.

[2] Gramont in his book (p. 212) does not say with whom the proposal originated, but only that when, at the close of the deliberations, the Emperor and the Ministers separated, the decision was still for a peaceable policy (although this conclusion was not reached without much hesitation and great sacrifice, p. 214). Why I designate the Emperor as the originator of the proposed measure will appear later.

submitted to the idea of a congress, consoling himself
with the reflection that, as he remarked, King William's
approval of the Prince's withdrawal would constitute
the necessary guaranty for the present, and the action
of the congress, which he had no doubt would be favorable, would furnish that for the future; this would
probably allay the excitement in the Chamber.

It was nearly six o'clock when the Cabinet Council
adjourned. To Ollivier was intrusted the duty of preparing the message by which the plan of a congress
was to be announced to the Chambers, and Lebœuf
received orders from the Emperor to defer the calling
out of the reserves. Immediately afterwards Napoleon
showed the Italian Ambassador, Nigra, a copy of the
proposal to be made to the Powers in the form in
which it was to be submitted to the Chambers, saying that thus, it was hoped, war would be happily
averted.[1]

With like cheerful anticipations of a peaceable termination of the difficulty, Ollivier sat in the office of
his Department busily engaged in preparing the message to the Chambers, when suddenly the door was
thrown open, and Gramont entered, showing evidences
of strong excitement, a stack of loose papers in his
hands, among them a despatch from Munich notifying
him that, according to Bismarck's instructions, the
Prussian representative had announced to the Bavarian
Court, that, owing to Benedetti's insulting demeanor,

---

[1] As related by Nigra to Beust, according to the "Memoirs" of the
latter, Vol. II., p. 359.

King William had refused to grant the Ambassador further audiences.[1] " This is nothing less than a slap in the face for France," cried Gramont; " I will resign my portfolio rather than submit to such dishonor! "

Ollivier was sorely distressed; in the midst of his labor for the preservation of peace he was suddenly called upon to face the probability of war forced upon him by this provocation; he did not, however, oppose Gramont's wish that a Cabinet Council should be immediately called.[2]

Meanwhile a like request had been received by the Emperor from another quarter. In the Department of War the order that mobilization should be postponed had raised a veritable storm of indignation, which soon swept through all military circles and then through the whole city. A report made by Lord Loftus during these hours of intense excitement stated that in his opinion the agitation in the army and among the people was so great that no Government which should decide for peace could hope to survive. Lebœuf at once hastened to the Emperor at St. Cloud, where he found the war sentiment quite as strong in the Court

[1] From this we conclude that the allusion here is to the despatch sent by the French representative at Munich, and cited by Rothan, p. 17. This states that in conversation with the Bavarian Minister the representative of Prussia had maintained that King Louis could not leave unnoticed the fact that Benedetti had addressed the King in a most unseemly manner upon the public promenade to demand of him the guaranty for the future.

The other French representatives, so far as we know, announced no more than the receipt of the despatch from Ems without any allusion to Benedetti's *manière provocante*.

[2] Rothan, in the work to which reference has been made, p. 19.

circle (of which I shall soon give an instance) as in
the army and city. Before returning to Paris he had
persuaded the Emperor to call the Cabinet together in
council at ten o'clock that night.

Concerning this consultation, so fateful for France,
we have the testimony of three of the participating Ministers, from which we get a vivid picture of that which
occurred.[1]

The Emperor's first utterance after the Ministers had
assembled was a complaint that the promise of silence
respecting the decision of the morning had not been
kept. " I have since then," said he, " been compelled
to listen to the reproach that, forgetful of that which
the plebiscitum ordained, I overstepped my authority
by, in a measure, forcing a peace policy upon those
who were to be my advisers. I recognize fully that
to-day I am a constitutional monarch," he continued ;
" it is my duty therefore to rely upon your wisdom
and patriotism in the decision we are now to reach regarding the steps which the latest developments make
necessary."

The deliberations then began. Lebœuf insisted with
impressive earnestness that the reserves ought to be
called out without further delay ; but even yet he could
not prevail on his colleagues to abandon their purpose
of confining their action for the present to diplomatic
measures. " But toward eleven o'clock," his testimony

---

[1] Lebœuf, " Dépositions," I., p. 47. Gramont, *ibid.*, p. 107. " France
et Prusse," pp. 223, 232, 244. Ollivier, according to Rothan, in the work
referred to, p. 20.

before the Investigation Committee of 1872 continues, " Gramont received a despatch which he read to the assembled Cabinet; its contents were such as to convince nearly all the Ministers that war, and consequently mobilization, was inevitable." It is to be regretted that in 1872 the unhappy General had forgotten the contents of this very important despatch also.

However, Ollivier and Gramont do not fail to give us full information regarding this message. Ollivier says very concisely: " During the deliberations of the council Gramont submitted the despatches from which we learned that the honor of France had been offended, whereupon the Cabinet complied with Lebœuf's request that the reserves be called out at once."

It is a suggestive circumstance that Gramont had not discovered this affront to the honor of France either in the Berlin despatch of the previous morning or in the fact of its publication; that such was the case we learned from what took place in the earlier Cabinet meeting of that day. Moreover, from the statements made in Benedetti's despatch Gramont knew very well that nothing in the nature of an insult had occurred at Ems, but that matters had been conducted in a quiet and formal manner. That which stung him was the official communication of the despatch to the other Courts of Europe, in order that immediately after the occurrence they all might receive formal confirmation of the newspaper statement that Prussia had categorically and irrevocably rejected the French demand. This procedure he regarded as a slap upon the cheek of

France, although in reality it was the most natural thing in the world, that, after all the fierce speeches and threats of war to which France had given utterance since July 6th, every one concerned (and who in Europe was not concerned?) should be notified of the storm which was threatening from the West. This did not occur to Gramont, however, and he was furious that a diplomatic defeat suffered by France should be so inconsiderately heralded forth into the world.

"After the evening session of the Cabinet Council had begun," is his statement to the Committee in 1872, "we learned from our diplomatic agents, first from Munich and Bern, then from every direction, that Bismarck had not only sent the Ems despatch to all the Courts of Europe, but in addition had caused the circulation of a fictitious story in Berlin, according to which the King and Benedetti had insulted each other." Since Gramont was aware that this statement by no means conformed to the facts, he looked upon it as a malicious fabrication invented by Bismarck for the purpose of so offending the national pride of the two peoples that war would become inevitable. The "fictitious story," an English translation of which Gramont submitted to the Investigation Committee of 1872, was the one which originated in Ems, and with which Bismarck had nothing to do whatever. In his book Gramont prudently omits this tale, and replaces it by an article from the *Times* written by the Berlin correspondent, in which the excitement caused in Berlin by the appearance of the Ems despatch is described.

However, unfortunately for him, he could lay neither the story nor the correspondence before the Cabinet Council holding its session on July 14th, 1870, for the very excellent reason that they were not published in England until a later date; so that one is tempted to conclude that perhaps he added them to his account of the night session of the council as a convenient embellishment.

But, as apt as Gramont has shown himself at such inventions, I am nevertheless inclined to believe the following explanation to be the more probable one. On the evening of July 14th the official *Norddeutsche Allgemeine Zeitung* contained a short article in bold type stating that Benedetti had so far disregarded the rules of diplomatic etiquette as to obtrude himself upon the King during his sojourn at Ems for the benefit of his health, and had addressed him upon the public promenade for the purpose of interrogating him about the Spanish affair, and of extorting promises from him. If immediately upon its appearance Le Sourd sent a telegraphic report of this article to Paris, it is quite possible that Minister Gramont may have received it at about eleven o'clock, if it was forwarded to him at the council, and that he then made use of it to spur his colleagues on to war. The article does not, to be sure, mention an insult of any kind on either side, although it does criticise Benedetti for his violation of diplomatic form; in addition to this, the article appeared in a semi-official paper, a circumstance which made it possible to represent it as another public affront offered

France by Bismarck. This may therefore have been the article to which Lebœuf alluded as the drop by which the cup of French displeasure was filled to overflowing.[1]

Gramont continues his account of the council with the words: "This message was soon followed by others, informing us that the Prussians were marching toward our frontier, and that their forces were being concentrated with remarkable rapidity. It was then that the

---

[1] Sorel ("Histoire Diplomatique," I.) advances the conjecture that the despatch mentioned by Lebœuf as the deciding influence was a copy of a report made by Lord Loftus regarding Bismarck's threatening utterances of July 13th, and which in some unrevealed manner reached Gramont; both Oncken and Delbrück eagerly accept this explanation as the most correct one. In that case, however, I can see no reason why both Ollivier and Gramont in their wholly independent testimony should have preserved such complete and inexplicable silence concerning the document which had so deciding an influence. That they should have refrained from mentioning it in connection with the public transactions in the Chamber on July 15th we can readily understand, since their knowledge of its contents, obtained in some irregular manner, might have seriously compromised Lord Loftus. But in 1872 Gramont gave the despatch publicity through the pages of his book, stating that he received a copy of the report through a secret channel which he was still not at liberty to reveal; in this connection he cites it as an evidence of Bismarck's hostility. Under these circumstances, what possible reason could he have had for concealing the use he had made of it and the effect it had produced from the Investigation Committee before whom he testified just previous to the appearance of his book?

Moreover, a conversation carried on between two people in Berlin in strictest privacy, and under the additional safeguard of official secrecy, cannot be classed among the affronts to the honor of France upon which Gramont laid so much stress; and furthermore, the despatch would have done little toward deterring the French Ministers from carrying out their project of a congress; for they were not so little acquainted with Bismarck's energetic mode of action as not to expect from the outset that they would meet with vigorous counter charges and counter complaints in the congress upon which they had determined.

Government realized the necessity of mobilizing, and decided to ask the Chamber to provide the means wherewith to prepare for an attack becoming more imminent with every day. I realized that peace was no longer possible, and, fully confident of victory, accepted the necessity of deciding for war."

That on the 14th of July not so much as the first step toward mobilization had been taken in Germany, much less any preparations made for an advance upon the French frontier, is not only established by the reports of the Prussian general staff, but may also be learned from French testimony through the statements made by Benedetti and Stoffel.[1]

Gramont was now fully resolved upon war, because he believed that by advocating a peace policy he would incur the danger of being forced to resign by either the Chamber or the Army, that he might be succeeded by a Minister who would be even less slow to precipitate a conflict than was he. Reflections of a similar nature now also put an end to Ollivier's long indecision. Should we be overthrown, he argued at this time, the war will be undertaken by a reactionary Ministry, and the victory won will then be utilized to re-establish the despotism of 1852.

Despite all this, the final decision of the council was not reached without a struggle. The Emperor made a last attempt to rescue his favorite plan of a European congress; but hardly had he uttered the word, when Gramont turned upon him with the angry exclamation,

---

[1] Benedetti, "Ma Mission," p. 9.   Stoffel, "Rapports," p. 453.

"Sire, if you so much as mention a congress again, I will throw my resignation at your feet."[1] As Lebœuf also left no opportunity for doubt that he entertained a similar intention, Napoleon relapsed into his usual impotent silence. Thus it was that shortly before midnight the majority of the Cabinet[2] determined upon the immediate issue of orders to mobilize, as also that on the coming morning Duvernois' interpellation should receive the exultant reply: Guaranties we could not get for you, but we bring you war instead.

On the morning of July 15th the Cabinet decided upon the form in which the fateful announcement was to be made. It began with an historic review of the recent negotiations, from their beginning to the King's rejection of the very moderate and courteously made claim for guaranties. "Although this refusal seemed wholly inexcusable to us," the writing continued, "our desire for peace was so great that we hesitated to break off the negotiations, when, to our utter surprise, we learned that the King of Prussia had notified our Ambassador by an adjutant that he would not give him another audience; and, that there might be no uncertainty with regard to the nature of this message, the Prussian Government had given official information of it to the other Cabinets of Europe; further, that Baron Werther had received orders to take leave of absence,

---

[1] As related by Gramont to Count Vitzthum on the next day, as will be seen later.

[2] According to Thiers (" Dépositions," p. 9), Ministers Chevandier de Valdrome and Segris had promised him to vote for peace.

and that military preparations had been begun in Prussia. Under these circumstances," were the concluding words, " any further attempt at conciliation would have been not only derogatory to our dignity, but a folly as well. We have done all in our power to avert war, and now prepare to hold our own in this conflict to which we have been challenged, by committing to every one his rightful share of the responsibility. Yesterday our reserves were called out; and with your co-operation we will promptly take all necessary measures to protect the interests, the safety, and the honor of France."

This message was delivered to the Senate by Gramont, and to the Legislative Body by Ollivier. At the same time the Minister of War introduced two bills, the one providing for the arming of the Garde Mobile, the other for the enlistment of volunteers; a preliminary credit of fifty millions was asked for the army, and one of sixteen millions for the navy.

Gramont's duty in the Senate was quickly and easily performed; in this exalted assembly of imperial favorites, pensioned dignitaries, and church magnates, the message was received with such unbounded enthusiasm that the President closed the session with the remark that the emotion by which the assembly was stirred was too intense to admit of the transaction of further business. Gramont then repaired to the Legislative Body, where his colleague had no such easy task before him.

Here, too, there could, of course, be no doubt as to a favorable majority; for the bellicose Extreme Right was now joined by the Chauvinists of both Centres, and by the men of the Right, who, although their hearts inclined to peace, were nevertheless the obedient followers of the Government. But they were opposed with passionate vehemence by the Extreme Left, the group of Republicans, among whom were Jules Favre, Arago, Picard, and their associates. Although these had only too often reviled the Emperor for his shameful lenity toward Prussia, now that war was actually to be faced, they were again seized with the old fear that a wholly unrestricted military *régime* would be established should Napoleon return from the campaign a glorious victor; and so we witness their sudden transformation into benignant apostles of peace.

Hardly had the reading of the Cabinet programme been concluded, when, first and foremost of them all, the veteran Thiers took up the battle in seeming contradiction to his entire past, and to the utter surprise of his hearers; for, in truth, he it had been who more than any one else in France had spread the doctrine that the growing strength of Prussia was a serious menace to the vital interests of France, and that Napoleon ought long ago to have interposed. Even now he by no means abandoned this opinion; he believed the time would inevitably come when France would be compelled to meet and undo the consequences of Sadowa. We have already seen him laboring with both Ministers and deputies for the preservation of peace immediately after it was learned that Prince Leopold had declined to be a candidate. Now, in a speech of surpassing eloquence, he poured forth his wrath at the inability displayed by the Ministry from first to last by grasping at one ground-less pretext for war after another, thus forfeiting the good opinion of Europe; by rendering mediation of any kind impossible through hasty and unreasonable action; by raising a vain dispute about words after the chief point at issue had been conceded in the Prince's withdrawal. " Not in defence of our country's vital interests do we go to war," he exclaimed, "but because of the mistakes made by the Cabinet."

By his very first words he provoked the anger of the Arcadians and Clericals, and their uproarious protests interrupted him at every sentence. " Traitor!" " Miserable Prussian!" "Shameful prater!" were some of the insulting epithets which were hurled at him amidst the wildest tumult. But the veteran of threescore years and ten neither faltered nor flinched ; he did not leave the orator's tribunal until his motion that the despatches and other documents concerned be submitted to the House had been recognized in spite of the confusion.

As this old antagonist of Prussia now demanded, with all the power of which he was capable, that the peace be kept, so Ollivier, the former friend of Germany, upheld the war policy of the Government. " We have done all that was reasonable to avoid a rupture," he explained. " Not even the King's rejection of our claim for guaranties for the future, nor his refusal to give our Ambassador another audience about the matter, encountered our protest; but when Count Bismarck, with unseemly haste and obviously malicious intention, announced this refusal to all the

other Cabinets of Europe, we were compelled to recognize in this proceeding an affront to France. We
felt constrained to defend our country's honor with the
sword; and dared hesitate no longer when we were
informed that mobilization had begun in Prussia, and
that its troops were approaching our frontier."

It was in this connection that he uttered those words
which will always cling to his memory: "We know
that hereby we assume a great responsibility, but we
accept it with a light heart." It was in vain that, in
response to an indignant exclamation from the Left,
he added, "No contention about words, gentlemen;
yes, with a clear conscience, and therefore with a light
heart, as I have said."

At this juncture, Gramont, who had just entered
the hall, came to his assistance, saying, "The honor of
France is involved; should I be compelled to witness
the incredible, namely, a Chamber insensible to this,
I would not remain Minister five minutes longer!" A
roar of applause was his reward for this high-sounding
phrase; and the Chamber at once nominated a committee of ten of its members to examine into and report
immediately upon the bills proposed by the Government, and the credits asked.

These gentlemen all belonged to the war party, which
was in the majority; but they had not failed to be impressed by Thiers' forcible criticism that, after Prince
Leopold's withdrawal, the Cabinet had made new and
unreasonable claims whereby peace had been disturbed
and the sympathy of Europe forfeited. After Lebœuf

had emphatically declared that France was ready for war, quite ready, and had the advantage over Prussia of being several days ahead in its military preparations, a statement, we can but observe, that accorded illy with the one by which it had just been averred that the Prussian forces had long been mobilized, and were marching toward France, the chairman of this Committee, the Duke of Albufera, asked Gramont whether it were true that the Government had from the outset made one and the same demand of the King of Prussia, since this point was one of paramount importance.

Hereupon the incredible really did happen; Gramont declared that from the beginning the Government had persistently pursued the one purpose of inducing the King's active concurrence in the Prince's withdrawal as constituting a guaranty for the future. Although thus far a formal lie had been avoided, still the real intent was to deceive the Committee; but the worst was still to come. When Albufera requested that the despatches in question be submitted, Gramont took from his portfolio several papers, but did not allow them to leave his hands; and then, without mentioning any dates, but simply distinguishing the despatches by the numbers one, two, etc., he read from number one this sentence: The Prince's withdrawal will be effectual only in case the King concurs in it, and at the same time promises to forbid the Prince to reconsider the candidacy at some future time.

This was obviously a deception in form as well as in

intent; for it was not from the first despatch sent Benedetti on the 7th that Gramont read, but from that of
the 12th of July, which was in reality the tenth, and
was the one by which the Ambassador was first instructed to make the new demand for guaranties. Of
course, no one could have read this despatch without
at once observing both the date and the opening sentence, which referred to the Prince's withdrawal as
announced by Prince Charles Anthony, whereby the
untruthfulness of the Minister's previous statement
would have been discovered at a glance. It was for
this reason that Gramont did not submit the writing
to the inspection of the deputies, and in reading it to
them omitted the first sentence.

In this way the Committee's solicitude regarding this
all-important point was set at rest; and with equal trust
Gramont's statements regarding the affront to which
Benedetti had been subjected, as well as his intimation
concerning the probability of alliances with Austria and
Italy, were accepted. Immediately afterwards the Committee recommended the desired credits and bills to the
House for its sanction, with the statement that all the
desired information regarding the documents in question
had been received from the Ministers.

All the opposition offered by Thiers, Jules Favre, and
Gambetta was of no avail; by an overwhelming majority the bills as approved by the Committee became the
decisions of the House.

Thus the war which required greater sacrifice than
any other of the century was occasioned on July 6th

by a suspicion for which there was not the slightest
foundation, was made inevitable on the 13th by an unreasonable demand, and was inflamed by a deception
perpetrated by the Ministry on the 15th.

That night the streets of Paris were again the scene
of boisterous demonstrations and jubilation. Organized
bands, with hundreds in their ranks, carrying flags and
colored lanterns, marched about singing the *Marseillaise*,
cheering for France, shouting, "Down with Prussia!
Hurrah for war!" and beating without mercy any one
who dared to shout for peace.

Similar expressions of the national spirit were reported from other cities of the provinces; there could
no longer be any doubt that public opinion in France
was eager for war. To be sure, the reports received
a few days later from the prefects, who were usually
very slow to make an adverse statement with respect
to any pronounced wish of the Ministry, announced
that in only sixteen departments had the people declared themselves decidedly in favor of war, whereas
in thirty-four the sentiment had been unquestionably
against it, and in thirty-seven opinions had been very
equally divided. But what could this avail? The will
of the Capital was the will of France; and the will of
the politically active element, the statesmen and party
leaders, the writers and newspaper men, and upon this
occasion that of the clergy and army officers also, was
the will of Paris.

After the signal for war had once been sounded, the
patriotic sentiment and enthusiasm to enter the conflict

natural to the young men of a nation everywhere asserted itself; for the past four years a feeling of resentment against Prussia had been systematically and persistently fostered, and now the land resounded with the cry: Prussia is seeking to deprive us of our leadership in Europe! Down with her!

Whilst thus the French Ministers were rushing headlong into war, their Emperor was making a last although hopeless attempt to preserve peace.[1]

On the 11th and 12th of July, Count Beust, as we know, had severely criticised Gramont's policy, and had urgently advised a more pacific course. Hardly, however, had he done so when he was seized with anxiety lest thereby he might have incurred both for himself and Austria the serious displeasure of the French Government; he therefore gave Count Vitzthum orders on the 13th to leave Brussels, and hasten to Paris to learn the actual state of affairs. Immediately after the Count's arrival he was told by Prince Metternich that matters were beyond salvation here, that war could be averted no more than could a convulsion of nature — than could an earthquake, for instance.

On the 14th Vitzthum made a fruitless attempt to obtain an interview with Gramont, whose attendance upon the three sessions of the Cabinet Council left him little time for diplomatic consultations. On the 15th Napoleon, however, gave the Count an audience at St. Cloud; he received him most graciously, and remarked

[1] What follows is based upon information derived from unpublished memoirs.

that the sudden change in the state of affairs had probably been a surprise to him. When Vitzthum confirmed
this supposition with considerable emphasis, the Emperor exclaimed, "What would you have? We had
gone too far; we could not draw back!"

He expressed some concern lest he should be overpowered by the great body of the German troops, and
made the suggestion that since Austria must prefer
France to be the victor, that country should station an
army of observation on the Bohemian frontier, thus compelling a division of the Prussian forces. When in reply
Vitzthum deprived the Emperor of all hope that Austria would act upon this suggestion, assuring him, however, that the Austrian Government would do all in its
power to avert the war by diplomatic means, Napoleon
expressed his gratitude, and formally authorized the
Count in his name to ask Emperor Francis Joseph to
propose a European congress for the adjustment of the
dispute.

On this day, too, Count Vitzthum's efforts to interview the Duke of Gramont proved unsuccessful until
late in the evening, when, just before the Count's departure, the desired opportunity presented itself. The
Minister was just leaving the Chamber, and was in a
most agitated frame of mind. "We have decided for
war," he exclaimed; "and if Austria realizes what is
best for her own interests she will join us!" To this
Vitzthum replied, "The audience which the Emperor
granted me this morning does not allow me to regard a
conflict as inevitable. His Majesty directly commis-

sioned me to request my Emperor to propose a congress
of the European Powers." At the mention of the word
congress Gramont became furious, and blurted out how
he had on the day before resented this proposal when
made to the Cabinet Council by the Emperor. "Our
reserves have been called out, and Lebœuf has assured
me that we are *archiprêts,*" was the remark with which
he concluded.

Vitzthum pursued the conversation no further, but
proceeded to the railway station. Metternich, who accompanied him, said: "It is well that you saw him
before you left; now you can bear out my statement
that it would be wasted effort to reason with a person
who has lost his head completely, and is no longer in a
responsible condition."

Under these circumstances there could be no further
thought of a congress. A few days later, Napoleon,
evidently in a most gloomy and despondent mood,
wrote to her who for years had been his most trusted
friend, and who was living in deep seclusion apart from
all political interests, Queen Sophia of Holland : "This
war was no wish of mine ; I was forced into it by the
pressure of public opinion." The Queen, who was one
of Prussia's bitterest enemies, wrote this comment upon
the margin of the letter: "It is true ; for this he is not
to be blamed ; his mistake was committed in 1866."

On the 15th of July, the day on which France,
through jealousy of its neighbor's growing power, determined upon an offensive war against Prussia, King
William left Ems for Berlin to prepare for defence,

should events make it necessary. If during the earlier stages of the negotiations individual voices had been heard to criticise the patience with which he had listened to the French demands, now, after his emphatic rejection of them, his people were grateful to him for the extreme forbearance he had shown, thus manifesting to the world Germany's real desire for peace and the fact that it entered the conflict with a clear conscience.

Wherever the royal train stopped, the stations were filled with a dense crowd of people by whom the venerable monarch was greeted with unceasing cheers. Here there was no distinction between young and old, between city and country, between old Prussian and annexed provinces; the patriotic enthusiasm was quite as marked and general in Hesse and Lower Saxony as in Brandenburg.

The Crown Prince, Bismarck, Roon, and Moltke had gone as far as Brandenburg to meet the King, that the most necessary arrangements might be discussed without loss of time. Even yet King William could not bring himself to believe in the reality of the war; he hoped that now, at last, the excitement in Paris would subside. But when the train had arrived in the Berlin station, which, like the others, was filled and surrounded by an impenetrable mass of people, Bismarck was met upon the platform by Herr von Thile, who handed him a despatch just received from Paris, containing the report of the announcement which the French Cabinet had made to the Chambers. It was read to his Majesty,

the King, who remarked: " Why, that has a very warlike sound. I suppose we shall have to mobilize three
army corps at once." To this Bismarck said: " Your
Majesty, that will not suffice; the French are mobilizing their whole army even now." In reply, the King
asked that the whole message be read to him again;
after hearing it he exclaimed, deeply moved: " In
truth, that is in itself a declaration of war; and are we
really to have another dreadful conflict?" And after
a moment he added, "It does, indeed, mean war; well,
then, so be it in God's providence."

The Crown Prince, turning to the group of officers
standing back of him cried out " War! We are to
mobilize! " whereupon the King, with tears in his eyes,
embraced the Prince.[1]

The news spread like wildfire among the expectant
people outside the station; and immediately a mighty
cheer went up that made the windows shiver, and that
was repeated along the entire route which the King's
carriage took to the palace. This, too, was surrounded
by an enthusiastic throng, cheering, and singing "God
Save the King." Toward eleven o'clock, after the
King had repeatedly appeared at the windows to bow
his thanks to the crowd below, an officer stepped out
in front of the palace to announce to the multitude:
" His Majesty is holding a council of war, and desires
to be undisturbed." Immediately from mouth to mouth
was passed the word: " The King wishes to be undis-

---

[1] As related by eye-witnesses. Compare the report made by Bismarck
in person on September 23d, 1888.

turbed;" and two minutes later the people had disappeared as though by magic, and the large square in front of the palace lay deserted and silent.

During the night the orders for mobilization were issued, and the corresponding despatches sent to the South German allies.

On the following morning this notice was posted up in all the cities and towns of North Germany: All reserves are to report for duty, guards as well as third augmentation. First day of mobilization, July 16th.

Speedily the call to arms was carried abroad, reaching even the remotest farms; it claimed the occupant of the most sumptuous palace and of the poorest hut alike, and everywhere it met with the same patriotic response. Of the German people as a whole may be said that which upon a former occasion was remarked of the Prussian kings: they are a race mighty in war, but not given to war. Here there was no talk of a position of preponderance in Europe, nor thought of aggression upon the neighbor in the West. Every one rejoiced in the hope of peaceful days, looked forward to enjoying the reward of successful labor, and desired to live by Goethe's maxim: "Morning's duty! evening's guest! Week day's labor! feast day's rest!"

Suddenly into this peaceful existence came the news of the French hostility occasioned by the choice of a Spanish king; at this attack, regarded by the Germans as an act of madness or of infamy, the Teutonic blood, which ordinarily coursed so tranquilly through their veins, seethed with bitter indignation, and, with the

strength of a giant, the ancient *furor teutonicus* rose
to give battle to the French vehemence. And for the
very reason that here the excitement had sprung from
the necessity of self-defence, it was more intense and
more general than in France. The ideal thought of
defending German unity, and the very practical necessity of protecting private interests, combined to form a
single mighty incentive.

The national guardsman, who in only too many instances left wife and child in bitter need, clenched his
fist in angry resentment as he marched away with the
thought: God have pity upon the Frenchman who
may fall into my hands. The young soldiers took
leave of their parents, who in anguish and with tears,
and yet with pride and gratitude, clasped their gayly
departing sons in their arms, perhaps for a last time.
The lecture-rooms of the universities grew silent and
empty; the students who as yet had not served in the
army travelled about the country in search of a regiment which they might enter, but usually without success, since all the corps were full and more than full.
In that case they either found admission into a reserve
battalion, or formed themselves into so-called emergency corps, not infrequently under the leadership of
professors whose sympathy with the general movement
would not suffer them to remain inactively at home,
notwithstanding their advanced age; the special duty
for which these corps were organized was to carry the
wounded from the battle-fields, — and plentiful and
dangerous was the work which awaited them.

In every community societies were formed for the purpose of establishing suitable hospitals, and of collecting materials for bandages, as well as food and clothing of every description to supply the needs of the soldiers in the field, and of the sick and wounded who would soon fill the hospitals. German industry had led many of the young men to take up their abode in the other countries of Europe; at the first note of alarm, without waiting for official notification, all of these now hastened to take their places in the regiments of their native land. The writers of the day called to mind the similar uprising in 1813; to the old martial songs of Arndt, Körner, and Schenkendorf, new ones were added by the poets of the land, among them some which were of the highest poetical ardor, such as Geibel's "Song of Victory;" there was not a newspaper in the land which did not seek from day to day to stimulate the national enthusiasm. For long centuries past Germans had been arrayed against Germans without realizing what they did; now at last the German nation had awaked to the consciousness of its unity and its strength, and with joyful resolve millions hastened to attest their allegiance to the newly found fellowship, and to repulse the bitter foe of old from whom so much had been endured. This conflict was to be no tournament for the display of knightly feats at arms or diplomatic skill; but, far from it, prince and peasant, statesman and soldier, were alike determined to fight until the last breath, or until the disturber of the peace had been utterly vanquished.

All other interests receded; party opposition and
religious differences were forgotten; social intercourse
was purged of its luxury, and of the petty jealousies
of the several coteries; no mean care, no selfish desire,
dared to manifest itself; it seemed as though in the
presence of the grandly dawning conception of their
fatherland the people had grown nobler and purer.   He
whose happy privilege it was to witness these first days
of a nation's uprising in Germany will his life long
cherish the remembrance of them as a sacred treasure.

At the same time that the notice to mobilize appeared, on July 16th, Gramont's empty pretexts for
the incitement of war were confuted by Bismarck in
his report to the Federal Council; in it he stated the
facts, showing that the thought of the Hohenzollern
candidacy had originated in Spain ; that a preliminary
inquiry, wholly unofficial in its nature and conducted
with utmost secrecy, had then been made by Marshal
Prim ; that, with regard to the answer to be given,
King William had been consulted only in his capacity
as head of the family ; that the final official negotiations had been conducted between Madrid and Sigmaringen without the King's concurrence; and that Prince
Leopold had accepted the offer of the Spanish crown
without the King's knowledge, which he was fully at
liberty to do, since the Hohenzollern family compact
gave the King no right either to forbid or to order the
Prince's action in this matter.   Accordingly the French
demand that the King should forbid any future candidacy had neither rhyme nor reason ; hence, the termina-

tion of the negotiations begun at Ems was unavoidable. The French Ambassador had, according to his own statement, been subjected to no indignity, nor had this been intimated in the now notorious despatch as published in the papers. The Prussian representatives had been given no further information regarding the incident than that which the despatch itself conveyed.

After hearing this exposition of the facts in the case, the Federal delegate from Saxony, Minister von Friesen, announced his Government's unqualified approval of the course pursued, concluding with the words: "France evidently seeks war; let us then carry it through with all the expedition and energy of which we are capable." And to this all the other members of the Federal Council agreed.

On July 19th Le Sourd presented the formal declaration of war, which was but a more concise form of the announcement made to the Chambers on the 15th. Hereupon the Reichstag was immediately convoked by the Presidium of the Confederation, and began its session on the same day.

In his speech from the throne the King, with earnest and dignified words, deplored the coming conflict occasioned by passionate excitement in France and declared upon a wholly groundless pretext; in conclusion he expressed his strong reliance upon the unanimity and self-sacrificing spirit of the German people. On the following day the House replied to this speech with a most enthusiastic address, adopted without a single dissenting voice, and closing with the declaration:

Upon the field of battle the German nation will become united.

The war loan of one hundred and twenty million thalers asked by the Government was approved quite as unanimously, both in its first and second readings, as well as in the final action on July 21st, after which the House decided, notwithstanding the opposition of the Party of Progress, to extend the present legislative period, which was to terminate in the fall, to the end of the year. This was not the time to think of elections, but of battles; a single mighty impulse swayed the hearts of the people, the desire to share in the protection of the fatherland by giving the strength of their support to its defenders and their leaders.

During these days the aspiration for nationality asserted itself as the predominant influence south of the Main also, although even now not without a hard struggle.

In the Lower House at Munich the army budget was the subject under discussion from July 13th to 15th, the very days during which the crisis in Paris was at its height. The Ultramontanes, or, as they styled themselves, the Patriotic Party (in their care for their own State, Bavaria), controlled the majority of the votes, and were for the time re-enforced by a number of Democrats. They maintained that the standing army, by draining the money and labor supply of the country, was ruining the land. The Bavarian people could not continue to expend fifteen million florins for military purposes; a change would have to be made to the militia system, requiring a service of only eight months, which was quite sufficient to give the necessary training, and would cost the country only half as much as the present method.

When both the Premier and the Minister of War, Von Pranckh, with great earnestness called attention to the immediate danger of a French war, they received the reply: At present we are deliberating upon a peace budget; in case of war, we will do our part; after the war is over there will again be days of peace, and it is for these that we are legislating to-day.

The men of the majority were especially eager that the action they advocated should be taken, since with the discontinuance of the standing army the hated Prussian alliance would lose all practical force; in the ardor with which this object was pursued, the fact was entirely overlooked that the Government, which had no intention of relinquishing the reliable system of defence inaugurated in 1867, was thereby forced into closer union with Prussia. At the close of the general debate, on July 15th, the President of the House had the good judgment to postpone the special debate. That his action was well founded was soon to appear; for the day's session had hardly closed when news was received of the announcement which had been made to the Chambers at Paris, and which was synonymous with war.

Regarding the attitude which the Bavarian Government would assume, there was even now not the slightest doubt. On July 16th, simultaneously with the

Prussian orders for mobilization, those for the Bavarian army were issued. Ultramontane and Democratic papers in which appeared abusive articles in denunciation of a war fought at the side of Prussia were seized by the police; although this precaution was hardly necessary, since the patriotic German sentiment of the population had by this time become so intense that in Munich the editor of an Ultramontane paper begged to be taken under the protection of the police to escape violence from the populace, by whom his life was threatened.

On July 17th the large square in front of the royal palace was thronged with a dense crowd of people, whose resounding huzzas gave expression to their appreciation of the firm stand which their King had taken. In Nürnberg, a mass-meeting of four thousand men, in which the Democratic element also was represented, drew up resolutions voicing the hope that in the face of the declaration of war, so wantonly made by France, the Representative Assembly would by unanimous consent sanction all measures necessary to an energetic conduct of the war, and that the young men of the country would cheerfully place themselves at the service of their fatherland. The latter half of the appeal was fulfilled even before it was heard, for from every part of the land the young men hastened to take up arms in defence of their flag.

But with the Representative Assembly matters stood very differently. On July 18th the Government presented a motion in the Lower House asking for a credit of five million florins to cover the expense of mobilizing, and of twenty-one millions more for the demands expected during the months intervening between this and the close of the year. Discretion suggested that this request be accompanied by the statement that as yet the Government did not recognize the existence of a *casus fœderis*, as also that attempts at mediation were in progress in which Bavaria had participated. (Bavaria had transmitted the proposition to Berlin that Prussia should recognize the principle that the princes of Great Powers were hereafter to be excluded from foreign thrones, a suggestion which under existing circumstances could, of course, receive no consideration in Berlin.) This attitude of reserve on the part of the Government, which at heart was fully resolved upon war, did not, however, make any impression upon the majority in the Chamber; but, on the contrary, encouraged the Ultramontanes to take a wholly unreserved stand against the Government. It was due to their votes that the motion was referred to a special committee; and in the evening, at their club, they pledged themselves to vote no money except for the purpose of maintaining an armed neutrality, and in much smaller amounts than those which had been asked.

In the afternoon session of the 19th, Deputy Jörg read the report of the Committee to the House. As editor of the *Historisch-politischen Blätter* he had written many articles upon the subject of foreign politics; he, himself, had a high appreciation of his ability in this field, and in his party he enjoyed the reputation of being an expert in matters of diplomacy. Upon this occasion, however, it was his fate not only to display a thoroughly anti-German spirit, but a remarkable deficiency in statesmanship as well.

Every seat in the Chamber was occupied, the galleries were filled with an intensely excited and eagerly attentive audience; outside, the streets were thronged with a dense mass of people so demonstrative in their disapproval of the course pursued by the majority that the Government had deemed it advisable to station a guard of soldiers upon the lower floor of the building. Amidst such surroundings Jörg developed his theory of armed neutrality, to the effect that it was the earnest and high-principled endeavor of a State to abstain from participating in the wars of other nations so long as it was not compelled to action by a danger threatening its own existence.

During the deliberations of the Committee, Count Bray had expressed the opinion that with the withdrawal of Prince Leopold the Spanish question had ended, and a German one had been opened. To this Jörg now replied that with regard to the demand subsequently made by France, and which he considered a perfectly just one, it would have cost Prussia only one little word to avoid the spilling of much and precious blood. The King, however, had taken it amiss that Benedetti had addressed him upon the public promenade; and so it was that a real or imagined transgression of the rules of etiquette had given rise to this war, which, therefore, had nothing whatever to do with

a German question. The Minister himself had advised
neutrality, provided the contending parties would respect it. " Very good; in the present case this condition is forthcoming," declared the speaker. " Prussia,
to be sure, has as yet not expressed itself upon this
point; but the advantages it would derive from the
neutrality of the South in the protection afforded its
left flank are so obvious that there can be no doubt
concerning its decision. France, however, has offered
to respect our neutrality; for Minister Gramont has
openly stated that France does not purpose to gain one
foot of German soil through this war ; in fact, it is the
intention to guarantee the Palatinate to us."

Here, again, was a man who claimed to be well versed
in these matters, and yet had no idea of the true state
of affairs, although to understand that which was under
consideration required no technical knowledge, but
only ordinary common sense; this had, however, been
impaired in the speaker by the inordinate party feeling
of the Ultramontane.

The true condition may be learned from the fact, that
when Gramont read the despatch sent him by St. Val-
lier, in which the latter reported the complaint made
by Minister Varnbüler that the course pursued by
France made the neutrality desired by the South German States impossible to them, Gramont testily wrote
upon the margin of the despatch: " As though we had
ever consented to such neutrality ; we need the Palatinate for our strategic march northward, and Swabia
and Bavaria for our further operations."   The last part

of his remark had reference to the union between the French forces and their Italian allies, for Gramont still hoped for aid from Italy.

Jörg could, of course, have no knowledge of this; but the man to whom the map of Europe did not reveal the utter impossibility of Bavarian neutrality in case of war between North Germany and France had forever forfeited all claim to statesmanship. As it was, the Ministers found it no difficult task to prove him in error; Count Bray on the ground of Bavaria's duty to Prussia and Germany, Herr von Pranckh by the argument that to-day there was but one course by which Bavaria could maintain her independence, and that was by identifying her own interests with those of Germany.

The exciting debate which ensued was continued until late into the night. During its progress it become evident that many of the Patriotic Party had been converted to true patriotism by the convincing power of facts. Professor Sepp, a thorough scholar, although at times of an oddly religious turn of mind, told the House that no longer ago than the evening before he had written out a speech advocating neutrality. "But," said he, "yesterday and to-day are separated as by a decade of ordinary events; since then the French declaration of war has been received; the King of Prussia in his speech from the throne takes our support for granted; who to-day is inclined to ask for the cause of the war? Yesterday the woes of 1866 were still remembered; to-day wrath against France is pre-eminent in the heart of every German. In the battle of Leipzig we Bavarians took no part; in the new battle of nations we want to do our share."

A storm of applause rang through the hall at the close of this speech, after which Deputies Fischer and Völk, both National Liberals, ardently advocated the German cause. Deputy Levi from the Palatinate declared : " With us all parties are as one ; we know full well what our province has to expect, but above all else we want to be Germans, and stand or fall with our German brothers." When hereupon the old advocate of the greater Germany, Deputy Edel, with a speech glowing with enthusiasm, joined the Nationalists, the triumph of their cause could no longer be doubted.

Despite the earnest warnings of the President that the rules of the House must be observed, energetic applause, and hisses too, had not infrequently interrupted the speakers ; at length, between ten and eleven o'clock, by a vote of 89 voices against 58, the House gave its decision against the motion presented by the Committee, and a little later rejected a modified form of it also by a vote of 76 against 72. Again cheer upon cheer rose from the galleries.

And now, since war was inevitable, the motion for a credit of five millions for the expenditures of mobilization was after all passed; hardly had the decision been announced when so deafening a roar of approval rang up from the street below that the President was compelled to pause in taking the votes upon the next question in order, but soon was enabled to declare that the further credit of twenty-one millions had also been granted. Before the close of the day's session the entire Government bill was accepted by 101 against 47 voices. When the deputies left the hall of assembly they found the streets thronged with thousands of people whose jubilant cheers rent the air.

On the morning of July 20th the decision of the Lower Chamber received the unanimous sanction of the Upper Chamber without previous discussion of any kind. The action which the Assembly had taken was then at once announced to Berlin by telegram, and by the same medium the two monarchs exchanged warm fraternal greetings.

The Bavarian people had shown that when put to the test their hearts, too, responded to Schenkendorf's immortal words: Germany, Germany above all else!

In Würtemberg matters took a very similar course. Here, too, the Democratic majority in the Lower Chamber had announced its intention in the coming fall session to force the introduction of the militia system by making sweeping reductions in the army budget, as a first step toward the dissolution of the Prussian alliance. The leading Ministers, Mittnacht and Varnbüler, were most anxious to avoid a rupture with the Chamber, and hoped to moderate the disposition of the House majority by making great concessions to the popular demand.

Upon King Charles, despite the various anti-Prussian influences that were brought to bear upon him, this Democratic attack upon his army had no other effect than to make him a stancher friend to the national cause than he had been before. He asked General Suckow, at that time Chief of the General Staff, whether he would be willing to undertake the administration of the Ministry of War with the stipulation that although the present organizations should be continued the expenditure should be reduced by a half million florins. Suckow consented, although with a heavy heart, and worked out a plan whereby the desired amount would be saved, in part by cutting every expenditure to the lowest possible figure, in part by making a great reduction in the number of privates in the army when on a peace footing, although the regiments as represented by the corps of officers were to remain intact, and the Prussian drill and manœuvre regulations, as well as the term of two years' service, were to be retained.

A draft of the army budget based on this plan received the King's sanction, and on June 14th was also approved by the Council of Ministers, although at the close of the deliberations Minister Varnbüler remarked, " Our new Minister of War will have to come down a little from his plans, I am inclined to think," which was hardly encouraging to Suckow. On the 29th of June the draft went into the hands of the Committee of the Lower House for preliminary examination; the final action, however, was not to be taken until the fall session. King Charles went to the Engadine for the summer.

Suddenly a complete transformation was wrought in this state of affairs by the new and unreasonable de-

mands which France made of the King of Prussia after
the Prince of Hohenzollern had declined to be a candidate for the Spanish throne.   Like a flash the discontent over the existing militarism, and the fear of
Bismarck's despotic rule, vanished.   As with the Bavarian so with the Swabian people ; indignant wrath at
the unjust French attack conquered every other feeling.
In many a Swabian city and village, where only four
short weeks before the accusation, You're a Prussian,
had been looked upon as an insult, the streets now rang
with cheers for King William.   On July 16th, the first
day of mobilization in Prussia, Bavaria, and Baden, an
immense mass-meeting, in which adherents of every
party participated, was held at Stuttgart, and unanimously adopted the following resolutions, greeted with
a roar of applause : The war between France and Prussia is a national war; it has been brought about by
France upon an utterly groundless pretext for the purpose of thrusting Germany back into its old state of
dismemberment and impotence.   In such a war there
can be no question of party among Germans; the hour
has come when the treaties of alliance are to be put to
the test; we expect the Government of Würtemberg to
give its unswerving support to the German cause by
every means at its command, and despite every danger.

The Government was not deaf to the voice of the
people.   The King returned to Stuttgart with all haste ;
upon his arrival there on July 17th, he ordered the immediate mobilization of the army, and convoked the
Chambers for July 21st.   Varnbüler went to Munich to

come to an agreement with Count Bray. Mittnacht recognized the change which had taken place; and as heretofore he had been an uncompromising particularist, so now he became the most unreserved of nationalists.

In the name of the Government, Varnbüler announced to the Lower Chamber, immediately after the session had been opened, that the Government believed it to be its duty to take an unwavering and vigorous stand in defence of the integrity and honor of Germany, which implied an open and close association with Prussia; accordingly it now proposed that the necessary credit be granted by the Representative Assembly.

The National Liberal leaders, Hölder and Römer, gave the motion thus brought forward by the Government their hearty support, in which they were again and again interrupted by ringing plaudits from the audience which filled the galleries.   The leader of the Extreme Left, Meyer, declared that although it had undoubtedly been the desire of his associates to abstain from participation in this war, and, together with Bavaria, to preserve an armed neutrality in reliance upon Austria, which to their unceasing regret had been thrust out of Germany, nevertheless, now that Bavaria had said No to this, nothing remained but to acquiesce in the Government's policy, and, as quickly as possible, without the waste of more words, to grant the necessary funds.

The rules of the House required that the bill should be referred to the usual Committee, whose report was made on the very next day, when the decision desired by the Government was given by the House with only one dissenting voice. To be sure, thirty-eight of the deputies could not deny themselves the satisfaction of accompanying their votes by the explanatory statement, that their action had been for the sake of maintaining Germany's integrity, although they believed that this war was but a consequence of 1866, and that they missed with heartfelt sorrow that member of the Confederation which had once been the most powerful one.

With the people this wail of regret uttered by the "People's Party" found no response; as matters had gone in Munich, so they went in Stuttgart; here, too, the cries that were raised by the multitude outside demanding participation in the coming conflict were heard within the walls of the Assembly hall; and when, at the close of the deliberations, the deputies stepped into the street, they were greeted with shouts of gratitude for the action they had taken.

Even greater, if possible, than the enthusiasm here, was that displayed in Baden, although this State would be the first to suffer by the war. But because of the very nearness of the danger the patriotic excitement was the more intense and enduring; and fierce and bitter was the feeling of indignation which reached its climax when on July 21st the Duke of Gramont announced to the Baden *chargé d'affaires* at Paris that he had been informed that, in violation of the law of nations, granades were going to be used by the Baden infantry, in consequence of which that State could expect no better treatment at the hands of France than the Palatinate had received from Melac and Duras; not even the women would be spared.

That the Baden Government could upon the spot prove the utter untruthfulness of this accusation only increased the wrath of the people who were so barbarously threatened. Baden had not participated in the uprising of 1813; now its people were reminded by the foe himself of the worst outrages which its flourishing provinces had suffered at the hands of the old arch-enemy. We can readily imagine what, after this, was the effect of Napoleon's war manifesto against Prussia, published on July 23d, and in which appeared the fine phrase: "Our quarrel is not with Germany; we respect its independence, and desire that its several peoples shall be free to decide their own destinies." The successor of Louis XIV. was posing as the guardian of German liberty against Prussian tyranny.

But only so much the more earnestly and quickly did Baden prepare for the conflict; mobilization was ordered for the 16th; the fortress of Rastatt was armed with all haste, and the Kehl-Strasburg bridge across the Rhine was destroyed. The Representative Assembly was not in session; but here the Government was so sure of the Assembly's unqualified approval that the members were spared the trouble of coming together. Not without anxiety, but with a feeling of strong reliance upon the promised help from their North German brothers in arms, did the people of Baden look forward to the war which was before them.

Here, as elsewhere, the fear entertained arose from the very natural conclusion that France would not have rushed so headlong into a contest unless, by long and careful preparation, it felt itself to be more than a match for its adversary; and that immediately after the declaration of war a French army would cross the Rhine, and inflict heavy losses upon the Germans, probably not so ready for war as were their assailants. Moltke, to be sure, was not troubled by any such apprehension; on one occasion, when addressed upon the subject, he replied with great calmness: "It is possible that before our forces can get to South Germany, its soil may be invaded by French troops, but I can assure you that not a man of them will ever get back to France."

The people, however, who had not his knowledge of the French conditions at that time, overestimated the strength of the enemy whose armies for more than half a century had been the victors wherever they had appeared, and whose success in this conflict also was fully expected by the rest of Europe. And yet, concerning the final issue there was little doubt in Germany; again and again in those days could have been heard the opinion: At first we may suffer defeat; but our strength will endure, and in the end we will conquer. The consciousness of a just cause, and the incentive of national unity, raised all hearts above the anxiety of the moment, and inspired them with the hope of victory.

CHAPTER V.

ATTEMPTS TO FORM ALLIANCES.

GERMANY was united, and was resolved to strain every nerve in a conflict for life or death. It was Bismarck's opinion, moreover, that after the course events had taken, Germany could count upon Spain's assistance, since it was through that country's repeated and importunate endeavor to obtain the object of its desire that Prussia had become involved in this deplorable conflict; he believed, therefore, that Spain would consider participation in the war to be a matter of national honor as well as a necessary protest against French interference. These expectations were, however, doomed to disappointment.

After Prince Leopold had withdrawn his acceptance, Spain felt relieved of all further responsibility with regard to the issue of the controversy, besides which, owing to the very precarious state of affairs prevailing at home, it felt itself to be in no condition to participate in a struggle with so formidable an opponent as the French Empire. Germany was destined to engage in the contest unaided from abroad, and thus in utter self-dependence to prove its strength.

To the French manifesto of July 23d, Bismarck replied by publishing the proposal of alliance made in
August, 1866, according to which the French Government was to receive armed assistance from Prussia for
the conquest of Luxemburg and Belgium, in return for
which the North German Confederation would be allowed to incorporate the South German States.

Despite Benedetti's cunningly devised refutation, the
untruthfulness of which was soon authentically established, the impression which this disclosure made upon
all Europe was a profound one. In South Germany it
raised to the utmost the indignant aversion with which
the people turned from all connection with France ; in
England, where every menace to Belgian independence
touched a most vulnerable spot, it won at a single
stroke the favor of public opinion for the Prussian arms,
without distinction as to political parties. The great
popular organs, *The Times*, *Daily News*, etc., violently
denounced the French policy. But the attitude of the
English Government was of a different type ; it carefully avoided the expression of any opinion except an
abhorrence of all the evils of war, as beseems good
Christians, noble philanthropists, and prudent merchants.
Still, it cannot be said that it adopted the course best
calculated to put this humane view into practice. If
on July 12th, — when, after the withdrawal of Prince
Leopold, Gramont told the English Ambassador of the
new demands he intended to make, — Lord Loftus had
been in a position not only to warn him that by such a
proceeding he would incur the reproach of the world,

but also to announce to him that Great Britain was firmly resolved to oppose every new disturbance of the peace by all the means at its command, Napoleon and the majority of his ministers would doubtless have found the strength successfully to withstand the bluster of the Arcadians. Such was the stand taken against Talleyrand and Thiers by Lord Palmerston in the Belgian and Oriental questions of 1831 and 1840, and again as late as 1869 by Lord Clarendon, when Belgium was menaced by Napoleon; and in each instance peace was preserved to Europe.

But who, indeed, would have expected so manly an attitude from men like Gladstone and Lord Granville? To threaten with hand on hilt, even for the purpose of maintaining peace, would have appeared barbarous and unseemly to them, especially since for reasons of economy they had greatly reduced England's armed force. Accordingly, at the last moment they made a hopeless attempt to see what diplomatic skill might accomplish.

We remember that on July 13th Gramont urgently solicited Lord Lyons to induce his Government to influence the Prussian king to forbid the Prince of Hohenzollern to reconsider the Spanish candidacy in the future, since that would end the difficulty. This suggested to Lord Granville a proposal which he transmitted to both Governments on July 14th; namely, that France should recall the demand for guaranties, whereupon King William should formally announce the Prince's withdrawal to the French Government. This proposition was somewhat belated as to its one half, and a little premature as to the other; for the King had already made the announcement on the 13th through Benedetti, and Gramont had not the least idea of withdrawing his demand. Consequently, on the 15th, the proposal was simultaneously declined in Paris and in Berlin. Lord Granville's next resort was to that clause of the Treaty of Paris concluded in 1856, which requires that before declaring war, contending Powers shall seek an adjustment through the good offices of friendly governments. To this Gramont replied that it was too late for mediation, war was inevitable; and Bismarck declared that since France was the aggressor, that country must be the one to take the first step toward conciliation.

Thus this attempt also ended in failure; and on July 19th, England published a manifesto, in which the Queen proclaimed her country's neutrality, declaring that every violation of it by her subjects would be punished according to the law. The English Ministers were sorely perplexed; they could not do otherwise than disapprove the course France had pursued since the 6th, and more especially since the 12th; nevertheless, in their hearts remained the old sentiments, — in Lord Granville's a warm inclination to France, in Gladstone's a strong dislike for Germany, — although they were evinced only in so far as was compatible with a prudent regard for the pressure of public opinion, and for the promotion of England's mercantile interests.

During the discussion of Belgian neutrality in the House of Commons, Disraeli warned against placing too great reliance upon fine phrases and old treaties, and advised that in any case England arm herself well. Moreover, he reminded his hearers of another guaranty which England had undertaken in the Vienna Congress of 1815; namely, Prussia's possession of the Rhine provinces. But Gladstone repelled this intimation as vigororously as possible by the unfounded argument that England had been absolved from this guaranty by the dissolution of the German Confederation and by Prussia's annexations. He carefully avoided every allusion to Disraeli's real meaning, namely, that Belgian independence would be of short duration after a French conquest of the Rhine provinces, and that therefore, if only for the sake of Belgium, English interests would be best served by the success of the Prussian arms.

But Bismarck's disclosures had after all made Gladstone somewhat apprehensive with regard to Belgium's future; and he now roused himself to the wonderful endeavor to induce the two contending Powers to enter into a new treaty for the maintenance of Belgian neutrality, with the additional provision that in the event of its violation by either party England would co-operate with the other to secure the integrity of the country, but would take no further part in the military operations. The thought does not seem to have occurred to him that a Power that had disregarded the compact of 1839 was little to be relied upon to hold to the conditions of a new treaty. To his present gratification, however, the two belligerents signed the treaty without further parley.

But more vexatious was the controversy between the

English and Prussian Cabinets to which the duties of neutrality gave rise, especially with reference to the obligations requiring that English commerce furnish neither belligerent with arms, ammunition, and other war-like stores, the so-called contraband of war. At the time of Napoleon I., when England was a belligerent Power, that country had sought to include as much as possible in that which was to come under the denomination of contraband of war, insisting that all useful commodities, such as grain, for instance, came under that category, and had even confiscated all such stores found upon neutral vessels bound for French ports. Now the tables were turned ; England was the neutral State, and was therefore desirous to preserve to its merchants the greatest possible amount of trade.

Immediately after the French declaration of war had been proclaimed, Bismarck received information that English merchants of Birmingham and Newcastle had delivered large supplies of coal to French war vessels destined for service in the North Sea, and that other English firms had made contracts with the French Government to furnish arms and ammunition. There could be no question that these articles were contraband of war ; and accordingly Bismarck transmitted the request to London, that in compliance with the Queen's proclamation the English Government forbid this traffic. But this demand met with an ill reception. Lord Granville replied that coal and ammunition were at all times valuable and profitable commodities of England's export trade, and were now as heretofore sent to every part of

the world. Under contraband of war, therefore, could
be included only the individual shipment when consigned to a belligerent Power; and since it was manifestly impossible for the Government to inquire into
this in every instance, it could comply with Prussia's
request only by general restrictions upon the export of
these goods, which was obviously inexpedient in every
way. Moreover, it was added, during the war of the
Crimea, when Prussia was a neutral, such articles had
constantly found their way from Belgium to Russia by
way of Prussian routes. Prussia must therefore at that
time have learned that it was hardly possible to prevent
such transportations.

Prussia admitted the truth of this; namely, the difficulty of putting a complete stop to smuggling of this
kind, but directed attention so much the more emphatically to another fact, equally true, that at the time referred to the Prussian Government had taken the action
now desired of England, and had most vigorously sought
to enforce it.

In this connection the Attorney-General, or chief
Government advocate, made the statement to Parliament, that in England it is not within the province of
the Government to decide the question what in individual cases is or is not to be considered contraband of
war; but that this falls within the jurisdiction of the
prize-courts, whose duty it is to decide with regard to
the character of the cargo found upon a captured ves-
sel. As applied to the impending war, this implied the
very friendly declaration that England would not in-

terfere should Prussian war-ships seize the English mer-
chantmen carrying contraband of war to French ports,
and the unlawful cargo be confiscated by the Prussian
prize-courts. It is hardly necessary to state that whether
theoretically there was legal foundation for this decision or not, practically it gave the English merchants
full liberty to convey war material of every description
to France; since, owing to the immense superiority of
the French naval force, there was not the slightest
prospect that the Prussian war-ships could stop this
unlawful traffic.   How grave were the consequences
of England's attitude upon this question, not for Germany alone, we shall soon learn.

If thus through England's mercantile interests, and
despite the freely expressed Prussian sympathies of the
Times, the English Ministry was influenced to a step
redounding to the great advantage of France, there
were in the wide field of English commerce other interests, a due regard for which resulted on the other
hand in the frustration of important French aspirations.
All warfare interrupts commerce: consequently commercial interests demand that when a conflict of arms
has become inevitable, it shall be restricted to as limited a region as possible. The English Cabinet did all
in its power, therefore, to localize, as it was called, the
German-French war; that is, to deter other States from
allying themselves with either belligerent. As in the
question regarding contraband of war, this may, from a
judicial point of view, appear to be eminently non-parti-
san; but in its practical effects it touched only one of the

contending Powers, — not Prussia this time, which had long ago concluded its alliances, but France, which was still endeavoring to form them. The disadvantage incurred by the French policy in consequence of England's diplomatic activity in this respect soon proved to be most momentous, especially so since the English endeavor was energetically supported by the Russian Government; although the incentives by which the Court of St. Petersburg was actuated were entirely different ones from those by which the English Cabinet was influenced.

In the first place, there existed between the Emperor Alexander and his royal Prussian uncle not only the tie of relationship, but the bond of a warm personal esteem and affection. The Czar had at the beginning disapproved the Hohenzollern candidacy as much as any one; but when, after Prince Leopold had withdrawn, Gramont made new difficulties, he indignantly condemned this course. To this were added important political considerations. He, too, feared that Germany might not be strong enough to withstand the armies of France; and nothing seemed more probable than that a French invasion of Eastern Germany would be followed by renewed revolt of the Poles, whom it had been so difficult to reduce to submission in 1863, and who were already noisily proclaiming to the world their French sympathies and the hopes they set upon that country. And further, we know how bitter a feeling of humiliation filled every Russian heart at the remembrance of how in 1856 the Black Sea was neutralized; and

also that in 1866 Prussia declared itself willing under
favorable circumstances to co-operate with Russia for
the removal of this obstacle which England and France
had placed in the way of Russian preponderance in the
East.   Since then the relations between Berlin and
St. Petersburg had grown more and more cordial, even
without the tie of a formal alliance; and the more it
was now feared by the Russian Court that the French
armies would prove superior to the Prussian, the more
eagerly did it endeavor to prevent their augmentation
by those of an ally.

Denmark was the first to discover this.   Immediately after France had declared war, the old hatred of
Germany entertained by a large part of the Danish
population was again wrathfully displayed.   In Paris,
too, a plan was at once devised, acccording to which
a powerful fleet, carrying thirty thousand soldiers, was
to be despatched to the Baltic; the troops were to
be landed at some point upon the coast, where they
were to be re-enforced by twenty thousand Danes, and
thus Berlin was to be threatened from a position in
its immediate vicinity.

This was quickly thought, but not so easily carried
out.   Without a moment's loss of time Prussia sent a
request to the Government at Copenhagen that Denmark declare its neutrality in the impending war; this
was followed immediately afterwards by a very courteous but unmistakable intimation that, at the first indication of Danish hostility, Prussian troops would occupy
the whole of Jutland.   King Christian, less inclined to

war than were his people, remembered only too well
the difficulties in which his land had become involved
through the ardor of the Eider Danes in 1864. And
when, in addition, he now received urgent appeals,
first from London and then from St. Petersburg, not
again to stake Denmark's welfare upon the possibilities
of a hazardous contest, he determined to follow the
promptings of his own inclinations, and sign the declaration of neutrality. It was not until after this that
Marquis Cadore, the special envoy sent by France, arrived in Copenhagen, bearing the proposition that Denmark become the ally of France. He had come too
late; he had his labor for his pains.

Meanwhile the Russian Government had proclaimed
its own neutrality, which, it declared, would be rigidly
maintained so long as this was at all compatible with
the interests of the country. This reservation was explained by diplomatic communications to the effect that
Russia would consider its interests imperilled in the
event either of a Polish insurrection, or of Austria's
participation in the war against Prussia; in either case
Russia would enter the contest to the full extent of
its ability. Although the Court of Vienna was not
officially informed of this intention, it was not left in
doubt with regard to it; this was a menacing danger
which Count Beust, surrounded by perils as he was,
could not afford to lose sight of for a moment.

As soon as war had been decided upon, on July
15th, France lost no time to invite the two friends
with whom she had discussed alliances during the past

year to join her in the coming contest. As we remember, in September, 1869, Napoleon had deferred the signing of the draft-treaty of alliance because Italy had insisted upon the proviso that the French garrison still remaining in the States of the Church be withdrawn, a stipulation to which Napoleon was not at the time willing to agree. Now, however, the handful of soldiers stationed there was of no practical significance whatever; for the great body of the French troops, being employed elsewhere, could render no support.

Accordingly Napoleon addressed an autograph letter to King Victor Emmanuel, stating that he was now ready to comply with Italy's desire; that he would authorize the withdrawal of his troops, thus returning to the basis of the convention of September 15th, 1864, provided that Italy would undertake the duty stipulated in the treaty; namely, to respect the independence of the Papal territory, and to protect it against attack from abroad. The Duke of Gramont then gave the Italian military *attaché*, Count Vimercati, detailed information regarding the proposed offensive triple alliance; this the Count was to convey first to Vienna and then to Florence. The King's decision with respect to the matter was likewise to be communicated first to Vienna. Prince Latour d'Auvergne was to be sent as envoy to Vienna to represent France in the negotiations.

As it was well known in Paris that Austria and Italy would require at least six weeks, and perhaps even a longer time, to mobilize their armies, it was understood that both these countries, although entering into an offensive and defensive alliance with France, would for the present remain neutral, their military preparations being only preliminary to a joint attempt at mediation. As soon as they were ready for war, assuming the *rôle* of mediator, they would propose unacceptable terms to Prussia, and upon their rejection would declare war. As demands suited to this purpose were mentioned the following: that no Prussian Prince would ever be permitted to acquire the Spanish crown; that the condition of affairs ordained by the Treaty of Prague, namely, the complete independence of the South German States, be guaranteed by Prussia; that Austria be reinstated in the German Confederation as bearer of the presidential dignity.[1]

This communication caused the Austrian Cabinet the deepest concern. We are aware how sadly in need of peace Austria was; how desirous its Government was that the equilibrium of power between France and

---

[1] That these negotiations were actually begun by France is fully established by the accordant testimony of Prince Napoleon (*Revue des Deux Mondes*, 1 avril, 1878, p. 496; Rothan's "L'Allemagne et l'Italie," II., pp. 57, 64), Guiccioli ("Sella," I., pp. 258, 282), and Beust in his letter to Prince Metternich, dated July 20th. In this letter it is mentioned that Vimercati had been in Vienna, but on the 20th was no longer there, having continued his journey; that his return was, however, expected. This quite agrees with Guiccioli's statement that Vimercati left Paris on July 15th, bearing the proposal of alliance, and that he arrived in Florence on the 20th; according to this he would have reached Vienna about the 17th or 18th.

One of the propositions to be made by the mediators is mentioned by Beust in his letter of the 20th, and another in his "Memoirs," II., p. 391. The third one I have taken from Guiccioli, p. 258, although, it must be confessed, under the supposition that the statements on this page stand in close connection with the contents of p. 262.

Prussia should continue as heretofore, thus preserving to Austria the possibility of subjecting South Germany more and more to Austrian influence. And now this suddenly declared war would end all these hopes. Should Napoleon be the victor, which Beust thought more than probable, South Germany would fall under his domination as protector of a new Rhenish Confederation. Should Prussia offer an unexpectedly obstinate resistance, he would most likely follow the promptings of his personal inclination, and conclude a peace as quickly as possible, perhaps at Austria's expense; that is, he would resign South Germany to Prussia upon the condition that in return the left bank of the Rhine be ceded to him.[1] To share in a war which would bring about such results, to add strength to the side which was already the stronger, and thereby even run the risk of an attack from Russia, — all this Beust was firmly determined to avoid from the outset.

But, on the other hand, might not the consequences be still worse if the mighty imperator's hopes of armed assistance were so completely and immediately shattered? For, although he could not demand assistance in fulfilment of treaty obligations, he nevertheless fully expected it for old friendship's sake. And, should the French troops in rapid march overrun South Germany as far as the Bohemian frontier, would it not in that case be more than likely that, after Austria had provoked the displeasure of the French Emperor, he would

[1] Beust, "Memoirs," II., p. 342.

make overtures to Russia, and the two would then come to an agreement regarding a common policy in the Orient, and again probably at Austria's expense?

In short, difficulties and dangers presented themselves on every side. Count Beust saw but one course open to him, which was to avoid any decided answer for the present, that time might be gained, and, far from breaking with the conqueror, to hold out flattering prospects to him, without, however, entering into any binding agreement; and in the mean time Austria must make vigorous preparations for self-defence. No effort must, however, be spared to bring this dreadful war to a close as speedily as possible by peaceful intervention in conjunction with some of the other Powers.

Nothing could be more excellently adapted to serve as an opening in this direction than was Gramont's proposal that Austria should invite Italy to join her in an attempt at mediation; although, in consenting to this, Beust's purpose was just the reverse of that which Gramont had in mind. The demands which the latter had suggested were therefore rejected by Beust as unsuitable in every respect — the Spanish question was disposed of; to demand the independence of South Germany while its armies were taking the field against France was an absurdity; and, finally, the readmission of Austria into the German Confederation was not at all desired in Vienna.

On July 18th a Cabinet Council of all the Ministers common to the two halves of the monarchy, together with the President of the Hungarian Ministry, Count

Andrassy, and of the Cis-Leithan, Count Potocki, was held in the Hofburg. In this assembly Count Beust proposed that neither alliance nor neutrality be decided upon, but that Austria await events, and meanwhile provide for defence by placing the army upon a semi-war footing. But herein he was opposed most vigorously by Count Andrassy, who argued: " Our action must be determined solely by consideration for the present needs of the country, without regard for sentiment of any kind, and there can be no question that these peremptorily demand an open and decided declaration of neutrality. Otherwise, if Napoleon triumph over Prussia, Austria will fall into a state of absolute dependence upon the conqueror, and may expect France and Russia to come to an understanding highly prejudicial to Austrian interests. On the other hand, if Prussia be victorious, our neutrality will have gained for us a valuable friend, between whom and us there exists no contrariety of interests; since Austria will, in all probability, not yield to the temptation held out by France, and seek to reacquire its former title to the presidium of the German Confederation, a relationship wholly outgrown, and one from which Austria never derived benefit, but often suffered loss.[1] In my opinion military preparations are nevertheless absolutely necessary under existing circumstances; " added Andrassy, " and I therefore propose that we ask for an appropriation of twenty millions for this purpose. But this sum

[1] A similar assertion made in the Hungarian Representative Assembly was received with loud and enthusiastic applause.

will never be granted by the Delegations except for the enforcement of our neutrality." [1]

He carried his point; the Emperor and the Council of Ministers decided upon the declaration of neutrality.

Accordingly Count Beust announced this decision on July 20th, although not like England and Russia, by a publicly proclaimed manifesto, but by a circular note to the other European Courts; this set forth that the safety of the land demanded the intended military preparations. This could arouse no one's suspicion; when a fire breaks out in a neighboring house, it behooves us to put our own extinguishing apparatus in readiness.

Beust had submitted to the will of the higher authority, but he was far from being either convinced, or relieved from anxiety. Whilst the copy of the circular note intended for Paris was being prepared for the courier, his old friend, Count Vitzthum, was with him. "Remember," said he to the Count, "that in eight days an army of three hundred thousand men may be at our Bohemian frontier; we must try to keep Napoleon well disposed toward us, and must, above all else, place Metternich in a position to emphasize the fact that our neutrality is one of benevolence toward France." [2]

Hereupon Vitzthum wrote out the draft of a private letter in confidential form to be addressed by Minister

---

[1] Compare Konyi's extracts from conversations with Andrassy, as well as Louyai's letters, *Deutsche Revue*, 1890. In addition, Beust's oft-repeated statements.

[2] Derived from unpublished memoirs.

Beust to his representative at Paris. It began with the words " Dear Friend," and ended with the expression, " Accept a thousand greetings," by which it was intended to convey to Prince Metternich that, although this was a confidential despatch, it was not an official message to be communicated, for instance, to Gramont or Napoleon ; but that it was meant exclusively for his personal instruction, and to suggest to him that, in making the verbal announcement of Austria's intended neutrality and the rejection of the proposed alliance, he should administer the bitter pill with as sweet a coating as possible.

Beust had no idea that the letter would find its way into other hands, and would thus lead to endless misunderstandings and misrepresentations of his policy. It seems advisable, therefore, that the letter be inserted here, accompanied by explanatory comments indicating the true sense. It said : —

" Count Vitzthum has made known to our Emperor the commission with which Emperor Napoleon personally intrusted him " (namely, his wish that a peace congress be proposed). " This imperial message, together with Gramont's statements, proves the utter incorrectness of a misapprehension to which the suddenness with which this unexpected war was brought about may have given rise " (namely, the misapprehension that personally Napoleon was eager for war). "You will therefore say to the Emperor and his Ministers that, true to our obligations as stated in the written promise which the two Emperors exchanged toward the close of the last year" (namely, that neither would conclude an alliance with a third party without previously informing the other), "we look upon the cause of France as our own, and will do all that lies within the limits of what is possible to contribute to the success of the French arms."

He then sets forth that armed assistance is no longer within the limits of that which is possible, but that, much to the regret of the Government, the declaration of neutrality had become an absolute necessity, owing to the attitude of Russia, of the Magyars, and of the German element in Austria. The Government could not therefore enter into an alliance with a belligerent Power, although it would gladly aid the French cause by diplomatic means. This is further developed in the letter as follows: —

"We resort to neutrality only as a means by which to accomplish the ultimate aim of our policy, our purpose being to complete our military preparations without exposing ourselves in a defenceless condition to a hostile attack" (which may be expected when we begin our diplomatic activity). "We have, nevertheless," the letter continues, "already begun negotiations with Italy concerning the mediation suggested by the Emperor Napoleon; will the basis upon which this is to proceed, as indicated to the Emperor, serve the purpose he has in view? In other words, will the conditions be regarded as unacceptable by Prussia? To us this is a matter of indifference; as I have already telegraphed you, we will accept these conditions if Italy agrees to them as the aim of our joint action." (At this point Beust discreetly refrains from designating the process and purpose of this action as contemplated by himself. Instead, he makes the negotiations with Italy conditional upon a stipulation absolutely odious to Paris. The letter continues) : —

" In the despatch referred to above I mentioned the evacuation of Rome. This question must now be settled ; the September convention no longer meets the requirements ; the Italians will never be heartily with us until we have plucked this Roman thorn out of their flesh. The day that sees the evacuation of Rome by the French troops must also witness its occupation by the Italians, with the sanction of Austria and France. And, to be candid, is it not better for the Pope to be under the protection of Italian troops, than to be exposed to Garibaldi's hostilities?

" If France would do us the honor of leaving to us the solution of the Roman question, the undertaking whose initiative it desires us to assume would be greatly simplified. By so liberal a proceeding it would deprive the enemy of one weapon, and would place an obstruction in the way of the Teutonic enthusiasm which Protestant Prussia has aroused in Germany, and which, because of its power of infection, we have double reason to fear. It is a fortunate circumstance," were the concluding words, " that Count Vimercati's return and Prince Latour's arrival here are coincident."

Meanwhile, in impatient suspense, Gramont was awaiting an expression of opinion from Beust. Day after day passed ; Prince Metternich had no further information to give than that the Austrian army could not possibly be placed on a war-footing before September, but that Count Beust had already opened negotiations with Italy. Gramont could do nothing further than to send Prince Latour to Vienna once more, with new proposals to be vigorously pressed.

Notification of the course determined upon at Florence was also expected for a week before it arrived, and Ambassador Nigra was from day to day compelled to admit that his Government had as yet arrived at no definite decision.[1] So much the greater was the rejoicing when the entirely favorable reply, written 'on July 20th, to Napoleon's letter concerning the September convention, did arrive. It had been wholly due to the dispute engendered by this question that the triple alliance had suffered shipwreck in 1869; and, after an agreement had now been reached upon this point, all Gramont's doubts regarding armed assistance from Italy were set at rest. And now, on July 23d, Prince Metternich presented to him Beust's confidential letter of the 20th,[2] together with the demand that Rome be simply resigned to the Italians, since otherwise they would never join the triple alliance.

If Beust had hoped to win favor in Paris by the obsequious tone of his letter, any such effect was completely counteracted by the closing sentences. " What a wicked heretic this Beust is ! " was Empress Eugé-

[1] Prince Napoleon's assertion that Nigra had persistently raised false hopes in Paris was emphatically denied by the latter. Rothan, II., p. 64.

[2] As asserted by Gramont. That he read the letter there can be no doubt.

nie's comment. Gramont could not believe that, forgetful of all her Catholic traditions, Austria was calling upon France to turn traitor to the Pope and his holy cause. He himself forgot Austria's bitter quarrel with the Curia, a state of affairs which the declaration of Papal infallibility just determined upon by the Vatican Council was surely not calculated to improve. He wondered whether Beust had been influenced to his impious proposal simply by his own Protestant inclinations, or whether it had been the suggestion of Italy. In either case he was resolved to interpose at once. " The Prussians in Paris rather than the Italians in Rome ! " was the highly patriotic maxim of the religious enthusiasts who frequented the antechambers of the Tuileries at this time.[1]

Before the close of the day Gramont sent a despatch to Baron Malaret, his representative at Florence, saying that Beust and Prince Napoleon had mentioned the abandonment of Rome ; he desired Malaret to oppose this intrigue most vigorously. At the same time a despatch was addressed to the Italian Government reading: The only basis upon which we can come to an agreement is the September convention ; we have already announced to His Holiness the Pope the intended withdrawal of our troops; this will, however, not ensue unless Italy and France reciprocally promise to observe the stipulations of the September convention.[2]

[1] Rothan, II., p. 66.
[2] Guiccioli, I., p. 270. The author states that for the contents of his ninth chapter, in which he tells of the negotiations concerning neutrality, he gained his information from statements made by Sella and from the

By this threat the scales at Florence were turned, but not as Gramont had expected.

Up to this time the situation there had been the following: Upon the receipt of Napoleon's communication of July 12th, declaring that through Prince Leopold's withdrawal peace had become assured, King Victor Emmanuel went to hunt in the Alpine valleys of Aosta. In this parliamentarily governed State, the Ministers enjoyed great freedom of action; and when now, during the King's absence, they learned of the breaking out of hostilities on the 15th of July, they decided upon a most important step. The Minister of Foreign Affairs, Visconti-Venosta, proposed to the English Ambassador that their two Governments enter into a treaty with Austria to preserve an attitude of neutrality, and then invite the other Powers of Europe to join them herein. But Lord Granville, distrustful of the peaceable intentions of the two Courts, feared that by concluding such an agreement he might be disturbed in the inaction so fully resolved upon and so dear to his heart, and therefore declined to accede to the proposal.

On July 17th Victor Emmanuel returned to Florence. In open opposition to his Ministers, he was ardently enthusiastic for the alliance with France, and

documents of the Ministry, all of which had been open to his inspection; although he had not had documentary evidence regarding the King's confidential correspondence. What he relates with respect to this he gathered from French sources, and everywhere qualifies his statements by such expressions as " in so far as we can see," " as it appears," " we may conclude," and the like. We shall have frequent occasion to refer to this distinction with respect to authenticity.

participation in the war, hoping by brilliant deeds of
valor to win a glorious reward from his imperial friend,
— perhaps Rome itself, or, failing that, the remaining
Papal territory up to the very gates of the Eternal
City; and, if as yet that could not be obtained, then
for the present other territory in which the Italian
tongue was spoken, — the Italian Tyrol and Nice, for
instance. But with these representations, the creations
of his excited imagination, he made not the least impression upon his Ministers. The Cabinet was no
longer, as in 1869, under the guidance of General
Menabrea, with sympathies enlisted for France. The
new President of the Ministry, Lanza, like Visconti-
Venosta, was a grateful admirer of France; but both
these gentlemen were of a cautious and practical turn
of mind; and in consideration of the weak condition
of the army, made necessary by the low state of the
finances, they now maintained that war must be avoided,
and for the same reason advised against an over-hasty
attempt to force or solve the Roman question. Their
counsel was to wait, and look forward hopefully to the
future.

The real leader in the Cabinet, the Minister of Finance, Sella, whose courage and energy exceeded his
caution and forethought, took a somewhat different
view of the situation. Like his colleagues, he rejected
the French alliance, and, like the King, his heart was
set upon Rome. He had spent some time in Germany
pursuing his studies, and thus had come to have a high
regard and admiration for German culture and ability.

He repelled with indignation the idea of an attack
upon the ally of 1866, with whose assistance Italy had
regained Venetia, and upon whom war was now to be
made because of the aspirations for nationality, the selfsame aspirations upon which rested Italy's strength, and
hopes for the future. Added to this was the bitter
resentment he felt toward the crowned priest who, for
the sake of retaining his political power, fast falling
into decay, was willing to see the historic capital of
Italy in the hands of foreign troops. Toward the imperial protector of this state of affairs he had a feeling
of deep aversion; for through his occupation of Rome
he held all Italy in subjection, and even demanded
gratitude for the war of 1859, although, had matters
gone as he desired, Italy would simply have found
herself vassal to a different foreign lord in consequence
of it.

And so Sella's relations to the King were of a
peculiar nature. Victor Emmanuel loved him and
valued him highly, not only as his able Minister of Finance, but, above all other reasons, for the resolute
stand he took upon the Roman question. And yet regarding the best course to be pursued in connection
with it, there were vehement altercations between them
almost daily. Should it be a French alliance or armed
neutrality? The two men did not spare each other.
"You are averse to war," said the King; "to be sure,
it requires courage to give battle." Ready of tongue,
Sella replied, "It takes more courage to oppose Your
Majesty than it does to go to war." — "It is evident,"

said the King, " that your ancestors were not warriors,
but wool merchants." — " Our firm," was Sella's quick
retort, " has always honored its obligations; but it is
Your Majesty's present wish to indorse a note which
you will not be able to pay." The King was provoked,
but the resolute Minister remained in favor.

The day after his return Victor Emmanuel received
Napoleon's letter proposing the revival of the September convention. The King looked upon the recall of
the French troops as the first step toward the realization of his desire, and gladly welcomed it as such; he
therefore determined at once to send a favorable reply.[1]
His Ministers also expressed their approval, for they
all were eager that the foreign flag flying over Rome
should be removed. It was for this reason that Sella
also gave his consent, with the reflection that by agreeing to the September convention no obligation to enter
into an alliance of arms was assumed.

Hardly, however, had this conclusion been reached,
when the proposition to form a triple alliance was received from Paris, and consequent on this, Beust's
proposal of joint mediation, together with that for the
surrender of Rome to the protection of the Italians.
The King and his Ministers entertained very different
opinions on this point, but were quite in harmony upon
another, namely, that, for the present, the so suddenly
developed European situation demanded speedy preparation for war. As a first step in this direction the
order was given to call into active service all the men

[1] Rothan gives its text, p. 93.

who had been added to the reserves within the last two years; as a result the army, whose numbers had been reduced to 130,000 men, would now have a strength of 200,000 men.

The execution of this order was at once followed by the wildest excitement among the people throughout the length and breadth of the country, for by it all their pent-up wrath against the French was re-aroused; in the larger cities the masses gave vent to their feelings in fierce riots; in Florence they threatened to mob the palace of the French Ambassador; everywhere was heard the cry: Death to the Frenchmen! Long live Prussia! [1]

In the Chamber the orators of the Left declared that never would the Government be allowed to give aid to the murderers of Mentana, not even if, in return, Napoleon would throw open the gates of Rome; that which ought now to be done was to disregard the will of France entirely, and with self-reliant resolve to take possession of Rome. If the monarchy would not do this, then it would be accomplished by revolution.

While thus abroad in the land the storm was raging, the King, who recognized the fact that his war policy was impossible of execution unless he could obtain Rome for the people to be their national capital, sent Count Vimercati back to Vienna on July 22d, there to announce the King's willingness to conclude the triple alliance, although only on the one condition that

---

[1] All paid for by Bismarck, .was the comment made by French reports.

this would secure for him an acceptable solution of the Roman question in the manner suggested by Beust.

And now, a blow to all these pleasing anticipations, came Gramont's peremptory despatch of July 23d, in which the recall of the troops was made dependent upon the renewed reciprocal recognition of the September convention, which implied the rejection of Beust's proposition, and deprived the King of all hope to procure better terms.[1] At this juncture Sella came to the front. " For the present," said he, " we must give the desired promise regarding the September convention; for first of all we must rid Italian soil of French bayonets. We must, however, do all in our power to retain as great freedom of action for the future as possible. But this is not enough. In Paris the opinion prevails that for even these meagre concessions Italy's armies ought to, and will, follow the flag of the Emperor; it would therefore be a folly to expect the fulfilment of our desire as a grateful reward at the close of the war. Let us not deceive ourselves; under such circumstances a French triumph over Germany would be synonymous with the Pope's triumph over Italy, of the syllabus over culture and freedom of thought, of the policy of intervention over the principle of national unity. We must therefore shatter this tyrannical illusion under which the French Government is laboring by openly and resolutely declaring our neutrality. Then we can calmly await further offers which France may be in-

[1] Ollivier obtained a like declaration from the Emperor on July 25th Ollivier, " L'Église et l'État au Concile du Vatican," II., p. 474.

clined to make for the sake of securing our armed
co-operation."

The King declared himself fully convinced that upon
this point the stand taken by Sella was the correct one.

On July 24th Italy's neutrality in the impending war
was proclaimed by a royal manifesto. At the same
time a preliminary reply was telegraphed to Gramont,
saying: Italy is ready to comply with the wish of
France, and exchange the reciprocal promises regarding
the September convention; although we realize that it
is beyond our power to send our armies abroad against
Prussia, and at the same time protect the Papal territory against attack from insurgents at home; nor do
we perceive any advantage to accrue to us through a
revival of the September convention, since this compact
has not proved beneficial, but harmful, to Italy.

Although a promise was hereby held out, yet, in the
same breath as it were, its fulfilment was declared to
be impossible, or at least incompatible with participation in the war. Gramont, hasty of conclusion as
usual, entirely overlooked this trifling circumstance;
it was sufficient that Italy was willing to revive the
September convention. The proclamation of neutrality
appeared to him to be no more than a preliminary to the
armed mediation which he had proposed. As soon as
the promised declaration had arrived he would consider
the offensive and defensive alliance as assured.

On the next day Visconti-Venosta announced to the
Chamber the intended policy of neutrality and return
to the September convention. With Sella the Left re-

joiced at the rejection of the alliance, the Right with
Visconti-Venosta at the postponement of the Roman
question; and so the Chamber expressed its full confidence in the Ministry by a vote of 282 against 63
voices.

How fully convinced the Ministers were that they
owed the King's consent to neutrality wholly to Gramont's categoric insistence upon the September convention, is clearly evident from the fact, that, in reply
to a notification from Vienna announcing that Beust
was still endeavoring to procure a more favorable clause
with regard to the Roman question, they sent a despatch to Gramont saying that in view of the irrevocable decision of the French Government they believed
Beust's clause to be neither practicable nor seriously
intended.   Thus it was that the Italian Ministers themselves advocated the sanction of the September convention so long as this served the purpose of deterring the
King from concluding the French alliance.   Alas, poor
Gramont!

The King made a last though rather faint attempt
to ascertain from Malaret whether it might not be possible to obtain Napoleon's consent to Italy's occupation
of some strategically important point within the Papal
States, to the end that the entire territory might be
protected, and yet the employment of only a small military force be made necessary.   Malaret was compelled
to give an absolutely negative reply; and so the King
returned to his policy of neutrality, to depart from
which, after the vote given by the Chamber, would

under any circumstances have been attended by much
difficulty. His biographer, Massari, says plainly: The
King was for war; the Ministers were against it; the
King gave way to his Ministry. At all events, he
determined, before taking any further steps, to await
developments.

And so, on July 25th, thanks to Gramont's clerical
policy, Italy had definitely withdrawn from the triple
alliance so eagerly desired in Paris.

On the same day a like decision was reached in
Vienna.[1]

On July 24th both Prince Latour from Paris and
Vimercati from Florence arrived in that city, and negotiations were begun without delay on July 25th. Latour renewed the proposal which Gramont had made
immediately after the declaration of war. An offensive
alliance between Austria and France, with the stipulation that Austria would remain apparently neutral
until such time as its military equipment should be
complete, when, assuming the *rôle* of armed mediator,
it would make certain proposals to Prussia, and as
soon as these were rejected would declare war against
that country.

Vimercati acceded to this, and expressed the hope
that the conclusion of the alliance would be made possible to Italy, and thus at length the long desired triple
alliance be realized.

But, as we know, this was by no means what Beust
contemplated. After Austria had, on the 20th, notified

[1] What follows is derived from unpublished memoirs.

all the Courts of Europe that it would remain neutral,
it could not now enter into an alliance with one of the
belligerent Powers, he said.   Neither could he approve
Gramont's proposal as to the purpose which the armed
mediation should serve.   Austria was, however, quite
willing to endeavor by mediation to bring about a
speedy termination of the war, and desired, with this
end in view, to enter into close relations with Italy
according to a definite understanding.

Vimercati declared himself ready to attempt such an
agreement.   On July 26th he and Beust decided upon
a treaty of alliance to be concluded between Austria
and Italy, according to which each of these two Powers
was for the present to complete its military preparations for the enforcement of its own neutrality; all
independent action on the part of either was to be
avoided; and all measures, whether for the purpose of
mediation or of war, were to be jointly undertaken
after being agreed upon by the two Powers.

Prince Latour announced that in this form he had
no objection to the treaty.   To make it as inviting as
possible to the Italians, Beust added another clause, to
the effect that Austria would seek to gain Napoleon's
consent to more favorable conditions in the Roman
matter.   In reply to a telegraphic report stating the
substance of the draft-treaty, Vimercati received Victor
Emmanuel's unhesitatingly and gladly given approval;
for by it the King hoped to have the way to an alliance
of arms again opened to him.   To raise the King's
hopes still higher, Beust, on July 27th, submitted to

the Vienna conference a despatch to Napoleon asking that Austria be intrusted with the adjustment of the Roman question and the protection of the Pope.

Concerning Count Beust's object in making these proposals, there can to-day be not the slightest doubt. He wished to hold Victor Emmanuel's eagerness for war in check, and to this end endeavored to make Italy's every movement dependent upon Austrian consent. Should Napoleon now leave even the decision in the Roman question to him, then Italy would be entirely subject to the will of Austria; not, however, for the purpose of removing the last obstacle in the way of the desired alliance, as the King, so eager to join in the impending contest, flattered himself, but for the exactly opposite end of binding Italy to Austria's policy of neutrality and mediation.

However, as well planned as was every thread in this diplomatic web, it became evident at once that it would not accomplish its purpose, either in Paris or in Florence. In Paris, Gramont insisted upon the re-establishment of the September convention, and that upon no other condition would the French garrison be withdrawn from Rome. In Florence, the Cabinet was more than willing to comply with this demand; since it served the double propose of removing the French soldiers from Rome, and of deterring the King from concluding the French alliance. The formal agreement for the re-establishment of the September convention, which had been promised Gramont on the 24th of July, was drawn up and signed on the 28th by the Italian Ministers and the French Ambassador; and Malaret at once sent a despatch announcing the happy event to Gramont.

Without losing a moment of time the latter now telegraphed to Vienna: Napoleon and Victor Emmanuel have come to an agreement upon the Roman question on the basis of the September convention. By which this astute diplomatist meant to imply that without further delay the triple alliance might now be concluded.

But in Vienna, where both Latour and Vimercati had been left in total ignorance of the negotiations which Gramont had been carrying on with Florence since the 23d of July, his despatch of the 28th created utmost surprise and consternation. What does the King want? it was asked. It was but yesterday that he accepted with eagerness Beust's offer to obtain better terms for Italy in the Roman question, and to-day he submits without further ado to Napoleon's demands. What are we to conclude from this? One thing is certain: if the King himself consents to the September convention, the clause inserted in the new draft-treaty regarding more liberal terms will certainly be excluded from it.

It was decided to obtain the solution of the riddle directly from the two monarchs themselves. A copy of the despatch sent Prince Metternich was to be conveyed to Napoleon by Count Vimercati, who was then to acquaint the Emperor with the substance of Beust's treaty-draft. But to Florence, Beust sent Count Vitzthum, with the commission to learn the true condition of affairs there, to discuss the treaty-draft with the King and his Ministers, and, should all go smoothly, to sign it for Austria. By this proceeding the situation was soon clearly revealed.

On the evening of the 28th Vitzthum and Vimercati left Vienna; on the 29th they both arrived in Mestre, where their paths parted, Vimercati hastening to Paris by way of Mailand, Vitzthum continuing his journey to Florence, which he reached late in the evening, finding country and city wrapped in peaceful repose. Early on the next morning he received a visit from his Majesty's private secretary, who had come to tell him that on the morrow he would call for him, and accompany him to an audience with the King, but that it was his Majesty's wish that his Ministers receive no information whatever of this. The suspense occasioned by this secrecy was, however, entirely dispelled on the following day.

The King received the Count with extreme graciousness. "Napoleon," said he, "asks me for assistance, and personally I am inclined to comply with his request. But this crisis has come about so suddenly that I must have more time. Moreover, my Ministers are disposed to raise objections, for which that vexatious September convention is to blame. Another impediment to a prompt decision is the slowness with which the French army moves, making it impossible to form an opinion with regard to coming events, whereby the difficulty of determining upon our own attitude, which must, of course, be regulated accordingly, is greatly increased."

To this Vitzthum replied that this slowness had also caused some surprise in Vienna. With respect to Rome, Count Beust had proposed to the Emperor Napoleon that the negotiations with Italy regarding the guaranties to the Pope be intrusted to Austria; concerning this point he had brought with him a despatch to be submitted in confidence to the Minister.

The King did not deem it necessary to discuss this question further, and dismissed the envoy with the promise to summon him again as soon as developments should allow further decisions and communications.

To so great a degree had "that vexatious September convention" already damped the King's ardor for the French alliance. If even now, whilst making the request for armed assistance from Italy, Napoleon was so little inclined to make concessions to the Italian aspirations for nationality, how peremptorily he would suppress these at the close of a victorious contest!

After this revelation of the King's attitude, Vitzthum did not consider it necessary to mention the audience he had received, nor the despatch, nor the treaty-draft, to Visconti-Venosta when he called upon the Minister, but confined himself to inquiries concerning the intentions which the Italian Government entertained with respect to the war. He found the Minister extremely reticent also. The Italian army, he said, was by no means prepared for war. The documents in connection with the negotiations of 1869 had been consigned by Napoleon to a place among the archives; Italy was, therefore, free from any treaty obligations. The only obligation remaining to Italy was that of gratitude for 1859; but by the presence of French troops in Rome, and by the blood shed at Mentana, this feeling of gratitude had been put to a severe test. For the present, before any decision could be reached, the next events upon the arena of war must be awaited.

And so Vitzthum waited; but no mention was made of negotiations. He had abundance of time in which to examine the art treasures of Florence.

On the 5th of August, Vimercati returned from Paris without having furthered the object of his mission in any way. On the 3d of August he had spoken with the Emperor at Metz, but the interview had been wholly without result; Napoleon had simply insisted upon the September convention. Victor Emmanuel heard Vitzthum's report with but slight manifestation of interest; so much the greater, however, was the impression made upon him by the telegraphic report of the engagement at Weissenburg, received on the evening of the same day.

At length, in the night from the 6th to the 7th of August, came the news of the battle of Wörth, and the die was cast. A few hours later the King received a despatch from Napoleon; its tone was sad but dignified; in it the Emperor said that, having suffered defeat, he could not and ought not to make any demands; but in this hour of trial he appealed to the friendship and chivalry of Victor Emmanuel.

The King was deeply moved. He summoned Lanza and Visconti-Venosta at once, and sent them to La

Marmora to ask whether there still remained a way to come to the Emperor's assistance. The General was in despair. "If it is the Government's intention to declare war against Prussia, I beg the privilege of commanding a company which will fight at the side of the French army," he exclaimed; "but if the question is put to me as general and statesman, I am compelled to say that Italy is at present in no condition to do anything for France." A few minutes later Sella found him in tears.

To the King this declaration brought great relief of mind. His easily aroused imagination was already busily engaged with the thought that Napoleon's defeat would open the way to Rome to him. On the morning of August 7th he sent for Count Vitzthum, and upon his arrival received him with the words, "We have had a narrow escape. That the French have no generals we knew ever since 1859; nevertheless, this demoralized flight from Wörth is incomprehensible. In a military way there is no longer anything to be done for France. I will see if I can aid poor Napoleon by diplomatic means." This ended Vitzthum's mission.

The Italian Ministers drew a breath of relief when the French domination under which Italy had groaned for eleven years was thus terminated. Immediately a despatch was sent to Minghetti at London, instructing him to renew the proposal of an alliance between England, Austria, and Italy for the maintenance of neutrality. But even now Lord Granville, still fearing by such an agreement to become involved in Continental quarrels, declined the proposal.   Hereupon Minghetti explained that in Florence the Government was apprehensive of further urgent appeals from France for military assistance, and therefore was very desirous of English support against such pressure.   This proved the Open Sesame to the sympathy of the Gladstone Cabinet.   On August 10th Lord Granville replied that England was ready to enter into an agreement with Italy to the effect that neither of these two Governments would depart from its policy of neutrality without first coming to an understanding with the other. The treaty was then concluded without further hesitation, and was soon afterward announced to the other Powers.   This was the way in which Italian diplomacy came to the relief of Napoleon in his hour of need.[1]

A last appeal made by Gramont through Malaret, asking that at the earliest moment possible the Italian Government send an army of one hundred thousand men to France by the way of Mont Cenis, the very road by which the French army had hastened to the assistance of Italy in 1859, did not, of course, meet with the desired response.   There was some further discussion of the subject between Malaret and Visconti-Venosta; but, although the Minister invariably expressed the most favorable opinions personally, the Cabinet decision communicated by him to Malaret was quite as invariably that Italy could not comply with the wish of France.   It would require six weeks to

[1] According to the English Blue Book, Guiccioli, I., p. 288.

place only sixty thousand men in the field; and in view
of the existing uncertainty in the military situation, tho
probability was that such a force would be exposed to
utter destruction.

For France the bitterness of the situation was increased
by the attitude of the Vatican, for whose sake Victor
Emmanuel's assistance had been forfeited, through insistence upon the September convention. The withdrawal of the French brigade, which had now become
unavoidable, was practically of no significance whatever to the Curia.   Should France be defeated by
Prussia, the small garrison in Rome could be of no
avail against an attack from the Italians; and, on the
other hand, should Napoleon be gloriously victorious,
Italy would not dare to venture an attack.   Nevertheless, the announcement that the French brigade
was to be embarked for France provoked only feelings
of consternation and resentment in the Curia.

"This simply means," said Cardinal Antonelli to the
French representative, "that you leave us to certain
destruction; for you know quite as well as do we that
the Italians will not allow the binding force of a treaty
to restrain them for so much as a single moment.   It
was a mistake to rely upon your protection."

The Pope would not further express his opinion, but
so much the greater was the lack of restraint with
which it was voiced in his official press. The *Civilta
Cattolica* declared that Napoleon was guilty of the
heinous offence of breaking his imperial word and of forgetting his duty as a Catholic; the *Unita Cattolica* set

its hopes upon Prussia, which, it assured its readers, was firmly resolved after Napoleon's defeat to restore the temporal power of the Pope in all its former splendor.

A few honeyed words dropped by the Prussian representative, quite equalled in sweetness, however, by those of his colleague at Florence to the Italian Ministers, sufficed to induce the Curia to display in the presence of the representative of Catholic France the hatred and contempt felt for Napoleon.[1]

In the year 1873 Victor Emmanuel visited Emperor William in Berlin. In the course of their first conversation, immediately after the reception at the railway station, if I mistake not, Victor Emmanuel said to the Emperor: "I must confess to Your Majesty that in 1870 I was upon the point of taking up arms against you. I thought that my obligations of gratitude to Emperor Napoleon required this of me. If I was deterred from drawing the sword, the reason for this lay in the unwillingness of my people and my soldiers to wage war against you. But that which more than all else prevented me from carrying out my intention was the rapidity with which Your Majesty won victory after victory."[2]

The perfect candor of the opening sentence, together with the well-turned compliment implied in the closing one, did not fail to make an impression, it is said. It was the man and not the king who spoke thus.

Ever since the 25th of July Italy's neutrality had

[1] Rothan, ii., p. 84.
[2] As related by the Crown Prince, who was present.

been quite as firmly resolved upon as had Austria's since the 18th. Both Powers had felt themselves compelled to this course by the condition of their armies and their finances. For Austria, it was placed beyond recall by the threat uttered by Russia, by the persistent opposition of the Hungarian Government, and by the excited condition of the German population; for Italy, it became irrevocable through the resolute stand taken by the Ministry, through the opposition of the great majority in the Chamber, and through the hatred which the people bore France.

What might have happened if Napoleon had been quickly and brilliantly victorious it is idle now to conjecture; in regard to it but one assertion can be made with confidence, namely, that both Powers would have sought in every way possible to circumscribe the benefits to be reaped by France as the result of success.

It was, however, to be otherwise. Despite the many projected alliances, the two combatants were destined to face each other in utter dependence each upon his own strength. So it had been in 1866. But whereas in 1866 Austria and Prussia were contesting for the same prize, — the leadership in the German Confederation, — in 1870 France and Germany had wholly different incentives,— France to defend the European hegemony it had so long asserted; on the strength of which it forbade Spain's free choice of a King, prevented Italy from taking possession of its national capital, opposed the consummation of German federal reform, threatened Holland on account of Luxemburg, and Belgium on account of the railway transactions, and even frowned upon Switzerland because of the St. Gothard undertaking. In Germany, on the other hand, there was no thought of acquiring a dominating influence over any of the other nations; in patriotic indignation the German people resorted to the sword for the purpose of ending for all time the foreign interference in German affairs which had been endured for centuries, and of securing the independence and union of the fatherland, let us hope forever.

France was going into the struggle in defence of an old position of honor; Germany to battle for its newly found existence.

NOTE TO CHAPTER V.

GRAMONT'S FABRICATIONS REGARDING THE ALLIANCE NEGO-
TIATIONS OF 1870.

THE account which the foregoing chapter gives of the unsuccessful attempt made by France to combine with Austria and Italy in
a triple alliance against Germany is in its every particular founded
upon authentic material.

If my narrative differs in many respects from those which have
preceded it, the principal reason for this is to be found in the fact
that the authors of the others consulted Gramont's publications as
the most important, nay, even indisputable, source of information ;
whereas, with the exception of a few statements which I found
corroborated elsewhere, I have entirely disregarded Gramont's writings, believing them to be utterly misleading.

I have already had occasion to refer to the astonishing power of
invention for which the imaginative faculty of the Duke was remarkable.   Individual instances of this are to be found in the preceding volumes of this work, as well as in Count Beust's "Memoirs."
But the most astounding, almost incredible, examples of that which
he could render in this line occur in connection with his account of
the events of 1870 ; and since, afterward, when an exile, he wrote
the history of his country in the same spirit as he shaped it whilst
Minister, it seems well worth while briefly to consider him as an
author.

After the close of the war which proved so disastrous to France,
Gramont was vehemently attacked for the rashness with which he
precipitated the contest, although he knew France to be without an
assured alliance of any kind.   In December, 1872, he replied to this
charge by declaring that, although it was true that no formal treaty
of alliance had been concluded, nevertheless the friendly utterances
of both Austria and Italy, together with their cordial relations to
France, fully justified him in relying upon their armed co-operation
as soon as war should be declared.

In 1872 Count Beust was no longer Prime Minister, but ambassa-

dor at London ; very naturally he did not wish it to appear that he
had shared in Gramont's policy ; therefore, in a letter written for the
press and dated January 4th, 1873, he reminded the Duke of the
despatch he had sent him on July 11th, 1870, in which he had so
severely criticised Gramont's course of action, and had told him
that Austria would in no way participate in it.

To this Gramont replied in a letter published on the 8th of January. In it he says that, although the Austrian Ambassador, Prince
Metternich, had not submitted the despatch to him, he had informed
him of its contents, which had occasioned him everal days of anxiety, and had led to vehement altercations. " Then, however," he
continues, " Count Vitzthum came to Paris, and now all traces of
the estrangement which the despatch had occasioned instantly disappeared. He obtained an audience with the Emperor, conferred
with me, and immediately after his return to Vienna you wrote to
Prince Metternich, on the 20th, as follows : —

" ' Count Vitzthum has made known to our Emperor the commission with which the Emperor Napoleon intrusted him. This imperial
message has removed every possibility of a misapprehension to which
the suddenness with which this unexpected war was brought about
might have given rise. Say to His Majesty and His Ministers, therefore, that, true to the obligations we assumed in 1869 through the
letters exchanged between the two Emperors, we look upon the cause
of France as our own, and will do all that is possible to contribute
to the success of the French arms.'

" On the 24th of July, therefore," Gramont continues, " the day
on which I received this despatch,[1] I had Austria's formal promise
to do all that was possible to promote the success of our arms. Or
was I to understand that this would be done by means of sympathy
and good wishes only, without unsheathing the sword in our behalf ?
I cannot take this view of it ; and, moreover, you add, farther on in
the despatch : —

" ' It is to our regret that under these circumstances imperative
necessity compels us to utter the word neutrality ; but this neutrality
is only to serve as a means to the end, the only means by which we
will be enabled to complete our military preparations without exposing ourselves to a hostile attack.'

" On the evening of the 24th," Gramont adds, " Metternich wrote
me that the Austrian army could not be ready to take the field before
the beginning of September. How, after this, could I have any
doubt of your co-operation ? Furthermore, I must direct your attention, although this would seem superfluous, to that which took

---

[1] Inaccurate; he read it on the 23d.

place after Count Vitzthum's return to Paris. Assisted by Prince Metternich, he and I now determined upon the basis and the several articles of a treaty in which it was positively stated that the armed neutrality of the contracting Powers [the reference here can only be to Austria and Italy, although in this case the absence of an Italian representative must occasion surprise] was resorted to for no other purpose than that of making a transition to active co-operation with France against Prussia possible. The manner in which this was to be accomplished was the suggestion of your own representatives ; namely, that after the necessary military preparations were completed, the promise would be demanded of Prussia that nothing be undertaken by that State which would tend to disturb the *status quo* established by the Treaty of Prague. It was again your representatives who expressed the opinion that Prussia would refuse to comply with this demand, and that Austria would thereby be given the occasion to declare war."

So much for Gramont's version. By some German writers this has been regarded as evidence sufficient to justify the conclusion that in 1869 there existed a great conspiracy of arms against Prussia. They hold that, in the passages quoted by Gramont, Beust himself admits that through the Emperor's letter Austria assumed the obligations of an ally in arms ; and, furthermore, that Beust twice sent his most trusted coadjutor, Count Vitzthum, to Paris ; the first time, to dispel any existing misunderstanding ; the second time, to indicate to the French Government the way which might lead to combined warfare.

This is to be assumed with so much the greater assurance, they contend, since Beust did not by so much as a single word refute the assertions made in Gramont's letter, and thus, by his silence, conceded the truth of the statements.

The latter argument may be met by the simple reply that the Ambassador, Count Beust, was at the time advised by the Minister who was his superior in office to discontinue the correspondence with Gramont. Moreover, upon closer examination, the facts related by Gramont will be found sufficient in themselves as evidence to the contrary. Namely : —

In the year 1869 the three sovereigns did not promise one another armed assistance, but only that no one of them would conclude an alliance with a third party without the knowledge of the other two.

From Beust's then unpublished letter of the 20th, which has, however, long since been made public, Gramont, for good reasons, selected only the portions quoted above, passing in silence over the rest of its contents. Had he made known the whole of its text, it would have appeared at once that armed assistance was refused, as we have learned, and that the promise of diplomatic mediation was made conditional upon Italy's willingness to join in it, and upon the further stipulation that Rome be relinquished to Italy. Furthermore, it would have been seen that the plan of making armed mediation serve the purpose of a transition from neutrality to war with Prussia, which Gramont ascribes to the Austrian representatives, was in reality a proposition originating with the French Government, and was transmitted from Paris to Vienna no later than the 16th of July.

In fact, these conferences with Vitzthum on July 24th, which Gramont so vividly describes, never took place at all ; for the Count left Paris on the 15th of July, and did not return thither until late in August.

The whole account is the invention of Gramont, cut out of the whole cloth. Equally glaring misrepresentations have been made by other writers; but it is characteristic of Gramont that, within two and a half years of the date of the alleged occurrence, he openly confronted Beust with the fabrication, and must, therefore, in the interim have convinced himself of its correctness as a historic fact. Out of his conviction that in 1870 he had reason to rely upon Austria's armed co-operation arose this picture in which people and events range themselves in such manner as to justify him in this belief.

When, in 1873, Beust's and Gramont's letters appeared in the papers, the Investigation Committee appointed by the French Parliament called upon Count Chaudordy, Minister of Foreign Affairs during the time when Gambetta was at the head of French affairs, for supplementary testimony. He declared that he could not discuss these letters, from which no definite conclusion could be drawn ; he would, therefore, simply relate what he knew. The Austrian Government [he said] did not urge France on to war, but in view of the growing complications sent Count Vitzthum to Paris for the purpose of securing every possible advantage for Austria. On July 15th [therefore previous to the declaration of war] the official negotiations were begun, France being represented by Gramont, Austria by Metternich and Vitzthum, Italy by Ambassador Nigra and the military *attaché*, Count Vimercati. At first a triple alliance was proposed, which was, however, soon abandoned, since thereby Austria and Italy would have become involved in a war for which they were not prepared. In its place there was suggested a treaty of alliance between Austria and Italy for the maintenance of neutrality, by which these two countries would be furnished the opportunity to place their armies on a war-footing ; this done, the next step, quite in harmony with Gramont's account, was to be armed mediation in September, which would then lead to the declaration of war against Prussia, provided that by this time the French troops had penetrated into South Germany. These negotiations were continued from July 20th to the 4th of August; and as South Germany was not then in the hands of the French forces, which, instead, had been defeated at Wörth, nothing more was heard of the proposed treaty.

To the question whether the treaty had been ratified, Count Chaudordy could give no definite reply ; to the further question, whether he could submit the text of the treaty, he answered, "No ; it is not in my possession."

He is, therefore, far from being a well-informed witness. His account differs from Gramont's in that he makes the Italian representatives participants in this conference which never took place, and in that he fixes upon the 15th instead of the 24th of July as the date of its occurrence, which has the advantage that upon this day Vitzthum was still in Paris, although we know that he did not confer with Gramont regarding a treaty of alliance.

In the spring of 1878 Prince Napoleon published an account of the attempts made in 1868 and 1870 to form alliances. His purpose was to vindicate his assertion that each time the Roman question was the rock upon which the attempt suffered shipwreck ; Napoleon's solicitude for the Pope's welfare had therefore cost France the provinces of Alsace and Lorraine.

This the ardently clerical Gramont sought to refute. He conceded that such was the case in 1869, but maintained that in 1870 Napoleon arrived at an agreement with Italy regarding the Roman question; and so it was not due to consideration for the Pope, but to the rapid succession of German victories that, to the misfortune of France, the Emperor was deprived of Austria's and Italy's assistance.

This was a new idea, and so the events of the past assumed a correspondingly changed aspect in Gramont's mind.

He begins by stating that, after the opening of hostilities, Napoleon decided to withdraw his troops from the States of the Church, and notified King Victor Emmanuel of the intended step, making it conditional, however, upon the King's promise, in conformity with the September convention of 1864, neither to attack the Pope's domain, nor to suffer it to be attacked. With this, he says, the King complied in a confidential letter addressed to Napoleon on the 21st of

July [the 20th is the correct date], the details of the arrangement being determined through further correspondence. By this agreement, Gramont continues, the obstacle which prevented the consummation of the triple alliance in 1869 was removed, whereupon Austria and Italy at once proposed that the negotiations concerning the alliance be reopened. Their wish was fulfilled, says Gramont, and then relates, precisely as in his letter of January 8th, 1873, how the two Powers proposed to prepare the way to a rupture with Prussia by means of their armed mediation. "In these negotiations there was no allusion to the Roman question," he says in conclusion, "for it had been disposed of in the correspondence between the two monarchs."

The King's letter was written on the 20th, therefore could not have been received in Paris before the 22d; the subsequent correspondence between the two sovereigns may have been telegraphic, but even in that case a day must have elapsed before it was concluded; the renewed negotiations which Gramont mentions could not, therefore, have been begun before the 24th.

At this point a difficulty presents itself. It was on the 23d that Prince Metternich received Count Beust's letter of the 20th, in which the latter makes an agreement between France and Austria conditional upon the stipulation that Rome be simply relinquished to the Italians. Is it at all probable that in the negotiations of the 24th Prince Metternich should have failed to present this categoric demand? How does Gramont surmount this obstacle? In the most artless manner possible. Just after stating that the negotiations were reopened after the arrival of the King's letter, therefore no earlier than the 24th, he says, with extreme ingenuousness, four pages farther on, that these negotiations were concluded before Count Beust's letter was received, therefore on the 18th of July, or five days previous to the day on which, according to his own statement, they were begun. The reader is left to picture to himself as best he may a transaction which began on the 24th and was concluded on the 18th of July.

This is, however, not the only discrepancy. As in his former version, Gramont mentions as his fellow negotiators the Austrian representatives, Vitzthum and Metternich, but now adds Vimercati and Nigra as the representatives of Italy. Now, as we are aware, Vitzthum could not have participated in the negotiations, for he left Paris on July 15th; and, unfortunately for Gramont's assertion, the same is true of Vimercati, who had gone from Paris to Vienna, and upon his arrival there had immediately started on his journey to Florence, which he reached on the 20th. It is impossible, therefore, that he could have been in Paris, either on the 18th or the 24th, to take part in the conference. Accordingly, the only remaining representatives who could have been present to determine upon a treaty-draft are Ambassadors Metternich and Nigra. Here, however, an objection of another kind arises. Count Beust in his "Memoirs" declares most positively that Metternich was never given the authority or power to act upon a proposition of this nature ; and, in fact, Beust himself peremptorily rejected the alliance when proposed to him by the French Ambassador at Vienna.

And in so far as Ambassador Nigra's participation is concerned, this gentleman publicly protested against Prince Napoleon's assertion that he had held out to the French Government prospects of Italy's armed co-operation ; this, he declared, he had never done.

Here, therefore, we have a conference with four plenipotentiaries, two of whom were at the time over a hundred miles distant from the place of assembly, while the other two were not empowered to act in the matter.

Any further comment seems unnecessary. These negotiations, alleged to have taken place at Paris, never occurred at all, as has already been said. Something further still remains to be told, however.

Immediately after receipt of Count Beust's letter, in which he not only insisted upon the withdrawal of the French troops, but, going even beyond the stipulations of the September convention, demanded the occupation of Rome by the Italians, Gramont sent a telegram to Florence, as has been related, in which he made the withdrawal of the French troops conditional upon the formal recognition of the September convention by the Italian Ministry.

To rid Italy of the French soldiers, the Ministry complied with Gramont's demand, but at the same time proclaimed their country's neutrality in the impending war, and prevailed upon the King passively to await events, and see whether Napoleon would not make a better offer for Italy's armed co-operation.

Since, according to his own plan, Italy was to enter upon the course which would lead her to the battlefield by a declaration of neutrality, Gramont now felt quite confident that the hoped-for alliance would be realized. When, on July 28th, he received the notification from Florence that the September convention had been confirmed, his mind was entirely relieved of its burden of anxiety, and he now expected from day to day that the treaty of alliance would be signed. Again his firm conviction on this point suggested to him an imaginary chain of events, the narration of which, as authentic history, he bequeathes to posterity with authoritative assurance.

After the 28th of July, he states, the day on which the September convention was formally recognized in Florence, the negotiations relative to carrying out that which had been agreed upon in Paris on the 18th proceeded rapidly and smoothly up to the very point of affixing the necessary signatures ; so little, he remarks, did the French insistence upon the September convention and the protection of the States of the Church prove a hindrance to the alliance of arms. King Victor Emmanuel, according to Gramont's further statement, even suggested that his army should proceed through the Tyrol to Bavaria several weeks earlier than the time at which it was first declared it would be ready to take the field ; but to this the Austrian plenipotentiary, Count Vitzthum, demurred, since thereby Austria would become involved in war before its preparations were completed.

Upon this occasion Count Vitzthum, who was usually miles distant from the places at which the conferences were held in which Gramont represents him as a participant, was really at hand. But this time his presence is quite as fatal to a belief in Gramont's statements as his absence has been heretofore.

Owing to Count Beust's inadequate knowledge of that which had been decided in Italy, he sent Count Vitzthum to Florence on July 28th to learn the true state of affairs. We know what Vitzthum's experience there really was. The King had decided to await further developments of the war ; there was not the slightest opportunity for negotiations ; and after the battle of Wörth, Victor Emmanuel told the Count that there was nothing he could do for poor Napoleon.

And so we see that this last transaction which Gramont describes had as little existence as the others. And, as Prince Napoleon very correctly avers, the " vexatious September convention " was the obstacle which, in 1870 as well as in 1869, prevented the alliance with Italy.

CHRONOLOGICAL TABLE.

1740–1786.	Reign of Frederick the Great, King of Prussia.
1786–1797.	Reign of Frederick William II.
1797–1840.	Reign of Frederick William III.
1840–1861.	Reign of Frederick William IV.
1858–1861.	Regency of William I.
1861–1888.	Reign of William I.
1806, July 12.	Formation of the Confederation of the Rhine.
Oct. 14.	Battle of Jena.
1807, July 9.	Peace of Tilsit, between Prussia and France.
1813, Oct. 16–19.	Battle of Leipzig.
1814, May 30.	First Peace of Paris.
Sept. 20–1815, June 10. Congress of Vienna.	
1815, May 22.	Constitutional Law granted in Prussia by Frederick William III.
June 8.	German Confederation constituted at Vienna.
June 18.	Battle of Waterloo.
Nov. 20.	Second Peace of Paris.
1816, Nov. 16.	First Session of the German Confederate Diet at Frankfort.
1819, Sept. 20.	Carlsbad Decrees adopted.
1820, June 8.	Vienna Final Act.
1830, July 27–29.	Revolution at Paris.
Sept. 7.	Revolution at Brunswick; flight of the Duke.
Sept. 13.	Revolution in Saxony; abdication of the King.
1830–1848.	Reign of Louis Philippe.
1831, Jan. 5.	New Constitution in Hesse-Cassel.
Sept. 30.	Elector William II. abdicates in favor of the Electoral Prince as Co-regent.
1832, June 28.	New Confederate Laws passed.
1834, Jan. 1.	Establishment of the Tariff-Union.
1835, March 2.	Death of Francis I. of Austria, accession of Ferdinand I.
1846.	Insurrections in Poland and Galicia.
July 8.	Christian VIII. of Denmark declares the integrity of the Kingdom, and the right of the Crown to Schleswig and Holstein.

1847, Feb. 13.   Summons issued to the United Provincial Diet in Prussia.

Sept. 12.   Meeting of Liberals at Offenburg.

Oct. 10.   Meeting of Constitutional party at Heppenheim.

Nov. 20.   Frederick William I. becomes Elector of Hesse-Cassel.

1848, Jan. 20.   Accession of Frederick VII., King of Denmark.

Jan. 28.   Frederick VII. proclaims a new Constitution, uniting the Duchies more closely with Denmark.

Feb. 24.   Outbreak of the Revolution in Paris.

March 13.   Insurrection in Vienna; flight of Metternich.

March 18.   Insurrection in Berlin.

March 24.   Eider-Danish Government declares the incorporation of the Duchies.

March 24.   Insurrection in the Duchies; Provisional Government established.

March 24.   The rebels in the Duchies seize the fortress of Rendsburg.

March 30–April 4. German Preliminary Parliament at Frankfort.

April 9.   Troops of the Duchies defeated near Flensburg.

April 23.   Danes defeated by Prussians, aiding the Duchies, at the Dannevirke.

May 2.   Capture of the fortress of Fridericia.

May 15.   Insurrection at Vienna; Emperor flees to Innspruck.

May 18.   Meeting of the German National Assembly at Frankfort.

May 29.   Archduke John appointed Vicar-General of the Austrian Empire at Vienna.

June 28.   Decree of the National Assembly concerning a Central Government.

June 29.   Archduke John chosen Regent of the German Empire.

July 12.   The Confederate Diet remits its functions to the Archduke John.

July 12.   Termination of the Confederate Diet.

July 25.   Italians defeated at Custozza by Radetzky.

Aug. 26.   Truce and Compact of Malmö signed.

Sept. 5.   Compact of Malmö rejected by the Committee of National Assembly.

Sept. 16.   Compact of Malmö accepted by the National Assembly.

Sept. 17.   Riot in Frankfort.

Oct. 6.   Insurrection in Vienna; murder of Count Latour.

Nov. 22.   Schwarzenberg appointed Prime Minister of Austria.

Nov. 22.   Austrian Diet at Kremsier.

Dec. 2.   The Emperor Ferdinand I. abdicates in favor of his nephew, Francis Joseph.

Dec. 10.   Louis Napoleon chosen President of the French Republic.

1849, Feb. 26.   Victory of Austrians over Hungarians.

March 4.   New Constitution proclaimed for Austria.

1849, March 7.	Close of the Kremsier Diet.
March 23.	Battle of Novara; abdication of Charles Albert, King of Sardinia, in favor of his son, Victor Emmanuel.
March 24.	The Prussian King formally recognizes the claims of the Duchies.
March 26.	End of the truce of Malmö.
March 28.	The German National Assembly elects the King of Prussia " Hereditary Emperor of Germany."
April 3.	The King declines the imperial crown.
April 3.	Hostilities with Denmark recommence.
April 8.	Wildenbruch's interview with the King of Denmark.
April 12.	The German National Assembly recognizes the Provisional Government of the Duchies.
May 26.	Formation of the League of the Three Kingdoms.
June 5.	The King of Denmark sanctions a new liberal constitution.
July 3.	The French enter Rome.
July 10.	Armistice renewed at Malmö.
Sept. 30.	Compact of the " Interim: " a treaty between Prussia and Austria for the formation of a new central authority for a limited time.
1850, Feb. 23.	Appointment of Hassenpflug, Minister in Hesse-Cassel.
Feb. 27.	Federation of the Four Kingdoms.
March and April.	Union Parliament meets at Erfurt.
May 8.	Meeting of Princes in Berlin.
May 10.	Confederate Congress, summoned by Austria, meets at Frankfort.
July 2.	Separate Peace between Denmark and Prussia.
July 14.	Official declaration from the King of Denmark.
July 24.	Battle of Idstedt; defeat of Schleswig-Holsteiners.
Aug. 2.	Protocol signed in London by the Great Powers, proclaiming the integrity of Denmark.
Sept. 2.	Restoration of the Confederate Diet at Frankfort; Prussia and her associates refuse to join it.
Oct. 11.	League formed at Bregenz by Austria, Bavaria, and Würtemberg against Prussia.
Oct. 17.	Brandenburg meets the Czar at Warsaw.
Oct. 26.	Brandenburg's first interview with the Austrian Emperor.
Nov. 2.	Ministerial Council at Berlin decides upon peaceful measures.
Nov. 6.	Death of Count Brandenburg.
Nov. 8.	Skirmish at Bronzell.
Nov. 9.	Schwarzenberg demands the abolition of the Prussian Union.
Nov. 9.	Prussian troops occupy the military roads in Hesse-Cassel.
Nov. 29.	Convention of Olmütz.

1850, Dec. 23–1851, May 15. Conferences at Dresden upon German affairs.

Dec. 24.   Prince Schwarzenberg's visit to the King of Prussia.

1851, May 30.   The re-established Confederate Diet assembles with its former membership.

May 31.   The Czar and the King of Prussia meet the Emperor of Austria at Warsaw.

Aug. 29.   Bismarck appointed deputy to the Confederate Diet.

Sept. 7.   Commercial Treaty signed between Hanover and Prussia.

Nov. 18.   Death of Ernest Augustus, King of Hanover; accession of George V.

Dec. 31.   The Emperor Francis Joseph revokes the Constitution of March 4, 1849.

1852, Jan. 28.   Royal Manifesto issued in a concessive spirit by the King of Denmark.

April 5.   Death of Prince Schwarzenberg.

April 13.   New Constitution proclaimed in Hesse-Cassel.

May 5.   Signing of the agreement concerning Neuchâtel.

May 8.   Signing of the London Protocol concerning the Danish succession.

June.   German fleet sold at auction.

Nov.–Dec.   Chastisement of Hesse-Cassel.

Dec. 2.   Napoleon III. proclaimed Emperor of the French.

1853, Feb. 19.   Treaty of commerce and navigation between Prussia and Austria.

April 8.   German States of the Tariff-Union agree to the conditions of the commercial treaty between Prussia and Austria.

1854, April 9.   Protocol concerning the integrity of Turkey signed by the Four Powers at Vienna.

April 20.   Treaty of alliance between Prussia and Austria.

July 31.   New Constitution for the Duchies proclaimed by the King of Denmark.

Dec. 2.   Alliance of Austria with the Western Powers.

1855, March 2.   Death of Czar Nicholas; accession of Alexander II.

Aug. 18.   The Austrian Concordat, increasing the Papal power in Austria.

Oct. 2.   New Constitution proclaimed in Denmark.

1856, March 30.   Treaty of Paris, at the close of the Crimean War.

1857, May 26.   Settlement of Prussia's troubles with Neuchâtel.

Oct. 23.   William, Prince of Prussia, appointed temporary regent.

1858, Jan. 14.   Attempted assassination of Napoleon III. by Orsini and others.

Feb. 11.   The Confederate Diet declares the Danish Constitution of 1855 to be illegal.

March 27.   Fortification of Copenhagen decreed.

Oct. 9.   William, Prince of Prussia, appointed permanent regent.

1858, Nov. 6.	Frederick VII. concedes that the General Constitution is invalid in Holstein and Lauenburg.
Nov. 6.	Resignation of the Manteuffel Ministry; succeeded by that of Prince Hohenzollern-Sigmaringen (Liberal).
1859, April 26.	Austrian Ultimatum rejected by Sardinia.
May 13.	Resignation of Count Buol; followed by Rechberg.
June 4.	Austrian defeat at Magenta.
June 11.	Death of Prince Metternich.
June 24.	Battle of Solferino.
July 11.	Preliminaries of Peace signed at Villafranca.
Aug. 14.	Meeting at Eisenach for the establishment of the German National Association.
Nov. 10.	Treaty of Zurich; the Italian Confederation established.
1860, Jan. 16.	Count Cavour returns to the Ministry.
Feb. 10.	Bills brought forward by the Prussian Government about military service and a military appropriation.
March 24.	Savoy and Nice ceded to France by treaty.
June 6.	Death of Cavour.
June 11.	Ricasoli forms a Ministry.
June 15.	Prussian Regent and other German Sovereigns meet Napoleon at Baden.
July 26.	Meeting of the Prussian Regent and the Austrian Emperor at Teplitz.
Sept. 11.	Sardinian troops enter the Papal territories.
Oct. 20.	Imperial Diploma promising to restore to Holstein its old Constitution.
Oct. 22.	The Emperor of Austria, the Czar, and the Regent of Prussia meet at Warsaw.
Dec. 13.	Ministerial Crisis in Vienna; Schmerling becomes Minister.
1861, Jan. 2.	Death of Frederick William IV.; Accession of William I.
Feb. 26.	New Constitution proclaimed for the whole Austrian Monarchy.
Feb. 27.	Tumult in Warsaw.
March 8.	Hohenzollern Ministry resigns; Von der Heydt succeeds.
March 17.	Victor Emmanuel proclaimed King of Italy.
July 14.	Attempt to assassinate the King of Prussia.
Oct. 18.	William I. crowned at Königsberg.
1862, March 8.	Austria and Prussia move in the Diet to demand from the Elector of Hesse the renewal of the Constitution.
May 11.	General Willisen sent to Cassel.
July 8–Aug. 10.	Meeting at Vienna of plenipotentiaries from German States.
Sept. 10.	Durando's Circular.
Sept. 23.	Count Bismarck-Schönhausen made President of the Ministry.

1862, Sept. 28.	Meeting of deputies at Weimar.
Sept. 30.	Bismarck informs the Chamber that the Budget is deferred till 1863.
Oct. 11.	Budget passed by the Upper House; Chamber of Deputies declare this to be unconstitutional.
1863, Jan. 22.	Austria's proposals rejected by the Confederate Diet.
March 24.	Commencement of the Minghetti Ministry.
March 30.	Eider-Danish proclamation by the King of Denmark, abandoning the basis of 1852.
July 9.	Confederate Diet calls upon Denmark to retract.
Aug. 2.	Visit of the Austrian Emperor to King William at Gastein.
Aug. 17.	Opening of the Assembly of Princes at Frankfort.
Aug. 26.	Denmark refuses compliance.
Sept. 28.	Special session of Danish General Council; Speech from the Throne.
Sept. 29.	Danish Government lays before Parliament a bill incorporating Schleswig.
Nov. 5.	The French Emperor proposes a European Congress.
Nov. 13.	New Danish Constitution adopted.
Nov. 15.	Death of Frederick VII.; accession of Christian IX.
Nov. 16.	Prince Frederick of Augustenburg asserts his claim.
Dec. 2.	Prussian Lower House upholds Frederick as Duke of Schleswig-Holstein.
Dec. 7.	Confederate Diet decides to execute federal chastisement upon Holstein.
Dec. 21.	Representatives of German States meet at Frankfort and resolve to support Frederick; appointment of the Committee of Thirty-Six.
Dec. 24.	German troops enter Holstein; Danes retire.
Dec. 25.	Federal Commissioners assume control in the Duchies.
Dec. 30.	Prince Frederick enters Kiel as Duke of Schleswig and Holstein.
Dec. 31.	Minister Hall retires; Bishop Monrad forms a Cabinet.
1864, Jan. 14.	Motion of Austria and Prussia to occupy Schleswig lost in the Diet.
Jan. 16.	The two Powers agree to go ahead independently of the Diet.
Jan. 20.	Marshal Wrangel takes command of the allied troops.
Jan. 31.	The two Powers issue a joint note.
Feb. 2.	Bombardment of Missunde.
Feb. 5.	Danes abandon the Dannevirke.
Feb. 7.	The allies occupy Flensburg.
Feb. 13.	Federal Commissioners protest against Prussian occupation of Holstein towns.
Feb. 18.	Prussians enter Jutland.
March 5.	New agreement signed between Prussia and Austria.
March 10.	Death of Maximilian II. of Bavaria.

1864, April 4.	Garibaldi arrives in England.
April 18.	Prussians take the fortress of Düppel by assault.
April 25.	Opening of Conferences at London.
April 29.	Danes retreat to Alsen and Funen.
May 9.	Danish naval victory off Heligoland.
May 12.	Beginning of one month's armistice.
May 18.	Prince Frederick Charles replaces Wrangel as Commander-in-chief.
May 28.	German Powers move in the Conference the establishment of Schleswig-Holstein as an independent state under Prince Augustenburg; English proposal to divide Schleswig at the River Schley.
June 9.	Armistice in Denmark prolonged a fortnight.
June 10.	Bismarck's interview with the Czar at Berlin.
June 22.	Emperor Francis Joseph and King William meet at Carlsbad.
June 25.	End of Conferences at London.
June 29.	Prussians bombard Alsen and capture the batteries.
July 8.	Fall of the Monrad Ministry.
July 11.	Formation of the Bluhme Ministry in Copenhagen.
July 18.	Truce agreed to in Copenhagen.
July 26.	Peace Conference at Vienna.
Aug. 22.	Visit of the King of Prussia to the Austrian Emperor at Schönbrunn.
Sept. 15.	Franco-Italian Convention signed.
Sept. 21, 22.	Riots in Turin.
Sept. 24.	Minghetti resigns ; La Marmora forms a Ministry.
Oct. 27.	Resignation of Rechberg; appointment of Count Mensdorff-Pouilly.
Oct. 30.	Treaty of Peace with Denmark signed at Vienna.
Dec. 5.	Withdrawal of troops from the Duchies decreed by the Diet.
Dec. 8.	Publication of the Papal Encyclical and Syllabus.
1865, Jan.	Great financial difficulty in Austria.
Feb. 22.	Prussian specifications sent to Vienna.
March 24.	Order to transfer Prussian Marine station to Kiel.
April 6.	Confederate Diet adopt the resolution of Bavaria and Saxony, requesting the transference of Holstein to Prince Frederick.
April 17.	Prussia asserts to Austria her determination to retain her power in the Duchies.
May 29.	Discussion about annexation in the Ministerial Council at Berlin.
June 27.	New Austrian Ministry ; Schmerling succeeded by Belcredi.
July 21.	Prussia decides to send an ultimatum to Austria.
July 23.	Interview between King William and Von der Pfordten at Salzburg.

1865, July 27.	Motion of Bavaria, Saxony, and Darmstadt, to summon the Estates in the Duchies and to admit Schleswig into the Confederation.
Aug. 14.	Convention of Gastein signed.
Aug. 19.	Meeting of King William and Emperor Francis Josepn at Salzburg.
Sept. 8.	Publication of the French Circular to the embassies.
Sept. 14.	Circular Despatch of Lord John Russell.
Sept. 15.	The King of Prussia takes formal possession of Lauenburg ; Manteuffel and Gablenz assume the administration of Schleswig and Holstein.
Sept. 20.	Suspension of the February Constitution in Austria.
Sept. 30.	Bismarck calls upon Drouyn de Lhuys in Paris.
Oct. 1.	Gastein Convention condemned by the Diet at Frankfort.
Oct. 4.	Bismarck's first interview with Napoleon at Biarritz.
Oct. 14.	Augustenburg's visit to Eckernförde.
Dec.	German States accept the Italian commercial treaty and recognize Victor Emmanuel as King of Italy.
Dec. 14.	Meeting of Manteuffel and Gablenz at Kiel.
1866, Jan. 20.	Bismarck demands from Austria the banishment of Prince Augustenburg.
Jan. 23.	Great mass-meeting at Altona.
Jan. 26.	Bismarck's despatch complaining of Austria's infidelity.
Feb. 7.	Austria's official reply to the above.
Feb. 24.	Revolution in Bucharest; deposition of the Prince.
March 7.	Napoleon replies to King William's letter of March 3d.
March 7.	Austrian Council decides to send more soldiers to the north.
March 14.	Govone arrives in Berlin.
March 16.	Mensdorff's circular note to the German Governments, referring the Schleswig-Holstein question to the Confederate Diet.
March 24.	Prussian Circular to the German States informing them of Austria's military movements, and asking what side they would take in the war.
March 27.	Prussian Ministerial Council decides to prepare for war.
March 29.	Prussia issues orders securing her frontiers.
March 31.	Pfordten's note to the two Great Powers.
March 31.	John Bratianu, an influential Roumanian statesman, visits Charles Anthony.
April 7.	Austria demands the demobilization of Prussian army.
April 8.	Treaty between Prussia and Italy.
April 9.	Prussia's motion in the Diet for a German Parliament.
Apr. 11, 14.	Government at Bucharest issues proclamations bearing imprint of French origin.
April 14.	England and Austria propose that definitive decision in relation to Roumania be postponed.

1866, April 15.	Prince Charles Anthony receives telegram from Bratianu.
April 19.	Bismarck counsels Prince Charles regarding throne of Roumania.
April 21.	Prussia agrees to a common disarmament.
April 21.	Austria decides to mobilize. Archduke Albrecht appointed Commander of the Army of the South; Benedek of the Army of the North.
April 22.	Prime Ministers of the Lesser States meet at Augsburg.
April 27.	Italy decides to mobilize.
May 1.	Bratianu presents himself to Prince Charles announcing result of plebiscitum.
May 3.	Thiers' speech in the French Chamber.
May 4.	Count Mensdorff declares negotiations about disarming to be at an end.
May 5.	Austria's proposal to exchange Venetia for Silesia laid before Nigra.
May 6.	Napoleon's speech at Auxerre expressing contempt for treaties of 1815.
May 7.	Attempt to assassinate Bismarck.
May 9.	Dissolution of the Prussian Chamber.
May 11.	It is decided to ask Prussia to specify her plans of reform.
May 11.	Prince Charles disappears from Düsseldorf.
May 12.	Alliance of Prussia and Italy.
May 20.	Prince Charles arrives in Roumania.
May 24.	Napoleon officially invites the contending Powers to a Congress; declined by Austria.
May 28.	Proposals of Anton Gablenz declined.
June 1.	Austria proposes to refer the matter of the Duchies to the Confederate Diet.
June 3.	Bismarck protests against the above.
June 7.	Prussians enter Holstein; Austrians retire.
June 10.	Prussia sends to all the German Governments her plans for a future Confederate Constitution.
June 10.	Prussia assumes the administration of Holstein.
June 11.	Austria's famous motion in the Diet, — to be voted upon in three days.
June 12.	Treaty of France and Austria.
June 12.	Imperial Manifesto in the form of an official letter from Napoleon to Drouyn de Lhuys, dated June 11th.
June 12.	Austria breaks off diplomatic relations with Prussia.
June 12.	Bismarck's Memorial concerning measures to be adopted.
June 14.	Vote in the Confederate Diet upon Austria's motion: declaring that Prussia by entering Holstein had broken the treaties, and calling for intervention by the mobilization of the whole Confederate army except Prussia's contingent, which should be demobilized. Voted for by Bavaria, Saxony, Hanover,

	Hesse-Cassel, Nassau, and others, 9 *vs.* 6. Prussia announces her withdrawal from the German Confederation, declares the same dissolved, and invites the members to form a new one exclusive of Austria. The Diet protests, and continues its functions.
1866, June 15.	Prussia declares war upon Hesse-Cassel, Hanover, and Saxony; Prussians advance.
June 16.	Prussia's note to the German Petty States requesting their co-operation.
June 17.	Prussian occupation of Hanover.
June 18.	Prussian occupation of Dresden.
June 19.	Prussian occupation of Cassel.
June 20.	Italy declares war upon Austria.
June 23.	The First Army, under Prince Frederick Charles, and the Army of the Elbe enter Bohemia.
June 24.	Italians defeated at Custozza.
June 26.	The Second Army, under the Crown Prince, enters Bohemia.
June 26.	Prussian victories at Liebenau, Turnau, and Podoll.
June 27.	Second Army repulsed at Trautenau.
June 27.	Encounter at Langensalza.
June 27.	Left Column of Second Army victorious at Nachod.
June 27.	Prussian victory at Hühnerwasser.
June 28.	Left Column of Second Army victorious at Skalitz.
June 28.	Battle of Münchengrätz.
June 28.	Second Army victorious at Trautenau.
June 29.	Victory of First Army at Gitschin.
June 29.	Surrender of the Hanoverians.
June 29.	Victory at Schweinschädel.
June 30.	Communication opened between the two armies.
July 1.	Command assumed by the King.
July 2.	Falckenstein leaves Eisenach to conduct the campaign of the Main against the Confederate army under the Princes Charles of Bavaria and Alexander of Hesse.
July 3.	Battle of Königgrätz, or Sadowa. Total defeat of the Austrians.
July 4.	Emperor Francis Joseph cedes Venetia to Napoleon, and requests his intervention.
July 4.	Prussian victories at Wiesenthal and Dermbach.
July 5.	Publication of the note in the *Moniteur.*
July 8.	Cialdini crosses the Po and enters Venetia.
July 10.	Victories at Hammelburg and Kissingen.
July 13.	Victory at Laufach.
July 13.	Archduke Albrecht assumes command of all the Austrian forces.
July 13.	Members of the Confederate Diet retire from Frankfort to Augsburg.
July 14.	Engagement at Aschaffenburg.
July 15.	Battle at Tobitschau.

1866, July 16.   Frankfort occupied by Falckenstein.

July 22.   Fight at Blumenau stopped by the news of the truce.

July 24.   Victories at Bischofsheim and Werbach.

July 25.   Engagements at Neubrunn and Gerscheim.

July 26.   Fight at Rossbrunn.

July 26.   Preliminaries of Peace signed at Nicolsburg.

July 30.   Armistice granted to the German states.

July 31.   Prussian army reviewed by the King fifteen miles from Vienna.

Aug. 4.   Bismarck's Circular to the states that had accepted the invitation to join a Northern Confederation.

Aug. 4.   Tariff Convention at Brunswick.

Aug. 5.   Opening of the Prussian Parliament.

Aug. 13.   Peace with Würtemberg concluded; Aug. 17, with Baden; Aug. 22, with Bavaria; Sept. 3, with Hesse-Darmstadt.

Aug. 17.   Bill of annexation brought before the Prussian Parliament.

Aug. 18.   Treaty of alliance, offensive and defensive, signed between Prussia and the following states: Saxe-Weimar, Oldenburg, Brunswick, Saxe-Altenburg, Saxe-Coburg-Gotha, Anhalt, Schwarzburg-Rudolstadt, Schwarzburg-Sondershausen, Waldeck, Reuss the (Younger Line), Lippe-Detmold, Schaumburg-Lippe, Lübeck, and Bremen; Aug. 21, with Mecklenburg-Schwerin and Mecklenburg-Strelitz; Sept. 3, with Hesse (for the country north of the Main); Sept. 26, with Reuss the (Elder Line); Oct. 18, with Saxe-Meiningen; Oct. 21, with Saxony.

Aug. 23.   Treaty of Peace signed at Prague.

Aug. 24.   Last sitting of the Confederate Diet at Augsburg; its dissolution.

Sept. 8.   Indemnity Bill passed.

Sept. 11.   Passage of the Annexation Bill.

Sept. 16.   Napoleon's Circular to the French embassies.

Sept. 27.   Loan granted by the Prussian Parliament.

Oct. 3.   Treaty of Peace between Austria and Italy signed at Vienna.

Oct. 6.   Prussia takes possession of Hanover.

Oct. 8.   Prussia takes possession of Hesse-Cassel, Nassau, and Frankfort.

Oct. 21.   Plebiscitum in Venetia concerning annexation to Italy, 641,758 *vs.* 69.

Oct. 23.   Electoral Law for the new German Parliament promulgated at Berlin.

Oct. 27.   Special treaty between Prussia and Oldenburg.

Oct. 30.   Baron von Beust becomes Austrian Foreign Minister.

Dec. 3-11.   The French troops quit Rome.

Dec. 15.   Plenipotentiaries from North German Confederation meet at Berlin.

1867, Jan.	Napoleon sends Gen. Fleury to Italy to demand renunciation of Rome.
Jan. 7.	Stephan submits draft of contract in relation to postal affairs.
Jan. 17.	Ricasoli ministry submits bill to Second Italian Chamber relating to Rome.
Jan. 24.	Schleswig and Holstein incorporated.
Feb. 3–5.	Conference for consideration of uniform organization of South German armies held at Stuttgart.
Feb. 9.	Draft of the new Constitution for North German Confederation settled.
Feb. 12.	Election for the Reichstag.
Feb. 14.	Opening of French Chambers.
Feb. 24.	North German Parliament meets at Berlin.
March 4.	Bismarck presents draft of Constitution for consideration by the House.
March 13.	First reading of the Constitution ended.
March 19.	Benedetti receives instructions to prepare Bismarck for surrender of Luxemburg to France.
March 26.	Prince of Orange sent to Paris with a letter to Napoleon.
March 28.	Prince of Orange delivers letter of King-Grand-Duke into hands of Napoleon.
March 30.	House completes section of Constitution relating to Reichstag.
March 31.	Moustier sends telegram to Benedetti.
April 1.	Benedetti calls upon Bismarck.
April 1.	Count Goltz informs Marquis Moustier of Bismarck's attitude.
April 1.	Reichstag begins its deliberations upon individual administrative branches.
April 2.	Despatches received at The Hague from Prussia.
April 4.	Ricasoli resigns.
April 5.	Lord Derby announces to the English Upper House the intentions of his government in relation to Luxemburg.
April 6.	Benedetti instructed to demand the real motive of Bismarck's speech on the 1st.
April 7.	Hesse-Darmstadt enters into offensive and defensive alliance with Prussia.
April 8.	Jules Favre interpellates the French Government.
April 11.	Ratazzi succeeds Ricasoli.
April 12.	Austrian ambassador calls upon Bismarck offering his government's good offices in connection with Luxemburg question.
April 15.	France sends circular note to St. Petersburg, Vienna, and London.
April 17.	Austria's formal proposals submitted to Napoleon.
April 17.	Federal Constitution adopted.
April 18.	Bismarck sends communication to London.

1867, April 21.	Malaret sends communication to French Government regarding Italian policy.
April 27.	The King of Würtemberg appoints Col. Von Wagner chief of the department of war.
April 30.	*Moniteur* declares French military measures justifiable.
May 3.	Lord Stanley forwards to the Powers draft of a proposed treaty.
May 7.	He receives communication from Prussian ambassador.
May 9.	Lord Stanley announces that English Cabinet would agree to Bernstorff's amendment.
May 11.	Prussia agrees to neutrality of Luxemburg.
May 17.	Bismarck rejects the Bavarian proposition.
May 30.	Conference held at Nördlungen.
May 31.	Ratifications exchanged.
June.	Great World's Fair in Paris. Arrival of Emperor Alexander of Russia.
June 1.	Denmark refuses Prussia's demands in relation to Schleswig-Holstein.
June 3.	Draft submitted by Prussian Government in relation to Customs Union.
June 6.	Arrival of King William and Bismarck in Paris.
June 14.	King William leaves Paris.
June 18.	Bavaria granted six votes in enlarged Federal Council.
June 18.	Bismarck replies to Danish refusal of Prussia's demands.
June 26.	Representatives of North German and South German States assemble at Berlin.
July 1.	Napoleon receives intelligence of shooting of Maximilian.
July 8.	Formal treaty of Customs Union signed.
July 14.	Count Bismarck nominated as Chancellor of the Confederation.
July 15.	Prussian ministry defends its action.
July 25.	Moustier sends despatch to his *chargé d'affaires* at Prussian Court.
July 30.	King William grants audience to committee of Hessian Assembly.
Aug. 4.	Bismarck arrives at Ems.
Aug. 12.	A Federal Chancery instituted to assist the chancellor.
Aug. 15.	First session of the Federal Council opened.
Aug. 15.	King of Prussia makes a *détour* through Frankfort.
Aug. 18.	Napoleon meets Francis Joseph at Salzburg.
Aug. 23.	The royal guests depart from Salzburg.
Aug. 31.	Elections for the Reichstag take place.
Sept. 5.	Grand Duke of Baden makes speech in favor of alliance with North German Confederation.
Sept. 7.	Bismarck sends circular note in consequence of meeting of emperors at Salzburg.
Sept. 10.	First regular session of North German Reichstag opens.

1867, Sept. 10.   First Chamber of Baden votes in favor of treaty with North German Confederation.

Sept. 17.   North German Reichstag elects its President.

Sept. 17.   Admiral Topete, commanding Spanish naval force, raises standard of revolt.

Sept. 20.   Andalusia in hands of Spanish revolutionists.

Sept. 27.   Resolutions adopted by National Party of Würtemberg.

Sept. 29.   Resolutions adopted by Democratic Popular Party of Würtemberg.

Sept. 29.   Treaty regarding Hanoverian funds signed and ratified.

Sept. 29.   Menotti Garibaldi opens hostility against Papal troops.

Sept. 30.   Bavarian Legislative Assembly convened.

Oct.   Isabella of Spain offers Napoleon assistance in protecting Pope.

Oct. 4.   Bavarian National Party adopts resolutions in favor of treaty with North German Confederation.

Oct. 5.   Second Chamber consents by unanimous vote.

Oct. 8.   Prince Hohenlohe advises Lower Chamber of Bavaria to confirm treaties.

Oct. 17.   Ratazzi tenders his resignation.

Oct. 21.   A debate of unusual violence takes place in Bavarian Chamber.   Customs Union treaty.

Oct. 22.   Bavarian Lower Chamber confirms the treaties.

Oct. 23.   Upper Chamber rejects treaty.

Oct. 26.   Upper Chamber reconsiders its action and accepts treaty.

Oct. 27.   Bavarian delegates arrive in Berlin.

Oct. 28.   First French battalions march into Rome.

Oct. 28.   North German Reichstag begins its final deliberations in regard to treaties.

Oct. 29.   Deliberations in Würtemberg Lower Chamber on treaties with North German Confederation.

Oct. 31.   Treaties approved.

Oct. 31.   Gives unconditional sanction to the treaties.

Nov. 1.   Treaties sanctioned by Upper Chamber.

Nov. 3.   Garibaldi fights with Papal and French troops.

Nov. 6.   Exchange of ratifications takes place in Berlin.

Nov. 7.   General elections carried by the Government.

Nov. 10.   Marquis Moustier sends circular note to European Courts.

Nov. 17.   Bismarck receives note from Mazzini.

Nov. 18.   Napoleon, in speech from throne, laments general feeling of apprehension.

Dec. 2.   Jules Favre criticises French Government for its defence of Rome.

Dec. 4, 5.   Discussions on French policy in Rome continue.

1868, Jan. 8.   Debate on the Constitution of North German Confederation.

1868,	Feb. 29.	King William closes session of the Assembly.
	March.	Prince Jerome Napoleon makes a tour to Berlin. Prussia accedes to request of Baden officers to receive instruction in Prussian military schools.
	March 2.	Customs Federal Council assembles.
	March 23.	Reichstag convoked in Berlin.
	April 2.	Reichstag organizes.
	April 22.	Committee in charge of bill regarding administration of Federal debt reports.
	April 27.	King William opens session of Customs Parliament.
	April 28.	Customs Parliament proceeds to election of officers.
	May 1.	Committee reports upon examination of Bavarian delegates.
	May 2.	Würtemberg elections discussed.
	May 6.	Suckow has an interview with Moltke.
	May 6.	Suckow has a conversation with Bismarck.
	May 7.	Bennigsen defends National Liberals.
	May 14.	Suckow discusses with Moltke probability of French attack on South Germany.
	May 18.	Commercial treaty with Austria discussed.
	May 19.	Finances receive careful scrutiny.
	May 23.	House proceeds to financial deliberation upon tariff bill.
	May 27.	Bismarck authorizes re-assembling of German Reichstag.
	June 9.	Special deliberation upon items of the budget begun.
	June 15.	Deliberation by the plenum begun.
	June 19.	Final deliberation on the budget takes place.
	June 22.	Pope condemns Austrian Constitution.
	Sept. 5.	Annual meeting of German working-men's societies in session at Nürnberg.
	Nov. 22.	Bismarck demands Prince Charles of Roumania to dismiss his ministry.
	Dec.	Belgian railway companies sign a preliminary agreement to give French Government possession and control of direct lines to Brussels and Rotterdam.
	Dec. 1.	Turkish Government sends ultimatum to Athens.
	Dec. 11.	Matter of railway control discussed by Second Belgian Chamber.
	Dec. 11.	Turkish ultimatum presented.
	Dec. 15.	Ultimatum rejected by Greece.
	Dec. 21.	Bismarck proposes that Turkish-Greek question should be settled by conference of Great Powers.
1869.		Belgian railway companies conclude final negotiations.
	March.	Vitzthum takes draft-treaty of triple alliance to Vienna.
	March 4.	King William opens session of Reichstag.
	April.	Vitzthum returns to Paris to open formal negotiations with regard to triple alliance.
	April 4.	Prim induces Spanish ministry to offer crown to King Ferdinand.

1869, April 6.	Spanish crown offered to Amadeo, Duke of Aosta.
April 9.	Prince Hohenlohe addresses circular note to the Powers.
April 13.	Federal Council submits budget for 1870 to Reichstag.
April 16.	Brilliant parliamentary encounter takes place in North German Reichstag.
April 22.	Frère-Orban comes to Paris.
April 27.	Protocol agreed upon to appoint commission to decide upon indemnity to Belgian railways.
May 1.	Beust gives Belgians advice in regard to their submission to France.
May 11.	Bismarck not averse to discussion on subject of Spanish crown.
May 15.	Gramont nominated to the French ministry.
May 19.	Napoleon submits Archduke Albert's plan of campaign to council of highest officers.
May 23.	Elections in France.
June 1.	At Madrid Cortes completes Constitution.
June 4.	Vitzthum returns to Brussels satisfied with his achievement.
June 11.	Prim addresses Cortes upon throne question.
June 14.	Prim sends Salazar to Sigmaringen.
June 20.	Prince of Hohenzollern promises to accept Spanish crown.
June 22.	Session of North German Reichstag concludes.
June 24.	Spanish Cortes adjourns.
June 28.	French Chamber convened in extraordinary session.
July 2.	Napoleon again laid upon a bed of suffering.
July 17.	Office of Secretary of State abolished in France by imperial decree.
Aug.	Menabrea requests Austria to influence Napoleon to remove troops from Rome.
Aug. 2.	Draft of *senatus consultum* submitted to French Senate for legislative action.
Aug. 12.	Napoleon suffers serious attack of illness.
Sept.	Period of great uncertainty and agitation in Spain. Salazar goes to Munich.
Sept. 10.	Napoleon removed from St. Cloud to Paris.
Oct. 6.	Prussian Assembly opens.
Oct. 7.	Crown Prince of Prussia arrives in Vienna.
Oct. 15.	Treaty between Switzerland and Italy.
Oct. 23.	Salazar advises placing Hohenzollern prince on Spanish throne.
Oct. 25.	Herr von der Heydt, Prussian Minister of Finance, resigns, and Otto Camphausen appointed his successor.
Oct. 26.	House appoints 29th as day for opening discussion on budget.
Nov. 4.	Discussion on Prussian budget begins.
Nov. 5.	Lasker's and Virchow's motions rejected.
Nov. 16.	Bill embodying completed plan of Minister of Finance submitted to Prussian House.

1869,	Nov. 29.	Interrupted session of French Chambers resumed.
	Dec. 8.	Œcumenical Council begins its sessions in the Vatican.
1870,	Jan. 2.	French empire receives responsible ministry.
	Feb.	Pope lays before Council draft of a decree claiming control of Church over State.
	Feb. 1.	Count Daru requests good offices of England with Prussian Government.
	Feb. 14.	Reichstag enters upon important session.
	Feb. 20.	Ollivier opposes a forcible note defending rights of State.
	Feb. 22.	Jules Favre interpellates French Government.
	Feb. 23.	Principle of Government candidatures made subject of further interpellation.
	Feb. 24.	Lasker eager to welcome Baden into Confederation.
	Feb. 24.	French Left applauds ministry for its stand against official influence in elections.
	March.	Bitter debate in French Chambers.
	March 9.	Ollivier announces draft of a decree making needful modifications in Constitution.
	March 19.	The Curia peremptorily upholds every paragraph of schema.
	March 22.	Napoleon expresses approval of Ollivier's views.
	March 28.	Ollivier submits completed draft to Senate.
	April 8.	Debate in Reichstag upon penal code closes.
	April 13.	French legislative body adjourns.
	April 14.	Buffet and Daru retire from French Cabinet.
	April 20.	French Senate approves draft of Constitution.
	April 21.	Session of Customs Parliament opens.
	April 23.	Imperial decree formulates the plebiscitum.
	May 8.	Voting on the plebiscitum.
	May 9.	Reichstag resumes its labors.
	May 21.	Final deliberation upon penal code begun.
	May 23.	Planck and associates introduce compromise motion.
	May 26.	Session ends.
	July 2.	Spanish ministers discuss situation with President of Cortes.
	July 3.	Telegrams received at Paris Foreign Office regarding Hohenzollern affair; Gramont directs French *chargé d'affaires* at Berlin to interrogate Prussian Government.
	July 4.	Council of Ministers decide to recognize Prince Leopold as candidate.
	July 4.	Gramont stimulates excitement in Paris by official announcements.
	July 5.	Notes of alarm sounded by Parisian press.
	July 6.	Gramont and Ollivier reply to Cochéry interpellation.
	July 7.	Gramont sends despatch to Le Sourd at Berlin; sends instructions to Benedetti.
	July 7.	Sagasta sends circular letter explaining position of Spanish Government.

1870, July 8.   Instructions sent to Prussian ambassadors.
July 8.   Benedetti arrives at Ems.
July 8.   Salazar issues pamphlet in relation to Hohenzollern prince.
July 8, 9.   Gramont telegraphs instructions to Benedetti.
July 9.   Werther calls on Benedetti.
July 9.   Benedetti has audience with King William.
July 10.   Bismarck makes announcement to Federal Council.
July 10, 11.   Gramont sends urgent telegrams to Benedetti.
July 11.   Gramont informs Chamber that he has no definite announcement to make.
July 11.   Gen. von Roon leaves country-seat for Berlin.
July 11.   Benedetti has second interview with King William.
July 11.   Count Beust condemns Gramont's quarrelsome attitude.
July 12.   Gramont telegraphs instructions to Benedetti.
July 12.   News of Prince Leopold's withdrawal carried to every part of Germany.
July 12.   Great tumult in Paris.
July 13.   King William learns of latest demands of France.
July 13.   French Cabinet meets in council at St. Cloud.
July 13.   Benedetti has interview with King William in Park.
July 13.   Gramont announces to French Chamber new claims against Prussia.
July 13.   Reports of feeling in Paris circulated in Berlin.
July 13.   Reports of occurrences at Ems made known in Berlin.
July 13–15.   Army budget under discussion at Munich.
July 14.   French Chamber discusses question of mobilization.
July 14.   Lord Granville submits proposals to France and Germany.
July 14.   Vitzthum makes fruitless attempt to obtain interview with Gramont.
July 14.   Despatch posted up in Ems.
July 14.   French Cabinet assembles in Council; orders issued to mobilize French army.
July 15.   Lord Granville's proposal declined in Paris and Berlin.
July 15.   Napoleon gives Vitzthum audience at St. Cloud.
July 15.   French Cabinet decides upon form of fateful announcement.
July 15.   King William leaves Ems for Berlin to prepare for defence.
July 16.   Orders for mobilization of Bavarian army issued.
July 16.   Mobilization in Baden.
July 16.   First day of mobilization in North Germany.
July 17.   Great crowds assemble in front of palace in Munich.
July 17.   King of Würtemberg orders mobilization of army.
July 17.   Victor Emmanuel enthusiastic for France.
July 18.   Cabinet council of Austrian ministers held.
July 18.   Debate in Bavarian Representative Assembly on war loan.

1870,	July 19.	Deputy Jörg reads report of committee to House.
	July 19.	England publishes manifesto of neutrality.
	July 19.	Le Sourd presents formal declaration of war.
	July 20.	Decision of Bavarian Lower Chamber receives sanction of Upper Chamber.
	July 20.	Count Beust announces Austria's neutrality.
	July 20.	Favorable reply to Napoleon's letter received from Italy.
	July 20.	Spanish Cortes convene for purpose of electing king.
	July 21.	King of Würtemberg convokes Chambers.
	July 21.	Reichstag takes final action on war loan.
	July 22.	Vimercati sent to Vienna in relation to triple alliance.
	July 23.	Bismarck replies to French manifesto.
	July 23.	Metternich presents Beust's confidential letter to Gramont.
	July 23.	Gramont sends despatch to Italy rejecting Beust's proposition.
	July 24.	Italy's neutrality proclaimed.
	July 25.	Italy withdraws from triple alliance.
	July 26.	Vimercati and Beust decide upon treaty of alliance between Austria and Italy.
	July 27.	Beust submits to Vienna conference a despatch from Napoleon.
	July 28.	Vitzthum and Vimercati leave Vienna.
	July 28.	Formal agreement for re-establishment of September treaty drawn up by Italian ministers and French ambassadors creates surprise and consternation in Vienna.
	Aug. 3.	Vimercati has audience with Napoleon.
	Aug. 5.	Vimercati returns from Paris, his object unaccomplished.
	Aug. 6, 7.	News received in Italy of battle of Wörth.
	Aug. 10.	England ready to enter into an agreement with Italy.
	Dec. 3.	The Imperial Crown offered to the King of Prussia.
1871,	Jan. 18.	Re-establishment of the German Empire; William I. of Prussia proclaimed German Emperor at Versailles.

INDEX.

ization of the army, 95; realizes his country's isolated position, 101; submits draft of triple alliance to Metternich and Vitzthum, 107; his proposition alarms Beust, 108, 109.; reads a sharp lecture to Belgium, 109; assumes a high tone with Frère-Orban, 110, 111; arrives at an agreement with Beust in relation to triple alliance, 117; declares that French troops shall not be removed from Rome, 119; has no objection to Italy's acquiring the Tyrol, *ib.*; importunes the Italians to content themselves with the imperial word, 121; resorts to every means to secure majority favorable to Government, 122, 123; holds the wavering emperor firm, 124, 125; members of the Chambers jealous of his great power, 126; gives decided advice to Napoleon, *ib.*; nominated to Presidency of Senate, 127; abuses under his administration had exasperated men, 242; invited to preliminary conference in relation to plebiscitum, 260; convinces the emperor and empress, 261; believes the plebiscitum would result favorably to the emperor, 264; his judgment correct in regard to plebiscitum, 271.

Roumania, proposed division of, disapproved of by Great Powers, iv. 341; revolution in, vi. 414; people of, called to decide their choice for sovereign in a plebiscitum, 420; they throng to the polls with eager enthusiasm, 421; receive Prince Charles with unbounded demonstrations of joy, 424; internal affairs in, 426; armed bands from, invade Bulgaria, 430; consignment of Prussian arms arrives in, *ib.*; Austrian possessions threatened by, 431.

Rousset, Camille, writings of, upon the volunteers of 1792, vi. 302, *note.*

Ruge, Arnold, on the re-establishment of Poland and of Italy, i. 237.

Ruland, Ultramontane, makes bitter speech against treaties with North German Confederation, vi. 327.

Russell, Lord John, on conscription in Warsaw, ii. 577; communicates his opinions to the Prussian Government, 626; makes a bold speech, 630; proposes mediation, iii. 117; sends another despatch to Copenhagen, 124; diplomatic attempt rejected by Rechberg, 147; sends numerous despatches and proposals, 150; against new constitution of Denmark, 160; indifferent as to conditions of peace, 188; eager to bring about a conference, 316; circular despatch from, on Gastein treaty, iv. 426.

Russell, William, "War Diary" of, referred to, vii. 299, *note.*

Russia, growth in the Napoleonic era, i. 40; proposes a conditional evacuation of the principalities, ii. 234; proposes a Congress of the Great Powers, 368; delight in, at prospect of Austria's humiliation, *ib.*; mobilizes four

corps *d'armée,* 371; favors a triple alliance with France and Prussia, 412; places her whole army on a war-footing, 586; patriotic enthusiasm in, 596; will not be dictated to by Western Powers, 601; army of, on a war-footing, *ib.*; declares to King Christian her readiness to support his policy, iii. 45, 46; urges settlement of question of Danish succession, 82; advises submission by Danish Government, 108; Russia and England recognize fairness of German demands, 116; recognizes appropriateness of English propositions, 119; wishes to see Denmark treated tenderly, 252; anxiety in, lest a Scandinavian union should be formed, 395; possibility of war with France and Austria, iv. 6; proposes European Congress, v. 395; intervenes in favor of Darmstadt, 447; Prussian annexations cause displeasure in, 448; not in favor of vigorous reorganization of Germany, vi. 4; proposes a conference of the Great Powers in London, 156; proposes that fortress of Luxemburg be evacuated by Prussians, 201; sympathizes with revolt in Crete, 215; entertains no thoughts of aggrandizement in Orient, 226; silent in regard to French interference in Germany, 236; not in favor of European Congress to settle affairs in Italy, 398; threatens to hold Roumania under military subjection, 415; strained relations of, with Austria and Turkey, 429; Government of, in sympathy with Prussia, vii. 457; proclaims its own neutrality, 458.

Russo-Turkish war of 1854, its influence on German relations, ii. 200 *et seq.*

Sadowa, battle of, see Königgrätz.

Sagasta sends circular letter concerning selection of candidate for Spanish throne, vii. 346.

Salazar y Mazarredo publishes memorial regarding candidates to Spanish throne, vii. 290, 291; receives permission from Prim to offer Spanish crown to Prince Leopold, 297, 298; has interview with the prince, 298, 299; reports the result of his mission at Madrid, 300; issues a revised form of his appeal to the country, *ib.*; urges upon Prim that refusal had not been an unqualified one, 302; admits that Napoleon would oppose a Hohenzollern prince, 303; again sent to Germany to reopen negotiations, *ib.*; takes letters to King William and Bismarck, 304; his pamphlets made the name of Hohenzollern famous, 312; sent to Sigmaringen, 312, 313; has favorable interview with the Hohenzollern princes, 313; preface to his pamphlet of July 8, 314, *note*; originated the Hohenzollern candidacy, 318; his pamphlet in relation to Prince Leopold reissued, 347.

Salt trade in Prussia monopolized by Government, vi. 297; tax on, discussed in Reichstag, 297-299.

ment, 341; received by the people with boundless enthusiasm, 399; attends the opening of Parliament, 404; speech of, 405; replies to letter of Emperor of Russia, 449; receives address from Chambers, 486; signs a bill asking for public loan, 506; urges Duke Bernard of Meiningen to abdicate, 514; accepts the imperial crown, 532; honors loyalty of Hanoverians to their hereditary house, vi. 20; manifests no inclination towards French alliance, 50; looks upon the protection of Luxemburg as his principal duty, 50, 51; unwilling to enter into an offensive alliance with France, 53; in speech from the throne announces proposed treaties between North and South Germany, 56, 57; declares stand taken by Allied Governments, 58, 59; doubts of, in regard to Luxemburg removed, 141; his acts based upon deliberate conviction, 143; opposed to war with France, 145; not his habit to cringe before a threat, 155; summons the Reichstag to the royal palace, 197; pays a high tribute to the patriotic zeal and labors of the Reichstag, 197, 198; visits Paris, 224; uninterrupted cordiality of his visit to Napoleon, 228; encouraged to undertake formation of the Federal Government, 274; seeks benefit from the waters of Ems, 283; sympathizes with Hesse, *ib.*, makes a détour through Frankfort, 284; greeted with demonstrations of delight at Cassel, *ib.*; undoes the mischief wrought by his Ministers, 284, 285; troubled at the resignation of Baron von der Heydt, Minister of Finance, 285; repays from his private chest the funds taken from Frankfort, *ib.*; his attitude gives satisfaction to the new provinces, 286; speech of, from the throne, at the first regular session of the North German Reichstag, 287; receives address from Simson at Castle Hohenzollern, 292; pays well-merited tribute to achievements of the session of the Reichstag, 334; through personal intervention preserves to Electoral Hesse its state funds, 354; makes the Conservatives feel his deepest displeasure, 361; closes session of the Assembly, 374; speech from the throne in relation to affairs in Italy, 397, 398; attitude of, towards the Roumænian question, 417–425; opens the Reichstag, vii. 3; opens the session of the Customs Parliament, 21; closes the session, 56; gives warm words of commendation to the Reichstag, 79; remains inaccessible, 114; finds no cause to interfere with existing conditions of state and church in Prussia, 165; in speech from throne discusses important political questions, 182; opens session of Reichstag, 186; expresses his appreciation of legislative activity of House, 207; approves Camphausen's financial plan, 210; announces impor-

tant bills in speech from throne in Reichstag, 218, 219; sees no occasion to change policy pursued by Germany, 220; reviews with gratitude results achieved by Reichstag, 231; opposed to Prince Leopold's accepting Spanish crown, 293, 294; receives letters from Spanish statesmen in relation to Prince Leopold, 304; refuses Salazar an audience, 305; as head of the family calls the Hohenzollern magnates together, *ib.*; allows Prince Leopold liberty to decide for himself, *ib.*; remains unshaken in his disinclination to the project, 308; believes the Hohenzollern candidacy to be disposed of definitively, *ib.*; Prim hopes to gain his object behind king's back, 309; has no thought of renewed overture to Prince Leopold, 312; receives communication from Prince Leopold announcing his acceptance of Spanish crown, 313; taken aback at the prince's communication, 313, 314; discusses the candidacy with Bismarck, 318, 319; calls Hohenzollern family council, 319; demands made upon him by Gramont, 340, 341, 349; Leopold's letter to him an act of courtesy, 347; waives formality in his intercourse with Benedetti, 353; rehearses events concerning the Hohenzollern affair, 354; Benedetti's attempts to make Gramont's proposal acceptable to him end in failure, 355; explains his Government's attitude, 356; anxiety of Bismarck in relation to his audience with French ambassador, 358; has second interview with Benedetti, 360; Benedetti's instructions to interview, 361; declines to comply with French exactions, 362; receives a telegram from Charles Anthony, 363; receives message from Bismarck, 364; accused of perfidy by Gramont, 369; his position explained by Baron Werther, 370; French Ministers demand a letter and guaranties from, 371–378, 381, 383; has important audience with Benedetti in public park at Ems, 386–388; receives Werther's report, 388; indignant at French demands, 389; declines further audience with Benedetti, 389, 390; notifies Benedetti of arrival of letter from Charles Anthony, 390; writes to Abeken, 394; good-natured mildness of, 395; directs that the French demand and its rejection be made public, 395; grants Benedetti a short audience, 399; enthusiastically cheered in Berlin, 400; his manly dignity extolled, 401; leaves Ems for Berlin, 425; greeted with cheers by the people, 426; could not believe in reality of war, *ib.*; deeply moved at prospect, 427; palace of, surrounded by enthusiastic throngs, *ib.*; deplores coming conflict, 432; visited by Victor Emmanuel, 488.

Willisen, Gen. von, sent against the Poles, i. 176; his action, *ib.*: Comman-